GALLIPOLI

When first published in 1965, when the author was thirty-two, Robert Rhodes James' history of the Gallipoli Campaign of 1915 was widely hailed as a master-piece of military history, and subsequent estimations have been equally enthusiastic. It is one of those rare books that have an enduring appeal, and are regarded as classics. Its special merit is that it describes the campaign in words written at the time by the actual participants, then regarded as a quite novel, indeed revolutionary, manner of writing military history. This admiration extends to Turkey, where it has been published in Turkish, and to Australia, where it has been described in the Preface to the latest edition of the Official History of Gallipoli as 'the best short history of the campaign'. Others regard it as *the* best. It has seldom been out of print for twenty-three years, and this new edition is exactly the same as the original, which was described by Field Marshal Lord Slim as 'by far the best history of the campaign' - remarkable praise from that eminent source, not given to superlatives, and himself a Gallipoli veteran.

By the time *Gallipoli* was published, Robert Rhodes James had already established a remarkable reputation as art historian and author. His biography of Lord Randolph Churchill, published in 1959 when he was twenty-six, caused a sensation, and the praise of Lord Randolph's son, Sir Winston Churchill; his biography of Rosebery (1963), which received the Heinemann Award of the Royal Society of Literature, and *Gallipoli* further enhanced his reputation. Since then this early established reputation has grown further with, amongst others, a study of Churchill's career up to 1939, published in 1970, *The British Revolution, 1860-1939* (1977), *Prince Albert* (1983) and *Anthony Eden* (1986). Of his thirteen books, ten are still in print. He is a Fellow of the Royal Society of Literature and the Royal Historical Society, is a former Fellow of All Souls College, and has received several awards and literary prizes. Astonishingly, all this has been achieved while engaged in a career of public service, as a Clerk in the House of Commons, as a senior official in the United Nations, as the Director of a Research Institute, and, since 1976, as Conservative Member of Parliament for Cambridge. Having served in the Conservative Government in the Foreign Office and then with special responsibilities for Higher Education, he is currently one of the Chairmen of the House of Commons. Of all his books, *Gallipoli* occupies a special place in his affections - as it does for the many who have read and appreciated what the British military historian John Keegan has described as 'a master's demonstration of how military history may be done'.

Robert Rhodes James is the youngest son of the late Colonel William Rhodes James, OBE, MC, is married with four daughters, and lives near Cambridge. His wife's stepfather served in the Manchester Regiment in Gallipoli.

GRAND STRATEGY

GALLIPOLI

ROBERT RHODES JAMES

PAPERMAC

To the memory of my Uncle, Brigadier L. R. Lemon (1890–1963)
who, while attached to the 1st Battalion, The 6th Gurkha Rifles,
served and suffered in Gallipoli, August, 1915

First published 1965 by B. T. Batsford Limited

Papermac edition published 1989 by
PAPERMAC
a division of Macmillan Publishers Limited
4 Little Essex Street, London WC2R 3LF
and Basingstoke

Associated companies in Auckland, Delhi, Dublin, Gaborone,
Hamburg, Harare, Hong Kong, Johannesburg, Kuala Lumpur,
Lagos, Manzini, Melbourne, Mexico City, Nairobi, New York,
Singapore and Tokyo

British Library Cataloguing in Publication Data
James, Robert Rhodes, 1933 –
    Gallipoli.
    1. World War 1. Gallipoli campaign.
    Military operations by Allied forces
    I. Title
    940.4'25

ISBN 0-333-48872-5

Printed in Hong Kong

Contents

No military campaign of modern times has had such an enduring fascination with successive generations than the epic but ill-fated attempt by the British, Commonwealth and French forces to take the Dardanelles in 1915, first by sea, and then by land by capturing the Gallipoli Peninsular. Why is this so? It is partly the glittering and exciting contrast with the mud-splattered bloody misery of slaughter on the Western Front in the Great War, partly the sheer drama of the enterprise, and partly that it so often came close to triumph, that gives Gallipoli its unique quality. For the Australian and New Zealand people it has a very special place in their histories and memories, not only because it was there that the Anzacs made their imperishable name and reputation for the first time, but because very few families in either country - and particularly New Zealand, with its tiny population - did not have a member of their family involved; too many of them never returned. Also, any operation associated with the name of Winston Churchill has a compulsively interesting power, however controversial his role may be regarded. For the Turkish people it was a glorious victory, although achieved at terrible cost, by which Kemal Ataturk first rose to fame. For the British, who suffered so severely, it remains a tantalising epic of might-have-beens. Whatever the causes may be, Gallipoli is still regarded as a very special campaign.

For students of military history it has a particular professional interest, as it was the first major amphibious operation in modern warfare, involving the novelties of aircraft, submarine and landing-craft, and revealing the inadequacies of naval bombardment on well-dug positions. It provided an immense storehouse of experience drawn on in the planning of the invasion of France in 1944 and the recapture of the Falklands in 1982, although, interestingly, some of the same mistakes were repeated on both occasions. Nonetheless, the importance of the study of military history by professional servicemen has seldom been so clearly justified, and the harsh experience of war rarely put to better use. In this sense, at least, it can be said with truth that Gallipoli was not all loss. The young Lieutenant Slim, for one, never forgot the lessons he learnt from Gallipoli to the immense benefit of those who were fortunate to serve under his command in North Africa and Burma. It was on Gallipoli, also that Slim first appreciated the great qualities of the Anzac and the Indian soldier, for whom he developed an admiration not far short of love, and which was fully returned by both.

My fascination with the campaign began early, as my father had very nearly served in it, and my beloved Uncle Roy had, with the 1/6 Gurkha Rifles, the regiment in which Slim, his son, and my eldest brother later served. Furthermore, he had been at Anzac and had taken part with Slim in the terrible August attack, in which, like Slim, he had been gravely injured. This book, like the original, is dedicated to him.

At the age of thirteen I went to the Oxford City Library and took out Aspinall-Oglander's two volumes of the British Official History, and was enthralled. For years I read everything I could about Gallipoli, including the C. E. W. Bean's superb Australian Official History, but without any intention of writing about it.

In 1956 Alan Moorehead's *Gallipoli* was published. It received immense praise, but my initial enthusiasm was tempered not only by the inaccuracies it contained but by many of the judgements, and by the realisation that it was thinly researched. It was, like all Moorehead's books, beautifully written, but the more I went into it the more I became convinced that it was, as a work of history, seriously flawed. I suppose it was then that the idea of writing a new history was born, but at the time I was a young official of the House of Commons and deeply involved in my biography of Lord Randolph Churchill, which was published in 1959, followed by my biography of Rosebery, which appeared in 1963.

It was just after the principal research on Rosebery had been completed in 1961 that I met Brian Batsford, Member of Parliament and publisher, in the Members' Lobby of the House of Commons to discuss the affairs of a little committee of which he was the Chairman and I was the Clerk (secretary). At the end of our chat he casually asked me what book I next had in mind, and I said that the book I really wanted to do was a new history of the Gallipoli Campaign, as the confidential British papers would be soon available under the then Fifty Year Rule. To my eternal gratitude Batsford commissioned it on the spot for his firm's 'British Battles' series for the then princely advance of £100. From that chance conversation much flowed.

My *Gallipoli* was published in 1965. When I had publicly appealed for papers relating to the campaign I had been swamped with old diaries, letters, and reminiscences. Also, at that time, many Gallipoli veterans were alive, including Slim and Lord Attlee, and were generous in their time and papers. Long before I got to the official British archives I had more material, all of it original, than I had ever bargained for, and it was this material that completely changed the course of the book: it became an exercise in describing the campaign from the vantage-point of the participants on both sides. I had not appreciated the sheer novelty of this approach until the reviews came in. I believe that it is this that has given the book a freshness and vitality that has kept it in print for virtually all the past twenty-three years and has made it, in terms both of sales and library borrowings, the most successful of all my works. It has been translated into Italian and Turkish, and has been as successful in America as it has been in Britain, Australia and New Zealand. The first edition is virtually unobtainable - which is sad, as it was lavishly illustrated with original photographs that were, unlike so many of the usual Gallipoli photographs, genuine.

Public interest in Gallipoli has never really faltered, but was certainly given an immense boost by Peter Weir's beautiful and brilliant film, *Gallipoli*. Sadly, the film was badly marred by an anti-British streak, culminating in a total distortion of the causes of the disastrous attack by the Ligh Horse at The Nek - a travesty that would have shocked Charles Bean as much as it did me, and which has recently been corrected in a fine documentary film on the campaign by the Australian Broadcasting Corporation. It is melancholy when so many myths of the campaign - especially in Australia - are perpetuated in this manner, especially as the heroism of the Anzacs requires no mythology.

When I first visited the Peninsular in 1962 it was utterly deserted. Access to it was virtually impossible as it was a military zone and in my case only granted through the intercession with the Turkish authorities by Sir Winston Churchill. There were only dirt roads, and paths negotiable only on foot or by Land-Rover. I could have taken home a ship-load of trophies from the battlefields, as the debris of the armies was everywhere — and also the skulls and bones of unburied soldiers. It was an eerie experience, and, certainly in Monash Valley, an unnerving one. When I wrote 'If ghosts walk, they walk in Monash Valley' I meant it. Over the years I have met many who had not believed me until they had visited that truly haunted and forbidding place, where strangers are *not* welcome. These include cynical professional soldiers as well as visitors, including my wife, who has also caught that grim atmosphere. Even now, when there are Tarmac roads and a museum, when the battlefields have been stripped of their mementoes and tourists made welcome (and some barbarian has built a house at V Beach where the *River Clyde* landed), Monash Valley keeps its own company.

Each reprinting of my book has been so warmly received that I hope this latest one will attract a new generation of readers who have, like me, fallen under the strange hold on the heart and the imagination that Gallipoli continues to exercise, over seventy years after the great enterprise ended.

Robert Rhodes James
1988

Acknowledgement

The Author and Publishers wish to thank the following for permission to reproduce the illustrations which appear in this book:

The Australian War Memorial, for figs. 3, 5, 7, 8, 15
The Imperial War Museum, for figs. 1, 3, 5, 11, 12, 14
Dr O. C. Williams, for figs. 2, 8, 9, 10

List of Illustrations

Maps

PART ONE

INITIATION

Who is to have Constantinople? That is always the crux of the problem.

Napoleon, May 1808

(*Above*) *The
Dardanelles Area*

*Southern Gallipoli
Peninsula: Principal
geographical features*

I

Prologue

My sentence is for open war: of wiles
More unexpert, I boast not.
Milton: 'Paradise Lost', Book ii, line 51

The problem of forcing the Dardanelles—the ancient Hellespont—had engrossed the attention and imagination of naval and military strategists for many centuries before the First World War. Although this famous narrow strip of water linking the Aegean Sea and the Sea of Marmara extends for about 40 miles, the critical area on which particular attention was devoted runs from the western entrance some 13 miles up to the Narrows. The western mouth of the Dardanelles is only some 4,000 yards wide; but as soon as one has passed the guardian fortresses of Sedd-el-Bahr at the tip of the Gallipoli Peninsula—the Thracian Chersonese—to the left and Kum Kale jutting out on a low promontory from Asia to the right, the channel widens considerably for about four miles. To the left, the Gallipoli Peninsula rises steadily from Cape Helles, and the western shore of the Dardanelles becomes tall and uninviting; to the right, the hills of Asia gradually come nearer. The Dardanelles then contracts sharply, and by the time that the Narrows, only 1,600 yards across, are approached, the Kilid Bahr plateau on the Gallipoli Peninsula rises sharply from the water, while to the right the hills behind the town of Chanak* are oppressively close.

Sedd-el-Bahr and Kum Kale guard the entrance to the Dardanelles; the forts of Kilid Bahr and Chanak dominate the Narrows; between the two, any advancing fleet would find itself under fire from the frowning massif of

* Its correct Turkish name is Çannakkale; but it is called Chanak in the British 1915 maps and I have therefore used this name throughout. All references to place-names are to those used by the British in 1915. Some place-names have been changed since 1915, or have reverted to older names. Thus Constantinople is now Istanbul, and Maidos Eçeabat.

I

the Gallipoli Peninsula and from the rising ground on the Asiatic shore. A five-knot current, sweeping perpetually down the Dardanelles from the Sea of Marmara, can whip the water up unpleasantly. In winter, it is bitterly cold; in summer, apart from an occasional storm which rushes fiercely down from the hills, the sun burns unrelentingly from the end of April to October.

In spring and early summer the Dardanelles and the surrounding countryside are exquisitely beautiful. The hills are ablaze with flowers, the ground appears soft and verdurous, the tiny towns have a toy-like charm in the delicious light, and the Marmara birds skim endlessly over the deep blue of the Dardanelles. But, as summer progresses, the flowers fade and vanish, the interminable stunted scrub acquires a parched, withered appearance, the grass dies on the hills, an almost perpetual breeze stirs up the bleached chalky drugget into an unpleasant spume which drifts lazily across the Peninsula; a film of dust covers everything, and an air of dispiriting ennui descends over the few small towns and villages. Apart from the town of Gallipoli, some 25 miles north of the Narrows, the Peninsula was sparsely populated in 1915. The few villages were small, bedraggled and poverty-stricken. There was little of a living to be scratched from the inhospitable soil, and the lack of fresh water in summer precluded any extensive grazing for cattle. The occasional cart-tracks were rocky, narrow, deeply-rutted and hazardous.

The southern end of the Peninsula is dominated by the relatively low, bald hump of a ridge known to the Turks as Alchi Tepe, and to the British (as a result of a map error) as Achi Baba. Although only about 700 feet high it bestrides the Peninsula and absolutely dominates the ground to the south. It rises so gently that the walk to the summit from Cape Helles, which barely takes an hour, does not prepare the climber for the view to the south. To the east of the summit, however, the Dardanelles is hidden from view until one walks a further mile and a half to the lesser summit of Tenkir Tepe. From here one can see most of the Dardanelles up to the Narrows. But two deep, plunging gorges—the Soghanli and Saghir Deres—lie between the Achi Baba ridge and the Kilid Bahr Plateau, some four miles away to the north-east. Thus, although distances are short on the Peninsula, the ground is so broken and rough and the paths so few that progress north of Achi Baba to the Kilid Bahr Plateau is very slow indeed.

About ten miles to the north-west from Achi Baba, a much higher ridge, nearly 1,000 feet high, dominates the sky-line. This is Sari Bair (Turkish for 'the yellow ridge') which forms the vertebrae, as it were, of this part of the Peninsula. It has three summits, all approximately the same height, separated from each other by about half a mile of undulating crest-line. The most northern summit, 971 feet high, is called Koja Chemen Tepe; the next, Besim Tepe, became known to the British as Hill Q; the third—850 feet high—is called Chunuk Bair. Between the southern Sari Bair foothills and the western extremities of the Kilid Bahr Plateau a low, bare, and almost flat plain stretches across the Peninsula from the blunt promontory of Gaba Tepe on the west coast to the small village of Maidos on the Dardanelles shore. The Sari Bair hills climb gently westwards away from the Dardanelles, but, on the west coast they collapse suddenly from the triple crests into an impossible tangle of steep ravines, washaways, and cliffs cascading abruptly down to the Aegean. To the north of Sari Bair lies Suvla Plain and a great Salt Lake, across which the carts of the villagers creep endlessly in high summer, collecting the salt, like flies crawling across a white marble table-top. A triangle of bleak hills surrounds Suvla Plain on three sides, giving it the appearance of an enormous natural arena. Far across the Aegean to the north-west, the jagged pinnacle of Samothrace can be seen on a clear day; to the west, the long island of Imbros lines, pencil-like, the horizon.

Since ancient times, when the Hellespont was the scene of the siege of Troy and Xerxes' crossing by a bridge of boats into Europe in 480 B.C., the world left the Gallipoli Peninsula undisturbed. The few large towns built on the Peninsula crumbled away and disappeared;* apart from the building of the two massive fortresses of Sedd-el-Bahr and Kilid Bahr in the sixteenth century, the centuries had done little to alter the face of the bleak, narrow, wind-swept and barren Peninsula.

All naval authorities agreed that an opposed forcing of the Dardanelles would be difficult and hazardous. In 1807 a British squadron under Admiral Duckworth made a successful opposed passage of the Straits, and although the return journey proved more difficult, returned to the Aegean without losing a ship. The vast improvement in gunnery in the nineteenth century made it improbable that this feat could be repeated. 'If the artillery material in the Dardanelles were set in proper order,' Moltke wrote in 1836, 'I do not believe that any Fleet in the world would dare to enter the Straits.' In 1878 a British squadron was sent to Besika Bay, in case the Russians attacked Turkey, and the Admiral in command did not conceal his apprehensions about making an opposed passage through the Dardanelles. One of his subordinates was the future Lord Fisher, who undertook several examinations of the problem while in command of the Mediterranean Fleet and at the Admiralty when he became First Sea Lord in 1904. His conclusion was that it was 'mightily hazardous', a view confirmed by a joint military and naval investigation in 1906, which stated that although a squadron of 'His Majesty's least valuable ships' might succeed in 'rushing' the Straits, the attempt was 'much to be deprecated'. In the March of 1911, Winston Churchill wrote in

* Unfortunately, little detailed archaeological work has been done on the Peninsula. It is believed that there was once a large town near Morto Bay, and during the campaign some valuable antiquities were unearthed by the troops digging trenches or as a result of shell-fire. The existence and location of the ancient towns on the Peninsula remain a subject of speculation.

a Cabinet memorandum that the days of forcing the Dardanelles by warships were gone; it should be remembered,' he wrote, ' that it is no longer possible to force the Dardanelles, and nobody would expose a modern fleet to such peril.'*

The exercise, which had particularly fascinated British sailors for so long, had been in the main an academic one. British diplomacy throughout the nineteenth century had applied itself to the preservation of the Ottoman Empire as a barrier to Russia's Mediterranean ambitions. The task was not a simple one; apart from the fundamental weaknesses of the Empire, British opinion became progressively more anti-Turk. A warm interlude in Anglo-Turkish relations had not long survived the Crimean War in the 1850's. The popular enthusiasm in Britain on Turkey's behalf, bolstered by a stream of cogently argued memoranda on Russian ambitions which descended on Ministers from the British Ambassador, Sir Stratford Canning, had propelled the Aberdeen Government into a war in the Crimea which it hated and which it grievously mismanaged. British troops were quartered at Gallipoli, and the British fleet sailed to Constantinople and filled the Golden Horn. Thereafter British enthusiasm for Turkey cooled. When the Russian armies again threatened Constantinople in 1876–7, the active intervention of the British Government on Turkey's behalf provoked intense opposition in England. Reports of Turkish atrocities in Bulgaria aroused a public revulsion in Britain which was re-awakened in the 1890's, when the Turkish massacres of the Armenians brought the aged Gladstone thundering out of his retirement. Carlyle had been in a minority when, at the outbreak of the Crimean War, he had categorised the Turk as 'a lazy, ugly, sensual dark fanatic'; by the beginning of the twentieth century this was the popular view in Britain. The Turk was no longer the brave underdog, gallantly standing up to the Russian colossus, the saviour of the Hungarian revolutionary, Kossuth, who had been given sanctuary in Constantinople in 1848 while the Russian armies brutally suppressed his followers; he was now 'unspeakable', the pariah of Europe, barbaric, incompetent and impotent.

In these circumstances, British policy towards the Ottoman Empire became increasingly ambivalent. The Empire was a supreme geographic, political and economic monstrosity which enveloped the eastern end of the Mediterranean, penetrated deep into Europe up to the Adriatic, plunged eastwards across vast tracts of territory inhabited almost solely by nomadic tribes, and lapped westwards far along the northern littoral of the African continent. But its political effectiveness as a barrier to Russian ambitions was invaluable, and was the basis of its precarious existence.

Although the Congress of Berlin of 1878 had emphatically affirmed the

* This document has never been published in full. It is not included in the recently published *List of Cabinet Papers, 1880–1914* (Public Record Office: H.M.S.O., 1964).

principle—first laid down in the Congress of London and confirmed by the Treaty of Paris in 1856—that the Dardanelles were not to be entered by the warships of any belligerent nation while Turkey herself remained neutral, and although Britain, France and Germany had also combined to guarantee the integrity of the Ottoman Empire, there was an increasing disposition in British political and diplomatic circles to adopt a cold and contemptuous attitude towards the Sublime Porte. British intervention in Egypt—theoretically part of the Ottoman Empire—in 1882, subsequently extended into virtual acquisition, provided an additional source of strain between the two Governments.

From 1880, when Gladstone summarily recalled Sir Henry Layard, the spiritual legatee of Sir Stratford Canning, from Constantinople, the calibre of British Ambassadors to Turkey, and the length of their tours of duty, declined in comparable proportions. At the same time, German influence was sedulously fostered. 'The new element, the German, in Eastern politics deserves our grave consideration', Layard had written to Beaconsfield as early as 1877, but the warning went unheeded. While Europe rang with denunciations of the Armenian atrocities, there was no echo in Berlin; the Germans financed loans, provided a military mission from 1883 to 1895, and encouraged hundreds of young Turkish officers and army surgeons to complete their training in Germany. Trade between the two countries was so actively fostered that Turkish exports to Germany rose from a value of two and a half million marks in 1880 to over 71 million marks by 1905, and this in a period when Turkish exports to other countries remained stagnant.

State visits to Constantinople by the Kaiser gave the opportunity for flamboyant public expressions of devotion to Turkish aspirations, while the formidable German Ambassador at Constantinople from 1897 to 1912, Baron Marschall von Bieberstein, pursued a dexterous course in the labyrinthine intricacies of Turkish politics to promote German influence. Two obscure but deeply informed Germans, Paul Weitz, who represented the *Frankfurter Zeitung* in Turkey for nearly 30 years, and the naval attaché, Humann, who had been born in Smyrna and who spent almost all his life in Turkey, provided von Bieberstein and his successor, Baron von Wangenheim, with accurate and up-to-date information of the greatest value. 'I am afraid I see no signs of any diminution of German influence here,' George Lloyd wrote from Constantinople in the March of 1906; 'It steadily increases and—through our own inactivity—it is gradually becoming out of our power to stop it.'

By the time that Europe began to mass itself into two uneasy camps in the first decade of the twentieth century, the separate interests of the Entente Powers—Britain, France and Russia—were causing tensions in the alliance in the Middle East. Although Russian eyes were still traditionally fixed on the gleaming minarets of Constantinople, they were reasonably content with a situation whereby Turkey was strong enough to hold the Straits as an international waterway to provide Russia with her vital access to the Mediterranean. As Sazonov, the Russian Foreign Minister, wrote to the Tsar in the December of 1913, 'to abandon the Straits to a powerful State would be synonymous with subordinating the whole economic development of southern Russia to this State.' The British, although they had no direct personal interest in the Straits, were very interested indeed in Persia, which was a perpetual sore in Anglo-Russian relations. The French were actively concerned to prevent the possibility of her two allies carving up what remained of the Ottoman Empire between themselves. These jarring interests were to have a profound effect upon subsequent events.

The unexpected deposition of Sultan Abdul Hamid in 1908 by a group of young army officers had caught all the great powers off balance. Discontent at Abdul's repressive and incompetent government had become so well established but had manifested itself so sporadically and feebly that it came as a considerable surprise when a number of officers, dubbed 'the Young Turks', raised the standard of military revolt in Macedonia and demanded the restoration of the constitution which had been suspended since 1877. The surprise was even greater when Abdul weakly capitulated and issued writs for elections. Liberal-minded men everywhere were enchanted; all Europe and the Young Turks themselves gazed with stupefaction at the simplicity and speed of it all.

Disillusionment followed swiftly on the morrow of elation. Bulgaria declared for independence. Austria-Hungary annexed Bosnia and Herzegovina. Crete proclaimed her union with Greece. This series of hammer-blows inflamed the volatile population of Constantinople and, far more seriously, powerful elements in the army itself. Those around Abdul judged that the opportunity for counter-attack had arrived. When the dust cleared, Abdul was exiled in Salonika, his tottering feeble brother had been proclaimed Sultan in his stead, and the Young Turks were back.

The dismemberment of the Ottoman Empire now gathered momentum. In 1911 the Italians invaded Tripoli and Cyrenaica. In the October of 1912 the highly improbable coalition of Bulgaria, Greece, Serbia and Montenegro fell on Turkey's European territories. After a series of military catastrophes the Turks were in danger of losing Constantinople itself before the western powers, with a belated realisation of what was involved, intervened to prevent the process of dismemberment to be carried to its logical conclusion. The victors then fell into bitter disputation over their booty, and the Turks managed to salvage something from the wreckage.

In these threatening circumstances the Young Turks searched eagerly for powerful allies. At home, all the early pretences of democratic government had been abandoned, and the atmosphere was sulphurous; abroad, the Empire was surrounded by avaricious neighbours. In spite of all von Bieberstein's efforts and the fact that the Germans had adapted themselves more quickly to the new situation created by Abdul Hamid's deposition than the British or the French, the failure of the German-trained Turkish armies in the First Balkan War had caused a sharp slump in the reputation of the Germans at Constantinople, and the Young Turks would have been prepared to involve themselves more closely with the British. Their approaches, however, were coldly received, and the Germans made continuous attempts to restore their somewhat tarnished reputation, achieving a considerable double success when they received final permission for the Bagdad Railway and secured the appointment of a military mission headed by General Liman von Sanders in December 1913.

The extent of German infiltration into Turkey now began to cause the Russians considerable and justifiable alarm. In spite of the series of disasters which had overtaken the Ottoman Empire since their accession, the position of the Young Turks had not been seriously challenged. Indeed, resentment at the perfidy of other nations had aroused in Turkey something in the nature of a feeling of nationalism. The Young Turks themselves were a bizarre collection of adventurers, opportunists and idealists whose background, aspirations and methods were grotesquely alien to pre-1914 Europe. The Sultan, Mohammed V, sat unhappily as the titular head of the precarious structure, his only asset to the government being the mystical concept of the Khalifate which was virtually the only bond which kept the Empire together, and which the Young Turks had wisely preserved. He had already been compelled to sign the death-warrant of his son-in-law by Talaat, the Minister of the Interior, on a trumped-up charge of conspiracy, and the body of the victim conspicuously dangling from a public gibbet in Constantinople dramatically emphasised where the reality of power lay. The nominal Prime Minister, the Grand Vizier, was, in the words of Lewis Einstein, then at the American Embassy, 'a rather pompous little man who speaks as if he ruled the Empire, whereas he is only a figurehead, ignores business, and takes his orders from Talaat'.

Talaat, however, was not the dominant personality. This was the 34-year-old Minister of War, Enver, of whom the American Ambassador, Morgenthau, has written that 'his nature had a remorselessness, a lack of pity, a cold-blooded determination, of which his clear-cut handsome face, his small but sturdy figure, and his pleasing manners, gave no indication'. His career since 1908, when he had led the march to bring Abdul Hamid to heel, had been tumultuous, spectacular, and dazzlingly successful. He was suave, cold-eyed, mercurial, with more than a touch of megalomania; his personal courage and utter ruthlessness were well known, and to none better than his colleagues. However much they might distrust Enver, there was no one in the Young Turk government who dared to challenge him.

It was on Enver, the most impressionable and volatile of the Young Turks, that von Bieberstein, and subsequently Wangenheim, most assiduously played. On the whole, the instinctively xenophobic Turks had no real liking for the Germans, and were uneasy at their growing influence. When the von Sanders military mission arrived at Constantinople in December 1913, representatives from the German Embassy were studiously absent. Von Sanders was angry, but Wangenheim had been right. The Russians, reluctantly supported by Britain and France, had protested at the mission, but it was not only to calm Entente alarm that Wangenheim had taken such care to avoid any public association with the mission, although he had been the prime instigator of its appointment.

Other elaborately-publicised efforts were made to play down the rôle of the mission. The visit to Constantinople of the almost brand-new battle-cruiser *Goeben* was a happier *succès d'estime*. She was the largest warship to pass through the Dardanelles, and, anchored off the Golden Horn, ablaze at night with lights from stem to stern, and the venue for numerous glittering receptions, her arrival did something to counter-balance the healthy respect felt by Turkish Ministers for the British fleet.

Nevertheless, as the calm, uneasy, torrid summer of 1914 passed, the Turks manifested little desire to become too closely enmeshed with the Germans. When some Ministers visited the Tsar at Livadia in May they were treated with unwonted consideration. A sharp decline in Anglo-Russian relations, caused by chronically divergent interests in Persia and by calculated leaking by the Germans of secret naval talks which provoked such a storm of British popular indignation that they had to be hastily abandoned, helped to lessen Turkish apprehensions about the presence of both Britain and Russia in the Entente.

Confidential discussions about a new Anglo-Turkish treaty began in London. Two modern battleships for the Turkish Navy were nearing completion in British shipyards; there was a British naval mission at Constantinople. Although the size of the German military mission steadily increased, a series of sharp personal differences about the re-equipping and reorganisation of the Turkish army between von Sanders and Enver aroused resentment and mistrust on both sides. Sir Louis Mallet, the British Ambassador, had no cause to alter his plans to go on extended leave in July. But by the time he returned on August 18th the situation had changed catastrophically for the Entente powers.

The series of events which sucked Turkey into the Great War have often been related. The Turks had everything to gain by playing off one side against another, and this, for a time, they managed to do. On August 2nd,

Enver and Wangenheim signed a secret treaty exclusively directed against Russia, but Britain's unanticipated declaration of war against Germany two days later resulted in a proposal to the Russian Ambassador by Enver for a Turco-Russian alliance aimed exclusively against Germany. But the brusque appropriation by the British Government of the two Turkish battleships, the *Sultan Osman* and the *Reshadieh*, being completed in British shipyards caused a wave of intense anti-British feeling not only in Government circles but throughout Turkey. The warships had cost the then colossal sum of seven and a half million pounds, much of which had been raised by public subscription, and although the British decision had strong military justification, the manner in which it was carried out was inept. No mention was made of compensation, and no suggestion was considered that two older ships might have been offered. Turkish reactions were bitter, and were inflamed by a fierce anti-British and anti-Russian press campaign financed by Wangenheim, who even purchased one newspaper—*Ikdam*—for the purpose.

Into this atmosphere of disillusionment and anger steamed the *Goeben*, with her attendant light cruiser, *Breslau*, commanded by Admiral Souchon, remembered by Lewis Einstein as 'a droop-jawed, determined little man in a long ill-fitting frock coat, looking more like a parson than an admiral'. For the warships to enter the Dardanelles with the connivance of the Turk government would be in direct contravention of no less than three international treaties, and even Berlin hesitated. Souchon, however, was determined to make for Constantinople, and, after a series of dramatic adventures in the Mediterranean in which he evaded the British squadrons with a combination of audacity and luck and which have been often described,* arrived off Sedd-el-Bahr on August 10th, determined, if need be, to shoot his way through the Dardanelles.

On the late afternoon of the 10th Enver was in conference with a member of the German military mission, Colonel Kannengiesser, when a Lt.-Col. von Kress was ushered in. Kress announced that *Goeben* and *Breslau* were at the entrance to the Dardanelles, and required permission to enter. Enver hesitated, and said that he must consult the Grand Vizier; Kress demanded an immediate answer. After a long pause, Enver said they could enter. Kress then asked for the forts to be ordered to open fire if the British warships, belatedly closing in, pursued them; Enver again tried to procrastinate, Kress again demanded an immediate decision, and Enver at length gave it. 'We heard the clanking of the portcullis descending before the Dardanelles,' Kannengiesser wrote. 'It was an incident in the world's history of which I chanced to be a witness. None of us had moved a muscle. Kress

---

* See R. K. Middlemas, *Command the Far Seas* and D. Woodward, *The Escape of the Goeben and Breslau* (*History Today*, April 1960) for two recent accounts.

took his leave, and I proceeded with my report as though nothing had happened.'

From the moment that *Goeben* and *Breslau* anchored in the Golden Horn, the Young Turks were trapped. On September 9th the British naval mission under Admiral Limpus was withdrawn, and Limpus himself was appointed to administer the Malta Dockyard, and not the British squadron off the Dardanelles, for the reason—not as stupid as some critics have made it appear—that his knowledge of Turkish naval matters might not arouse suspicions about Britain's professions of friendship, now being eagerly pressed by Mallet. On the previous day (September 8th) Enver, although under strong German pressure, had refused to authorise the closing of the Dardanelles, and the majority of the Ministers were strongly in favour of non-intervention. *Goeben* and *Breslau* had been nominally handed over to the Turkish Navy, although they still had their German crews—who went through the farce of wearing fezzes when going ashore—but the Entente Powers were by now prepared to accept almost anything provided Turkey stayed neutral.

The age-old question of forcing the Dardanelles was reopened in London by Sir Louis Mallet himself towards the end of August. Mallet, on the information at his disposal, had no doubt that a British squadron could shoot its way through, but urged that examination should be given to providing an army to occupy the Dardanelles area after the fleet had passed through. The Russians, meanwhile, had asked King Constantine of Greece if he would supply an expeditionary force to assist in an attack on the Dardanelles, and had received guarded assent. On August 19th the Greeks offered the Entente their full naval and military resources, and on August 31st, the subject was discussed by Winston Churchill, the First Lord of the Admiralty, and Lord Kitchener, the newly appointed Secretary of State for War. On September 1st, Churchill asked the Chief of the Imperial General Staff to examine and work out with two officers from the Admiralty a 'plan for the seizure of the Gallipoli Peninsula, by means of a Greek army of adequate strength, with a view to admitting a British fleet to the sea of Marmara'.

The report of the Director of Military Operations, General Callwell, was submitted two days later. On the hypothesis that the Peninsula was garrisoned by about 27,000 men, with further reinforcements at hand, a force of not less than 60,000 would be required to effect its capture. Even in these circumstances, Callwell emphasised, the attack 'is likely to prove an extremely difficult operation of war', and Kitchener's attention was drawn to a decision of the Committee of Imperial Defence in 1907 that the only possibility of success lay in a combined operation. 'My exposition was intended to be dissuasive,' Callwell subsequently wrote, 'and I think Mr. Churchill was disappointed.' Nevertheless, on September 4th, the chief of the British naval mission to Greece, Rear-Admiral Kerr, was instructed to open discussions with the Greek military authorities.

The Greek plans for capturing the Peninsula were detailed and had been carefully prepared. 60,000 men would be landed south of the promontory of Gaba Tepe on the west coast, to strike eastwards across the Maidos plain to take the Kilid Bahr batteries from the rear and then to attack south towards Sedd-el-Bahr. Meanwhile, a smaller force would be landed on the Asiatic shore to seize Kum Kale. Following the success of these operations, another army would be landed near Bulair to seize and hold the isthmus.

Churchill, who had wanted to chase the two German warships up the Dardanelles and sink them in the Marmara but had been overruled by his colleagues, was now enthusiastically pressing the project for seizing Gallipoli. Alone of the Cabinet, he cherished few hopes that the Turks would remain neutral for long. A succession of intercepted messages between Wangenheim and Berlin were evidence enough. 'Winston [is] violently anti-Turk', the Prime Minister, Asquith, noted on August 21st. On September 6th Churchill was urging Grey, the Foreign Secretary, to ask the Russians for an army corps to join in the attack. 'The price to be paid in taking Gallipoli would no doubt be heavy,' he wrote, 'but there would be no more war with Turkey. A good army of 50,000 men and sea power—that is the end of the Turkish menace.'

These highly ambitious projects collapsed. The Greeks had made it clear that their intervention was based on the proviso of a simultaneous attack on Turkey by Bulgaria, and King Constantine now drastically extended this stipulation by declaring that Greece would not attack unless Turkey attacked her first. The Balkan imbroglio which had tormented western diplomats for over a decade, and now exacerbated by the influence of Constantine's Queen (a sister of the Kaiser), was already exercising its baleful influence on the war which it had itself precipitated. The Russians had no army corps to spare. The Gallipoli project receded into the background.

Nevertheless, an important step forward had been taken. No one in the Admiralty or the War Office had said that the idea was madness, and the Greeks had been very confident. Churchill himself, like most military students, had been profoundly impressed by the effect of modern artillery on forts, and the Dardanelles forts were very old indeed. Subsequently, in *The World Crisis*, Churchill waxed very sarcastic about those critics who had accused him of confusing the effects of land-based howitzers with low-trajectory naval guns, but his own evidence to the Dardanelles Commission emphasises the extent to which he had been justifiably impressed by events in Europe. 'Like most people,' he said, 'I had held the opinion that the days of forcing the Dardanelles were over, and I had even recorded this fact in a Cabinet paper in 1911. But this war had brought many surprises. We had seen fortresses reported throughout Europe to be impregnable collapsing after a few days' attack by field armies without a regular siege.' Callwell was very struck by Churchill's immense enthusiasm for the project, even at this very early stage. 'Mr. Churchill was very keen', he subsequently said, 'on attacking the Dardanelles from a very early stage . . . he was very keen to get to Constantinople somehow.' Churchill was also becoming intrigued by the possibilities of a purely naval attack if troops were not forthcoming, and discussed these at length with his naval secretary, Commodore de Bartolemé; the latter was strongly of the opinion that such a project was doomed to failure, and there, for the moment, the matter lapsed.

Churchill's gloomy prognostications about the chances of keeping Turkey neutral were quickly fulfilled. In Europe, everyone's plans had gone dramatically wrong. The Germans had not reached Paris; the French had not recaptured Alsace and Lorraine; the Russian advance into Prussia had been overwhelmingly thrown back at Tannenberg; the opposing trenches of the Anglo-French and German armies writhed from the Flanders coast to the Swiss frontiers. The casualties on all sides had been unimaginably terrible. The first atavistic fury of the war was over.

It was now even more vitally important for the Germans to jerk Turkey out of her twilight neutrality and for the Allies to keep her out of the war. On September 27th the British squadron off the entrance to the Dardanelles ordered a Turkish torpedo-boat to turn back. There was no justification whatever for this high-handed action, and it gave the Germans the opportunity they needed. The Turkish Admiral commanding the Straits was persuaded by the Germans on the spot to close the Dardanelles; after the torpedo-boat episode he was not disposed to challenge the suggestion. Lighthouses were extinguished, mines sown, and warning notices appeared on the cliffs. The Turkish Ministers met in consternation, but there was nothing they could do. The Entente Ambassadors delivered strong protests, and were supported vigorously by the Americans, but the reality of power no longer lay with the Turkish Government. Russian ships filled the Golden Horn for several weeks, and then had to go back to their ports; they were destined never to return. What had been one of the most busy and animated shipping thoroughfares in the world quickly assumed a deserted and hang-dog air, the water only occasionally ruffled by ferry-boats and *caiques*.

More and more German officers were now to be seen everywhere in Constantinople; Morgenthau has described how General von der Goltz would make 'a kind of viceregal progress through the streets in a large and madly-dashing automobile, on both sides of which flaring German eagles were painted. A trumpeter on the front seat would blow loud, defiant blasts as the conveyance rushed along'. The wives and children of British, French and Russian officials and businessmen began to leave the capital. The

Entente Ambassadors stepped up their offers to guarantee the Ottoman Empire, while, on the other hand, Wangenheim worked tirelessly to impress the Turks with the reality of German strength. His most powerful argument rode at anchor in the Golden Horn. By now, there were several thousand Germans in the capital; French and British ships were being detained and having their wirelesses removed; minelaying in the Straits continued; a battery of field guns, heavy howitzer batteries, thousands of rifles and over 3,000 shells for *Goeben* arrived by devious routes at Constantinople. Turkey was slithering helplessly into war.

The decisive act of war came on October 28th, when Souchon took the Turkish fleet into the Black Sea and bombarded Odessa, Sebastopol and Feodosia under the Turkish flag. The available evidence, although conflicting and confusing, makes it reasonably clear that only Enver of the Turkish Ministers knew of this deliberate act of belligerency, and it is doubtful if even he was fully aware of what Souchon intended to do.

Hostilities began on October 31st. On November 3rd the British squadron in the Aegean, on Churchill's orders but contrary to the urgings of Admiral Limpus, opened fire on Sedd-el-Bahr and Kum Kale, with impressive results. A lucky shot hit the magazine at Sedd-el-Bahr, which blew up with a shattering detonation, destroying almost all the heavy guns in the vicinity. A dense pall of smoke hung in the short November afternoon over the entrance to the Dardanelles as the British warships turned away, with a few Turkish shells splashing harmlessly in the sea.

For nearly six weeks, nothing of importance occurred at the Dardanelles. In spite of the dramatic warning given by the brief bombardment, the work of repairing the forts and garrisoning the area was not carried forward energetically. On December 13th Mr. Engert, the American vice-consul at Chanak, was enjoying the warm morning in a small rowing boat in the Straits when the old battleship *Messudieh*, anchored south of Chanak in Sari Sighlar Bay, was suddenly rent with a gigantic explosion and sank in under seven minutes. The tiny British submarine B11, only 143 feet long and with a maximum submerged speed of $6\frac{1}{2}$ knots, manned by two officers and eleven ratings, eventually limped out of the Straits to the open sea, safety, and the first submarine V.C. for her commander, Lt. Holbrook. It was, as a German naval officer ruefully admitted to the enthralled Mr. Engert, 'a mighty clever piece of work'.

Thus ended the prologue to the Gallipoli expedition.

2

The Drift to the Dardanelles

Expeditions which are decided upon and organised with insufficient care generally end disastrously.
Lloyd George, Memorandum to the War Council, December 1914

The Dardanelles fortifications which ran along both shores from the Aegean
up to the Narrows were based on three groups of defensive positions. The
Outer Defences consisted of the batteries at and around Sedd-el-Bahr and
Kum Kale, with a total of four long-range and 20 medium-range guns. The
Intermediate Defences were between the entrance to the Dardanelles and
Kephez Point, and at this stage comprised only seven medium-range guns
in two batteries and one or two field batteries. The Inner Defences at the
Narrows, grouped in batteries around Kilid Bahr on the Gallipoli shore and
Chanak on the Asiatic, consisted of nearly 80 guns, of which only eight were
long-range. The distribution and grouping of these batteries was poor. All
were uncovered, the inexperienced gun crews had little protection, and
magazines were adjacent to the guns and almost unprotected; range-finding
equipment was obsolete and inefficient, telephone communications were
haphazard and unreliable, all the batteries were conspicuous from the sea,
there were several types of guns in many batteries using different ammunition, the ground equipment was so bad that the guns had to be re-aligned
whenever they were moved, and the guns themselves were old and had been
poorly maintained.

The effortless destruction of the Sedd-el-Bahr guns on November 3rd
shocked even the lethargic Turks, as well as arousing over-confidence
among the British. The warships had been able to destroy the Outer Defences
without danger or even inconvenience, and in fact the Fleet had caused
more damage in this brief bombardment than they achieved in the rest of the

14

naval campaign. The balance of the Dardanelles defences was therefore shifted to the Intermediate and Inner Defences, although the Outer Forts were not abandoned. The emphasis was also moved from the guns to the mines, a decision which was to alter the nature of the defences completely. 'The basic principle on which the defence of the Dardanelles was based,' Djcvad, the Turkish commander of the Straits, subsequently stated, 'was to have the minefields concentrated high up the Straits, and to have the field of fire of the principal forts some distance below the minefield, so that a barrage could be maintained on ships entering the Straits before they could reach or interfere with the minefields.'

Reduced to its essentials, the purpose of the guns was to protect the minefields. Mines were of a poor quality and in short supply, but in November five lines were laid, with a total of 191 contact mines. By March these had increased to 11 lines, with a total of 344 contact mines; three 18-inch torpedo tubes, the result, ironically enough, of Admiral Limpus' advice on the defence of the Dardanelles, were installed on a pier at Kilid Bahr, which could fire across the Straits. When howitzers began to arrive at the Dardanelles they were grouped and deployed in mobile batteries on both sides of the Straits; their purpose was to cover the minefields and prevent sweeping operations, and great emphasis was placed on their mobility and careful concealment. By the beginning of March 1915 there were no less than 24 of these mobile batteries established on both sides of the Dardanelles, with buffalo teams established near each one to drag the guns to new emplacements when they were located by the British. To increase the difficulty of locating the guns from the sea, smoke canisters were established at certain points, designed to emit puffs of black smoke at intervals and draw fire. Much was done to improve the range-finding and communication systems, and to train the crews; German technicians and gunnery experts brought an urgently required professionalism to these matters and achieved great improvements.

Until the February of 1915 there was only one infantry division in the Dardanelles area, which was split up into tiny detachments at Bulair, Gaba Tepe, Maidos, Cape Helles, and Kum Kale. On February 19th another division arrived, and the two divisions were concentrated on the Gallipoli Peninsula and the Asiatic shore respectively.

Between the November of 1914 and the February of 1915, therefore, a major change had taken place in the defensive system of the Dardanelles. The guns, either in the conspicuous fortresses and batteries or in the hidden mobile howitzer formations, were protecting the minefields, which were skilfully situated. The battleships could not pass through the Dardanelles, nor even close with the Narrows forts, until the mines were swept; until the guns were silenced the sweepers could not clear the minefields. This was the problem confronting any purely naval attempt to force the Dardanelles. It was a situation which was never fully grasped by the British, and which has not been understood by some historians of the campaign. The British, both in London and at the Dardanelles, persisted in treating the forcing of the Dardanelles in terms of knocking out the main established batteries at the Narrows.

For the first hectic months of the war the British had been wholly pre-occupied with events in Europe to worry much about the Turks. On December 18th the light cruiser *Doris* landed a party of sailors north of Alexandretta to cut the railway line; the Turks were extremely co-operative, and assembled the locomotives for destruction while parties of unhindered sailors blew up a bridge and a station. The torpedo-lieutenant in charge of the demolition party agreed to a Turkish request to become a Turkish officer for the day, and Turk soldiers assisted in the blowing up of the locomotives. This *opéra bouffe* episode understandably persuaded many people—including Churchill—that Turkish military competence was not very highly developed.

Early in 1915 events took a more serious turn. The British position in Egypt was ambiguous and difficult. Theoretically Egypt was part of the Ottoman Empire, and although the British had been firmly established for over 30 years, there had been signs of nationalist forces stirring even before the war. The Khedive, Abbas Hilmi, was bitterly opposed to the British régime, and on the outbreak of war was instrumental in proclaiming the *Jehad*—the Holy War—against the infidels. The British promptly deposed Abbas, appointed a more congenial nominee in his place, declared Egypt a Protectorate, and imposed martial law. Outwardly, everything was calm, but Sir John Maxwell, the commander of the forces in Egypt, estimated that there were some 70,000 Turkish subjects in the country, and it was necessary to give frequent demonstrations of military strength.

On top of this worrying situation in Egypt itself, Maxwell now began to receive alarming reports of Turkish troop concentrations in the Sinai Desert. A force of 20,000 men, with nine batteries of field artillery and one howitzer battery, under the command of Djemal, left Beersheba in mid-January. The real organiser of the expedition was the German, von Kress, who had presented the *Goeben* ultimatum to Enver. Instead of following the traditional route to Egypt along the shore of the Mediterranean, the Turks struck out boldly into the desert, and, assisted by friendly Bedouins, reached the eastern side of the Suez Canal on February 3rd.

This daring stroke did not take the British entirely by surprise, as some writers have stated. Maxwell had been half-expecting an attack on the Canal, and a remarkable series of reconnaissance flights over the desert by French seaplanes gave him ample warning.

The attack on the Canal, which began on February 3rd, and which lasted for a week, was repulsed remarkably easily. The total British casualties were 32 killed and 130 wounded; the Turks admitted to 192 dead, 371 wounded, and 727 missing, but this was probably an under-estimate. Djemal had confidently expected a rising of Egyptian nationalist forces in Egypt on his appearance on the banks of the Canal, but there was little response. Djemal withdrew his force, only leaving a small force of three battalions, a squadron of cavalry, and two mountain batteries under the command of Kress in the Sinai.

In spite of its complete failure, this attack had given both Maxwell and Kitchener a bad fright, and another long-range flight by a French seaplane on February 21st revealed that there was still a large army at Beersheba. To the west of Egypt, there was another potential threat; a powerful and ambitious religious leader, Sayed Ahmed, who called himself the Senussi, had been fighting the Italians with some success, and although Sayed professed friendship towards the British, Maxwell was uneasy. When he heard that he had been joined by Enver's half-brother, Nuri, his apprehensions increased. In the Sudan there were ominous reports of unrest. Although the British had some 70,000 troops in Egypt, most of them were inexperienced Dominion and British Territorial units. If the Turks maintained their threat on the Canal and there were difficulties in Egypt and the Sudan, the British would be fully stretched to maintain their position.

Meanwhile, on Turkey's eastern borders with Russia, an even more alarming event had occurred. A Turkish army of 100,000 had advanced into the Caucasus in December, and had moved across very difficult country with remarkable skill and speed. By this time, the Russian situation was becoming disquieting. Within three months of the outbreak of war the much-vaunted 'Russian steamroller' had been brought to an abrupt halt in Prussia. The Russians had lost over a million men, barely one week's supply of shells remained in the initial reserve, over a million rifles had been lost, and new supplies were being produced very slowly. Colonel Knox, the British representative at the Russian headquarters, was sending a series of unsparing reports to the British Government. And now came the reports of the daring Turkish invasion of the Caucasus. At the beginning of January 1915 the Grand Duke Nicholas appealed to the British Government to arrange for a demonstration against the Turks to draw at least part of their army away from Russia.

By the time that this message was received in London, a pitched battle had developed between Russian and Turkish forces near Sarikamish. It was fought with barbaric ferocity in a violent blizzard at an altitude of 10,000 feet in a temperature 30 degrees below zero. At one point the Turks were close to an overwhelming victory, but Enver, who had taken command, attempted an impossible wheeling movement in the deep snow, and the chance was missed. Over 30,000 Turks literally froze to death, and most of the survivors were forced to surrender. Enver and about 12,000 men managed to extricate themselves from the disaster. All news was rigidly suppressed in Constantinople, and Russian reports merely stated that a large Turkish army had surrendered; to a Europe familiar with Turkish military disasters this came as no surprise. But the Grand Duke's appeal for assistance, coming as it did on the heels of Colonel Knox's bleak reports on the corroding Russian military machine, coincided with a remarkable shift in opinion in the British Cabinet about the conduct of the war. The first link in the chain which brought the British to the Dardanelles had been forged.

It is necessary at this point to examine the machinery through which the British were endeavouring to exercise control over the conduct of the war. Until the end of November 1914 the higher direction of the war was vested in the Cabinet, consisting of 22 members, assisted by the Committee of Imperial Defence. This was essentially a peace-time system, which proved incapable of adaptation to war conditions, and after four months a War Council was formed at the end of November. It consisted of H. H. Asquith, the Prime Minister, Sir Edward Grey, the Foreign Secretary, David Lloyd George, the Chancellor of the Exchequer, Winston Churchill, the First Lord of the Admiralty, Lord Kitchener, the Secretary of State for War, Sir Archibald Wolfe Murray, the Chief of the Imperial General Staff, Lord Fisher, the First Sea Lord, and Arthur Balfour, who had no position in the exclusively Liberal Administration, but who was a member of the Council in view of his long membership of the Committee of Imperial Defence, his close friendship with Asquith and Churchill, and his position as an ex-Premier and, until 1911, leader of the Conservative (or Unionist) Party. Balfour was the only representative of the Opposition on the Council. In fact, until the Liberal Government which had been in power since the beginning of 1906 fell in May 1915, the Unionist leaders attended only one meeting of the War Council (on March 10th), and the experiment was not repeated. Lord Crewe, Lord Haldane, Reginald McKenna and Lewis Harcourt (all Liberal Ministers) joined the War Council between December and March, and the Service representation was subsequently increased by the addition of Admiral Sir Arthur Wilson.

It was a most remarkable collection of personalities. Asquith, Prime Minister since 1908, presided over the affairs of the nation at this terrible time with a calm and judicial skill. Unflustered, meticulous and resolute, never indolent yet not energetic by nature, he did not live, eat and breathe politics as did Churchill and Lloyd George, and consequently possessed an exceptional capacity to cast aside the cares of his office completely. A familiar figure in public life for nearly 30 years, his quiet confidence and magisterial competence in the House of Commons had as yet stilled any nagging doubts about his qualities as a war leader.

Sir Edward Grey, the deeply respected and conscientious Foreign Secretary, belonged to the same generation as Asquith, and shared many of his skills and prejudices. Nurtured in Foreign Affairs in 1892–5 under the considerable shadow of Lord Rosebery, he had been Foreign Secretary since 1906. Differing views may have been entertained of his competence and far-sightedness; no doubts were ever raised of his sincerity, public-spiritedness and integrity. But after nine years of office the physical and mental strain of his burdensome responsibilities had sapped his vitality and spirit, and the shadow of the blindness which was to end his career two years later was already gathering over him.

Arthur Balfour, aloof, genial but politically cold-blooded, moved in the same social circles as Asquith and Grey. A Member of Parliament for over 40 years, the one-time languid collaborator of the ebullient and tragically unstable Lord Randolph Churchill in the gay irresponsible days of the 'Fourth Party' in 1880–3, the blandly ruthless Chief Secretary for Ireland from 1887 to 1891, Prime Minister from 1901 to 1905 and leader of the Unionist Party in Opposition for the following six years, he had a lifetime's experience of public life, and concealed beneath a highly agreeable façade a degree of cunning and heartlessness which had proved the downfall of many more glittering rivals. In 1914 he was in the political shadows as far as his own party was concerned; but in the most inner councils of the Liberal administrations he was a welcome and respected counsellor.

Significantly, Balfour's successor to the Unionist leadership, Andrew Bonar Law, was not in the War Council. He was cast in a very different mould to Balfour, and was not highly esteemed in Ministerial circles. A Glasgow businessman of modest Ministerial experience, Law's elevation to the leadership of the party in 1911 had been totally unexpected. He was in, but not of, the London political world. Political small-talk bored him, he detested the social side of politics, and was totally uninterested in food and drink. In the House of Commons and on the platform he was a brisk, methodical, sharp and incisive speaker, with a distinctive professional no-nonsense manner. To men like Asquith and Churchill he was a disagreeable phenomenon, inexplicably raised to the leadership of the Unionist Party, which he had subsequently led into a series of harsh and inflammatory disputations with the Government in which the traditional conventions on which British public life is maintained had been stretched to breaking-point. The less seen of Mr. Law, it was generally considered in Government circles, the better.

Lord Kitchener of Khartoum, summoned from the Consul-Generalship of Egypt amid public acclaim to be Secretary of State for War on the outbreak of hostilities, was a national talisman, to the people of Britain what General Gordon had been to the generation of 30 years before. Only the aged Lord Roberts—who had succumbed to pneumonia while visiting the troops in France early in the war—had rivalled Lord Kitchener in universal esteem and confidence. For 20 years, amid stirring events and fluctuating fortunes in Africa and the Sudan, Kitchener's star had glittered ever more brightly. When Commander-in-Chief in India he had triumphed in a famous disputation with the Viceroy, Lord Curzon, after a battle of wits and intrigue which remains one of the most singular episodes in modern Imperial history. In 1914 and 1915 he was the personification of the resolution and integrity of the British people. His face stared sternly from a million posters, with the phrase 'Your Country needs YOU', and his finger pointing both accusingly and appealingly. By nature taciturn, he sat uneasily in the presence of experienced and resourceful politicians in Cabinet and War Council, a wary and uncomfortable professional soldier in the midst of one of the most brilliantly intellectual Cabinets in British history.

He had already given remarkable demonstrations of his formidable administrative ability and military prescience. While all declared that the war would be brief, Kitchener sombrely remarked that it would be long. His preparations were based on that calculation. To the amazement and awe of his Cabinet colleagues, huge new volunteer armies began to materialise out of nowhere, to be equipped, armed and trained. But Kitchener had long been out of touch with the drastic reorganisation of the War Office recommended by the Esher Committee of 1903–4 and carried through by Haldane from 1906 to 1911. The General Staff system so carefully established had been fatally damaged by the dispatch of its most able officers to the front at the outbreak of war; Kitchener assumed the enormous burdens of the War Office with composure and authority. The new Chief of the General Staff, Wolfe Murray, trembled in his presence, and had little or no influence on the conduct of military strategy. Murray subsequently explained rather pathetically that he regarded himself as Kitchener's Chief of Staff, to give advice and information when asked; he was never asked. The new General Staff, mainly composed of relatively inexperienced officers at this stage, was kept in almost complete ignorance of the vital matters of policy and strategy on which it was its statutory function to advise the Government.

But Kitchener's colleagues in the Cabinet were thankful to place so much responsibility in his capable hands. No whisper of criticism of his methods or tactics had yet been heard. His colleagues were often bewildered, and even offended, by his lengthy, heavy silences and by his disconcerting inability to argue briefly and coherently in Cabinet, but of his outstanding capacities they entertained few doubts. Even if there had been any such reservations—and Lloyd George, for one, was becoming uneasy—Kitchener's public reputation was so dazzling that he was quite indispensable. 'All-powerful, imperturbable, reserved, he dominated absolutely our counsels at this time', Churchill has written. Lloyd George, with one of those brilliantly true flashes of imagery which occasionally illuminate his *War Memoirs*, subsequently compared Kitchener with 'one of those revolving lighthouses which radiate momentary gleams of revealing light far out into the surrounding gloom and then suddenly relapse into complete darkness'.

The Admiralty was represented on the War Council by the First Lord, Winston Churchill, and the First Sea Lord, Lord Fisher of Kilverstone. Churchill, like his father, Lord Randolph, was the stormy petrel of English politics of his day. He was just 40 years of age, yet his political career had been one of turbulence since his entry into the House of Commons as a young Unionist in 1900 after a much-advertised and ebullient apprenticeship in the Army and military journalism, which included an escape from a Boer prisoner of war camp which entranced his fellow-countrymen. He had crossed the floor of the House to join the Liberals within five years, and even in 1914 was still viewed by many of his quondam colleagues with all the exclusive hatred reserved in the House of Commons for the turncoat. Brave almost to a fault, impulsive, possessed of a formidable vocabulary of invective and contempt, he asked for and gave no quarter in his political battles. While he rapidly advanced from subordinate Minister to the Cabinet in 1908 and from the Home Office to the Admiralty in 1911, his detractors and foes remorselessly increased.

In spite of much competence and imagination in his conduct of naval affairs, his reputation had not been increased by the events of the war at sea. The British public, eager for a dramatic and overwhelming demonstration of naval supremacy, were disconcerted and angered by the apparent inactivity of the Royal Navy. The sinking of three cruisers—*Aboukir*, *Hogue* and *Cressy*—by the submarine U.9 on September 22nd off the Dutch coast, with the loss of 1,459 officers and men out of a total of more than 2,200, had stunned the nation. In a series of minor engagements the Royal Navy, far from gaining the expected sweeping victories, had been checked and even defeated. Ships were lost in apparently futile operations; in the South Atlantic von Spee's squadron roamed at will over that vast expanse of sea, utterly destroying Admiral Cradock's inadequate force off Coronel. In the Indian Ocean the *Emden* almost paralysed the movement of Allied vessels, and aroused terror on the Indian coast. *Goeben* and *Breslau* were anchored in the Golden Horn. When the new super-Dreadnought *Audacious* was lost towards the end of October, the Cabinet decided that the news must be rigidly suppressed. The belated dispatch of the half-trained units of the Royal

Naval Division to Antwerp in the October of 1914 had failed to avert the loss of the city and had ended in near-disaster for the Division. The R.N.D. was Churchill's own idea, and its formation had aroused intense opposition in the Navy as well as in the Army; Churchill's own Assistant Director of Naval Operations, Captain Richmond, described it as 'foolery' and as 'Winston's tuppenny untrained rabble'. 'It is a tragedy,' the same officer wrote on October 4th, 'that the Navy should be in such lunatic hands at this time.' Churchill's personal appearance at Antwerp and his offer to take command of the operations brought further criticism and derision on his head. The Press was also hostile to him; *The Times*, in particular, rarely lost an opportunity of linking his name with any naval reverse. Powerful elements in the Navy distrusted and disliked him. In Parliament, the Opposition was implacably suspicious. Some of his colleagues were entertaining strong doubts of his judgement and capacities.

Churchill's First Sea Lord on the outbreak of war had been Prince Louis of Battenberg. A vicious campaign against his foreign background had grown to such intensity that Battenberg's position had become impossible, and, at the end of October, he had resigned. The episode reflected little credit on anyone, and *The Times* even managed to imply that Churchill's part had been dubious; 'honest men', it remarked sourly, 'will prefer the brevity of the retiring Admiral to the rhetorical document which accepts his decision.'

For Battenberg's replacement, Churchill had turned to the formidable, gnarled and explosive Lord Fisher. Churchill and 'Jacky' Fisher had first met at Biarritz in 1907, when Churchill was a very young Under-Secretary of State at the Colonial Office—'They bought me cheap', he growlingly complained to Lord Rosebery of his reward for joining the Liberal Party—and Fisher was First Sea Lord. It was the beginning of a remarkable friendship. The Navy was then riven with the notorious and savage personal disputes between Fisher and Lord Charles Beresford, which culminated in 1909 in the circulation by Fisher of some private letters from a Captain Bacon containing highly uncomplimentary accounts of Beresford's command in the Mediterranean. The document fell into hostile hands, was speedily communicated to a London evening newspaper, and both Fisher and Bacon were obliged to retire. This deplorable episode had not dimmed Churchill's great admiration for the old Admiral; he admired, above all, the questing and cajoling spirit which Fisher had brought to the Navy, and which had led to his downfall. It was Churchill's view, supported by subsequent events, that the Fisher-Beresford vendetta had been a relatively small price to pay for the transformation of the Navy's complacent slumber into the intense activity and re-thinking which had marked Fisher's term as First Sea Lord.

After Churchill went to the Admiralty in 1911, with clear instructions to effect drastic changes in the senior administration of the Navy, he kept in close touch with Fisher, whom he found 'a veritable volcano of knowledge and inspiration'. They kept up a voluminous correspondence; they met frequently. For all his 73 years, the old Admiral's fires still burned fiercely. Above all, and it was clearly this factor which entranced Churchill, he was bubbling over with ideas. So long as he was not in an official position, Churchill was not obliged to accept all of Fisher's plans, but as soon as Fisher became First Sea Lord the proximity of the volcano could be disconcerting. An idea put to the First Lord by a close friend with lengthy experience but no official position was one thing; the same idea projected by the First Sea Lord was quite another.

It is extremely difficult to decide what Fisher really thought of Churchill, so varying and kaleidoscopic were his judgements. His letters reflected completely the whim of the moment, and Fisher's whims tended to be violent. Early in the war he wrote to Lord Rosebery that 'Winston has the courage of Satan (*and some of his other attributes!!*)'; shortly afterwards he complained that Churchill's great weakness was snobbery. When Rosebery asked him why he did not openly challenge some of Churchill's tactics (which had reduced the old man to vehement excoriation), he replied that it was because Churchill had kept his word by promoting Jellicoe to the command of the Grand Fleet; 'a sprat to catch a whale!' Shortly after returning to the Admiralty, Fisher was again writing to Rosebery that 'Winston, like every genius (*and he really is a genius!*) will not brook criticism and idolises power and so has surrounded himself with 3rd class sycophants'; Churchill's visits to the Western Front and his enthusiastic interest in all aspects of the conduct of the war maddened Fisher. 'It is magnificent, but it is not War!' It would be easy to demonstrate, by a careful selection of Fisher's correspondence, either that he worshipped Churchill or loathed him. In fact, on Fisher's side, it was an almost classic love-hate relationship.

At first, everything went marvellously well. Fisher fell on the Admiralty like a thunderbolt. In five incredible days he summoned all the naval constructors in the country to London, barked dates, quantities and prices at them, and hurled them back to their desks and shipyards with a gigantic programme of over 600 ships. His personality was felt in almost every sector of naval administration; his letters sped from his desk, exhorting, extolling, cursing, and lamenting; his fierce memoranda, with the famous 'F' scrawled in red ink at the bottom, flashed out like the signals from a frenzied heliograph.

The price which Churchill had to pay for the arrival of this aged demon was to be heavy, yet Churchill himself never had any regrets. It is doubtful if he ever realised, until too late, the fact that he and

Fisher were incompatible under the same roof. 'Churchill co-opted Fisher to relieve the pressure against himself, but he had no intention of letting anyone else rule the roost', Lord Beaverbrook has succinctly commented: 'Here, then, were two strong men of incompatible temper both bent on an autocracy.'

In the War Council, the position of David Lloyd George was difficult to define. After a career more lengthy but almost as meteoric as Churchill's, the effervescent, darting, quicksilver little Welshman, who had first risen to national prominence and notoriety through his courageous opposition to the Boer War, was not at home in these novel and awful waters. Superficially compared with Asquith, Grey, Balfour, Haldane and Churchill, his intellectual qualities may have appeared inferior, but he possessed an intuitive common sense, what Churchill has called 'the seeing eye', to an extent only perhaps shared by Kitchener. In him alone, as he fretfully surveyed the bleak prospects of a war of attrition in France, grave doubts about the conduct of the war were germinating. He had as yet no sane alternative to offer, and his personal knowledge of war did not exist; it was almost a reflex action. But the future War Leader—the only member of the Asquith Government who served in office throughout the war—carried, at this time, little direct personal responsibility. He was the cynical but apprehensive observer of the great struggle, who refused to be impressed by alleged triumphs, and who challenged any facile optimisms with cold questionings.

The War Council's conduct of affairs unhappily belied its impressive title. It did not meet regularly, did not forward its conclusions to the Cabinet, kept its proceedings in manuscript, received very few departmental memoranda, did not work to an agenda, and was summoned only when the Prime Minister deemed it desirable. In no way did it superintend, or even discuss, the day-to-day conduct of the war. When it did meet, the Service representatives apart from Kitchener were invariably silent, a fact which subsequently brought them heavy censure. From the very beginning there was a fundamental lack of understanding between the political and Service members of the Council concerning the latter's position. The Council met in the Cabinet room at 10 Downing Street; its proceedings were conducted by Asquith on the lines of Cabinet meetings; it was composed almost entirely of Cabinet Ministers, who also treated its meetings as Cabinet conclaves. The whole atmosphere was one of a Cabinet meeting to which Service representatives had been invited to attend in order to answer specific questions directed to them. As Lord Crewe subsequently remarked, 'the political members did too much of the talking, and the expert members too little'. 'It is a mistake to call us members of the War Council,' Fisher told the Dardanelles Commission; '—it was no such thing. We were the experts there who were to open our mouths when told to.' This was also the understanding of Sir Arthur Wilson and Wolfe Murray, but not that of the politicians. Speaking of the rôle of the Service members of the War Council in the Commons on March 20th, 1917, Asquith said that 'they were there—that was the reason, and the only reason, for their being there—to give the lay members the benefit of their advice'.

But it is possible to exaggerate the effects of the inarticulateness of the Service members of the Council, while acknowledging the fact that the basic misunderstanding about their position had unfortunate results. The critical deficiency of the War Council did not lie in the fact that it was an administratively untidy body nor in the fact that it was dominated by politicians, but in the total absence of strong leadership. Lloyd George has complained that 'there was no co-ordination of effort. There was no connected plan of action. There was no sense of the importance of time'. 'No man had the power to give clear, brutal orders which would command unquestioning respect,' Churchill has written. 'Power was widely disseminated among the many important personages who in this period formed the governing instrument.' Asquith was a master of the art of juggling strong personalities and conflicting proposals. These artifices might keep a Cabinet together, but were unsuited to the utterly novel conditions of war.

The decline in his own position and the relatively feeble showing of the Navy was causing Churchill real anxiety. Richmond, the Assistant Director of Naval Operations, was very struck by Churchill's concern when he dined with him on October 24th. 'He was in low spirits,' Richmond recorded in his diary, '[and] . . . oppressed with the impossibility of *doing* anything. The attitude of waiting . . . and the inability of the Staff to make any suggestions seem to bother him. I have not seen him so despondent before. . . He wanted to send battleships—old ones—up the Elbe, but for what purpose except to be sunk I did not understand.'

When the War Council held its first meeting on November 25th, Churchill at once brought forward the desirability of a joint military and naval attack on the Dardanelles. The suggestion arose after Kitchener had opened a discussion on the defence of Egypt, and Churchill argued that the best way of defending Egypt would be to threaten Turkey in a decisive area. Kitchener pointed out, and the argument was incontrovertible, that there were simply not enough troops available to be diverted to another front; the army being built up in Egypt was not large enough nor sufficiently prepared for such an operation as Churchill proposed.

The Council rejected Churchill's suggestion that the Admiralty should start to assemble ships for the enterprise, and passed to other business.* 'There was, however, one important result,' the Council's Secretary,

* Notwithstanding this, Churchill gave instructions that the ships which had transported the newly raised Australian and New Zealand divisions to Egypt should remain there.

Colonel Hankey, later wrote; 'namely, the planting of an idea into the minds of the members of the War Council'.

At the end of December 1914 (before the receipt of the appeal from the Russians), Hankey, Lloyd George and Churchill, each acting independently, were coming to similar conclusions about the war situation. All were alarmed by the prospect of an interminable war of attrition in France, and were anxious to bring in new allies in the Balkans to increase the pressure on Turkey and Austria-Hungary and relieve that on Russia. Each agreed that the decisive theatre was France; but none considered that progress could be made there unless the Central Powers were seriously engaged in other sectors. They had a strong ally in Kitchener, who was becoming equally depressed by the policies being pressed on him by Sir John French and Joffre, which amounted to a series of gigantic frontal offensives—which, although gigantic in numbers and material, would be hardly decisive in effect, even if successful. Hankey, in a prescient and well-argued paper subsequently known as 'the Boxing Day Memorandum', proposed an attack on Turkey with the triple purposes of removing one of Germany's most important allies, opening the vital sea-route to Russia, and drawing the wavering neutral Balkan States—particularly Greece, Rumania and Bulgaria—into the Entente. Lloyd George, in his memorandum to the Council, stressed the urgent importance of a decisive victory 'somewhere' to raise morale and convince the neutrals of the strength of the Entente powers. He pointed out that half a million men would shortly be available for service, that the time had come to realise that the Western Front was impregnable, and that the new armies should not be thrown away on hopeless offensives in Flanders. His arguments ignored the fact that the Allied line on the Western Front (as the events of April 1915 demonstrated) was far from impregnable, and also failed to take account of the serious lack of munitions for the new armies. His proposals were even more startling, as they included a vast attack on Austria from Salonika or a landing on the Syrian coast to sever Turkish communications with the army threatening Egypt; but he struck a wise note of warning by stressing the vital necessity of careful preparation. 'Expeditions which are decided upon and organized with insufficient care and preparation,' he wrote, 'generally end disastrously.'

After perusing these papers, Churchill wrote to Asquith that 'We are substantially in agreement, and our conclusions are not incompatible. I wanted Gallipoli attacked on the declaration of war.*... Meanwhile the difficulties have increased. ... I think the War Council ought to meet daily for a few days each week. No topic can be pursued to any fruitful result at weekly intervals.'

* It should be noted that neither Lloyd George nor Hankey had mentioned an attack on the Dardanelles in their papers.

Coinciding with this remarkable shift of opinion in the War Council came the Grand Duke's appeal on January 2nd. Churchill and Kitchener at once discussed the situation at length, and although they agreed that a successful attack on Constantinople would have far-reaching effects, Kitchener made it clear that no troops could be made available. Later the same day Kitchener wrote to Churchill that 'We have no troops to land anywhere. . . The only place that a demonstration might have some effect in stopping reinforcements going East would be the Dardanelles. . . . We shall not be ready for anything big for some months.' On January 3rd Fisher wrote to Churchill to urge a joint naval and military attack on Turkey, 'But ONLY if it's IMMEDIATE. However, it won't be! Our Aulic Council will adjourn till the following Thursday fortnight! (N.B. When did we meet last and what came of it???) We shall decide on a futile bombardment of the Dardanelles, which wears out the irreplaceable guns of the *Indefatigable*, which probably will require replacement. What good resulted from the last bombardment? Did it move a single Turk from the Caucasus? And so the War goes on! You want ONE man!' He envisaged a sudden assault by 75,000 'seasoned troops from Sir John French's Command' at Besika Bay, while the Greeks landed on Gallipoli, the Bulgarians marched on Constantinople, and 'Sturdee forces the Dardanelles at the same time with "Majestic" class and "Canopus" class! God bless him! But as the great Napoleon said, "CELERITY"—without it "FAILURE".'

This grandiose and impracticable plan—involving the active participation of two neutral countries and the transfer of a large part of French's army at a time when he was badgering Kitchener for vast reinforcements—was not put forward as the result of a serious consideration of the problems or issues involved. Churchill's initial reactions seem to have been cautious. 'I think we had better hear what the others have to say about the Turkish plans before taking a decided line', he replied. 'I would not grudge 100,000 men, because of the great political effects in the Balkan peninsula; but Germany is the foe, and it is bad war to seek cheaper victories and easier antagonists. This is, however, a very general question.' Nevertheless the suggestion about the old battleships at once re-awakened his personal interest in the prospects of a purely naval attack on the Dardanelles. The idea of using old battleships was not new, and had been considered by the joint staffs in 1906; Churchill, as his conversation with Richmond in October has revealed, had been thinking along these lines in considering an attack on the Elbe. Furthermore, the definition of 'His Majesty's less valuable ships' had drastically changed since the joint study of 1906-7. The advances in naval construction and gunnery since then had been so phenomenal that the super-Dreadnoughts of 1909 were markedly inferior to the *Queen Elizabeth* class of battleships nearing completion in 1915. The Navy had a considerable number of battleships which, although not capable of taking on the German High Seas Fleet, were relatively modern in construction and design. Most of these were due to be scrapped in 1915, and the prospect of using them more usefully to achieve a decisive victory in the Eastern Mediterranean was alluring.

The story now took a strange turn. Churchill sought, and received, Fisher's permission to discover the views of the Admiral commanding the British squadron in the Aegean, Admiral Carden. He did not show Fisher, nor did the First Sea Lord ask to be shown, the telegram which he then sent, on January 3rd, within a few hours of receiving Fisher's letter.

> Do you consider the forcing of the Dardanelles by ships alone a practicable operation? It is assumed older battleships fitted with mine-bumpers would be used, preceded by colliers or other merchant craft as mine-bumpers and sweepers. Importance of results would justify severe loss. Let me know your views.

Churchill states that this 'purely exploratory' telegram was sent 'with the active agreement of Lord Fisher': Fisher's account is that he agreed in general terms to Carden's views being ascertained, but did not actually see the telegram. 'Churchill talked to me about it,' he has stated; 'I was quite conversant with it.'

The telegram sent to Carden was curiously phrased. The local commander, who had little knowledge of the Dardanelles defences, was being invited to give his views on a matter of high policy. The first sentence was the critical one; it placed upon Carden the invidious responsibility of giving an opinion on the very wide question of whether the Dardanelles could be forced by ships alone. As Churchill subsequently admitted to the Dardanelles Commission, it was deliberately phrased to produce a favourable response. Understandably, Carden replied extremely cautiously on January 5th:

> With reference to your telegram of 3rd instant, I do not consider Dardanelles can be rushed.
> They might be forced by extended operations with large number of ships.

There was nothing in this very guarded message to inflame hopes in London, but it gave Churchill the lead he required. 'I did not mean directly that they *could* be forced,' Carden later explained; '. . . I thought it *might* be done.' But the War Council, which met on the afternoon of January 5th, was definitely interested. On his return to the Admiralty, Churchill saw his Chief of Staff, Admiral Oliver, and Admiral Sir Henry Jackson. Both, like Carden, favoured a gradual assault on the Dardanelles as opposed to a 'rush', although Jackson considered that troops would be required at some stage. Fisher's attitude is difficult to determine. 'He seems at this time not merely to favour the enterprise in principle,' Churchill wrote in *The World Crisis*, 'but to treat it almost as a matter practically decided.' But in evidence to the Dardanelles Commission Churchill said that 'Lord Fisher gave no opinion one way or the other. He was seeking more information, and considering his views.' As Fisher subsequently made clear, he was startled and rather nonplussed by Carden's reply. Churchill might have discerned the dawn of new apprehensions in a letter he received from Fisher on January 6th. The First Sea Lord was becoming alarmed by another of Churchill's schemes, to attack and block the Zeebrugge Canal, and he wrote: 'Have we the margin of ships in view of impending great operations? *and the men and officers?*'

Churchill did not summon the Admiralty War Staff Group, described by Fisher as 'the supreme and isolated centre of naval war direction', which consisted of Churchill, Fisher, Oliver, Wilson, Sir Graham Greene (Secretary to the Admiralty) and de Bartolomé, to consider Carden's telegram. The views of Oliver and Sir Henry Jackson had been sought verbally; Churchill says that Fisher saw the draft of his next telegram to Carden, and made no comment; Fisher later said that he had no recollection of having seen it. This telegram ran:

> Your view is agreed by high authorities here. Please telegraph in detail what you think could be done by extended operations, what force would be needed, and how you consider it should be used.

Once again, the ball was firmly in Carden's court. The phrase 'high authorities' had a magic ring about it, and Carden naturally assumed that this meant much more than the guarded agreement of Sir Henry Jackson—who was not even a member of the War Staff Group—and the verbal approval of Oliver. As Churchill frankly told the Dardanelles Commission, 'it would not have been fair to involve Lord Fisher' as one of the 'high authorities' favouring Carden's plan. Churchill was in fact playing off one side against the other with great skill; it requires considerable credulity to believe that this was entirely fortuitous.

Even the possibility of an Allied offensive elsewhere than on the Western Front had aroused apprehension in France. Joffre was suspicious and hostile. Sir John French replied to Kitchener, who wrote to him on January 2nd seeking his views on the desirability of operating elsewhere than on the Western Front, that 'in the most favourable circumstances it could only cause the relaxation of pressure against Russia in the Caucasus and enable her to transfer two or three corps to the West—a result quite incommensurate with the effort involved. To attack Turkey would be to play the German game and to bring about the very end which Germany had in mind when she induced Turkey to join in the War, namely, to draw off troops from the decisive spot, which is Germany itself. . . . There are no theatres, other than those in which operations are now in progress, in which decisive results could be attained.' These arguments could not be denied. French had raised the fundamental issue which was never to be resolved throughout 1915: where was the war to be fought?

French appeared before the Council on January 7th to urge a massive onslaught on the Western Front, but Ministers were not impressed. Kitchener was coldly sceptical. On the following day Lloyd George urged the Council to adopt his plan of attacking Austria-Hungary from Salonika, but received little support. Kitchener then read out a War Office appreciation of the various theatres in which an Allied offensive would have good results, and picked out the Dardanelles 'as an attack could be made in co-operation with the fleet'; he considered that the operation would require an army of 150,000 men, and only Lloyd George expressed surprise at the lowness of his estimate. The Council, its interest now thoroughly aroused, authorised the War Office and the Admiralty to proceed with its examination of the matter, but resolved that 'for the present, the main theatre of operations for British forces should be alongside the French Army, and that this should continue as long as France was liable to successful invasion and required armed support'.

On the 11th Carden's detailed plans, prepared by his staff and the gunnery experts of *Inflexible*, reached the Admiralty. They envisaged a four-stage attack, involving direct and indirect (i.e. over the Gallipoli Peninsula from off Gaba Tepe) bombardment of the forts, the clearing of the minefields, and eventual advance into the Marmara. Carden emphasised that aerial reconnaissance was indispensable, that ammunition expenditure would be heavy, that it was impossible to estimate the time required to complete the operation, and that the weather—notoriously unreliable at that time of year in the Aegean—was of crucial importance. He asked for a fleet of 12 battleships, three battle-cruisers, three light cruisers, 16 destroyers, six submarines, four seaplanes, 12 minesweepers and other miscellaneous craft.*

This plan created a highly favourable impression on all who studied it. Churchill subsequently described it as '*the* most important telegram', and said that 'it was in its details an entirely novel proposition.' Instead of 'rushing' the Dardanelles, which Churchill says that he originally envisaged, the fleet was to reduce the forts one by one to a methodical plan. The Admiralty War Staff Group even proposed that the mighty *Queen Elizabeth*, the most powerful battleship afloat, should carry out her final gunnery and calibration trials on the Dardanelles forts. This was an immense material and psychological addition to Carden's fleet, and, indeed, to the whole enterprise. Fisher raised no objections, although his suspicions that Churchill would steadily increase the Dardanelles fleet to the detriment of Jellicoe began to nag again even more keenly as soon as the decision had been taken. Richmond saw Fisher on January 19th, and thought him 'old and worn-out and nervous'.

In his account of these stages in *The World Crisis* Churchill laid great emphasis on the fact that Fisher and the Admirals were absolutely united on

---

* His force in January 1915 consisted of two battle-cruisers, four French battleships, three light cruisers, 15 destroyers, four submarines, one torpedo depot ship, and some merchant auxiliaries.

the feasibility of the naval attack. 'The genesis of this plan and its elaboration were purely naval and professional in their character', he has written. 'It was Admiral Carden and his staff gunnery officers who proposed the gradual method of piece-meal reduction by long-range bombardment. It was Sir Henry Jackson and the Admiralty staff who embraced this idea and studied and approved its detail. Right or wrong, *it was a Service plan*.'* It is at this point that Churchill's account begins to lose its convincing character through over-statement of a good case. Whatever might be said on the 'elaboration' of the Dardanelles project, its 'genesis' lay entirely with Churchill. His eyes had been on the Dardanelles from the moment that Turkish intervention on the German side appeared probable; he had been the first to call for professional views on the military problems involved in an attack on the Gallipoli Peninsula; he had been the first to urge such an operation; it was, above all, he who had inspired and sent the first vital telegram to Carden. It was Churchill, furthermore, who informed the Grand Duke as early as January 19th that it was the intention of the British Government to 'press the matter to a conclusion,' before the British Government had seriously considered the matter in this light. While it is reasonable for Churchill's admirers to applaud his strategic genius, it is hardly reasonable for them, almost in the same breath, to cast the burden of failure upon his advisers. This does not excuse Fisher and his colleagues from their responsibility, and Fisher, at least, never attempted to deny it. But the impelling force was Churchill's; the initiative was solely his; and the responsibility for what ensued must be principally his. Churchill's account in *The World Crisis* must therefore be approached with caution. To take one example. Sir Henry Jackson wrote on January 15th that although he 'generally' concurred with Carden's plans, he considered that a final decision must depend on the results of the early operations against the Outer Forts and in the Straits. This was a fairly basic qualification to the plan, and hardly merited Churchill's subsequent statement that Jackson had 'embraced', 'studied', and 'approved' it. Oliver thought that 'we should push on slowly till either we overcame the enemy's defence, or till the enemy's defence brought us to a standstill'. There was thus a fundamental gulf of attitude towards the enterprise between the Admirals on the one hand and Churchill on the other. This cleavage, which did great harm, was exacerbated by a failure to bring all the Sea Lords into the preliminary planning. The Board of Admiralty met only 12 times between the outbreak of war and May 17th, 1915, a period of ten months. There was discontent and resentment among the junior Sea Lords who were not members of the War Staff Group; the Third Sea Lord subsequently related that he had only once discussed the Dardanelles with Churchill; it was an entirely informal conversation, and 'was not welcomed and had no effect.'

* *World Crisis*, II, 121. (My italics.)

The War Council had a prolonged and exhausting session on January 13th, which lasted almost all day. French again argued for a new Western offensive, and was so persuasive and confident that even Kitchener wavered. Only Balfour and Lloyd George were unimpressed, but approval was eventually given on the understanding that if the attacks failed the Allies would have to look elsewhere for decisive results. After a lengthy discussion on these and other points, the meeting seemed to be drawing to an end, and Hankey has vividly described the scene.

> The War Council had been sitting all day. The blinds had been drawn to shut out the winter evening. The air was heavy and the table presented that rather dishevelled appearance that results from a long session. I was looking forward to release from the strain of following and noting the prolonged and intense discussion. I suppose the Councillors were as weary as I was. At this point events took a dramatic turn, for Churchill suddenly revealed his well-kept secret of a naval attack on the Dardanelles! The idea caught on at once. The whole atmosphere changed. Fatigue was forgotten. The War Council turned eagerly from the dreary vista of a 'slogging match' on the Western Front to brighter prospects, as they seemed, in the Mediterranean. The Navy, in whom everyone had implicit confidence and whose opportunities so far had been few and far between, was to come into the front line. Even French with his enormous preoccupations caught something of the general enthusiasm.
>
> Churchill unfolded his plans with the skill that might be expected of him, lucidly but quietly and without exaggerated optimism.

The crux of Churchill's proposals to the Council was that the Admiralty 'believed that a plan could be made for systematically reducing all the forts within a few weeks. Once the forts were reduced the minefields could be cleared, and the Fleet would proceed up to Constantinople and destroy the *Goeben*. They would have nothing to fear from field guns or rifles, which would be merely an inconvenience.' This was a subtle but considerable extension of Carden's proposals in that the hazards and heavy *matériel* requirements of the operation were skilfully obscured, and the impression was given that Carden's plans were further advanced than in fact they were. Balfour spoke strongly in favour of the project. 'He was beautiful!' Fisher later told the Dardanelles Commission. 'He has got the brain of Moses and the voice of Aaron. He would talk a bird out of a tree, and they were all carried away with him. I was not, myself.'

After Churchill and Balfour had finished, there was a brief discussion in which Fisher did not participate—'I made it a rule that I would not at the War Council kick Winston Churchill's shins,' as he told the Commissioners; 'he was my chief, and it was silence or resignation, that was my *métier*'— during which Asquith was seen to be writing.

At length he read out the conclusions which he proposed. French was to have two more Territorial divisions, but the final decision concerning the new offensive was to be postponed until the beginning of February; the Admiralty should consider action in the Adriatic against the Austrian Navy; and 'the Admiralty should also prepare for a naval expedition in February to bombard and take the Gallipoli Peninsula, with Constantinople as its object.' Of almost as great significance—although little remarked upon by many historians of the campaign—was the decision of the Council 'that if the position in the Western theatre of war becomes, in the spring, one of stalemate, British troops should be dispatched to another theatre and objective, and that adequate investigation and preparation should be undertaken with that purpose.' As Hankey subsequently commented: 'Although this conclusion does not mention the Dardanelles as an objective . . . . it is of some importance as an indication that, in the opinion of the War Council, troops might be employed in some theatre of war other than the Western Front. Even the early investigations which preceded this decision had shown . . . . that there were only two alternative theatres of war to the Western Front at that time in the region of feasibility, namely the Dardanelles and Serbia.' The meeting, which had opened with a victory for French and the Western Front advocates, thus ended with their implied defeat.

'Nearly everyone was well satisfied,' Hankey has written. '. . . Fisher alone, whose silence had not meant consent as was generally assumed, was beginning to brood on the difficulties of his position.' Fisher had already had serious second thoughts about the naval attack, and had described the notion as 'damnable' in conversation with Kitchener on January 7th. As the affair moved forward with an unexpected speed and enthusiasm his alarm increased. His knowledge of the problem of forcing the Dardanelles was considerable. He had studied it again and again since serving under Admiral Hornby in 1878, and had always come to the same conclusion. The hazards and difficulties fascinated him, and there is no doubt that, like Churchill, the prospect of forcing the Dardanelles had an almost hypnotic effect. But his eyes were fixed on the North Sea and the Baltic. A large number of highly secret landing barges capable of carrying 500 men each, armour-plated and equipped with ramps for rapid disembarkation, had been ordered for the Baltic landings, and were now nearing completion. 'The Baltic was the real focus of all my purposes at the Admiralty,' he subsequently explained. 'Mr. Churchill dropped it for the Dardanelles. That was the real point of separation.' But this was only part of the matter; the position in the North Sea was the principal factor. On January 19th he wrote to Jellicoe that 'the Cabinet have decided on taking the Dardanelles solely with the Navy, using 15 battleships and 32 other vessels, and keeping out there three battle cruisers and a flotilla of destroyers—*all urgently required at the decisive theatre at home!* There is only one way out, and that is to resign! But you say "*no!*", which simply means I am a consenting party to what I absolutely disapprove. *I don't agree with one single step taken*, so it is fearfully against the grain that I remain on in deference to your wishes. *The way the War is conducted both ashore and afloat is chaotic! We have a new plan every week!*' On the 21st he again wrote to Jellicoe that he considered the sending of more warships to the Mediterranean 'a serious interference with our imperative needs in Home waters, and I've fought against it "tooth and nail". But, of course, if the Government of the Country decided on a project as a subject of high policy, one can't put oneself up to govern the diplomatic attitude of the nation in its relation with foreign powers, and apparently the Grand Duke Nicholas has demanded this step. . . . I just abominate the Dardanelles operation, unless a great change is made and it is settled to be made a military operation, with 200,000 men in conjunction with the Fleet. I believe Kitchener is coming now to this sane view of the matter.'

Everyone seems to have come to a different interpretation of the decision of January 13th. Churchill, as has been related, regarded it as a positive step towards the major offensive against Turkey which would be pressed to a decision; Asquith understood it to be 'merely provisional, to prepare, but nothing more. . . . It was a very promising operation, and the Admiralty ought to get ready for it . . . . [But] no more than that'. Lord Crewe and other members of the Council thought that the operation 'was approved subject to the occurrence of any unforeseen event which might have made it from one point of view unnecessary'. Sir Arthur Wilson did not realise that any definite decision had been arrived at; 'It was not my business,' he subsequently explained. 'I was not in any way connected with the question, and it had never in any way officially been put before me.' Jackson and Admiral Oliver thought that the War Council had only sanctioned a 'probing' action; Commodore de Bartolomé subsequently said that 'my impression was always that the naval members . . . only agreed to a purely naval operation on the understanding that we could always draw back—*that there should be no question of what is known as forcing the Dardanelles.*'*

Admiral Carden was informed on January 15th that the Government approved his plans, and that, in addition to the ships he had requested, he would have *Queen Elizabeth* as well. Churchill informed the French of the plan on January 18th and the French Government agreed to send a squadron under Admiral Guépratte to serve under Carden. On January 19th the Russians were informed of the attack on the Dardanelles, and were asked to prepare for a simultaneous attack on the Bosphorus. The Russians also agreed to send a light cruiser, *Askold*, to the Aegean. It was decided that the fleet should assemble in the neighbourhood of the island of Lemnos at the end of the first week in February. Carden, becoming uneasy about all this strength and speed, urged that he should not be ordered to begin operations until his force was assembled and fully prepared. Churchill replied that the

* My italics.

date chosen for the opening bombardment was February 15th, and for political reasons it was imperative that it should take place on that date. On February 5th Carden was told that great care should be taken with *Queen Elizabeth*'s new guns, that salvoes should not be fired by her except in emergency, and that she should under no circumstances sail in waters unswept of mines. 'It is not expected nor desired that the operations should be hurried to the extent of taking large risks and courting heavy losses,' he was instructed. 'The slow, relentless creeping forward of the attacking force mile after mile will tend to shake the morale of the garrisons of the forts at Kephez Point, Chanak and Kilid Bahr, and will have an effect on Constantinople.' This was a subtle, but significant, change of emphasis in his orders. Having been told that the enterprise was so important as to justify heavy losses, he was now urged to be cautious. Carden was far from being a reckless or adventurous leader; he was, furthermore, a sick man, and, trying to assemble his fleet in the storm-tossed Aegean, oppressed with conflicting exhortations from Whitehall, and ignorant of the condition of the defences he was to assault, he understandably became a prey to grave doubts and anxieties.

Fisher's differences with Churchill came to a head on January 28th. Asquith had been warned by Hankey a week earlier that Fisher was extremely unhappy about his relationship with Churchill in general, and with the Dardanelles operation in particular. 'I am not in accord with the First Lord,' Fisher wrote to Asquith, 'and do not think it would be seemly to say so before the Council. . . I say that the Zeebrugge and Dardanelles bombardments can only be justified on naval grounds by military co-operation, which would compensate for the loss in ships and irreplaceable officers and men. As purely naval operations they are unjustifiable. . . I am very reluctant to leave the First Lord. I have a great personal affection and admiration for him, but I see no possibility of a union of ideas, and unity is essential in war, so I refrain from any desire of remaining as a stumbling block. The British Empire ceases if our Grand Fleet ceases. No risks can be taken.'

Churchill, after consulting Asquith, urged Fisher to meet them that morning before the meeting of the War Council, and his letter continued; 'You have assented to both the operations in question, and so far as I am concerned there can be no withdrawal, without good reason, from measures which are necessary, and for which preparations are far advanced.' Fisher had submitted a lengthy memorandum on the naval situation on January 25th which was clearly not his own composition, but to which he gave his complete support. Churchill later said that this was the first serious intimation he had that Fisher was opposed to the naval attack; it would probably be more accurate to say that it was the first indication he received of the extent of

Fisher's hostility. 'We play into Germany's hands if we risk fighting ships in any subsidiary operations such as coastal bombardments or the attack of fortified places without military co-operation,' the most significant passage of the memorandum ran, 'for we thereby increase the possibility that the Germans may be able to engage our fleet with some approach to equality of strength. . . . *Even the older ships should not be risked, for they cannot be lost without losing men and they form our only reserve behind the Grand Fleet*. . .* Being already in possession of all that a powerful fleet can give a country we should continue quietly to enjoy the advantage without dissipating our strength in operations that cannot improve the position.' Fisher wanted this document to be circulated to the War Council, but Asquith—who received a strong counter-memorandum from Churchill—refused to do so. This was a serious error of judgement.

Asquith, Churchill and Fisher met on the morning of January 28th. Fisher briefly described his objections to the Zeebrugge and Dardanelles operations, and indicated his strong preference for his Baltic scheme or an attack on the Belgian coast in co-operation with the Army. All accounts agree that Fisher did not criticise the Dardanelles operation on its own merits, and gave no reason for Asquith to believe that he would resign if over-ruled. Churchill urged that both the Zeebrugge and Dardanelles operations should be under-taken, but if either had to be abandoned, it should be Zeebrugge. Asquith, characteristically, proposed a judicial compromise; Zeebrugge should be abandoned and the Dardanelles operation endorsed. Fisher was silent, but both Asquith and Churchill assumed that he was satisfied. In fact, he had assumed that the discussion was adjourned, and that no actual decision had been reached.

At the meeting of the Council which immediately followed this conclave Fisher broke his silence. After Churchill had reported that preparations for the attack on the Dardanelles were well advanced, Fisher intervened to say that he had understood that the matter was not going to be raised, and that the Prime Minister was well aware of his views. He then left the table and made for the door. Kitchener, however, got there first, and, taking him over to a window, quietly asked him what he was going to do. While the puzzled Ministers carried on their discussion, Fisher told Kitchener that he was going to resign. Kitchener, of course, was well aware of Fisher's hostility to the purely naval operation, and, as Fisher subsequently wrote, 'knew I was bloody-minded and would resign'. Kitchener pointed out that he was the only member of the Council against the scheme and ought to abide by the Prime Minister's decision. Fisher later said that the pause gave him the opportunity to think of the great shipbuilding programme now under way, and of the manifold schemes of strategy and organisation which, he

* My italics.

believed, would collapse if he left the Admiralty; eventually Kitchener persuaded him to return to the table, where Ministers were vying with each other in enthusiastic prognostications about the outcome of the operation. Grey said that 'the Turks would be paralysed with fear when they heard that the forts were being destroyed one by one'; Kitchener declared that the operation was vitally important, and that 'if satisfactory progress could not be made, the attack could be broken off'. Fisher, however, maintained what Asquith described as 'an obstinate and ominous silence'.

That afternoon, however, Fisher and Churchill had another long discussion, in which Fisher agreed to support the operation. 'I am in no way concealing the great and continuous pressure which I put upon the old Admiral,' Churchill later wrote. Fisher's objections to the scheme were imprecise and largely intuitive, and Churchill had little difficulty in combating his arguments. As Fisher complained to Hankey at this time of Churchill, 'he always out-argues me'. To J. A. Spender he kept saying, revealingly, 'I am sure I am right, I am sure I am right, but *he* is always convincing me against my will. I hear him talk and he seems to make the difficulties vanish, and when he is gone I sit down and write him a letter and say I agree. Then I go back to bed and can't sleep, and his talk passes away, and I know I am right. So I get up and write him another letter and say I don't agree, and so it goes on.' On January 28th Churchill convinced him that he must support the operation, and he agreed. He even added two more battleships to Carden's fleet, and Churchill informed the War Council later in the afternoon that the Admiralty was now agreed, and that the plans would be set in motion. 'This I took as the point of final decision', Churchill wrote. 'After it, I never looked back. We had left the region of discussion and consultation, of balancings and misgivings. The matter had passed into the domain of action.'

'When the operation was undertaken,' Fisher told the Dardanelles Commission, 'my duty from that time onwards was confined to seeing that the Government plan was carried out as successfully as possible with the available means. I did everything I could to secure its success. I put my whole heart into it and worked like a Trojan. Although I had been against it, I felt it my duty to go in for it *con amore*—No, I can hardly say "*con amore*", but I did my best.'

Fisher's position was unenviable and difficult. He had been enthusiastically in favour of a joint operation but against a purely naval attack. He had made his position on this issue clear to the First Lord, the Prime Minister, and his Admiralty colleagues. He later wrote that his views were known 'even to the charwomen at the Admiralty'. But events had moved with an altogether unexpected and disconcerting swiftness, and he was now presented with a virtual *fait accompli*. If Churchill had enjoyed Fisher's complete confidence all might have been well; but he did not. In 1916 Fisher wrote in defence of his attitude on January 28th:

> In my judgement it is not the business of the chief technical advisers of the Government to resign because their advice is not accepted, unless they are of opinion that the operation proposed must lead to disastrous results.
> The attempt to force the Dardanelles, though a failure, would not have been disastrous as long as the ships employed could be withdrawn at any moment, and only such vessels were engaged, as in the beginning of the operations was in fact the case, as could be spared without detriment to the general service of the Fleet.

The final qualification was the all-important one, and Churchill was left in no doubts as to Fisher's views. *'The more I consider the Dardanelles the less I like it!'* he wrote to Churchill on March 4th. 'No matter what happens it is impossible to send out anything more, not even a dinghy! and why the hostile submarine has not appeared is a wonder.' Thus Fisher was haunted by three menaces: the torpedoes in the German submarines if any reached the Aegean; the casualties which might be caused to precious skilled naval personnel in the Dardanelles attack; and, above all, the lurking shadow of the German High Seas Fleet across the shrouded turbulence of the North Sea. On this latter apprehension Jellicoe assiduously played. At the end of March Fisher repeated his fundamental objection to the Dardanelles, which was that a victory or defeat in that area was irrelevant. *'A failure or check in the Dardanelles would be nothing,'* he wrote to Churchill. *'A failure in the North Sea would be ruin.'* On April 5th he wrote: 'You are just simply eaten up with the Dardanelles and cannot think of anything else. Damn the Dardanelles! They will be our grave!'

But on January 28th, albeit with many misgivings, Fisher had definitely agreed to the naval attack. 'To forbid, before it had been tried, *an experiment** on which rested so many sanguine hopes, would have been an impracticable step', he later declared. 'The experiment had to be made, and I did accept in that connection, responsibility, though reluctant responsibility.' There can be little doubt that Fisher accurately reflected the majority view in the Admiralty when he described the operations as 'an experiment'. As the official historian has remarked, 'it was felt by the Admiralty War Staff that, if immediate action was a political necessity, there would be little harm in making a naval attempt. . . If unsuccessful, the operations could be regarded as a mere demonstration and broken off at any moment.' The gulf between the First Lord and his Service advisers could hardly have been wider.

* My italics.

3

Naval Prelude

Try and take an opportunity of examining Gallipoli. One never
knows what may happen, and it is just as well to know all about
places.
Lord Randolph Churchill to Joseph Chamberlain, Oct. 4th, 1886

Up to the beginning of February, all plans had been prepared in the light of
Kitchener's repeated statements that no troops could be made available for
the Dardanelles. But the weight of opinion in the War Office and in the
Admiralty itself propelled Ministers uneasily in the direction of at least some
degree of military participation in the forthcoming operations. Kitchener
himself began to waver. He had at his disposal in England the 29th Division,
which consisted of 11 regular and one Territorial battalions, and it was
around this magnificent division that the controversy raged.

Like most great politico-military controversies, it started stealthily. On
February 9th, after Churchill had been over to France to see Sir John
French, the War Council agreed in principle to send the 29th Division to the
Middle East, probably to Salonika. This was a political rather than a military
decision, whose purpose was to strengthen the pro-Entente Venizelos
Government, but it was rejected by Venizelos himself within a few days.
Nevertheless, it had been a momentous decision. If the 29th Division could
be spared to bring Greece into the war, could it not be used to drive Turkey
out of it? The principle of providing limited military assistance for the Fleet
was also admitted by the decision on February 6th to send two battalions of
Marines to the Aegean to provide landing parties to demolish the guns of the
Dardanelles forts.

On February 15th Sir Henry Jackson circulated a remarkable document,
which accurately reflected Lord Fisher's apprehensions. 'The naval bombardment', it concluded, 'is not recommended as a sound military operation

unless a strong military force is ready to assist in the operation, or at least to follow it up immediately the forts are silenced.' Ministers were thus for the first time presented with a disconcerting professional estimation of the nature of the adventure into which they were drifting. On February 16th Asquith, Lloyd George, Grey, Kitchener, Churchill and Fisher met informally, and agreed that the 29th Division should be sent to the Greek island of Lemnos in the Aegean, and that units of the Australian and New Zealand Army Corps (A.N.Z.A.C.)* in Egypt should also be prepared for dispatch to the same destination. It was also decided that the Admiralty should collect suitable transport for the conveyance and landing of a force of 50,000 men to any point where they might be required. Rear-Admiral Wemyss was instructed to proceed to Lemnos to assume the title of Governor with Venizelos' connivance for the purpose of making preparations for the arrival and accommodation of the Army. Although no decision was reached as to the employment of these troops, their concentration in the neighbourhood of the Dardanelles represented a considerable step in the direction of supplying military support for the Fleet.

Some idea of the muddle which was rapidly overtaking the entire project can be glimpsed from Wemyss' account of what followed. He saw Churchill and Fisher at the Admiralty, but was given only a most vague description of his responsibilities. He was told by Churchill that he would receive his instructions from Carden when he reached the Aegean, but when Wemyss arrived he discovered that the harassed Admiral was bewildered by this new development. 'He gave me to understand that some 10,000 troops might shortly be expected,' Wemyss has related, 'but of any plans for combined operations he appeared to be as ignorant as I was. . . . And so I entered into my kingdom with but vague ideas of what I had to prepare for, but always hopeful that I should shortly receive some further instructions, however indefinite they might be.'

In this nonchalant manner, Wemyss was dispatched, without instructions, staff, or means, to establish a base on an arid, thinly-populated island, nearly 3,000 miles from Britain, 700 from Malta, and 575 from Alexandria, whose only asset was the enormous but exposed natural harbour of Mudros. The local Greek officials were considerably taken aback when Wemyss announced himself as the new Governor. He found that there were no facilities for loading and unloading ships; that there was only one tiny pier, no depot ship or supplies of any kind, no accommodation on shore for the Army when and if it arrived, and wholly insufficient water resources. He installed himself on

---

* Two Australian sergeants, Little and Millington, had cut a rubber stamp with the initials 'A. & N.Z.A.C.' for the purpose of registering papers at the Corps headquarters, situated in Shepheard's Hotel, Cairo. When a code name was required for the Corps, a British officer, a Lt. White, suggested 'Anzac'. Little later claimed that he made the original suggestion to White. It was in general use by January, 1915.

an old gunboat converted into a yacht, and on March 4th received a first detachment of 5,000 equally baffled Australian troops sent from Egypt, most of whom had to remain on board their ships as there was no accommodation on shore. On March 9th a French officer arrived with the interesting information that a French division was on its way; three days later units of the Royal Naval Division arrived, and had to be immediately sent off to Alexandria as there were no wharves, piers or boats with which to disembark them.

In London, on the morrow of Wemyss' departure for the Aegean, matters became more confused than ever. On February 19th Kitchener suddenly changed his mind about the 29th Division. The Russians were crumpling on the Eastern Front, and it was probable that a substantial part of the German armies could shortly be released for the Western Front; in these circumstances, the margin of numbers between the opposing armies would be markedly in the favour of the Germans, and the 29th Division was Kitchener's one remaining experienced division. His decision to countermand the orders to the division were therefore prudent in the context of the potentially critical situation on the Western Front, but increased the fog which was enveloping the whole enterprise.

Churchill's personal position was becoming extremely difficult. The same enthusiasm and persuasiveness on the prospects of the naval attack which had so impressed the War Council now made it difficult for him to convince Kitchener and his colleagues of the importance of having an army available in the Dardanelles area. As he subsequently remarked, 'I had no right at this stage to complain if Lord Kitchener had said, "I am not going to land on the Peninsula." I could not have said, "Oh! you have broken faith with the Admiralty." On the contrary, we had said we would try it without committing him to that, and he would have had a right to complain if we had turned round and immediately demanded that he should undertake this very serious military operation.' There is no doubt that Kitchener had been a too-willing recipient of Churchill's glowing enthusiasm and confidence about the naval operation. On February 16th he summoned Captain Wyndham Deedes, who had served with the Turkish Army and who was now working at the War Office as an intelligence officer, to seek his views on the prospects of a purely naval attack on the Dardanelles. Deedes said that the operation was fundamentally unsound, but when he began to develop his arguments Kitchener turned on him angrily, told him brusquely that he did not know what he was talking about, and signified that the interview was at an end.*

At this point, four days late, Carden opened his attack on the Outer

---

* Nine months later, at the Dardanelles, Kitchener characteristically sought Deedes out from the throng of Staff officers to apologise.

Defences on February 19th. From a military point of view it was a fiasco, as the warships kept moving while they fired, and caused little or no damage. The Admiralty *communiqué*, however, created a vast international sensation. The Bulgarians hastily broke off their flirtation with the Central Powers; the Greeks offered three divisions for an attack on the Gallipoli Peninsula: the Russians, anxious not to be out of the dismemberment of the Ottoman Empire, spoke of attacking Constantinople from the east and bringing up an army corps for the purpose; the Italians made distinctly friendly noises. In Constantinople itself there was almost a panic. 'On all hands,' Morgenthau recorded, 'there were evidences of the fear and panic that had seized not only the populace but the official classes.' Von der Goltz considered that, for the sacrifice of ten warships, the British must get through; Wangenheim nervously prepared for his personal effects to be transferred to the American Embassy; the members of the Government hastened to make their arrangements for an immediate departure from the capital. Only Enver seems to have kept his head, but his jaunty desperado-optimism carried little conviction. Constantinople was tense and expectant, acutely conscious of the proximity of the wolves gathering for the death agonies of the Ottoman Empire. In the subterranean world of secret operations, news reached London that certain members of the Turkish administration would welcome a clandestine discussion with British representatives on the subject of a peace treaty. At the first gentle push, the Ottoman Empire rocked on its heels. From this moment there could be no going back.

Acting entirely on his own responsibility, Kitchener had telegraphed to Sir John Maxwell, Commander-in-Chief in Egypt, on February 20th:

> . . . In order to assist Navy a force is being concentrated in Lemnos Island to give co-operation and to occupy any captured forts. At present 2,000 Marines in the Island, to be followed about 13 March by 8,000 more.
> You should warn a force of approximately 30,000 of Australians and New Zealand contingent under Birdwood to prepare for this service. We shall send troopships from here to convey these troops to Lemnos, which should arrive Alexandria about March 9th. You should, however, communicate through Navy with Admiral Carden, commander at the Dardanelles, as he may require a considerable force before that date and in order that you may send him what he most requires.
> You should not therefore wait till the transports arrive from here, but should take up any transports you can obtain and despatch units to Lemnos immediately. . . .

Maxwell accordingly telegraphed to Carden for instructions, and Carden replied on the 23rd:

> I have been directed to prepare for landing force of 10,000 men, if such a step is found necessary; at present my instructions go no further. If such a force is sent, I would propose landing it at Sedd-el-Bahr, with the object of occupying the Gallipoli Peninsula as far east as the line Suandere-Chanalvasi. The garrison of the Peninsula is about 40,000. . . .

Maxwell was understandably startled by this response to his request for detailed instructions. 'Admiral Carden's telegram strikes me as being so helpless that I feel unless military authorities take the initiative, no progress is likely to be made,' he telegraphed to Kitchener.

When the War Council met on the following day (February 24th), Kitchener, acting in the spirit of Maxwell's telegram, robustly declared that if the Fleet failed to get through 'the Army must see the business through.' Only Lloyd George, rapidly assuming the rôle of the Jeremiad of the Council, expressed dissent. Kitchener also ordered the commander of the Australian and New Zealand Army Corps in Egypt, Lt.-General W. R. Birdwood, to proceed to the Dardanelles and report back confidentially on the situation. But he still refused to order the 29th Division to proceed to the Aegean, and on the 26th Churchill took the extreme step of disclaiming responsibility for the consequences of the operations in these circumstances, and unavailingly urged Asquith to overrule Kitchener.

In Egypt, Maxwell's mystification increased. On February 23rd he was told that the force of Anzacs and Marines would have the task of 'taking the forts in reverse'. On the next day, Kitchener was writing that 'the operation is to be effected mainly by naval means; when successful will doubtless cause retirement of Gallipoli garrison. According to our information, it would not be a sound military undertaking to attempt landing in force on Gallipoli Peninsula—whose garrison is reported 40,000 strong—until the naval operations for the reduction of the forts have been successful and the passage has been forced. . . . To land with 10,000 men in face of 40,000 Turks while naval operations still incomplete seems extremely hazardous'; meanwhile, the Anzacs were to be held ready at Alexandria, and the Marines should be available at Lemnos if required. On the 26th Kitchener repeated that the troops would be limited to minor operations, while, on the same day, he told Birdwood to train his troops in rapid embarkation and disembarkation 'on any beaches available under service conditions and in face of pretended opposition. You might specially earmark one brigade and perfect it in this work.' On March 4th Kitchener wrote to Maxwell that there was no intention of using the troops to capture the Gallipoli Peninsula, but that they might be wanted for the advance on Constantinople when the Fleet had reached the Marmara. Maxwell complained on February 23rd that he made his suggestions for the employment of the troops—he favoured a landing at Besika Bay—'considerably in the dark as I have no knowledge of the deep study which must have been made of the whole question of the forcing of the Dardanelles by the Imperial General Staff and the Navy for many years past, the result of which must be in the War Office and résumé of which I should much like. . . . Meanwhile I recommend that troops be despatched from here and concentrated at Lemnos as shipping permits so as to be ready for eventualities.' On the 28th he again protested that 'I am very much in the dark as to the intentions and objects of the Fleet in forcing the Dardanelles. . . . The Admiralty seem to me to be over-sanguine as to the capacity of the Fleet to force the passage without an expeditionary force.' To Kitchener's military secretary, Colonel Fitzgerald, Maxwell wrote despairingly on March 8th, 'who is co-ordinating and directing this great combine?'

The weather in the Aegean was characteristically bleak, wild and un-certain. A day of almost glassy calm would be followed by a tempest of rough seas, lashing rain, gloomy scudding clouds, and, on more than one occasion, brief blizzards. The puzzled Maxwell in Egypt, still occupied by the vague but sinister menace of the Turkish army within striking distance of the Canal, made the best arrangements he could for the transporting of Birdwood's Anzacs to Lemnos; on that island the hapless Wemyss was struggling to create modern harbour facilities with virtually no materials; Birdwood was with Carden, already under the impression that he was the designated future commander-in-chief of any military force which might be required to assist the Fleet;* Carden, unsure about the position of the soldiers, but concentrating on the immediate naval problems, was becoming increasingly uneasy about the whole operation. In London, Fisher was still consumed with nagging doubts and suspicions; Churchill was pressing for military reinforcements; Kitchener, although half-persuaded that the Army would be required, still remained obdurate on the question of the 29th Division; in the War Office, the vague possibility of military requirements in the Dardanelles was known only to a few officers. At a time when the British Army in France was gravely deficient in trained men and adequate munitions—as the events of April in the Ypres sector were so graphically to emphasise—in Sir William Robertson's brutal and laconic sentences, 'the Secretary of State for War was aiming at decisive results on the Western Front; the First Lord of the Admiralty was advocating a military expedi-tion to the Dardanelles; the Secretary of State for India was devoting his attention to a campaign in Mesopotamia; the Secretary of State for the Colonies was occupying himself with several small wars in Africa; and the Chancellor of the Exchequer was attempting to secure the removal of a large part of the British Army from France to some Eastern Mediterranean theatre.' And thus did the mighty enterprise advance!

Carden renewed the bombardment of the Outer Forts on February 25th with more satisfactory results. The long-range guns were silenced, and the others abandoned by the crews. On the next day the bombardment of the Intermediate Defences was opened from inside the Straits by three warships, when, for the first time, some inconvenience was caused by the concealed

* The question of his appointment as such was in fact discussed by the War Council on February 24th.

mobile howitzer batteries. Meanwhile, parties of Marines had been landed at Sedd-el-Bahr and Kum Kale, had met little serious resistance, and had destroyed 20 guns before being disembarked with the loss of one man killed and one wounded. For the following ten days these landings became almost daily occurrences, and between February 27th and March 3rd the Marines put 30 more guns out of action.

On March 4th, however, a company of the Plymouth Battalion, landed at Sedd-el-Bahr, met unexpectedly fierce resistance, and had to be evacuated by the Navy. To cover the withdrawal, the old battleship *Majestic* pounded the castle and village of Sedd-el-Bahr, and, as an officer related with satisfaction, 'in a few minutes there was in place of a village a smoking ruin.'

The Kum Kale operation, carried out by another company of the Plymouth Battalion, was equally unsuccessful. The landing was opposed, but the Marines eventually landed under the walls of the fort; a demolition party and covering platoon sent out to destroy the guns in a small battery were badly held up by Turkish snipers, and became detached from the men in the fort. A young officer was instructed to run the gauntlet and to order Colonel Matthews, who was with the advance parties, to retire. When he arrived, after wading in the sea to reduce the target to the Turks, he found that Matthews had come to exactly the same conclusion. Eventually, and with considerable difficulty, the men were withdrawn, doubling across the bullet-swept gap between their position and the fort. Twenty-two men were killed and 22 wounded in this operation, which barely merited passing reference in most histories of the campaign. It was, however, a grim portent. The disembarkation of troops under fire, their deployment when landed, their handling on largely unknown beaches; all these were novel problems, not only for the men of the Plymouth Battalion, but for everyone. The Turks, although few in number, had not been cowed by the guns of the warships and had kept their heads; some officers and men of the British detachments had found the unexpected resistance extremely disconcerting, and a Captain found one platoon whose officer was 'pale with funk and afraid to move . . . it was not until I said that I proposed standing there until they did and that it was unusual for Marines to watch their officers being killed that a fellow got up and said "I'll come with you, sir!". . . . Unluckily he was shot in the chest as I got him up, but we succeeded in moving the platoon.' The Marines re-embarked, shaken and silent.

Although the fall of the Outer Defences had created a great sensation throughout Europe, the difficulties of the Fleet were steadily increasing as it penetrated further into the Dardanelles. Co-ordination was rendered more difficult by the number of bases in the Aegean; 'one of the curses of the present complete lack of organisation is that we have *six* bases!' one officer complained; 'and no one knows where ships are.' The ships themselves, being old, were giving trouble, and difficulties were experienced in some ships in achieving reasonably accurate gunnery with worn guns. With several notable exceptions, the crews were not of the highest quality, as the best had been taken by the Grand Fleet. As Admiral Brodie has written, 'some of this residue was first class, more was green, mostly with age.' The weather was bad, and the difficulty of navigating in the confined waters of the Dardanelles against the fierce currents from the Marmara added to the hazards of the operation. Although the warships were manoeuvred with great skill and enthusiasm, one detects in the reports from senior officers to Carden a mounting concern about the progress of the operations. Seaplanes from *Ark Royal*—a merchant ship converted into a seaplane carrier—were proving so unreliable and their observers so inexperienced that, in spite of the great gallantry and resolution of the pilots, they were almost useless for reconnaissance purposes.

Bombardments on the Inner Forts were carried out on February 26th, March 2nd and 3rd, but with little effect. The mobile howitzer batteries, skilfully positioned and handled, kept the warships moving, with the consequence that their firing was inaccurate. The howitzers could not hope to cripple, let alone sink, any of the warships except the North Sea trawlers brought for minesweeping duties, but a howitzer shell landing on an old warship was not something to be laughed off, and their fire was harassing and disconcerting. One officer reported that 'a most careful watch failed to locate the howitzers, and I am not even certain whether they were on the north or south side of the Straits'. The dummy batteries emitting black smoke drew the ships' fire and increased their difficulties. If a battery was definitely located one day, it was in another place on the next, and, in any event, the chances of scoring a direct hit on one of these batteries were minimal. 'I found extraordinarily divergent views among naval officers as to their chances of success', Birdwood reported confidentially to Kitchener on March 2nd. 'Some made light of it, but the majority seemed to think they had the toughest of knots before them and couldn't say when they could hope to get through.'

On the same day, however, Carden informed the Admiralty that, given fine weather, he hoped to be in the Marmara in about a fortnight. Only Kitchener did not share the general elation among Ministers at this forecast. Birdwood, a trusted confidant, had been profoundly struck by the hazards of the enterprise and by the complete lack of real progress being made by the Fleet. Carden, he reported to Kitchener, was 'very second-rate—no "go" in him, or ideas, or initiative'; he was 'too sanguine'; it was at best doubtful if the Fleet could get through by itself. When Kitchener told him on March 4th of Carden's expectations, and forbade him to undertake any military operations without further orders, Birdwood replied somewhat sharply that 'I have already informed you that I consider the Admiral's fore-cast too sanguine, and I doubt his ability to force the passage unaided. . . . I have no intention of rushing blindly into the Gallipoli Peninsula, and I quite realise that my movements must depend entirely on the navy's progress.' These apprehensions were not confined to the soldiers. Brodie has written: 'Looking back at the start of the Dardanelles campaign the size of the im-provised staff seems microscopic, and the amateurishness of the Navy in general, and staff-work in particular, quite amazing.'

Birdwood was a man whose judgement could not be discarded lightly, and his reports finally persuaded Kitchener that an army was likely to be required, but he still refused to sanction the departure of the 29th Division. The French, although refusing to move a soldier from France, had agreed to provide a force commanded by General d'Amade consisting of troops taken from North Africa. Maxwell, it may be remarked in passing, only learnt of this fact from a chance conversation with a French officer attached to the military mission in Cairo in the middle of March; the Turks, however, were so well informed that a divisional order dated March 11th described the French force in considerable, and accurate, detail.

Kitchener's anxieties and apprehensions were strengthened by the events of the following week. On March 5th *Queen Elizabeth* opened up an indirect bombardment of the forts at the Narrows across the Gallipoli Peninsula from a point off Gaba Tepe at 14,000 yards' range. The utterly unexpected arrival of her enormous shells from this angle flung the Turks into consider-able confusion, as the limited protection which their batteries had was designed on the basis of an attack from the Straits. Fortunately for the de-fenders, the British reconnaissance aircraft failed again; of the three seaplanes used, one crashed after take-off, another was hit by rifle-fire and the observer wounded, and the third sent back only one correction. When *Queen Eliza-beth* arrived off Gaba Tepe on the following morning to repeat the operation, she was shelled by a battery which had been rushed there overnight by the Turks, and was forced further out to sea, with seriously adverse effects on her gunnery.

On March 7th and 8th, unaware of the extent to which the indirect bom-bardment had disconcerted the Turks, Carden renewed the direct bombard-ment of the forts from inside the Straits, but with little effect. Apart from the mobile batteries, which were an irritation and were virtually impossible to detect, the Fleet was experiencing difficulty in hitting even the located batteries. Fort Dardanos, for example, south of Chanak on the crest-line of a hill, was plastered almost daily, but although the area around the battery resembled a moon-landscape with craters, none of the guns themselves was put out of action. Even the 15-inch shells of *Queen Elizabeth* hardly dented the vast medieval superstructure of Kilid Bahr. The morale of the Turkish and German gunners was rising with every day that passed. Morgenthau saw a practice firing at Kilid Bahr at this time, and was greatly impressed by the proficiency and enthusiasm of the Turkish gunners. 'Everything was quickness and alertness; evidently the Germans had been excellent instructors, but there was more to it than German military precision, for the men's faces lighted up with all that fanaticism which supplies the morale of Turkish soldiers. . . . Above the shouts of all I could hear the sing-song chant of the leader, intoning the prayer with which the Moslem has rushed to battle for thirteen centuries. "Allah is great, there is but one God, and Mohammed is his Prophet!"'

By March 11th deadlock had been reached at the Dardanelles. The Intermediate and Inner Defences, although battered, were still protecting the vital minefields; the hidden howitzers were still unlocated.

Unknown to the Cabinet, the Foreign Office, or the War Council, secret negotiations had been proceeding between Turkish and British emissaries about the bloodless surrender of Turkey which had come very close to success. The details of this curious episode have only recently come to light.

On the personal instructions of Admiral Sir Reginald Hall, the Director of Naval Intelligence, a Mr. George Eady, a contractor who knew the Middle East well, and Mr. Edwin Whittall, assisted by Gerald Fitzmaurice, who had been attached to the British Embassy at Constantinople for several years, had been secretly conveyed to Turkey to contact leading members of the Turkish Government who were thought to be prepared to negotiate a peace treaty. An unspecified Turkish Minister sent emissaries to the remote Thracian coastal town of Dedeagach. The British were instructed to negotiate a treaty with the Turks whereby Turkey would withdraw from the war, retain strict neutrality, and open the Dardanelles to Allied shipping; Hall gave the British agents a letter guaranteeing a sum of £3,000,000 to be paid to the Turks, with authority to go to £4,000,000 if necessary. At the beginning of March it became necessary to press for a quick decision, and Hall telegraphed that each day's delay would bring with it a lowering of the subsidy; on March 5th he offered £500,000 for the complete surrender of the Dardanelles with all mines removed, with a similar sum for the surrender of Goeben if undamaged. The fatal flaw in the position of the British negotiators was that they were not permitted to give any undertaking that Constantinople should remain in the hands of the Turkish Government. Whittal and Eady were unaware of the fact that their Government had promised the capital to the Russians, and could not understand why their appeals to Hall to be permitted to guarantee Constantinople's integrity were refused. Another meeting was arranged for March 15th, and it was becoming clear that the Turks required positive assurances about the capital's future if the negotiations were to continue. On March 15th, however, a signal from Berlin to Constantinople was intercepted by the British which revealed that the Dardanelles forts were short of ammunition; Fisher's fading confidence in the naval attack was at once restored, and he ordered Hall to break off the negotiations. As Admiral Sir William James, Hall's biographer, has recently revealed, Fisher 'had been completely taken aback when Hall told him he had guaranteed £4,000,000 without informing his own superiors, the Foreign Office, or the Cabinet, but it was the kind of initiative that appealed to him'. It is not clear whether Hall did instruct Whittall and Eady to end the negotiations, or whether the Turks ended them, but the fact was that on March 17th, the British emissaries left Dedeagach for Salonika. Eady wrote in 1919: 'The whole country desired peace, and their leaders would have accepted almost any terms had we been able to assure them on Constantinople. They knew full well that signing away that city would also mean signing their own death warrants.' Thus ended one of the most strange episodes of the Great War.*

None of this was dreamed of in the Fleet at the Dardanelles, whose officers were becoming increasingly concerned by the skilful and obstinate resistance being put up by the Turks. The most disconcerting fact was the effect of the mobile howitzers on the minesweepers. These were small fishing trawlers, manned by civilian crews from the North-East ports of England, and were so slow and under-powered that they could barely make three knots against the Dardanelles current. The quality of their civilian crews was mixed, and the naval officer sent from England to command them had no previous experience of sweeping. The draught of the trawlers, furthermore, was greater than the depth of the mines from the surface, and this knowledge did little to improve the morale of the crews. The principle of sweeping was to move in pairs over the mines, 'trawling' them to the surface with a wire dragged behind the boats. Thus, if the trawlers went over the minefields they stood a good chance of being blown up; if they did not, they had little hope of bringing up any mines. Reduced to its essentials, this was the problem. Barely able to make any progress against the fierce current, illuminated by powerful searchlights at night and even more conspicuous by day, working under almost constant fire from no less than 74 guns at close range, it was hardly surprising that the nerve of the civilian crews broke. On March 1st they did not reach the Kephez minefield; on March 2nd, under a bright moon and heavy fire, no progress whatever was made; on March 3rd the trawlers fled down the Straits with shells splashing about them; on March 10th, at the seventh attempt, they actually reached the minefield, but after one trawler

---

* The incident has only recently been revealed by Eady's son-in-law, Capt. G. R. G. Allen, D.S.O., R.N. (Retd.) in the May 1963 issue of *The Royal United Service Institution Journal*. Admiral Sir William James added further details in the November issue of the Journal.

had hit a mine and blown up, the others hastily withdrew. On the following night they turned back as soon as the first shells dropped into the water.

Commodore Roger Keyes, Carden's Chief of Staff, exasperated by this series of disastrous fiascoes, took charge of the sweeping force, called for naval volunteers, and offered the civilian crews handsome financial inducements to persevere. On the night of March 13th a determined attempt, supported by a cruiser, was made to sweep the Kephez minefield; four out of the six sweepers engaged were badly damaged by shellfire, the cruiser—*Amethyst*—was hit, and lay out of control for 20 minutes or so in the Straits with damaged steering-gear, a perfect target for the Turks. 'A watch of stokers had been washing themselves in their bathroom', an officer reported. 'A shell burst right among them, so that all the walls and roof were plastered with flesh and blood. The remains of the victims were put into sacks, but, on mustering, it was discovered that instead of twelve men having been in the room (as thought), there had been nineteen.' Of the 27 men killed and 43 wounded in the operation, 22 of the dead and 28 of the wounded were on *Amethyst*. The minefield had hardly been touched.

As a result of this final failure, Carden decided to reverse his strategy. The suppression of the Turkish batteries by the heavy guns of the battleships must precede, rather than follow, the sweeping of the channel. Spurred by anxious telegrams from Churchill, Carden replied that he was about to launch his major attack, possibly on March 17th. Fisher, who 'had a sort of feeling that the thing was rather too much for Carden', offered to go out to take personal command, but Churchill persuaded him to abandon the idea.

The vexatious delays suffered since March 4th, although not amounting to an actual reverse, had had important consequences. The attention of the belligerents had been effectively diverted from the titanic but temporarily quiescent struggle in Flanders and Prussia. Admiral von Tirpitz noted on March 12th: 'It is a dangerous situation. The capsizing of one little State may affect fatally the whole course of the war.' On the 21st he wrote: 'The forcing of the Dardanelles would be a severe blow to us. . . . We have no trumps left.' But the Balkan States remained in their hazardous neutrality until events became clearer.

The Russians, fired by the expectation of the imminent downfall of the Ottoman Empire, were adamant in refusing to sanction any Greek participation in the campaign, and the immediate downfall of the Venizelos Government on March 6th was the consequence of this intransigent attitude. On the following day the new Greek administration, reflecting the views of King Constantine and his consort, peremptorily demanded of the British Government an explanation for its occupation of Lemnos. On March 10th the British felt obliged to agree to further Russian demands that Constantinople, the European side of the Bosphorus, the Marmara and the

Dardanelles should be handed over to Russia when they were captured. This was a formidable diplomatic achievement for the Russians; committed to nothing save a naval bombardment of the Bosphorus,* they had assured themselves of vast territorial gains after the British and French had done the hard work. It was not until many years later that the true consequences of the Russian attitude could be appreciated. But the short-term effects were equally important, as the signing-away of Constantinople had destroyed Whittall's and Eady's mission at Dedeagach.

Kitchener now came to two important—indeed, crucial—decisions. On March 10th he at last told the War Council that the 29th Division was under orders to proceed forthwith to the Aegean, although no decision had been taken as to how the British force, now amounting to nearly 70,000 men when the 29th Division arrived, was to be employed. As Hankey has commented, 'up to this point the only officially recorded object in sending out military forces was to help the Navy to reap the fruits of success. Actually, we were drifting inevitably into a major campaign in the Peninsula.' On March 11th Kitchener informed his colleagues that he had appointed General Sir Ian Hamilton, then commanding the Central Force in England, to command this force.

Kitchener must have been giving great attention to this matter long before this announcement, as he told Churchill on March 3rd that he was seriously considering the claims of General Sir Leslie Rundle as Commander-in-Chief of what was already being tentatively described as 'the Constantinople Expeditionary Force'. Birdwood, in the meantime, was still under the impression that the task was to fall upon him, and was preparing detailed plans for landing at Cape Helles with a vigorous feint at Bulair to deceive the Turks, and then a rapid advance on the Achi Baba ridge and the Kilid Bahr plateau. These plans were well advanced, and his troops either at Mudros or en route from Alexandria, when he learnt on March 13th that the command had been given to Hamilton. Apart from any personal considerations, the immediate effect was to negative all the considerable staff work which Birdwood, his staff, and Maxwell had undertaken.

It is clear that a considerable amount of discussion, and a certain personal manoeuvring took place before Kitchener decided on Hamilton's appointment. In particular, Churchill—a close and devoted friend of Sir Ian—was active on his behalf, and in a letter to Kitchener on March 4th said that no choice would give greater satisfaction to the Admiralty. In making Hamilton Commander-in-Chief of the new army, Kitchener did not make any other changes in the Middle East Commands. Maxwell remained as G.O.C.-in-C,

---

* The effect of these should not be underrated, although they are almost completely ignored in British and French histories of the campaign. They tied down a large Turkish army in the area until the end of April, and a correspondingly large amount of guns and ammunition.

Egypt, with the responsibility of defending the country—and above all the Canal—from the threatened Turkish attack. Thus, from the beginning, there was a divided military command in the Middle East, a situation which was to have unhappy consequences. Carden, of course, had complete control over the activities of the Fleet, so that there were, in effect, three separate commanders in the area. Birdwood, his dreams of supreme command dashed, was to revert to the command of the Australian and New Zealand Corps.

Hamilton was summoned to the War Office on March 12th.

> Opening the door I bade him good morning and walked up to his desk where he went on writing like a graven image. After a moment, he looked up and said in a matter-of-fact tone, 'We are sending a military force to support the Fleet now at the Dardanelles, and you are to have Command'. . . .
> Although I have met K. almost every day during the past six months, and although he has twice hinted I might be sent to Salonika, never once, to the best of my recollection, had he mentioned the word Dardanelles.
> I had plenty of time for these reflections as K., after his one tremendous remark had resumed his writing at the desk. At last, he looked up and inquired, 'Well?'
> 'We have done this sort of thing before, Lord K.,' I said; 'we have run this sort of show before and you know without saying I am most deeply grateful and you know without saying I will do my best and that you can trust my loyalty—but I must say something—I must ask you some questions.' Then I began.
> K. frowned; shrugged his shoulders; I thought he was going to be impatient, but although he gave curt answers at first he slowly broadened out, until, at the end, no one else could get a word in edgeways. . . .

After describing the forces at Hamilton's disposal, which consisted of the 29th Division, the Anzac Corps, the Royal Naval Division, and the French Corps—totalling over 70,000 men—Kitchener emphasised that the 29th Division was only on loan, and should be returned as soon as its services were no longer required. When told by General Callwell, the Director of Military Operations (who had joined the discussion), that the Greeks had estimated that 150,000 men would be necessary, Kitchener remarked to Hamilton that 'half that number will do you handsomely; the Turks are busy elsewhere; I hope you will not have to land at all; if you *do* have to land, why then the powerful Fleet at your back will be the prime factor in your choice of time and place.'* When General Walter Braithwaite, who had been appointed Hamilton's Chief of Staff without Hamilton being consulted, remarked that an efficient air force was essential, 'K. turned on him with flashing spectacles and rent him with the words, "*Not one!*".'†

---

* This account of Kitchener's attitude is in such marked contrast with a letter Kitchener wrote to Churchill on the following day, when he described the operations as 'a difficult undertaking, in which severe fighting must be expected', that Hamilton's version may exaggerate Kitchener's actual words.

† Hamilton: *Gallipoli Diary, I.* Almost every historian of the campaign has made the understandable error of treating this book as a day-to-day diary. It was in fact a memoir in diary

Churchill was feverishly anxious that Hamilton should be dispatched to the Dardanelles that very day, but Kitchener replied that he could not leave 'until we have thoroughly studied the situation with which he may be confronted. . . . "More haste, less speed".' In fact, no 'thorough' study was attempted. The Chief of the Imperial General Staff had no idea of what was in Kitchener's mind until he joined the discussions with Hamilton and Callwell on March 12th. General Braithwaite, who had been Director of Staff Duties until the previous afternoon, was given less than forty-eight hours in which to assemble a staff. Inevitably, he had to take whatever lay at hand, and a number of considerably startled officers in the War Office were ordered to prepare for an immediate departure to the Middle East. On going to the Intelligence Branch to seek information on the Dardanelles, Braithwaite was given an out-of-date text-book on the Turkish Army and two small guide-books on western Turkey, one of which contained such illuminating observations as 'the road leading up to the Kilid Bahr Plateau becomes very steep where a dog fox once ran across it.' Captain Aspinall, who was destined to be the campaign's official historian, was given 24 hours in which to work out the establishments for Hamilton's headquarters and the transport and supply requirements of the army, without being given any precise information as to what the army was to do or what the current situation was. It was not until he was in the train with Hamilton en route for the Dardanelles on the following evening that he discovered what was going on. As he subsequently wrote: 'I shall never forget the dismay and foreboding with which I learnt that apart from Lord Kitchener's very brief instructions, a pre-war Admiralty report on the Dardanelles defences and an out-of-date map, Sir Ian had been given practically no information whatever.'

One of the unexplained mysteries of the whole Gallipoli enterprise is why the detailed reports on the Dardanelles defences which had been sent to the War Office since 1911 by successive military attachés at Constantinople and vice-consuls at Chanak were not made available to Braithwaite. The military attaché at Constantinople from the end of 1913 until the outbreak of war had been a Lt.-Col. Cunliffe-Owen, who later fought at Gallipoli. In the spring of 1914, apparently on his own initiative, he had carried out a careful survey of the Dardanelles area, and has related that throughout the year 'a stream of information went home to the War Office, dealing with new armaments arriving or projected, alterations of sites of batteries and minefields, and ancillary matters pertaining thereto'. Important data concerning the topography of the Gallipoli Peninsula and the Asiatic shore were also reported to the War Office by Cunliffe-Owen and the vice-consul at

___

form. Hamilton usually wrote down a few comments in a diary, or dictated them to his batman while he shaved. This document has been made available to me by Mrs. Shield, Sir Ian Hamilton's literary executor.

Chanak; this was never seen by Braithwaite or his staff, who were only given the most vague information about the area. Cunliffe-Owen, on his return from Constantinople, made himself available in the event of operations being undertaken against Turkey, but was ignored. At no stage of the preliminary planning of the operations was he consulted, and his detailed reports of the Dardanelles defences and the Turkish Army were permitted to moulder in some dark recess of the War Office.

Hamilton's instructions were handed to him by Kitchener on the morning of March 13th. They had not been approved by, or even shown to, the War Council or the Cabinet. As Hankey has justly emphasised, they 'constitute the real decision which originated the first landing on the Gallipoli Peninsula. It was taken by Kitchener.'

Hamilton was ordered to undertake military operations 'only . . . in the event of the Fleet failing to get through after every effort has been exhausted'; he was to await the assembly of his full force 'before any serious undertaking is carried out in the Gallipoli Peninsula'; 'Having entered upon the project of forcing the Straits, there can be no abandoning the scheme. It will require time, patience, and methodical plans of co-operation between the naval and military commanders'; military operations in Asia, the instructions concluded, were greatly to be deprecated. In conversation with Hamilton, Kitchener was emphatic on this last point: 'Once we begin marching about continents, situations calling for heavy reinforcements would probably be created.' Kitchener, therefore, still thought of the military operation essentially in the light of a large landing party, going ashore on the Gallipoli Peninsula in a kind of cutting-out rôle after the Fleet had got through. As Hamilton later told the Dardanelles Commission, Kitchener repeatedly said, 'I do not expect you to do it at all. I hope to get through without it.' South of Kilid Bahr, he told Hamilton, 'the Peninsula is open to a landing on very easy terms. The cross-fire from the Fleet lying part in the Aegean and part in the mouth of the Straits must sweep that flat and open stretch of country so as to render it untenable by the enemy. Lord K. demonstrated this cross-fire upon the map. He toiled over the wording of his instructions. They were headed "Constantinople Expeditionary Force". I begged him to alter this to avert Fate's evil eye. He consented and both this corrected draft and the copy as finally approved are now in Braithwaite's despatch box more modestly headed "Mediterranean Expeditionary Force". None of the drafts help us with facts about the enemy; the politics; the country and our allies, the Russians. In sober fact these "instructions" leave me to my own devices in the East.'

Hamilton left London with his hastily assembled staff on the same evening. 'A sense of boyish enthusiasm for adventure had been in the air,' the new chief cipher officer, Orlo Williams, who had been jerked dramatically from a Clerkship in the House of Commons into uniform within 48 hours, has written; 'and in this our Chief, that most friendly and accessible of men, had set the tone. The rest of the War Office, so said some of my new acquaintances, were green with envy.' 'My staff still bear the bewildered look of men who have hurriedly been snatched from desks to do some extraordinary turn on some unheard-of theatre', Hamilton wrote. 'One or two of them put on uniform for the first time in their lives an hour ago. Leggings awry, spurs upside down, belts over shoulder straps! I haven't a notion of who they all are.' Cunliffe-Owen, although in London and available for duty, was not included in the staff. Of the party, only Jack Churchill, the First Lord's younger brother, had seen active service in the war, and he, in Williams' account, 'conveyed tremendously the hardened warrior, with a vicious bludgeon in his hand and a large revolver sticking out of his belt.' Winston Churchill and 'a few dazed wives' saw the party off from Charing Cross station. Churchill had urged Hamilton to land with all available troops as soon as possible, but Hamilton replied that he felt bound to obey Kitchener's injunction to wait for the 29th Division.

With mounting exultation Hamilton and his staff were urgently conveyed across the Channel in a destroyer, whisked through France in a luxurious special train, and embarked on the cruiser *Phaeton* at Marseilles; they then, in Orlo Williams' account, 'resisted the Dionysiac hospitality of the *Phaeton*'s tiny wardroom, drowsed on her deck as the Mediterranean, summer-smooth, turned purple and orange, passed all one morning among the Cyclades, and together experienced that marvellous moment when, after steaming through a lovely sea to the white cliffs of Tenedos, we rounded the island's southern point and a whole new world—the bristling, threatening world of a British battle fleet—burst upon our astonished view. . . . As we paced the tiny quarter deck of *Phaeton*, throbbing from stem to stern, who thought of failure? Not the Chief, certainly.'

Churchill had written of Hamilton some 15 years before:

Ian Hamilton is a man of rather more than middle height, spare, keen-eyed, and of a commanding aspect. His highly nervous temperament animating what appears a frail body imparts to all his movements a kind of feverish energy. He is a singularly good and rapid judge of character. He takes a very independent view on all subjects, sometimes with a slight bias towards or affection for their radical and democratic aspects, but never or hardly ever influenced by the set of people with whom he lives. . . . He has a most happy gift of expression, a fine taste in words, and an acute perception of the curious which he has preserved from his literary days. But it is as a whole that we should judge. His mind is built upon a big scale, being broad and strong, capable of thinking in army corps and if necessary in continents and working always with serene smoothness undisturbed alike by responsibility or danger. . . It is evident that here is a man who in the years to come will have much to do with the administration of the British Army in times of peace and its direction in the field.

Churchill was writing of 'Johnny' Hamilton when his career was at its height in the South African War; Lord Roberts wrote in 1900 that 'Ian Hamilton . . . is quite the most brilliant commander I have serving under me . . . I would select him before all others to carry out any difficult operation.' Possessed of exceptional physical courage—he had been recommended thrice for the Victoria Cross—he had also demonstrated great administrative ability in Burma and Chitral in the 1890's and as Kitchener's Chief of Staff in South Africa. Quickly spotted by Lord Roberts in the 1880's as an outstanding officer, he had transformed the musketry of the Indian Army. Mr. Alan Moorehead has incorrectly stated that 'Kitchener was Hamilton's star'.* Roberts was Hamilton's star. His career was closely and intimately linked with Roberts' fortunes, and he was a leading member of Roberts' entourage. Between 'the Wolseley ring' and Roberts' admirers there was a deep and unbridgeable gap. 'I would gladly have given away all my belongings provided thereby Roberts could be hoisted up and Wolseley brought low', Hamilton later wrote in reminiscence.

In spite of—and, indeed, partly because of—Hamilton's ability, charm and independent outlook, his career had suffered since the Boer War. He urged the development of mobile heavy artillery, revised infantry tactics, a reduction of the rôle of the cavalry, and the construction of 'steel shields on wheels' to protect advancing infantry against rifle and machine-gun fire. Without entering into the wearying controversies which rent the Army after 1902 about the respective rôles of the infantry, artillery and cavalry, the views of Hamilton, unhappily, did not gain general acceptance. He wrote a book called *The Fighting of the Future* which attracted the unfavourable attention of some of his superiors; his reports on the Russo-Japanese fighting in Manchuria, where he was the official British observer, contained numerous jeering references to the efficacy of cavalry in modern warfare which were officially removed from the published version. Something of his recklessness in the field was transmitted to his pen. His published writings invariably produced a storm of strong reactions, almost equally distributed between praise and censure. *A Staff Officer's Scrap Book*, published in two volumes between 1905 and 1907, excited wide interest; volume two, unfortunately, contained a jest in doubtful taste about the pock-marked Japanese general, Oyama, which drew on Hamilton a magisterial snub from King Edward VII. 'Ever since the reign of Edward the Confessor it had been known that the touch of a king would instantly cure scrofula', Hamilton ruefully related many years later; 'but it was left to me to prove that a king's frown will give scrofula.

* *Gallipoli* (1956), 114. On pages 112–13 of the same book there is a somewhat unwise attempt to depict Hamilton's character from a photograph taken on the yacht *Triad* 'somewhere about this time—April 1915'. In fact the photograph was taken several months later, when Hamilton was in poor health, and on the day he relinquished his command.

The King looked clean over my head when I bowed and did not seem to see me, but society with its hundred eyes saw that he did not see me.' So severe was the Royal disapprobation that volume two was actually withheld from publication until President Roosevelt, eager to have an acute assessment of the Japanese military machine available in the United States, intervened with the King. The more mundane features of the book aroused interest and enthusiasm in some quarters, but seemed to confirm in many minds the suspicion that Hamilton was altogether too eclectic a personality for comfort.

As the stars of John French, Henry Wilson and Douglas Haig rose, that of Ian Hamilton waned. His known friendship for Winston Churchill, his literary activities,* his perhaps somewhat too fluent personal charm, and his independent views did not help. From 1905 to 1910 he was outstandingly successful as G.O.C. Southern Command; blessed with a handsome private income, a charming wife, and the glories of Tidworth House, he entertained admirably, and the conversation at the Hamiltons' was of a standard not normally to be found at the tables of senior officers of the British Army.

In appearance he was slight, alert and eager. His eyes had a delightful twinkle, and his smile could be enchanting. His men in South Africa called him 'old full compliments and half rations', but liked and admired him. The fingers of his left hand were shrivelled, unbendable and virtually without feeling, a result of an injury received at Majuba Hill in 1881, where he was severely wounded, taken prisoner by the Boers, and recommended for the V.C. His left leg had been badly shattered in the Tirah Campaign as a result of a fall from a horse, and hurriedly set; it had to be re-set later, and was slightly shorter than the other. He had seen more active service than any other senior serving officer in the British Army, and probably in any army in Europe. In India, the Sudan and South Africa he had always somehow managed to be in the thick of things, yet, as his record showed, his experience extended far beyond the skirmishes which in late Victorian times were blown up by the popular appetite into great battles.

But, in the Army itself, the rising men did not regard Hamilton as a possible future Commander-in-Chief. His charm and lavish hospitality, allied to his skill in handling politicians—particularly Churchill and Haldane —aroused mistrust in many quarters. These doubts were fully confirmed by a now-forgotten incident in 1910, when Hamilton's pen once again drew him into unwise controversy.

Before leaving to take over the Mediterranean Command he had been invited by Haldane, the Secretary of State, to prepare a memorandum against the principle of compulsory service, at that time being eagerly advocated by

* Moorehead (Gallipoli, 112) refers to Hamilton as being 'in the long tradition of British poet-generals', and that he 'wrote much poetry'. In fact, he seems to have written very little actual poetry.

Roberts. Haldane was so impressed by Hamilton's memorandum that he had it published, with a foreword by himself, commending its sentiments to the public. The intervention of a serving officer into what was largely a burning political issue excited considerable surprise and much criticism. Roberts, who justifiably regarded Hamilton as his protégé, was pained and indignant, and penned a sharp riposte entitled *Fallacies and Facts* which dealt at length with Hamilton's arguments. The episode, apart from its effects on Hamilton's reputation in the Army, earned him the lifelong hatred of the shifty Henry Wilson, who, with Sir John French as a not unwilling accomplice, conspired to prevent Hamilton even visiting the Western Front after the outbreak of war.

In 1914 Hamilton was 62, aide-de-camp general to the King, and apparently gliding into a dignified and agreeable retirement. But one of Kitchener's first actions on going to the War Office had been to appoint him to command the Central Force in England. His office was in the Horse Guards, and he saw Kitchener frequently. 'Every day, almost, I used to run in and burst into a sweat from the two blazing fires and the antics of that poor untamed bull in the china shop', he has whimsically related. At one point Kitchener seriously considered appointing him to replace French, but the news reached French himself, and Kitchener had been forced to disclaim the project.

Hamilton's appointment as Commander-in-Chief of the Mediterranean Expeditionary Force was a wonderful and unexpected advancement, and he was naturally exultant. As he had written in *A Staff Officer's Scrap Book*: 'Are not the best moments in life those in which it is borne in to a poor mortal that some immortal has clearly designated the field of action, wherein he has only to be true to his convictions and himself, and advance confidently by word of command to the accomplishment of some predestined end?'

He sailed, with his hurriedly assembled General Staff, without an army and with only Kitchener's instructions to guide him, into a disagreeable atmosphere of confusion and irresolution. Birdwood, although he bore his disappointment well, was naturally depressed at having had the cup brusquely dashed from his lips. Both he and Maxwell were in despair about Carden, whose habit of simply not providing adequate answers to quite simple questions had forced them to turn to London for advice. 'Both Birdwood and I would like definite instructions', Maxwell had telegraphed to Kitchener on March 16th. 'Is the base [for the army] to be formed at Lemnos or Alexandria? . . . I have heard nothing from Admiral Carden.'

At this critical moment, and before Hamilton arrived on the scene, Carden had collapsed from the accumulation of strain and worry, and the conduct of the imminent operations developed upon Vice-Admiral de Robeck, who had been Carden's second-in-command. Wemyss, still marooned on Lemnos, was senior to de Robeck but at once waived all claims he justifiably had upon the command of the Allied fleet.

De Robeck's bearing and manner conveyed an air of calm confidence. Throughout his career he had taken little interest in the great technological developments in naval design and gunnery which had taken place since the 1890's, and was primarily distinguished for his seamanship. 'One could not feel,' Churchill has written, 'that his training and experience up to this period had led him to think deeply on the larger aspects of strategy and tactics.' 'De Robeck was simple and slow-thinking (unread, too),' a junior officer on his staff has related in a private memoir, 'but a fighting leader if ever there was one. . . . I loved Roger Keyes but (perhaps like Nelson) he could be almost crooked, he felt so sure he was right. De Robeck was utterly straightforward.' At the outbreak of war he had been on half-pay, but had been recalled to command the Ninth Destroyer Flotilla in the North Sea, with considerable success, before being sent to the Dardanelles. Thus, as in the cases of Carden and Hamilton, the turmoil of war had restored a career which had been virtually ended.

It would be difficult to conceive a more remarkable contrast between the new naval and military commanders, now gathered in the Aegean. De Robeck was stern, authoritarian, phlegmatic and calm, and, as Churchill has written, 'his character, personality and zeal inspired confidence in all.' Hamilton was spare and spry, alert, springy of stride and quick of smile, genial, acute and charming to everyone. De Robeck's Chief of Staff was the zestful, indefatigable and engaging Roger Keyes of whom one officer, very close to him at this time, has written: 'To me he was like Nelson in his simplicity, love of danger, and greed for glory. He worshipped valour for its own sake, but his judgement was apt to be overwhelmed by his enthusiasm when hazards were high. He could be exasperating, but he was the most lovable leader I have ever served. . . . Offensive Operations, not to say "stunts", interested him more than the routine work of a Chief of Staff.'

Hamilton's Chief of Staff, Braithwaite, was a man about whom it was easy to hold strong views. He quickly irritated Birdwood, who was told in so many words that events had overtaken him and his plans, that his views on the situation and the plans prepared by his staff were obsolete, and that he himself should now conduct himself as the commander of a corps and nothing more. Birdwood wrote to Kitchener on March 23rd that 'I am rather inclined to think (though I may be wrong) that Johnny's staff—*not* himself— think that now I am no longer in command they want little help or advice from me, and think I and [my] staff should confine ourselves to my Army Corps—so we will.' But the snub rankled. In spite of his many abilities, Braithwaite's facility at getting people's backs up was to become notorious;

there are some people, who with the best intentions, can go through life sowing mistrust and resentment wherever they go without ever being remotely conscious of the fact; Braithwaite, unfortunately, was such a man.

Birdwood, until shortly before the commander-in-chief designate, was, after Hamilton, perhaps the greatest enigma of all the Allied commanders. His nickname, 'Birdie', suited him admirably. He had something of Hamilton's alertness and vivacity, without its gentleness. Small, pugnacious, practical and determined, it was difficult not to like him. But his considerable flair for self-advertisement had the result that there were some officers who felt that there was something not quite genuine about him. There was undoubtedly a considerable element of jealousy in this; Birdwood was a 'Kitchener man', and extremely ambitious. Birdwood was subsequently incensed when, at the end of the war, he was not honoured with the peerage and substantial money grant given to the other Army Commanders and was with difficulty dissuaded from making his chagrin public by refusing the K.C.M.G., which was his sole reward. He also nurtured deep ambitions to become Governor-General of Australia after the war, and lost no opportunity of letting this be known in the highest political and diplomatic circles in England and Australia. His visits to Australia in connection with ex-Servicemen's organisations were numerous and well-advertised. He kept every letter of praise and gratitude he ever received, and was known to thrust them at complete strangers with the cry, 'Well, what do you think of that?' It was all to no avail. Birdwood never became Governor-General, and this wound never healed. Keyes, for all the accusations of showmanship which have been levelled at him, was fundamentally modest and shy, and was incapable of dissimulation; 'Birdie', on the other hand, was perpetually on show, and even Kitchener had his doubts about him. Nevertheless, it was a happy accident which gave Birdwood the command of the Australian and New Zealand Army Corps. He had a real feeling for his Anzacs, and a quick appreciation of their great potentialities beneath what was, at that time, a rather rough-and-ready exterior.

On March 18th, having given Churchill an assurance that he wholeheartedly supported the enterprise and Carden's plans, de Robeck ordered the Allied fleet to advance to the attack on the Dardanelles.

No less than 18 battleships, surrounded by an armada of cruisers and destroyers, swept majestically across the glittering waters into the Straits. It was an unforgettable picture of aloof grandeur, and made an immense impression on all who saw it; 'It looked as if no human power could withstand such an array of might and power,' one officer subsequently related. At 11.30 a.m., in brilliant sunshine, the four most powerful ships in Line A,

Queen Elizabeth, Agamemnon, Lord Nelson and *Inflexible*, opened fire on the Narrows forts at just over 14,000 yards' range; within a few minutes the supporting ships in Line A, *Triumph* and *Prince George*, joined in the long-range bombardment. Shortly after noon, Line B, commanded by the gallant and aggressive Admiral Guépratte, and consisting of *Suffren, Bouvet, Charlemagne, Gaulois, Cornwallis* and *Canopus*, passed through the Line A battleships and engaged the forts at closer range.

The warships were subjected to a determined and fairly accurate fire as they steamed slowly up the Straits amidst gigantic splashes from the great shells and a fearful thunder as the cannonade reverberated from the hills. One of Hamilton's staff officers, Guy Dawnay, wrote of the scene to his wife a day or two later that over the Narrows there was 'a great browny-black column of smoke, where the conflagration from the ships' guns was still blazing. The battleships, looking rather small in the middle distance; and a few minesweepers and destroyers dotted about. Inland on the Asiatic side, a great range of snow clad mountains in the far distance; on the European side, only higher ridges of undulating country, white and brown and green and olive, as far as one could see. And over the whole the blue sky flecked with white clouds, and the bright sun of an early summer day in England.'

Shortly after the Line B battleships engaged the forts, the first setback occurred. At 12.30 *Gaulois* was forced to retire when a heavy shell damaged her under the waterline, and was eventually beached on a small islet just beyond the mouth of the Straits. *Inflexible* was hit several times, her fore-top was destroyed, and she was forced to leave the line temporarily to put out fires and repair the damage to the fire-control station. But by 2.30 she was back in the line. *Agamemnon, Lord Nelson, Albion* and *Charlemagne* had been hit several times, but the damage had not been serious. By 2 p.m. the fire from the forts had slackened, and de Robeck ordered the minesweepers to go forward and the ships in Line B to withdraw.

Up to this point, so far as could be judged, things were going very well for the Allied fleet. 'By 2 p.m. the situation had become very critical', the official account of the Turkish General Staff states. 'All telephone wires were cut, all communications with the forts were interrupted, some of the guns had been knocked out, others were half buried, others again were out of action with the breech mechanism jammed; in consequence the artillery fire of the defence had slackened considerably.'

But now, as the battleships swept round to the right in a great arc and started to withdraw, *Bouvet*, travelling fast in Eren Keui Bay, was suddenly rocked by a great explosion, heeled over, capsized and disappeared in a cloud of smoke and steam with almost her entire complement of over 600. 'She was at the turning point,' Brodie relates, 'and under fire; all of us who

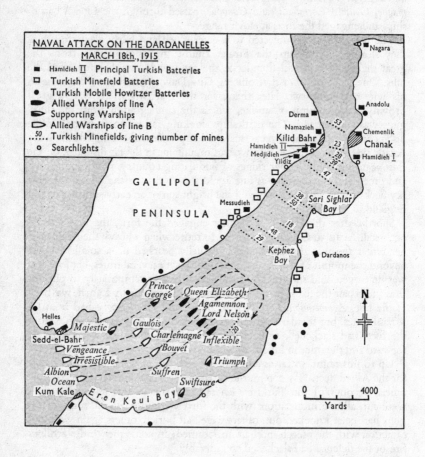

NAVAL ATTACK ON THE DARDANELLES
MARCH 18th., 1915

- ■ Hamidieh II Principal Turkish Batteries
- □ Turkish Minefield Batteries
- ● Turkish Mobile Howitzer Batteries
- Allied Warships of line A
- Supporting Warships
- Allied Warships of line B
- ..50.. Turkish Minefields, giving number of mines
- o Searchlights

Nagara

Anadolu

Derma

Namazieh

Chemenlik

Kilid Bahr

Chanak

Hamidieh II
Medjidieh

Hamidieh I

Yildiz

53

23

28

39

47

GALLIPOLI

Messudieh

Sari Sighlar
Bay

PENINSULA

38

161

18

Kephez
Bay

48

29

Dardanos

N

Prince
George

Queen Elizabeth

Agamemnon
Lord Nelson

Helles

Majestic

Gaulois

Charlemagne

20

Inflexible

Sedd-el-Bahr

Vengeance

Bouvet

Irresistible

Triumph

Albion
Ocean

Suffren

Kum Kale

Eren Keui Bay

Swiftsure

0   4000

Yards

saw it thought a shell had reached her magazine. It was one great explosion, not a thud like a mine followed by a magazine explosion.' 'One man got out of the hole in the bottom of a turret when it turned upside down and was saved', an officer on *Lord Nelson* wrote. 'The others that were saved ran down her side and across her bottom as she went over, like squirrels in a wheel.' The sinking of *Bouvet* was never properly explained. The Turks say that she first hit a mine, and then was struck by a heavy shell which plunged into the magazine. At the time it was thought that she had been sunk by a shell. Whatever the cause, she had vanished in under a minute.

From this moment, everything began to go wrong. The minesweepers, greeted with a storm of howitzer shells, wavered and then fled. At 4.11 *Inflexible*, manoeuvring near where *Bouvet* had gone down, reported that she had struck a mine and began to list badly. Three minutes later *Irresistible* was seen to be listing and flying a green flag at her starboard yardarm, indicating that she had been torpedoed on her starboard side.

These developments naturally caused great consternation on *Queen Elizabeth*. It was confidently believed that Eren Keui Bay had been swept of mines, and it was surmised that the series of mishaps had been caused either by floating mines, being swept down by the fierce current, or by hidden torpedo-tubes firing across the Straits. Admiral Limpus, when in charge of the Naval Mission, had not only recommended the installation of torpedo-tubes on the shore but had prepared plans for the Turkish Admiralty, and it was not known if his plans had been carried into effect.* De Robeck accordingly decided to break off the battle. *Inflexible*, surrounded by a protective gaggle of destroyers, crept out of the Straits and eventually reached Tenedos. *Suffren*, struck by a plunging shell, was also seriously damaged, and the condition of *Irresistible* was critical.

Keyes was sent in the destroyer *Wear* with orders from de Robeck to direct the captain of *Ocean* to take *Irresistible* in tow, but the captain took no heed of Keyes' requests and *Ocean* steamed about, blazing away at the forts until she was torn with an internal explosion at 6.5, took on an ugly list, and began to career around in a huge circle with her steering gear jammed. The destroyers raced in to save the crew, and the battleship was left to drift for another four hours before she foundered. Having ensured that the crew of *Irresistible* was also safe, Keyes returned after dark in the destroyer *Jed* to finish off the two drifting battleships, but could find no sign of them, and was eventually satisfied that they had sunk.

'Except for the searchlights,' Keyes has related, 'there seemed to be no sign of life, and I had a most indelible impression that we were in the presence of a beaten foe. I thought he was beaten at 2 p.m. I knew he was beaten at

---

* The one torpedo-tube installation at Kilid Bahr had been hit by a chance shot, and was out of action for about ten days.

4 p.m.—and at midnight I knew with still greater clarity that he was absolutely beaten; and it only remained for us to organise a proper sweeping force and devise some means of dealing with drifting mines to reap the fruits of our efforts. I felt that the guns of the forts and batteries and the concealed howitzers and mobile field guns were no longer a menace. Mines moored and drifting must, and could, be overcome.' The official German account of the situation on the evening of March 18th confirms Keyes' impression:

> Most of the Turkish ammunition had been expended. The medium howitzers and minefield batteries had fired half their supply . . . Particularly serious was the fact that the long-range high explosive shells, which alone were effective against armour, were nearly used up. Fort Hamidieh had only 17, Kilid Bahr but 10. Also there was no reserve of mines. What, then, was to happen if the battle was renewed on the 19th and following days with undiminished vigour?

The Turkish account is more prosaic. They had fired nearly 2,000 shells; out of 176 guns only 8 had been hit, of which only four had been put out of action; their losses amounted to 40 men killed and 70 wounded. The account concludes: 'The Turks viewed the period after the attack with apprehension because most of the ammunition available for the long-range guns had been expended and there was a shortage of ammunition. On the other hand the enemy had cleared only one (or at the most two) lines of mines.' In fact the Allies could not even claim this degree of success. For the loss of nearly 700 men killed, three battleships sunk and three crippled, the Allied fleet had merely succeeded in making the Turks fire away almost all of their heavy ammunition. The price paid had been a heavy one, but Churchill, at least, had never expected an easy victory, and although the door to Constantinople was far from open, it now only needed one more decisive push.

At first there was no thought, either at the Admiralty or the Dardanelles, of not pressing forward with the operations, although even Keyes admitted that the action could not be renewed until the sweeping force had been drastically overhauled, which he anticipated would take about a fortnight. As he has written, 'there was never any question of taking battleships through unswept minefields.' Fisher at once ordered the battleships *London* and *Prince of Wales* to the Dardanelles, in addition to *Queen* and *Implacable* which were already on their way, and the French sent the ancient battleship *Henri Quatre*—dubbed 'the Angry Cat' by the British—to replace *Bouvet*. The War Council on March 19th authorised the Admiralty to instruct de Robeck to 'continue the naval operations against the Dardanelles if he thought fit'. 'We are all getting ready for another "go",' de Robeck wrote to Hamilton on the 19th, 'and not in the least beaten or down-hearted.' In telegrams to the Admiralty on March 19th and 20th, he gave no hint that the attack would not be resumed as soon as the sweeping force had been re-organised.

If the sailors did not admit to being discouraged by the events of March 18th, the soldiers were pessimistic. Birdwood, of course, had expected this débâcle since he had arrived at the Dardanelles, and Hamilton completely shared his appreciation of the situation. He wrote at once to Kitchener that 'it looks at present as if the Fleet would not be able to carry on at this rate, and, if so, the soldiers will have to do the trick.' On the 19th he wrote again to Kitchener that 'I am being most reluctantly driven to the conclusion that the Straits are not likely to be forced by battleships as at one time seemed probable and that, if my troops are to take part, it will not take the subsidiary form anticipated. *The Army's part will not be a case of landing parties for the destruction of forts, but rather a case of a deliberate and progressive military operation carried out in force in order to make good a passage for the Navy.*'* Hamilton then asked de Robeck on March 20th for permission to remove his troops to Alexandria for re-organisation, but the Admiral asked him to wait 'until our attack is renewed in a few days' time.'

Kitchener's reply to Hamilton's message of the 19th was of decisive importance. 'You know my views—that the passage of the Dardanelles must be forced, and that if large military operations on the Gallipoli Peninsula by your troops are necessary to clear the way, these operations must be undertaken after careful consideration of the local defences, and they must be carried through.' Hamilton later told the Dardanelles Commission that he regarded this as a 'peremptory instruction that he was to take the Peninsula'; he replied to Kitchener on March 20th that he 'understood his views completely.' It is doubtful if Kitchener had intended Hamilton to understand his telegram in the way that he did, but it is difficult to see what other interpretation Hamilton could reasonably have put upon it. Hamilton subsequently told the Commission that he did not regard Kitchener's telegram as entirely depriving him of all discretion in the matter, although 'if I had chosen to say "this is altogether an impossibility", I might have said so, but I did not think so.'

De Robeck, meanwhile, was brooding over the events of March 18th. To Keyes and Wemyss he spoke mournfully of 'disaster', and could not be lifted out of his gloom. Not only had he lost one-third of his force, but he had no idea what had caused the catastrophe. He did not know, nor was it known until after the war, that the battleships had blundered into a row of mines laid in Eren Keui Bay only a few nights before. The naval pilots, whose reports had come to be regarded as authoritative, had seen nothing in the clear waters. Brodie had spent the night of March 17th–18th in a picket boat

* My italics.

with a creep wire in Eren Keui Bay, and was convinced that he could not have missed a new row of mines.

At a hurriedly convened court of enquiry on March 19th on *Queen Elizabeth* conducted by Brodie evidence was taken from those survivors of the sunk battleships who were immediately available. One reliable witness from *Irresistible* said that he had seen the track of a torpedo just before she was struck; the evidence of those who had seen *Bouvet* go down was to the effect that she had been hit by a shell. Commander Ramsay, described by Brodie as 'the best brain of the whole party, but moody and difficult', submitted ominous figures of the dwindling supplies of ammunition. On the other side, Keyes triumphantly produced a memorandum on the operations prepared by one of his favourites, Captain Godfrey, which depicted the events of March 18th in the light of a brilliant success only marred by a few unfortunate mishaps. It was the view of some staff officers that Godfrey had written this appreciation more for Keyes' approval than as an accurate factual summary of the situation. Keyes was delighted with it, and it seems to have temporarily cheered de Robeck up, but facts were facts, and the longer de Robeck studied them, the more unreal Godfrey's and Keyes' calculations appeared to be.

De Robeck had a high admiration and affection for Keyes, which were warmly reciprocated, but had strong doubts about his judgement. As Brodie, who was devoted to Keyes, has written: 'Keyes . . . was not capable of cool reasoning. The most dangerous way was best to him. Surprise and the offensive spirit has, and might have, achieved a miracle, but he thought it the answer to every problem. . . . At the blackest moment on the bridge of the *Queen Elizabeth* on the 18th, when Keyes was a bit excited and darting off to the stricken ships, de Robeck was rock-like, and a tower of strength to all. . . . At our end, de Robeck had come to the conclusion that Keyes was too much of a visionary, and in London the Cabinet felt the same about Winston.'

In spite of Keyes' inspiriting optimism, the facts were that the fire from the forts and the unlocated howitzers had seemed as heavy as ever after the sinking of *Bouvet*; and de Robeck could not forget Limpus' warnings to Carden about the possibility of concealed torpedo-tubes, now apparently strengthened by the evidence of the survivors from the warships. Had Wemyss taken a different line, however, de Robeck would probably have ordered the renewal of the attack, although with great reluctance. But Wemyss, although not as depressed as de Robeck, agreed that the mobile howitzers would have to be silenced and that some form of military intervention was necessary. Wemyss thought that the Army would have to be used; Hamilton and Birdwood were anxious for the Army to play its part.

On the 22nd de Robeck and his staff met Hamilton and Birdwood on

Queen Elizabeth. Accounts of the conference vary slightly. Hamilton says that 'the moment we sat down de Robeck told us *he was now quite clear he could not get through without the help of all my troops.*' De Robeck's version is that he had been prepared to continue with the naval attack until Hamilton told him that he regarded a joint attack as 'a sound operation of war', and would be in a position to begin operations by the middle of April. Birdwood's account, in his diary for March 22nd, confirms Hamilton's version. 'I went on board Cunard liner *Franconia* to meet Sir Ian Hamilton and discuss plans. Found he quite agreed with me in all plans I had made to attack etc. . . . Went with Sir Ian and Braithwaite to call on Admiral de Robeck, who had come in on *Queen Elizabeth* and he told us he did not consider fleet could get through without co-operation of army which I had always thought must be the case.'

This dispute about who actually proposed the joint attack first at the meeting on *Queen Elizabeth* is not really as significant as some historians of the campaign have suggested. In a sense, it was the soldiers who had forced the pace. Until the evening of the 21st, de Robeck had thought that Hamilton's instructions were extremely limited, and were confined to occupation of the Peninsula after the Fleet had passed through. When he realised that they were much wider, and furthermore that Hamilton appeared to be positively eager to take the initiative, his relief was manifest. Wemyss has written that 'the decision of the conference *confirmed the conclusion de Robeck and I had come to on the 19th,** viz. that combined action must be postponed until plans had been developed and perfected.'

Keyes is not an entirely reliable witness of the events of March 18th–22nd, but his subsequent explanation of de Robeck's change of front seems the most convincing:

> I am not sure that the Admiral would have renewed his attack if the General had decided to land at Bulair, or had made it clear . . . that there would be no question of a landing in force until the Fleet was in the Marmara, or finally failed. But the General's readiness to land at the toe of the Peninsula entirely altered the situation from the point of view of the Admiral, who was not as sanguine of a naval success as I was.

Another important factor was that of dates; Keyes estimated that his sweeper force would not be ready until April 4th, and Hamilton said that he could land on April 14th. As de Robeck pointed out to Keyes, who admitted the force of the argument, it was a matter of only waiting ten days.

There was thus absolutely no disagreement between de Robeck and Hamilton; the discussions were principally on methods and timing. Birdwood was in favour of an immediate landing with all the available troops——'a scratch affair' as Hamilton put it—but this proposal, apart from its intrinsic unsoundness, was of course contrary to Kitchener's instructions.

* My italics.

The weather was another critical factor, which by itself precluded any possibility of an early landing. On the night of March 18th a gale had blown up, and did not fully abate until the end of the month. When Keyes heard what had been decided on *Queen Elizabeth* he implored de Robeck to reopen the discussions, but at this second conference Keyes was obliged to admit that his reorganised sweeping force could not be ready until April 4th at the earliest. De Robeck accordingly telegraphed to the Admiralty that Hamilton would not be able to undertake military operations until April 14th, and that 'it appears better to prepare a decisive effort about the middle of April rather than risk a great deal for what may possibly be only a partial solution.'

Both Churchill and Kitchener were dismayed by this news. Churchill drafted a telegram ordering de Robeck to resume the naval attack as soon as possible, but the Admiralty War Staff Group was adamant. 'For the first time since the war began,' Churchill has written, 'high words were used around the octagonal table.' Fisher, supported by Wilson and Jackson, argued fiercely that as the men on the spot had come to the decision that a joint operation was essential, he would not permit this attempt of the First Lord to overrule their judgement. Although supported by Admiral Oliver and Commander de Bartolomé, Churchill realised that a major Admiralty crisis was imminent unless the telegram was fundamentally amended. The best that he could achieve was a reasoned telegram which, in effect, left the decision to de Robeck.

It had, of course, already been made by the men on the spot. Hamilton had decided to return to Alexandria to re-organise his army; de Robeck to abandon the Carden plan. When Churchill announced these facts to the Cabinet 'with grief' on March 23rd, Kitchener at once declared that the Army would carry the operation through. 'So here again there was no decision,' Churchill has remarked; 'the agreement of the Admiral and the General on the spot, and the declaration of Lord Kitchener, carried all before them. No formal decision to make a land attack was even noted in the records of the Cabinet or the War Council . . . the silent plunge into this vast military venture must be regarded as an extraordinary episode.'

In making his promise that the Army would see the matter through, Kitchener was under the impression that the men could be landed quite quickly—within about a week—and that in the meanwhile de Robeck would batter away at the forts. He was accordingly dismayed to learn that the operations could not start before April 14th at the earliest, but Hamilton replied unanswerably to Kitchener's protest that he had enjoined him strictly not to begin operations until his army was fully assembled. 'The Turks will meanwhile be kept busy by the Admiral', his letter to Kitchener ended. This was part of the understanding, but although de Robeck assured the Admiralty on the 25th that he would resume 'a vigorous offensive' until the army was ready by means of indirect fire on the forts, extensive reconnaissance flights, and sustained and determined sweeping operations, in the event for three weeks the mighty fleet which had advanced so confidently to the assault six weeks before, virtually disappeared into the Aegean.

And thus, by the end of March, three months since the project had first been seriously discussed, the decision to undertake a combined operation had been taken, not by the Cabinet or the War Council, but by Hamilton and de Robeck. The exact nature of the operations had not been defined, and never was defined. Hamilton and de Robeck were themselves under a misapprehension. Hamilton assumed that the operations to be undertaken by his army were to be in conjunction with another naval assault on the Dardanelles; de Robeck, however, had made up his mind that his ships would not again attack the forts until the army had occupied the Gallipoli Peninsula. The fatal weakness of the divided command of the Gallipoli Campaign was already becoming dimly apparent.

In spite of an almost minatory memorandum submitted by Hankey to the War Council urging precise definition of the campaign and a detailed examination of the forces required to carry out the operation—'Up to the present time so far as I am aware, no attempt has been made to estimate what force is required. We have merely said that so many troops are available and that they ought to be enough'—matters were permitted to drift onward. The War Council did not meet again until May 19th. In this period of two months, the subject was discussed eleven times in the Cabinet, but, as Sir William Robertson later commented, 'this, however, was a very poor substitute for the constant and systematic supervision which the competent management of a great expedition required.' Furthermore, the decision as to where the war was to be fought had been fatally postponed. Sir John French had been told to co-operate with the French armies in the recapture of Belgium, while Hamilton was to capture the Gallipoli Peninsula. The question of whether the British Empire had adequate resources to undertake both these operations simultaneously was not examined; the relative importance of each operation was not determined; neither French nor Hamilton was given any indication of the Government's priorities. 'There are two fatal things in war', Asquith had sagely written in his diary on January 21st: 'One is to push blindly against a stone wall; the other is to scatter and divide forces in a number of separate and disconnected operations. We are in great danger of committing both blunders. Happily K. has a good judgement in these matters'. Unhappily, K. had not, nor had the Prime Minister who had penned these wise observations. The Gallipoli operations, insofar as they were the subject of serious examination at this stage, were envisaged in the most disastrous terms; a major campaign run with resources appropriate to a subsidiary operation.

To the Turks and the Germans at the Dardanelles the days of peace which followed March 18th in unbroken succession aroused amazement and then elation. Morale was extremely high, and although damage to the forts and batteries had been easily repaired, the ammunition situation of the heavy batteries was grave. There was subsequently a sharp division of opinion among the Turkish commanders at the Dardanelles as to whether the Allied fleet could have got through if it had resumed the attack, but the shortage of heavy ammunition meant that it was a question of how long the howitzer batteries could keep the minesweepers away from the minefields. So long as the British sweepers were old trawlers poorly led the delay to the Fleet could have been almost indefinite, but if the sweeper force were drastically reorganised an entirely new situation would have arisen. But it never did arise, and we are presented with one of the most perplexing and tantalising of all military 'ifs'.

As the days passed and it was clear that the British had temporarily been checked, there was a great shift of opinion in the Balkans. The impact of their victory had a dramatic effect on the Turks themselves. As Morgenthau has written: 'The hesitating and fearful Ottoman, feeling his way cautiously amid the mazes of European diplomacy, and seeking opportunities to find the advantage for himself in the divided counsels of the European Powers, now gave place to an upstanding, almost dashing, figure, proud and assertive, determined to live his own life, and absolutely contemptuous of his Christian foes. I was really witnessing a remarkable development in race psychology—an almost classic instance of reversion to type.' The immediate result of the British defeat was a brutal and pitiless persecution of the Armenians in Turkey on a scale greater even than the massacres of the 1890's.

While the eyes of Europe remained riveted on the hypnotising spectacles of the armies locked grimly on the Western Front, those of the avaricious but nervous Balkan states were fixed on the gleaming waters of the Dardanelles.

4

Preparations for Battle

Now all the youth of England are on fire,
And silken dalliance in the wardrobe lies.
                              Henry V. Chorus

On March 24th Enver summoned Liman von Sanders to his office in Constantinople and invited him to take command of the Fifth Army at the
Dardanelles. 'I assented at once,' he wrote later, 'and informed him that the
troops there would have to be reinforced at once as we had no time to spare.'
He left on the following day, taking only his Turkish Chief of Staff, and two
German captains, Prigge and Mühlmann; the party arrived at Gallipoli town
on the morning of March 26th.

Von Sanders' first task was to inspect the troops at his disposal and the
ground which had to be defended, 'He had to travel hundreds of kilometres
in cars, by torpedo-boats, on horseback, and frequently for stretches on
foot,' Prigge has written. 'The 24 hours' day seemed all too short'. He found
that the Fifth Army consisted of five divisions—soon reinforced by a sixth,
which arrived at the end of the first week in April—scattered somewhat
haphazardly around the Dardanelles 'like the frontier detachments of the
good old days', as he subsequently remarked. 'The enemy on landing would
have found resistance everywhere, but there were no reserves to check
a strong and energetic advance.' Officers were ordered to concentrate their
forces, and send only 'the most indispensable security detachments' to guard
the coast. Von Sanders' task was not made simpler by the fact that there were
separate Turkish commanders in charge of the coastal defences and the Straits
respectively, each of whom was equal in status and responsibility to himself.

His task was to defend nearly 150 miles of coast with approximately
84,000 men, of whom, according to Turkish records, about 62,000 constituted
fighting strength. This was hardly adequate for the task which it was expected

to undertake, but even at this critical stage the vital importance of the Dardanelles had not been sufficiently appreciated in Constantinople. Turkey had nearly 400,000 men under arms, most of whom were on the Eastern Front, tied down by a fear of a Russian advance, and many troops were scattered throughout the Empire, separated from each other by large distances and a primitive and inefficient transport system which made troop movements difficult. It has so often been stated by historians that 'the Turks rushed every available man and gun to the Dardanelles' that the inaccuracy of these statements requires emphasis. The general dispositions of Turkish land forces in April 1915 were roughly as follows: The remnants of 3rd Army on the eastern frontier; 4 divisions in Sinai desert, Palestine, Syria; approximately 3 divisions in area north of Persian Gulf, between Basra and Bagdad; 6th Army (6 divisions) around Constantinople and Bosphorus; 4-5 divisions guarding the northern frontier; 5th Army (6 divisions) at the Dardanelles; 1 division in the Smyrna area; an unspecified number of reserve divisions in Anatolia. Out of a total of over 50 available divisions, only 6 (some eleven per cent of the total Turkish army) were in the Dardanelles area.*

Apart from its paucity in numbers, the Fifth Army was seriously deficient in artillery and ammunition, had no aircraft, and could expect little practical assistance from the Turkish fleet, a subject on which von Sanders was subsequently caustic. The troops themselves, although many were tough and experienced fighters, were poorly equipped, and exhibited a fatalistic lethargy which constantly exasperated the Germans. 'It was a daily battle to force the Turks to do that which was necessary for their own protection', writes Kannengiesser. ' . . . "If the English come we will deal with them all right. Why all this worry and oppression?" These were their thoughts, and often they expressed them quite openly. The Turkish soldiers' clothing was almost unbelievably bad, although we were only at the commencement of the war—summer and winter alike, torn and ragged. The covering for the feet differed widely, often only a piece of cloth tied round with a string. String was often used to replace leather in the equipment.'

Not unnaturally, von Sanders' account of his work in Gallipoli makes much of his own achievements in preparing for the attack on the Peninsula, and he has been fortunate in that most British commentators have judged him at his own valuation. 'Up to 25th February,' the Turkish official account states, 'it would have been possible to effect a landing successfully at any point on the Peninsula, and the capture of the Straits by land troops would have been comparatively easy.' But by the time Hamilton arrived on March 17th the British were already becoming seriously alarmed by the great activity being shown by the Turkish troops, and were soberly impressed

* See map on page 73 for the approximate deployment in the principal areas of Turkish forces in April 1915.

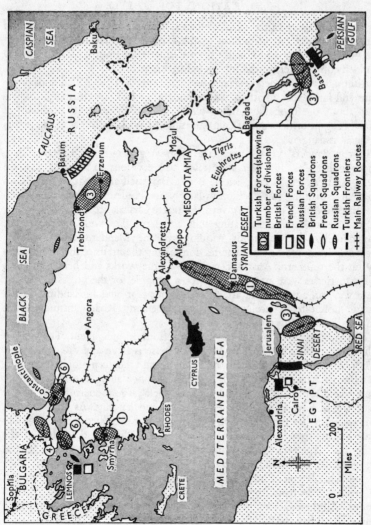

Turkey in travail, April 1915, showing principal Turkish and Allied dispositions

by the skilful siting of the beach defences. It in no way derogates from von Sanders' important contribution to the Dardanelles defences to emphasise the point that they had already been dramatically improved by the local Turkish commanders in the month before his arrival.

Although von Sanders received frequent reports of the Allied concentrations and knew that an attack was imminent, he had no information whatever about the probable landing-places. It was therefore a problem of establishing priorities, and of concentrating his available forces at the points of greatest danger.

In von Sanders' view, 'the place of greatest danger' was Besika Bay, opposite Tenedos, and he concentrated two divisions—a third of his total force—in this area, placing one at Besika Bay itself and another near Kum Kale. In explaining this decision in later years, he described the area which the British would have to traverse to reach Chanak from Besika Bay or Kum Kale as 'fertile undulating hills and large flats with meadow-land, traversed by the numerous windings of the Mendere River. . . . The most important works and batteries dominating the straits of the Dardanelles lay on the southern, Asiatic, coast . . . . As the works and heavy batteries of the fortresses were arranged only for a struggle for the possession of the waterway, an advance and attack against our rear after his landing on the Asiatic shore offered excellent chances to the enemy. Road communications here were tolerably good.'

This was probably von Sanders' most serious misjudgement. The ground which the British would have had to traverse is large and difficult, and is overlooked both from the Gallipoli Peninsula and the steep mountains which run from Chanak to the south-east. An advance along the Asiatic shore would be a formidable undertaking even for a large modern army, and in 1915 would have been extremely arduous and lengthy. As an American commentator has remarked: 'the country which an allied advance would have had to traverse is even more ragged and difficult than that of the Peninsula.* The rocky ridges, higher than those of Gallipoli, run in general perpendicular to the line of advance. The route of march would have been considerably longer. Both Allied flanks would have been exposed, the left to artillery fire from the Peninsula, and the right to attack by Turkish troops.' All these factors, of course, were better reasons for Hamilton not to land in Asia than for von Sanders to neglect the defence of this area.

Von Sanders concentrated two more of his divisions at Bulair. His obsession with this area is more understandable, although a lively controversy subsequently arose—actually sparked off by the semi-official German

---

* Although in general agreement with Captain Sherman Miles' comments (*East Coast Artillery Journal*), I do not wholly agree with this particular statement. The ground could be described more accurately as 'nearly as ragged and difficult as that of the Peninsula'.

account written by Captain Mühlmann—as to whether the loss of Bulair would have had decisive results. Mühlmann considered that if Bulair was captured by the Allies, 'the Turks on the peninsula would then be in a critical position. Their natural rearward communication would be broken, the road to Constantinople cut, and transport by sea more questionable. Success at Bulair would not, however, entail the collapse of resistance or the fall of the Narrows. However heavy a blow on the rear of the Fifth Army it might be, it would not cut a vital artery; there was always the possibility of changing the line of communication, and of supplying the army from the Asiatic side.' Nevertheless, it was evident that the loss of the Bulair isthmus would have had very serious effects on the defence of the Dardanelles, and von Sanders' concern for this area was justified.

Having safeguarded what he considered to be the two most critical areas, von Sanders situated his two remaining divisions on the Gallipoli Peninsula. The beaches on the southern tip at Tekke Burnu and Sedd-el-Bahr were evidently very vulnerable to naval fire, for which the Turks and von Sanders had a very considerable respect at this time. Achi Baba was clearly a vital point in the defence of the south of the Peninsula, even though it did not command the view of the Narrows forts that von Sanders himself and the British thought it did.* The activity of British warships off the southern beaches convinced the local officers that the main efforts would be made there, but von Sanders only allocated one division to the whole of the Peninsula south of Gaba Tepe. The dispositions of this division were contrary to all his general principles of concentration, units being scattered along the coasts, with the divisional reserve actually established north of the Achi Baba ridge, admirably situated to repel a landing on the eastern coast near Gaba Tepe, but a considerable distance away from the southern beaches. The entire area south of the small village of Krithia was defended by only one regiment and one field battery, and the beaches were defended by only two companies—with two more in reserve—and four machine-guns. Von Sanders makes no explanation of this decision, although he lays great stress on the importance of the Achi Baba ridge.

Von Sanders' final division, commanded by the thirty-four-year-old Lt.-Col. Mustafa Kemal, was concentrated near Boghali, a village about two miles to the north-west of Maidos, charged with the prime function of containing any landing in the Gaba Tepe area and preventing an advance across the plain to the Dardanelles.

These dispositions—and, above all, the emphasis on light coastal defences and concentrations inland—considerably perturbed many of the senior

---

* Roger Keyes, after a visit to the Peninsula long after the campaign, described Achi Baba as 'a gigantic fraud'. From its summit one can see hardly anything of the Dardanelles, and the Narrows forts are completely hidden by the massif of the Kilid Bahr plateau.

Turkish officers, who felt that von Sanders' plans did not make sufficient allowances for the peculiar features of the coast to be defended, of which the most significant was the smallness of the beaches on which landings could be made and the extremely poor roads, particularly on the Gallipoli Peninsula. Kemal was dismayed when von Sanders, after a very rapid inspection of the area around Gaba Tepe, ordered him to concentrate his division inland near Boghali and to leave only outposts on the coast itself; the 27th Regiment guarding the coast was to be sent to Maidos, and another regiment across the Straits to Chanak. Kemal complained to Colonel Sami, commanding the 9th Division, but von Sanders refused their joint protests, although the regiment destined for Chanak was permitted to remain at Boghali. 'Liman Pasha's preparations', one Turkish account states, 'had grave faults. There was no centre of gravity, there were insufficient reserve forces to drive landing forces into the sea immediately, and it was impossible to concentrate these forces because they were distributed equally over three areas and were dispersed in these areas. There were insufficient means of transport to move troops from one shore to the other and no harbours were designated for this purpose. . . . These mistakes', this Turkish historian sourly and ungratefully concludes, 'will not be forgiven by history.' These judgements are harsh and unfair, but, as subsequent events at Helles were to prove, von Sanders had underestimated the vulnerability of troops landing on a small beach opposed by even relatively small well-entrenched forces, and overestimated the destructive effects of a naval bombardment. But so did the British.

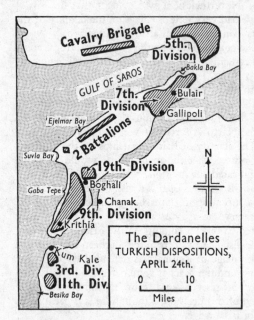

The Dardanelles
TURKISH DISPOSITIONS,
APRIL 24th.

0   10
Miles

Urgently prodded by their officers, the Turks began to dig hard. Although materials were limited, some beaches were wired, a few mines were constructed out of torpedo-heads and sown, and gun-emplacements and trenches dug near the beaches and on the Kilid Bahr Plateau. A programme of road construction and repair was pushed forward, and a flotilla of small boats assembled at Kilid Bahr and Chanak to ferry troops across the Narrows as soon as the British plan was revealed. All troop movements were carried out at night, and, on the whole, the Turkish concentrations were well concealed from the British reconnaissance aircraft which were now flying regularly over the Peninsula. The troops themselves were trained in target-shooting and bomb-throwing and sent on long marches to shake them out of their lethargy.

'The British', von Sanders later wrote, 'allowed us four good weeks of respite for all this work before their great disembarkation. . . . This respite just sufficed for the most indispensable measures to be taken.' Sixty-five days elapsed between the opening of the naval attack and the landings on April 25th, and in that time the Turk defences had been transformed. The deficiencies in men and material meant that it was virtually certain that the Allies could effect a successful landing at any point except, perhaps Besika Bay or Bulair. The problem was to contain the principal landings until the full Turk forces could be deployed, and great stress was laid on the importance of flexibility of plans and mobility of troops. It was constantly emphasised to the troops themselves that the only way to defend was to attack. 'Be sure', one order of the day read, 'that no matter how many troops the enemy may try to land, or how heavy the fire of his artillery, it is absolutely impossible for him to make good his footing. Supposing he does succeed in landing at one spot, no time should be left to him to co-ordinate and concentrate his forces, but our own troops must instantly press in to the attack and with the help of our reserves in the rear he will forthwith be flung back into the sea.'

April was particularly unpleasant that year, with hardly two fine days in succession. The Turks dug or marched by night, bivouacked by day. Occasionally one of the British warships lurking off the coast opened up a brief bombardment, or an aeroplane flew over on a reconnaissance mission. For days on end nothing in particular happened, the wind howled over the Peninsula, gusts of rain washed down parts of the new trenches and turned the newly dug earth into a glutinous marl, high seas crashed against the wire entanglements sown in the water, while the Turk soldiers stared out across the turbulent, sinister, empty Aegean.

Hamilton's difficulties when he returned to Alexandria on March 24th were infinitely greater than those confronting von Sanders. As he has himself said, his personal knowledge of the Turks and the Dardanelles area 'was nil'. His army was scattered around the Mediterranean in spectacular confusion; battalions were split up, wagons were separated from their horses, guns from their ammunition, shells from their fuses. An officer of the 29th Division reported that 'the arrangements for the embarkation had been made, and the ships taken up, in such a hurry that it was almost impossible to tell in what ships the various stores and vehicles of the Division were situated.' Wemyss, struggling to transform Mudros into the expedition's base, wrote more bluntly that 'the slipshod manner in which the troops have been sent out from England is something awful'. It was not until April 11th that Hamilton's administrative staff arrived in Egypt, by which time the entire burden of drawing up the landing and administrative plans had been borne by the General Staff officers, few of whom had any previous administrative experience. To add to these difficulties, the naval and military staffs were now divided by several hundred miles of water.

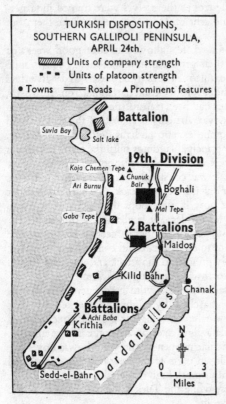

Every day that passed further illuminated the unprepared state of the expeditionary force. The artillery levels laid down by the War Office bore no relation to what Hamilton actually had at his disposal. In theory, the British divisions should have had 304 guns; in fact, they had only 118, and ammunition supplies were minimal. The Royal Naval Division, which had been hanging about at Mudros for weeks, arrived at Alexandria with a bizarre collection of equipment, which included Rolls-Royce armoured cars, motor-cars, motor-cycles, some machine-guns of varying degrees of antiquity, two 12-pounder guns, one 6·7-in. howitzer, three 4·7-in. guns mounted on pontoons for river operations—to be returned after the campaign for use against the cruiser *Königsberg* —and rifles of a different pattern to that of the rest of the M.E.F. The force had no grenades, and an official of the Cairo arsenal, a Mr. Garland, designed a rudimentary bomb-thrower and some equally rudimentary bombs, of which he promised a limited supply. At a comparatively late stage in the preparations it was discovered that the 18-pounder guns were only supplied with shrapnel shells and that the Navy also was running short of high-explosive ammunition.

There were no engineers apart from the divisional field companies, no headquarters signal company, no trench stores of any kind, and no materials for the construction of piers and jetties. Small craft for landing troops, horses, mules* and stores had to be bought for cash by British officers throughout the Middle East, and in most cases were quite unsuitable for the purpose for which they were to be used; apart from this, the fact that they were bought in neutral ports gave further information to the enemy of the preparations for invasion. Hamilton learned through a junior member of his staff of Fisher's armoured landing-craft, each capable of carrying 500 men, which he had had built for his Baltic adventure, but when a strong hint was dropped in a telegram to Kitchener that such craft would be invaluable he was curtly told that they were not available.

Matters were not improved by conditions in Egypt. Although the relationship between the British and the Egyptians was not comparable with that in the dark days of the north African campaign in the Second World War, there was a strong current of nationalist hostility towards the British troops. In addition, Maxwell was now oppressively alarmed by reports of Turkish activity in the desert east of the Canal and was demonstrating an increasingly evident lack of enthusiasm for the whole Gallipoli enterprise. Hamilton sensed this, as did many of his staff officers, but there was little that could be done about it.

Security had utterly collapsed. Letters addressed 'c/o, The Constantinople Expeditionary Force' arrived through the ordinary post, and the Egyptian press daily announced the arrival of new units and speculated freely on the outcome of the forthcoming campaign. When Hamilton protested, he was told that the authorities possessed no powers to censor the Egyptian newspapers, a reply which resulted in increased suspicions that Maxwell and the most senior British officials in Egypt were not prepared to enter wholeheartedly into the venture. A high point was reached when d'Amade gave an interview to an Alexandria newspaper, in which he discussed at great length the possibilities of a successful landing on the Gallipoli Peninsula. 'The attack was heralded as few have ever been', Dr. Bean, the Australian official historian attached to the Anzac Corps, subsequently wrote: 'No condition designed to proclaim it seems to have been omitted.' British

---

* A Mule Corps, with 750 mules, was recruited from Russian Jews who had fled from Palestine on the outbreak of war with Turkey; known as the Zion Mule Corps, it rendered heroic service at the Dardanelles.

agents were instructed to spread rumours that this was all a colossal bluff and that Smyrna was the real objective, but no one was deceived. When the transports started to leave for Mudros, some of the captains did not even bother to open their sealed orders.

'The landing of an army upon the theatre of operations I have described', Hamilton subsequently wrote in his first despatch, ' . . . involved difficulties for which no precedent was forthcoming in military history, except possibly in the sinister legends of Xerxes'. A more recent precedent was the expedition to Walcheren Island in 1809, which had many painful similarities with the Gallipoli enterprise. The idea of landing on Walcheren, blocking the Scheldt, and destroying ships and harbour installations in Antwerp and Flushing, was an old one; when it was seriously proposed in Cabinet in March 1809 the Army said that it had no troops. By June it agreed that it had. The expedition was authorised. The press gave it full publicity. There was virtually no co-operation between the naval and military commanders. The Army medical authorities, who knew that the island was disease-infested in late summer, were not consulted. Ministers hopefully sat awaiting good news. The expedition sailed in a blaze of publicity, with a Commander-in-Chief who had not even got a map of the defences of Antwerp; the enemy, well-warned, was ready; the troops were smitten with disease, and, after weeks of havering, the Cabinet agreed to their evacuation. There was a Parliamentary inquiry, the Commander-in-Chief was sacked, the Government all but fell. The similarity with Gallipoli is almost complete.

As well as making the administrative arrangements for the expedition, Hamilton's General Staff had to prepare their appreciation on which the plan of attack would be based. The staff worked in a large rambling Alexandria house which had been a brothel in a previous incarnation, without drainage, light or water; after seven in the evening, the staff worked by the light of candles stuck on to old envelopes. They had only a 1905 hand-book on Turkey and a map which was vague and—it was later discovered—inaccurate. They also had a Manual of Combined Naval and Military Operations compiled in 1913, which was virtually useless since, as the joint-services confidential Report stated simply in 1919, 'no organisation existed for providing the personnel and material required to carry out the operation'. The staff did not know about the 1907 joint-staff inquiry and report, nor—more seriously—did they have Cunliffe-Owen's memoranda on the Dardanelles defences. Of greater significance than any of this was the division between the senior naval and military staffs. One example of the consequences of this separation may be cited. The naval pilots and observers operating from *Ark Royal* and Tenedos were asked to give close attention to the beach defences. A report was submitted. It was not until several weeks later that the pilots realised that, almost without exception, the beaches which they had described as being particularly well defended had been selected for the landings. It is not clear what happened to their report, except that it was never seen by the General Staff officers preparing their appreciation.

The business of preparing the General Staff appreciation thus resolved itself into a series of guesses. It was assumed that the Turkish forces in the Dardanelles area amounted to about 170,000 men, of whom 'between 40,000 and 80,000' were on the Gallipoli Peninsula, with 30,000 on the Asiatic shore, and another 60,000 in reserve. If these estimates were anything like accurate it was evident that the expeditionary force would be heavily outnumbered unless full use could be made of naval power and the incalculably important weapon of surprise. Once the army was landed, the General Staff had no information about such elementary matters as water facilities or roads. It was assumed that water would be scarce, and Egypt was scoured for skins, tanks, oil-cans and any conceivable receptacle for carrying fresh water; in addition, a condensing boat and a tank steamer were chartered. It was also assumed that the roads would be bad, but the number of boats available was so limited that it would be impossible to disembark any quantities of horses and fodder for at least twenty-four hours after the original landings, with the result that until then everything would have to be carried by hand. This realisation threw out the schedules for landing the artillery, and so the staff had to start again.

The General Staff appreciation which eventually emerged envisaged an ambitious and hazardous *coup de main* on the Peninsula. The French had originally favoured an Asiatic landing or one at Bulair, but Hamilton and his staff had been profoundly impressed by the glittering rows of barbed wire at Bulair, and the Besika Bay project—also favoured by Birdwood, now that the element of complete surprise had gone—was rejected on military and naval grounds, quite apart from the fact that Kitchener had forbidden Asia. The elimination of Bulair and Asia left only the Peninsula itself, and the number of practicable beaches further reduced the choice to Suvla Bay, a long narrow beach running about a mile to the north of Gaba Tepe, and the southern end of the Peninsula, near Cape Helles. The General Staff, like Birdwood in his original appreciation, favoured the latter because the Fleet could give active assistance not only during the landings but in the subsequent advance to Achi Baba, in the rear and on both flanks.

Hamilton's three senior commanders—Birdwood (Anzac), Sir Aylmer Hunter-Weston (29th Division), and General Paris (Royal Naval Division)—strongly disapproved of these proposals. Hunter-Weston's appreciation, written at Malta en route for Egypt, was extremely pessimistic, and concluded by remarking that cancellation of the whole enterprise, although it might bring derision, was preferable to a disaster. Paris, although he did not damn the Helles plan completely, was equally despondent. Birdwood now considered that the Asiatic shore was the most promising area, in which he was strongly supported by Maxwell. Birdwood's Chief of Staff, Walker, was so opposed to the entire operation that Birdwood threatened to leave him behind. In reply to a detailed memorandum submitted by Birdwood on April 1st, Hamilton wrote: 'I am still all for taking the bull by the horns. First of all, I have no roving commission to conquer Asia Minor. Indeed, the most positive part of my instructions specifically denies me the whole of that country ... I have not come here for any other purpose whatsoever but to help the Fleet through the Dardanelles. The War Office think the Gallipoli Peninsula occupation is the best way to effect this purpose. So do the Admiralty, and so does the Admiral in executive command.' Birdwood was irritated by the tone of this reply, and Maxwell strongly sympathised with him. 'No one talked of conquering Asia Minor,' he wrote to Birdwood on April 3rd. 'The question is the best way to co-operate with the Fleet to force and open the Dardanelles. Obviously, if you are *held up* in Gallipoli you retard instead of helping the Navy. I see nothing convincing in Hamilton's instructions. ... Gallipoli gives us no liberty of manoeuvre, you are cramped and very liable to be held up and have a sort of miniature Flanders to fight.' Birdwood entirely agreed, but Hamilton was obdurate.

He was curiously irritated by the opposition of his senior commanders to his basic plan, which augured ill for the future. His private letters at this time often refer with resentment to what he considered to be their pusillanimity. 'All goes well,' he wrote to Kitchener on April 3rd, 'and my chiefest worry is that my three or four senior officers (excepting Braithwaite) now seem, for the first time, to see all the difficulties with extraordinary perspicacity. In fact, they would each apparently a thousand times sooner do anything else except what we are going to do.' The private letters of the commanders themselves show that the resentment was reciprocal. Even at this very early stage, personal rivalries were becoming important. Wyndham Deedes was asked privately by Hunter-Weston to provide information about possible landing-places in the vicinity of Bulair; Braithwaite found this out, and not only sternly reprimanded the amazed Deedes but expressly forbade him to give Hunter-Weston any information on the matter. Deedes refers to this small incident in his diary as 'the first little rift within the lute'; a fortnight later he was writing, more seriously, of 'the feeling of apprehension and to a certain extent of indecision which is beginning to make itself felt amongst the Staff and leading members of the Expedition.'

Everyone writes, with varying degrees of admiration, of Hamilton's infectious enthusiasm at this difficult time, but some officers were beginning to entertain doubts as to where Hamilton's enthusiasm ended and wishful thinking began. Over the matter of reinforcements he showed himself to be timid in his dealings with Kitchener. Hamilton subsequently explained to the

Dardanelles Commission that he regarded Kitchener as his military commander-in-chief and not as a Secretary of State for War; he had seen how, in South Africa, Kitchener would react to appeals for reinforcements by actually withdrawing troops from the appellant; even the 29th Division, it had been emphasised, was only on loan. His requests for more troops were deprecating and hesitant. When he asked for a Gurkha brigade in Egypt he offered to leave four Australian mounted brigades in exchange; when he heard that the French might send another division he wrote at once to Kitchener to make clear that he had never asked for it, and ended his letter, 'just in case there is truth in the report you should know that Mudros harbour is as full as it will hold'.

In spite of his remarks about an easy victory to Hamilton on March 12th, Kitchener—perhaps beginning to recollect the high quality of the Turkish troops in the past, of which he had personal experience—was having anxieties about the operation, and ordered the 2nd Mounted Division to proceed to Egypt to be available to Hamilton. He also telegraphed Maxwell:

> You should supply any troops in Egypt that can be spared, or even selected officers or men that Sir Ian Hamilton may want, for Gallipoli. . . . This telegram should be communicated by you to Sir Ian Hamilton.

Something of a mystery has been created about the fate of this message, which never reached Hamilton. Like most mysteries, examination of the available records quickly disposes of it. On March 4th Maxwell was reporting to London that it was 'all bluff about Turkish preparations in Sinai. They are short of coal, they are badly off for aircraft, and rain pools within 20 miles of the Canal are drained'.

Three weeks, however, had wrought a remarkable revival in Maxwell's estimation of the Turk menace to Egypt. As his biographer has frankly stated, Maxwell 'never had any appetite for the Gallipoli enterprise'. With a relatively large body of Turks still within striking distance of the Canal, Maxwell's apprehension had a considerable foundation of reality. He responded to Kitchener's telegram of April 6th with a black portrait of an imminent attack on the Canal, railways being built in the Sinai Desert, huts for aeroplanes mysteriously appearing, and hostile patrols everywhere. On April 11th he was again writing to Kitchener that 'the Turks are up to some devilment on the Canal; I expect they will pop a mine or two into it. It is hard to prevent, but we will do our best'. In these circumstances, Kitchener did not press his telegram of April 6th, and Maxwell did not pass it on to Hamilton.

This episode was a foretaste of events. Throughout the campaign, whenever Hamilton directly or indirectly sought troops from Maxwell, the Turks mysteriously became active in the Sinai Desert, new roads and encampments were detected, hostile tribesmen became threatening. Even when—as in the case of General Cox's Indian Brigade and the 42nd (East Lancashire) Division—Kitchener came down robustly on Hamilton's side, Maxwell released the troops with an ill grace and gloomy prognostications of disaster on the Canal. 'Please realise that after the despatch of these Territorials', he wrote glumly on April 28th after having had the 42nd Division wrenched from his grasp, 'I shall have no infantry left in Cairo or Alexandria and no artillery on the Canal'.

It was by no means Maxwell's fault. Gallipoli took from him all his best units and most of his materiél. He was an independent commander, responsible for the defence of Egypt, and, above all, the Canal, and Djemal's electrifying hit-and-run appearance had been unnerving. He did not like Hamilton personally, and was jealous of the immense preparations being made for the Gallipoli expedition. If Kitchener had insisted on his telegram of April 6th being carried out, and had made it plain that priority rested with the Gallipoli expedition, the course of events would almost certainly have been very different; but he did not.

This was not the only serious misunderstanding. Of equal significance was the basic misconception about the landing held by both the military and naval commanders. The staff appreciation, and all Hamilton's plans, were based on de Robeck's Admiralty telegram of April 29th that 'directly the army is landed on the Peninsula the fleet will renew its attacks on the Narrows. . . . No matter where the army effects its landings, its extreme objective of both Services must be the forts at the Narrows, and the intention is to attack them simultaneously with all our forces'. Hamilton interpreted this to mean that as soon as his army was ashore the Fleet would resume its aggressive assault on the Narrows, this time supported by the army on the Peninsula, providing the Turks with a double thrust at their heart. In 1924 an American historian commented that: 'Certainly General Hamilton did not suspect that naval co-operation would be so limited, and to a large extent his plans during the following month were based . . . on the assumption of a combined attack with the Fleet'. In the margin Hamilton wrote: 'Correct'.

Quite apart from the question of what was going to happen after the troops got ashore, there was considerable dismay among the senior soldiers at the relative inactivity of the Fleet before the landings. On March 22nd de Robeck had told Hamilton that the Fleet would make the Turks 'think more of battleships than of landings'. But although the Fleet was now immensely stronger than it had been on March 18th, it henceforth occupied a secondary rôle in the operations. By the middle of April, 38 new sweepers had joined the Fleet, 24 destroyers had been converted for sweeping—all manned with the crews of the ships sunk on March 18th—a naval aerodrome had been established at Tenedos by a Commander Samson, and the lost capital ships had been replaced. But, apart from occasional forays, the Fleet did not undertake any major aggressive operations in this period. After April 7th all sweeping operations in the Straits were stopped. A week later, a bold attempt was made by two picket boats from *Triumph* and *Majestic* to clear a path for submarines through the Kephez minefield and cut a suspected underwater cable. On April 17th the new E class submarine, E.15, tried to get through the Straits to the Marmara, but was caught in a violent eddy off Kephez Point and driven ashore; when she surfaced, a lucky shot penetrated her conning tower and killed her captain* and six of her crew, the remainder being taken prisoner. After several unsuccessful attempts to destroy the grounded submarine, she was torpedoed on the night of April 18th by picket boats from *Triumph* and *Majestic* which carried torpedo-dropping gear, one of the bravest exploits of the entire campaign. On April 19th the cruiser *Bacchante*, working with the kite-balloon ship *Manica*, shelled a Turkish camp near Gaba Tepe, and there were other sporadic bombardments.

This was the sum total of the activity of the Fleet in the five weeks which elapsed between the attack of March 18th and the landing of the army on April 25th. While it was true that the Navy was heavily occupied protecting convoys and carrying out many other duties in this period, and the supplies of ammunition were not sufficient to permit continuous aggressive activity against the Turk defences, it was a lot less than Hamilton had been led to expect.

Hamilton's basic plan, to 'take a good run at the Peninsula and jump plump on—both feet together', was subject to several important amendments. The smallness of the Helles beaches and the shortage of small craft suitable for landing troops meant that there would have to be more than one major landing. Even if everything went according to plan, it was calculated that the landing of the 29th Division alone could not be completed within two and a half days, and it was eventually decided to land Birdwood's Anzacs about a mile to the north of Gaba Tepe, an area thought to be lightly defended, although Gaba Tepe itself was known to be wired and entrenched. Once ashore, the Anzacs were to secure the Sari Bair heights and push across the Peninsula to Mal Tepe, a commanding hill to the north-west of Maidos. It was hoped that by the evening of the first day the 29th Division would occupy the Achi Baba ridge, while the Anzacs would be astride the Peninsula, thus cutting off the Kilid Bahr defenders from north and south. There was a tendency at G.H.Q. to regard the Anzacs as enthusiastic, indisciplined amateurs, and they were deliberately entrusted with what was considered

* T. S. Brodie, the twin brother of C. G. Brodie; the latter, flying on a reconnaissance mission over the Straits, was the first to see the thin silver hull, lying like a piece of straw caught in the side of a stream.

to be the most simple part of the whole operation. The Royal Naval Division, meanwhile, was to carry out a diversion off Bulair which, it was hoped, would delay the movement of reinforcements to the south for at least forty-eight hours. Hamilton subsequently regretted having ignored the coast from Gaba Tepe to the south, and wrote in 1925 that 'I would think very seriously of landing a force there were I to throw the dice over again.' But the absence of suitable landing-places, and the great difficulties of supplying any landing force from the sea, would have provided objections to such a proposal which would almost certainly have proved insuperable.

In spite of all the difficulties and uncertainties of the operation, an extra-ordinary exhilaration swept through the Mediterranean Expeditionary Force at the prospect of battle. The troops were young and inexperienced, but their enthusiasm and eagerness were warming and infectious. There is something both stirring and poignant of the accounts of those who were in Egypt at that time of the excitement in the air, the zest of the men, the gaiety which was everywhere. 'Those who formed part of the original Expeditionary Force were united by an extraordinary sense of exhilaration and adventure, by a thrilling prospect of almost inconceivable possibilities, by a consciousness of being engaged in an affair incredibly more adventurous and romantic than the majority of them ever dreamed of', Orlo Williams later wrote. 'From the Commander-in-Chief down, this romantic sense of adventure spread through the whole force.' The young bloods of the Royal Naval Division brought copies of the *Iliad* and wrote rapturously of the romantic possibilities of the campaign. 'I only hope I may be able to nip over and have a look at Troy', wrote one of them, Patrick Shaw-Stewart. 'I don't think this is going to be at all a dangerous campaign—we shall only have to sit in the Turkish forts after the Fleet has shelled the unfortunate occupants out of them.' On another occasion, Shaw-Stewart wrote in a letter that 'it is the Dardanelles, the real plum of the war.' This was the feeling which surged through the expeditionary force, capturing the tall, bronzed Australians, the blue-uniformed and white-helmeted French, and even the habitually cynical British regulars. It was an occasion for the commanders for fine speeches and dramatic gestures, and for the men of high hopes of a quick and glorious victory. 'We approached the job of landing on the shores of Gallipoli with our traditional swagger', an Australian private has written: 'Who could stop us? Not the bloody Turks!' 'We were rather keen to have another go,' a New Zealand subaltern wrote more soberly, 'as his poor showing at the Canal gave us a contempt for the Turk's fighting.' 'It will be a grim work to begin with,' one of Birdwood's staff officers, Lt.-Col. Skeen, wrote on April 21st, 'but we have good fighters ready to tackle it, and an enemy who has never shown himself as good a fighter as the white man.'

By the beginning of April the army began to embark at Alexandria. The chartering of civilian transports and their crews led to many difficulties, and the relations between the merchant crews and their passengers were frequently very strained, but the troops were glad to leave Egypt.

Hamilton sailed for Mudros on April 8th in *Arcadian*, a luxury liner converted for his use, and two days later the naval and military staffs were at last reunited around a table on *Queen Elizabeth*. The fact that his army had been disembarked, re-organised, and re-embarked in a matter of a fortnight was one of the most outstanding achievements of improvisation, sheer professional competence and hard work ever achieved by the British Army. At Mudros, even though his personal staff consisted of two able seamen, an officer's cook, a steward and a sub-lieutenant, Wemyss had also wrought miracles. 'Truly I am surprised at the results we obtain,' he wrote in his diary on March 25th, 'and lost in admiration at the resources of my people.'

Of course, it was all relative. Mudros possessed nothing like the facilities for handling the armada of ships of all descriptions which now began to stream into that vast natural anchorage, and hardly any for the troops which they carried. The fact that everything had fallen on Hamilton's General Staff was unfortunate in two respects; in the first place, the fact that they had done so much so well greatly increased Hamilton's strong predilection for a small Staff and his unfortunate antipathy for a large administrative staff at headquarters; in the second, far too much was left to individual initiative. Important details were too often bungled, with very serious consequences, and the administrative staff were left in no doubt as to their minor rôle in events. Almost all the newly-arrived administrative staff were left behind in Alexandria; the Adjutant-General, the Director of Medical Services and the Quartermaster-General probably knew less about the destination and purposes of the expedition than anyone in Egypt, and no attempt was made to enlighten them. It was not until several days later that the Director of Medical Services even saw the proposed arrangements for handling the wounded, and by the time that his lengthy memorandum on the inadequacy of the steps proposed was in the hands of the General Staff—where it was ill received—it was too late to do anything of importance.

Birdwood was extremely perturbed by this attitude towards the administrative staff at G.H.Q., and wrote to Fitzgerald on April 19th: 'Braithwaite and Sir Ian are I think, as you say, a good combination, but it is most unfortunate that they have not got their Q staff with them here, for neither of them seem to have considered (at all events [not] thoroughly) the difficulties of supply, transport, etc. . . . the question of supplies and ammunition [is] extraordinarily difficult, and this, it seems to me, is not receiving anything like full attention at Headquarters. I do not know that my people have a great opinion of the Staff here, as, when I send them over to talk over matters, they generally come back saying they did not seem to be wanted, which seems to me a mistake.' 'The increasing size of the Staff is getting on my nerves', Hamilton wrote to Kitchener on the 23rd. Thus were the seeds of disaster sown.

After a series of conferences, Hamilton's basic plan was adopted. On de Robeck's advice, it was decided to land the covering forces not from merchantmen but from warships; a mile or so away from the beaches, the men would be put into ships' cutters, towed by tugs in groups (or 'tows'), while the warships bombarded the defences; the cutters would then be cast off from the tugs, and would be rowed ashore. As soon as the covering troops had secured the beaches and the high ground above them, the main force would arrive in transports, and be ferried to the shore in the cutters.

The Helles landings would be made by the 29th Division on three tiny beaches, named X, W and V. X beach was on the west coast, about three-quarters of a mile north of Tekke Burnu, and although it was hardly a beach at all, there was a small strip of sand, a fair path up the cliff, and the area was known to be only lightly defended. W beach lay between Tekke Burnu and Cape Helles, and V Beach, a mile to the east, was a natural amphitheatre, with the ruined castle of Sedd-el-Bahr on the east and Cape Helles itself on the west. The British knew both these beaches well, and the Navy was confident that a massive bombardment would effectively crush the defenders. This confidence was contrary to the practical experience gained from the Marine landings in the previous month; 'the naval guns do not seem able to knock the Turkish infantry out of their deep trenches, although they can silence their fire for a while', Hamilton had noted on March 17th after his first meeting with de Robeck, Keyes, Guépratte, d'Amade and Wemyss. On April 15th he went into the Straits on *Triumph* to observe the effects of naval fire on the trenches and barbed wire; once again, the effects were negligible, and the rows of barbed wire were hit only once, with no discernible result.

Commander Unwin, then commanding the destroyer *Hussar*, came forward with the novel proposal that an innocent-looking collier carrying two thousand men should be run ashore at V Beach; the men would emerge from holes cut in the sides—called 'sally ports'—run along specially built gangways down to a bridge of lighters connected to the shore by a steam hopper, and thence on to the beach. By this method, the number of men to be landed in the first wave would be doubled, but the naval and military staffs were doubtful, for the sensible reason that one unlucky shell might send two thousand men to the bottom of the Dardanelles. Wemyss, however, was very enthusiastic, and managed to persuade the staffs to adopt Unwin's scheme. Unwin was instructed to take charge of this part of the operation, and he selected a ten-year-old collier, *River Clyde*, as this modern Trojan Horse.

As a result of these amendments, the V beach landing was assuming such important proportions that it was decided to land a detachment of French troops on the Asiatic shore at Kum Kale, to provide the Turks with a major distraction and prevent them shelling V beach while the British were landing there. As a kind of further consequential addition, it was decided to land a British battalion at the eastern extremity of Morto Bay, at a point subsequently called S Beach; this project had been abandoned earlier in the formation of the plans, as it was thought that the Asiatic batteries would cover Morto Bay completely. A second major feint, by the French, at Besika Bay, was also agreed upon.

Rather late in the day, Hamilton produced a major amendment of his own by proposing to put ashore a force of about 2,000 men on the western coast at a point—designated Y beach—about a mile to the west of Krithia, where there was a passable path up the cliff and where there were known to be no Turks. Hunter-Weston, who was to be in executive command of the landing of the 29th Division, did not welcome this late addition to his plans, but raised no major objections.

The plan as a whole was bold, intelligent and ambitious. Hamilton calculated that von Sanders would not dare to concentrate his forces for at least forty-eight hours, by which time the decisive battle should have been fought and won. The whole operation was based on the reasonable assumption that the only really hazardous part of the operation was actually getting ashore, and that once this was achieved it would merely be a matter of rolling up the Turks and eliminating pockets of resistance. As Hamilton himself wrote in 1924: 'In my mind the crux was to get my army ashore. . . . Once ashore, I could hardly think Great Britain and France would not in the long run defeat Turkey. . . . the problem as it presented itself to us was *how to get ashore!*' No emphasis was accordingly laid in the orders to the 29th Division on the vital importance of moving inland rapidly after the disembarkation; the orders to individual commanders were so detailed on trivialities that they were almost incomprehensible, while at the same time they were excessively vague on the really important points, and left no margin for the unexpected, with the result that they inevitably seriously damped the initiative of individual officers. The plans for the landings were prepared with an almost microscopic attention to detail. This was not the kind of work that the staff needed to have been doing, nor that they ought to have been doing, but which they had to do while the administrative staff languished, ignored, in Alexandria. The General Staff officers, particularly Aspinall and Dawnay, spent hours in devising snags which might arise, and their solution. Orlo Williams was so fascinated by these parleys that he drew a caricature of Dawnay and Aspinall in grave conclave and an imaginary dialogue which ran:

> G.S.O. II (dreamily): Then two tugs come alongside, one to port and one to starboard, with four boats each, to take off the remainder, No I Field Laundry less one platoon, and . . .
>
> G.S.O. III (crossly): Yes, but that leaves 29 men, two hot water cans and a piece of sealing wax that can't get off at all. I say you *must* have two destroyers . . .

It was a good jest, and very near the mark. At the same time as the staff was embroiled in details of assembling and equipping men, matters such as the treatment of the wounded, fresh water supplies and sea-to-shore communication, vital to the success of any amphibious operation, were relatively cursorily treated. This was not surprising when it is realised that the staff of the Principal Naval Transport Officer consisted of his steward, cook and coxswain; he was established in the saloon pantry of *Arcadian*, charged with the responsibility of making all the transport arrangements for the landings. When five other officers joined the P.N.T.O., they also were incarcerated in the pantry.

It was not until the eve of the landings that any serious thought was given to what was to be done if part of the assault was held up. The success of the operation rested on successful landings being made at every point, and this was perhaps too much to expect. Furthermore, although the commanders were haunted by the nightmare of the soldiers being butchered before they had got ashore, all their plans assumed that headquarters, supply dumps, hospitals and communications centres would be established on the Peninsula within a few hours. Although the operation depended on the support of the naval guns, no adequate system of fire-control, identification, or communication from shore to ship was laid down, with consequences which might have been more clearly anticipated. Little attention had been given to the problem of turning the beaches into proper harbours, and in this respect there was a revealing and little-known episode. A British engineer, Colonel Joly de Lotbinière, designed and built eight floating piers, four for use at Anzac and four at Helles. These piers could be locked together and anchored, and for the trip to the Peninsula were to be ballasted with 4,000 sealed tins of fresh water each; thus, not only would the army have an adequate landing stage within a few hours of going ashore, but a considerable quantity of fresh water to hand. It was in effect the modest precursor of Mulberry, the great prefabricated harbours which were set up on the Normandy beaches in 1944, and an inspired piece of individual initiative. Of the eight piers, only one reached Mudros; the Navy had taken the responsibility of getting them from Egypt, but had entrusted them to merchant ships, which had cast them off in the Mediterranean. As little official enthusiasm had been shown about the plan, no one except the distraught de Lotbinière was particularly worried.

Many other similar stories are to be found in official and semi-official records of the campaign. They all point the same lesson, that modern warfare is essentially a matter of administration and organisation, and by neglecting this aspect of the operation the strategic planning of Hamilton and his talented but over-worked General Staff was increasingly divorced from the realities of the situation. In brief, they over-reached themselves; the enthusiasm and optimism which pulsated through the army and the Fleet had carried the senior commanders too far in the direction of an ambitious operation which was beyond their means to carry out.

Although, as Major John North has tartly remarked, 'it is easy to take the Gallipoli Peninsula on paper—in the light of later knowledge', the conspicuous feature of the plans of von Sanders and Hamilton was that whereas von Sanders' were essentially flexible, Hamilton's were rigid. The Turks knew that they would have to fight at a place chosen by their opponents, and would have to rely heavily on the initiative of individual commanders; the British plans—except, perhaps at Anzac, where Birdwood proposed to hurl his fiery Anzacs ashore and impressed on all the vital importance of speed and enterprise—left no room for initiative.

In Mudros Harbour the armada of assorted tramp steamers, ocean liners, tugs, hospital ships and warships gathered. The only incident which occurred on their passage from Alexandria was an attack by a Turk torpedo-boat on the transport *Manitou* off Smyrna on April 16th. It was a farcical episode with tragic consequences. The ship's captain was below when the torpedo-boat unexpectedly appeared, and all negotiations were handled by the senior soldier on board; the Turks gave him three minutes to get his men off, and, although he had a gun trained on the enemy, he decided not to fire, partly because this might precipitate the firing of the torpedoes, but mainly because he thought the Turks had behaved so well in giving him warning that 'it would be rather a dirty trick to shoot him'. Someone suggested sending off an SOS, but the senior soldier had no idea of the ship's position; meanwhile, some lifeboats were being hurriedly and inexpertly lowered, and some men were diving straight into the sea; at this precise moment an N.C.O. stepped smartly up to the bridge to report that he had watered and fed the horses! The Turk then closed on the defenceless transport, but, incredibly, missed with all three torpedoes at point-blank range; two British destroyers caught up with it as it returned to Smyrna, and chased it until it was beached on the island of Chios. In the general panic on *Manitou*, several soldiers were drowned, but the episode as a whole did little to raise the general estimation of the Turks' fighting qualities.

'In fine weather in Mudros,' John Masefield has written, 'a haze of beauty comes upon the hills and water till their loveliness is unearthly, it is so rare. Then the bay is like a blue jewel, and the hills lose their savagery, and glow, and are gentle, and the sun comes up from Troy, and the peaks of Samothrace change colour, and all the marvellous ships in the harbour are transfigured.' By April 20th there were over 200 ships at Mudros, and the French and the Royal Naval Division had to be sent to Trebuki Bay in the island of Skyros. The weather was unsettled and often surprisingly cold, which caused considerable difficulties in communications. A midshipman was sent with an important message across the harbour in a small launch, and was not re-covered until some 24 hours later, by which time his launch, whose fire had been swamped, was several miles offshore. 'Nobody who remembers the fortnight spent in Mudros Bay will forget the irksome confinement and nightmare difficulty of inter-communication', Orlo Williams writes. After a fortnight in *Arcadian*, he wrote in his diary: 'One is separated absolutely even from a transport to which a loud shout would almost carry.... There is no telephone communication with other staffs, and we have to rely a good deal on naval signallers.... With preparations for this historic enterprise proceeding at fever heat, with the force that is to carry it out, the com-manders and their staffs lying close by, yet so far away, with the fleet of fifteen British battleships, five cruisers, twenty destroyers within our view, it is a strange, isolated life, in an isolated ship, inevitable but curious ... little coming and going, no give and take, no opportunity of fraternizing. It is the same for us all, whether our ship holds a staff, or a regiment, or a collection of stores.' Although attempts were made to practise landings, the poor weather and lack of small boats hindered these exercises, and many of the troops never left their ships from the time when they embarked at Alexandria to their disembarkation on the Gallipoli Peninsula some three weeks later. 'Thus we whiled away the weeks of waiting', one subaltern wrote shortly afterwards, '—a tedious, anxious, gnawing time, when nobody did any work to speak of, because nobody knew exactly what was required of him.'

In these circumstances it was increasingly difficult to co-ordinate the planning of the operation. Hamilton had decided to take his General Staff with him on *Queen Elizabeth* when the operations began, leaving the administrative staff on another transport, completely out of touch with the situation. Hamilton was subsequently criticised for establishing himself on *Queen Elizabeth* for the period of the landings. It has been suggested that he should have put himself aboard 'some fast detached command vessel like the *Phaeton*, with adequate signalling equipment.'* These criticisms ignore the central problem which confronted Hamilton throughout the campaign,

---

* Moorehead: *Gallipoli*, 129. Moorehead states that Hamilton thus 'cut himself off ... from his staff'. But the General Staff officers, to their acute discomfort, were also on board *Queen Elizabeth*.

the division of command. Things were likely to be difficult enough without a physical separation between himself and de Robeck at critical moments. Experience also showed—and was confirmed by the events of April 25th—that it was hazardous to rely on wireless communications over long distances in a battle of this nature. It was an unsatisfactory arrangement, but it was a more sensible and practicable solution to the problem of liaison between the Navy and the Army than has often been implied.

The Adjutant-General, Brig.-General Woodward, and the Director of Medical Services, Surgeon-General Birrell, had now arrived at Mudros with their staffs, less than a week before the operations were due to begin. They had been horrified by the inadequacy and sketchiness of the plans for evacuating the wounded, and particularly by the fact that there were only two hospital ships and no provision had been made for converting other transport for removing casualties to Egypt. Woodward submitted a detailed memorandum of recommendations, but was far too late to achieve any significant improvements in the plans. What was even more disconcerting was the coldness with which the administrative officers were treated by Braithwaite and Hamilton. They were left in no doubt that they were considered to be a tedious encumbrance, and were isolated on a transport without any contact with the General Staff, and as much use as if they had stayed in Alexandria.

By April 20th everything was deemed to be ready, and the men were keen to be off. The force radiated with enthusiasm and confidence. A conscious effort was made by the senior officers to impress on the men the fact that the Turk could be a formidable foe, and Hunter-Weston perhaps carried this rather too far in his message to the 29th Division by laying great stress on the fact that 'heavy losses by bullets, by shells, by mines and by drowning', could be expected. But all the existing information which the Allies possessed showed that the Turkish army was poorly equipped, inefficient and demoralised by successions of defeats. Shortly before the expedition left Mudros, Hamilton received significant intelligence from Kitchener about a sharp engagement near Basra, where the Turks had shown an unexpected and disconcerting skill and courage. But as soon as they had been dislodged from their positions, they had retreated and had not stopped; this was exactly what G.H.Q. expected to happen at Gallipoli.* The final report circulated by G.H.Q. on the eve of the landings accurately reflected the views of the senior commanders.

> It is the general opinion that the Turks will offer an energetic resistance to our landing, but when once we are firmly established on the Peninsula it is thought possible that this opposition may crumble away, and that they may then turn on their German masters. The

---

* As Hamilton told the Dardanelles Commission, 'I did not know, to tell you the truth, that they were nearly as good as they turned out to be.'

average Turk has always been most sympathetic to the British Nation, and it is known that many look with envy on the prosperity which Egypt enjoys under British rule.

In London, only Hankey seems to have had any premonition of disaster. In a memorandum discussed by the War Council on March 19th, he urged the appointment of a technical naval and military committee —the first germ of the subsequent chiefs of staff committees—'so as to avoid repetition of the naval fiasco, which is largely due to inadequate Staff preparation'. The paper was only perfunctorily discussed, and no action was taken. Hankey returned to the point with a memorandum to Asquith, asking that at least the objectives of the operations should be established, so that a proper appreciation of the forces needed to carry them out could be made. 'Up to the present time, so far as I am aware,' he wrote, 'no attempt has been made to estimate what Force is required to make sure of success. We have merely said that so many troops are available, and that they ought to be enough.' Hankey had, of course, put his finger on the fundamental defect in the whole enterprise, but his warnings went unheeded. When he told Churchill that at least the landings would be 'of extraordinary difficulty', Churchill remarked 'that he could not see that there was any difficulty at all.' In a last attempt, Hankey sent Asquith another memorandum on April 12th, which concluded: 'The military operation appears, therefore, to be to a certain extent a gamble upon the supposed shortage of supplies and inferior fighting qualities of the Turkish armies.' The War Office estimated the likely casualties for landing and capturing the Peninsula at about 5,000. 'At the outset,' as the Dardanelles Commission subsequently commented, 'all decisions were taken and provisions based on the assumption that, if a landing were effected, the resistance would be slight and the advance rapid.' Optimism and enthusiasm, although great military qualities, had been carried in London and Mudros to an unreasoning myopia.

On the eve of the expedition, the force suffered one of its first, and most famous, losses. Rupert Brooke, the darling of the 'new Georgians' who seemed to fill all the senior positions in the Royal Naval Division, died on a French hospital ship off Skyros from blood-poisoning caused by an insect bite. 'He died at 4.46,' his friend, Denis Browne wrote, 'with the sun shining all round his cabin, and the cool sea breeze blowing through the door and the shaded windows. No one could have wished a quieter or calmer end than in that lovely bay, shielded by the mountains and fragrant with sage and thyme.' He was buried that evening in an olive grove high above Trebuki Bay, with Bernard Freyberg, Denis Browne, Charles Lister, Clegg Kelly, Patrick Shaw-Stewart, Arthur Asquith (the Prime Minister's son) and Johnny Dodge by his graveside. Of that remarkable company of hand-picked young men, Browne and Lister were destined to die at Gallipoli, and Shaw-Stewart and Kelly in France; Asquith never fully recovered from the wounds he received in the war, and Freyberg, a winner of the Victoria Cross, was the last survivor, dying in 1963. Hamilton was deeply moved by the news of Brooke's death. 'Death grins at my elbow,' he wrote. 'I cannot get him out of my thoughts. He is fed up with the old and sick—only the flower of the flock will serve him now, for God has started a celestial spring cleaning, and our star is to be scrubbed bright with the blood of our bravest and our best.'

There had already been one postponement on account of the weather when de Robeck, not without misgivings, gave the order for operations to begin on April 23rd. It was the kind of delicious morning, still, hot, clear and gentle, which one finds only in the eastern Mediterranean in spring or in England in May. One by one, the dowdy transports, the sinister warships, the aloof liners and humble colliers raised steam, and began to slip out of the enormous harbour into the open sea. Few who saw the departure of the armada were not stirred by the scene. Some describe the gaiety of the men, the roars of cheering from the packed transports, the bands playing; others remember the poignant quietness. 'The silent procession impressed us as nothing else could,' a New Zealander, Brereton, has written; 'the stillness only broken when a ship passed close to another, and then a sudden burst of cheering broke out and immediately died away. Noiselessly the warships approached, and passing we could hear their bands playing our old national airs.' For the Australians and New Zealanders, embarking on the first major military operation in the histories of their young countries, it was a particularly moving moment. In his diary, Orlo Williams wrote:

> The River Clyde, with her extra gangways tacked on to her side and her sand-bagged upper structure, left Mudros for Tenedos, carrying her gallant company and Doughty-Wylie* away, a great many of them for ever. An atmosphere of intense excitement begins to be felt, and the emotion as the transports, crammed with troops all cheering, moved down the roadstead in procession, as if proudly parading before action in front of the assembled shipping, was overwhelming. Tears rolled down my cheeks as those men went so gaily to their desperate enterprise.

By the evening of April 24th, over 200 ships moved through the Aegean waters, bearing the Royal Naval Division to the Gulf of Saros for the Bulair diversion, the Anzacs for Gaba Tepe, the 29th Division, after assembling off Tenedos, for Cape Helles. A young officer of the Lancashire Fusiliers, charged with the duty of storming W Beach on the morrow, boarded the cruiser Euryalus off Tenedos in the evening. 'Nature was so peaceful,' he has written; 'a dead flat calm, an oily sea, a silent, beautiful rock-crowned island, with its replica in the bay beneath, no sound or movement in water or in air, no sign of the prodigious eruption of metal and

* Lt.-Colonel C. M. H. Doughty-Wylie, C.B., C.M.G., had joined G.H.Q. as an Intelligence Officer on March 18th; he and another staff officer accompanied the V Beach force as liaison officers.

men which was to greet the dawn. Those long grey ships, with the faint smoke curling from their funnels and reflected in the mirror-like surfaces below, seemed like some fantastic fleet from dreamland.'

As darkness fell, and the ships moved into the open sea, the weather still seemed to be unsettled, and the sailors anxiously scanned the sombre skies, the scudding clouds and the restless sea. It was particularly unpleasant for the sailors already in the 'tows', bobbing along in long, sinister lines in the black sea. 'The night was cold and the boats uncomfortable, and the prospects gloomy', a very young midshipman later wrote in his diary; 'we were all

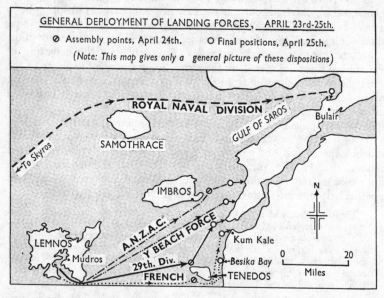

GENERAL DEPLOYMENT OF LANDING FORCES, APRIL 23rd-25th.

⊘ Assembly points, April 24th.   O Final positions, April 25th.

(Note: This map gives only a general picture of these dispositions)

more or less numb with cold.' But soon the sky cleared, and the moon shone on an almost perfectly calm flat sea, across which the ships slid silently. On board, there was little sound save for the throb of the engines, but few slept. A lance-corporal of the Lancashire Fusiliers on *Euryalus* has recorded that 'we had little sleep, for all were keyed up for the great adventure—spending our time talking and letter-writing, lying on the decks with our equipment by our sides.'

Between 1 and 2 a.m. on the morning of Sunday, April 25th, the warships with the covering force had reached their battle stations, and stopped in the calm sea. The troops were roused, given a hot meal, and then—'all very cold and expectant' as the young midshipman relates—embarked in the boats which were to take them to the beaches. The organisation and discipline were alike remarkable; 'the impression conveyed', Wemyss has written, 'was that of a phantom force.' Off Gaba Tepe, where the landing was to take place just before dawn, the Anzacs could see the dark mass of the Peninsula whenever a searchlight in the Straits arced into the pitch-dark sky. The warships then began to glide forward again, each with its covey of 'tows' behind, every small boat packed with tense and silent men. 'Almighty God,' Hamilton wrote, 'Watchman of the Milky Way, Shepherd of the Golden Stars, have mercy upon us. . . . Thy Will be done. *En avant*—at all costs—*en avant!*' It was an occasion for high hopes and fine rhetoric. Brigadier-General Hare, placed in command of the Helles covering force, addressed the 86th Brigade on the eve of the landing as follows:

> Fusiliers! Our brigade is to have the honour to be the first to land and to cover the disembarkation of the rest of the division. Our task will be no easy one. Let us carry it through in a way worthy of the traditions of the distinguished regiments of which the Fusilier Brigade is composed . . . in such a way that future historians may say of us, as Napier said of the Fusilier Brigade at Albuhera—'Nothing could stop that astonishing infantry.'

PART TWO

EXECUTION

Farewell happy fields
Where joy for ever dwells: Hail horrors, hail
Infernal world, and thou profoundest Hell
Receive thy new possessor: one who brings
A mind not to be changed by place or time.
The mind is its own place, and in itself
Can make a Heav'n of Hell, a Hell of Heav'n.
Milton: 'Paradise Lost', Book I

5

April 25th, 1915

The herdman wandering by the lonely rills
  Marks where they lie on the scarred mountain flanks,
Remembering that mild morning when the hills
  Shook to the roar of guns, and those wild Franks
Surged upward from the sea.
                    Lester Lawrence, 'The Anzac Book'

Late on the afternoon of April 24th, Liman von Sanders left the area near Besika Bay, where he had attended a divisional field exercise, to return to his headquarters in the old French consulate in Gallipoli town. A few miles to the west, beyond Tenedos, but not spotted by the Turks, the Allied transports and warships carrying the troops of the 29th Division and the French were making their final preparations.

At 5 a.m. on the following morning von Sanders was hurriedly awakened, to be informed that the Allies had landed on the Gallipoli Peninsula at Gaba Tepe, Sedd-el-Bahr, Tekke Burnu and Morto Bay and that more landings seemed imminent at Kum Kale, Besika Bay and Bulair. Bulair! von Sanders immediately ordered the troops encamped near Gallipoli town to march north and he himself rode at once to the threatened area. His staff had been amazed by the extent of the enemy attack. 'From the many pale faces among the officers reporting in the early morning it became apparent that although a hostile landing had been expected with certainty,' he later wrote, 'a landing at so many places surprised many and filled them with apprehension. . . . It seemed improbable to me that extensive landings would take place at all of these places, but we could not discern at the moment where the enemy was actually seeking the decision.'

From the high ground above the Gulf of Saros, von Sanders had a wonderful view of the diversion being carried out with great spirit and ingenuity by the Royal Naval Division and the warships. 'About twenty large enemy ships, some war vessels, some transports, could be counted in front of us', he wrote. 'Some individual vessels were lying close in under the steep slopes of the coast. Others were farther out in the gulf or were still under way. From the broadsides of the warships came an uninterrupted stream of fire and smoke and the entire coast including our ridge was covered with shells and shrapnel. It was an unforgettable picture.' Von Sanders remained on the ridge all day, while the Gallipoli troops made their way with all possible speed to the threatened isthmus. From time to time the transports put out boats covered with brushwood to conceal the fact that they held no troops, but when the machine-gun and rifle fire mounted in intensity they withdrew again. As the hours passed, von Sanders' suspicions were aroused that this was only a diversion, and eventually he ordered two battalions of the troops coming from Gallipoli to turn south to Maidos. Essad Pasha, commanding the Bulair divisions, was ordered south to take command.

Reports reaching von Sanders from Gaba Tepe, Helles and Kum Kale were bad. At Helles, the Turkish commander reported that the British were ashore, were landing reinforcements, and that his last available reserves had been committed; from Colonel Sami's headquarters it was reported that the enemy was ashore near Gaba Tepe and advancing up the Sari Bair ridge. The reported presence of a British submarine in the Straits meant that all plans for ferrying troops over from the Asiatic shore had had to be abandoned. All reports spoke with awe of the 'frightful fire' from the naval guns, of heavy losses, and enemy gains. Unable to tear himself away from Bulair until evening, von Sanders could only trust to the skill of his divisional commanders and the courage of his men.

The first landing had taken place near Ari Burnu just before dawn.

Birdwood's plan, in its conception, was reasonably simple and straight-forward. The covering force of about 4,000 men of the 1st Australian Division was to land in three successive waves on a broad front of 2,000 yards, with the southern boats landing at a point about a mile north of Gaba Tepe; as soon as the men were grouped, they were to fan out in three groups towards the summit of Chunuk Bair to the north, an eminence called Scrubby Knoll to the east, and Gaba Tepe to the south. These three positions in their hands, the way was open for a rapid advance across the comparatively easy ground to Mal Tepe and Maidos by the main body, who would land immediately after the covering force.

The battleship *Triumph*, showing a single light, marked the position off Gaba Tepe. The three battleships carrying the first wave of troops—500 to each battleship—reached their rendezvous about five miles west of Gaba

Tepe at 1 a.m. The boats were lowered, and the men silently clambered down into them. The scene was extraordinarily eerie, with the gentle green-black sea, the rows of silent forms, the muffled orders, an occasional splash of a rope or oar in the sea, the sombre silhouette of the Peninsula dimly perceptible to the east. 'Even the groaning and wrenching of the chains and cables seemed subdued and ghostly', an Australian private later wrote. 'A ghostly sort of light everywhere,' Lt.-Col. Skeen wrote, 'and myself sick with anxiety.' So silent was the embarkation that Admiral Thursby, commanding the landings, was wondering when it was going to begin when he was told that it was completed.

Just before 3 a.m. the three battleships, *Queen, Prince of Wales* and *London*, steamed slowly towards the Peninsula, followed by the 12 'tows' of small boats. The faint breeze died away, and the surface of the sea became as smooth as glass. At 3.30 a.m. the battleships stealthily came to a stop, and the 'tows' crept past them towards the invisible shore, now about two and a half miles away. The phosphorescence glistered from the bows of the boats. 'The green waters had turned to black,' one Australian has related; 'you only knew your comrades were with you in the same boat by the press of their swinging bodies against your shoulders and your ribs.' The throb of the engines of the pinnaces seemed loud enough to alert every Turk on the Peninsula, whose forbidding outline was occasionally visible. The first faint streaks of dawn were touching the sky when the 'tows' were cast off some 50 yards from the shore and the 48 little boats crept towards it. The men had been sitting cramped and silent for nearly three hours, and the strain was intense; it seemed impossible that they could not have been seen.

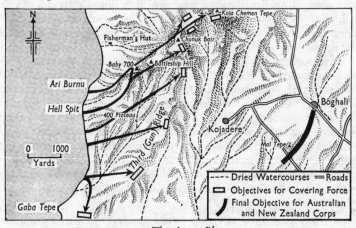

The Anzac Plan

It came almost as a relief when a flare shot up from a low headland, a silhouetted figure on the skyline shouted a warning, and a scattered fire broke out. Every boat landed where it could, the bullets striking sparks off the shingle, and the men splashed ashore; 'Come on boys,' a young subaltern yelled as he leapt from the boat; 'by God I'm frightened!' In many cases the Australians were led ashore by diminutive midshipmen* in their teens; unhappily, the legend of one clambering over his enormous charges, brandishing a large revolver and squeaking 'Come on, my lads!' is only a legend. Hardly any casualties were suffered. The picturesque story, first created by the war correspondent Ellis Ashmead-Bartlett,† that a party of Turks charged down to the beach and were repelled by a bayonet charge seems to be one of the many legends of the landings. So firmly had it been drilled into the men that everything depended on moving quickly inland that within a few minutes a party of Australians had scrambled up an unexpectedly steep slope in front of them and arrived at the top of a small plateau—subsequently known as Plugge's (pronounced 'Pluggy's') Plateau—to see a detachment of Turks hastily disappearing down the precipitous slopes into a vast scrub-covered ravine, later called Shrapnel Gully. Somewhere inland, a gun barked, and the first shrapnel shell burst over Plugge's.

The light was steadily improving and it was becoming obvious that something had gone wrong. The officers had been told that they would find a low sand-bank on landing, but in fact were almost immediately confronted with almost sheer scrub-covered cliffs. The officers on Plugge's could see what some realised to be 400 Plateau about 1,000 yards to their right instead of on their left. Below them, and to their right, the boats which had landed to the north of Ari Burnu had been faced with an almost sheer cliff of yellow sandstone. 'What are we to do next, Sir?' one soldier inquired of an officer. 'I don't know, I'm sure,' was the reply; 'everything is in a terrible muddle.'

The subsequent official account of what had occurred was that the tows had been pushed off course by an unexpected northerly current, and that when the naval officer responsible for positioning the landing, a Lieutenant-Commander Waterlow, had been able to discern the Peninsula, he had mistaken Ari Burnu for Gaba Tepe. Mistakenly thinking he was too far to the south, when in fact he was well to the north of the intended landing place, he had at once steered his tow—on the extreme right (or south)—sharply to the north. Commander Dix, in charge of the landing of the covering force, was leading the northern tow, and his unpublished account of what then trans-

* Two of them—Eric Bush and Charles Dixon of *Bacchante*—were first-term cadets from Dartmouth.

† And repeated by Moorehead (*Gallipoli*, 136). The Anzac landing is a mass of legends, and I am particularly grateful to Mr. H. V. Howe for his extremely clear, precise and factual account of the landing, which was also of great value to Dr. Bean in his Australian official history.

pired (made available to me through the kindness of his widow), describes his part:

> We gradually drew clear of the ships, and at first all seemed to be going well, but when three-quarters of the way ashore I saw that the right wing was steering across the bows of the centre, who were conforming to the movement, thus crowding the left wing away to port. By this time I was awake to the fact that we were already some way to port of our objective, and in order to save as much ground as possible I took the left wing at full speed under the stern of the other column and hailed them to keep to starboard. I felt that as soon as the first boat got ashore every other boat would at once put her helm over and do the same, and that the quicker we got there the less would be the error. The first approach of dawn was another reason for speed.

The result of this manoeuvre was that the boats finished up in a cluster around Ari Burnu. 'Tell the Colonel', Dix yelled in the eerie silence that preceded the actual landing, 'that the damn fools have landed us a mile too far north!'

Until recently, this very plausible version of events has been implicitly accepted by all historians of the campaign. It has however been challenged by H. V. Howe, himself a survivor of the landing.* Howe suggests that Birdwood or Thursby, together on *Queen* that night, may have made a last-minute change of plan, and ordered Waterlow to land further north; owing to the impossibility of signalling to *London*, Dix would not have known.

It is quite clear from the papers of Birdwood and Skeen—who were responsible for the executive planning of the landing—that they had no knowledge whatever of such a change of plan. Thursby, on the other hand, told Wemyss that 'the southern tow landed within a hundred yards of its assigned position'.

Indeed, something very odd had occurred. While making every possible allowance for the strain and difficulties under which he was attempting to position the landing, Waterlow's error was strange. He and Dix had made a very careful study of the coast only a few days before; all accounts agree that the Peninsula was visible for nearly half an hour before the boats grounded; and the silhouette of the Peninsula around Gaba Tepe could hardly be more different than that above Anzac Cove. Dix, certainly, knew where he was. Howe states that the outline of The Sphinx—a jutting cliff which was a notable landmark—was conspicuous for some time before the landing.

Another oddity, to which Howe attaches considerable significance, is the position of the three battleships as given in the official Australian history. All accounts state categorically that the 'tows' were ordered to steer due east, yet the battleships, which had anchored in a dead flat sea when the Peninsula was clearly visible, are positioned well to the north-west of the intended landing place. The notorious 'northerly current' to which so much blame was attached, does not seem to have affected the other 'tows' to

* H. V. Howe: 'Belated Query' (*Stand-To*, Canberra, September 1962).

anything like the same extent as it did to Waterlow's. When all these factors are considered, the theory that Thursby did give Waterlow revised orders at the last moment and told him to aim for Hell Spit, which Waterlow confused with Ari Burnu—a very understandable mistake—cannot be lightly dismissed, particularly as there *had* been a change on the very eve of the landing, when Thursby had moved the intended landing place of the southern 'tow' from a point 'about one mile north of Gaba Tepe' to a new point 'about 800 yards north of Gaba Tepe'. The two 'intended landing places', the actual landing place, and the probable positions of the three battleships and the approximate courses taken by the 'tows', are shown below.

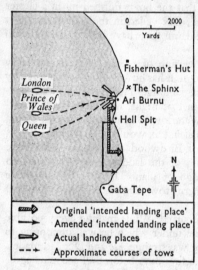

Anzac: 4.30 a.m., April 25th

Highly improbable though it may appear that Thursby, on his own initiative, and without telling either Birdwood or Skeen, would switch the landing at the last moment, it would seem possible that the three battleships themselves were out of position before the 'tows' left them. In this respect, a curious story from the Turkish side has recently been disclosed in a Turkish military journal. According to this account, soldiers on Gaba Tepe noticed a British marker buoy on April 24th. It was recovered by four of the regiment's best swimmers, who put it back in the sea a mile or so to the north. It would be dramatically satisfying to say that this act of ingenuity by a few Turkish soldiers wrecked the Anzac landing, but there is no mention whatever in the British naval archives of a marker buoy. The task of marking the rendezvous off Anzac had been given to *Triumph*, and Thursby's written orders to the captain show that her position was to be fixed by normal navigational methods:

On the night before the landing takes place, on a date that will be communicated later, you will proceed to a position latitude 40 deg. 13 min. N., longitude 26 deg. 10 min. E., and anchor your ship on that spot.

It is absolutely essential for the success of the expedition that your ship should be accurately in this position.

After anchoring you are to verify it by every possible means in your power. You should also note the directions and strength of the current, and communicate both—this and your position—to me by boat on my arrival at the rendezvous.

    You are to arrive at this rendezvous by 11 p.m., and should be careful to approach it unobserved by the enemy. . . . At 12 midnight you are to exhibit a light of sufficient strength to show about five miles over an arc extending from N.W. to S.W. . . . .

Queen, 21st April   Cecil F. Thursby, *Rear-Admiral Commanding, 2nd Squadron*

A probable explanation is that the curious divided responsibility between Dix and Waterlow, when combined with the change of plan on the evening of the 24th, made the chances of error far greater than they need have been. No evidence has come to light to the effect that *Triumph* did not mark the rendezvous correctly, but it seems possible that, by the time they were within a mile or so of the shore, the battleships were too far to the north-west, whether propelled there by the mysterious northerly current or as a result of inaccurate navigation it is not possible to say. Although the remote possibility that Thursby had a last-minute change of mind cannot be entirely dismissed, the real answer seems to lie in the general confusion and imprecision which bedevilled all known orders about the landing of the covering force. The men had no idea where they were meant to land nor the terrain they could expect to find when they had landed; some, when they saw The Sphinx, thought it was Sedd-el-Bahr Castle!

They only knew that the operation had opened in great confusion. Those who landed in Anzac Cove were, relatively speaking, lucky, and the climb to the top of Plugge's, although steep, was not severe. But those who landed north of Ari Burnu were confronted with almost sheer cliffs. Breaking into small groups, they hacked and cursed their way up. Machine-guns opened up from the direction of Fisherman's Hut, and almost completely destroyed a landing attempted near there.

In spite of the intermixing of units, the general confusion and the difficult ground, the Australians had been so imbued with the urgency of moving inland rapidly that small parties, admirably led, were quickly making rapid progress. By 6 a.m. they were in complete possession of First Ridge, parties were moving across Second Ridge, and on the left the Turks were falling back in disorder up Baby 700. About 4,000 Anzacs were ashore, and it is doubtful if the Turks in the vicinity totalled 700. Near The Sphinx, a monstrous cliff jutting from Russell's Top, a party of entrenched Turks flung down their rifles and fled when a small group of perspiring Australians hauled themselves grimly over the crest. By 7 a.m. small detached parties of determined men had crossed Legge Valley and had reached Third Ridge; a Lieutenant Loutit climbed up to Scrubby Knoll and looked down on the gleaming waters of the Narrows, barely three miles away. The capture of all the covering force's objectives seemed imminent.

It has been often stated that the Turks had never expected a landing in this wild and desolate area; while it is true that the main apprehensions were for a landing just north of Gaba Tepe, the coast from there to Fisherman's Hut was picqueted by a battalion of the 27th Regiment; as has been mentioned on page 76, the rest of the regiment was stationed near Maidos on von Sanders' orders, contrary to the advice of the local commanders. The area where the Anzacs landed was defended by two companies, reasonably well dug in. At about 2.30 a.m. the local company commander, in the words of the Turkish official account, 'surmised that a landing [was imminent] and had informed battalion headquarters. Thus the force had not been attacked unawares.' The strict orders to the men not to fire until the boats grounded—which had such shattering effects at Helles—was a mistake at Ari Burnu; the boats, very clear in the water as they approached the shore, vanished from the sight of many of the Turks when they ran aground under the promontory; 'the well-trained and courageous Australians,' one Turkish account states, 'taking advantage of this situation, easily broke this weak Turkish resistance.' This was not entirely true; although the detachments on the coast were easily pushed back or overrun, the ground was so difficult to traverse, and afforded such perfect concealment for a few snipers, that the momentum of the Anzac advance began to falter.

The remainder of the Turkish 27th Regiment had spent the evening of April 24th practising night exercises near Gaba Tepe, and had returned to Maidos at 2 a.m. Within two hours the regiment was aroused by the sound of firing and was ordered to stand to. Although the Turks thought that the Ari Burnu landing might be a feint attack to draw troops from Gaba Tepe, it was eventually decided to send the regiment into action; it made contact with small parties of Australians while advancing north-east across the southern fringes of Third Ridge. Although very tired, the men were well trained and confident. 'It was a calm day,' the Turkish historian relates, 'and the sea was smooth. Not a sound was to be heard except for a few occasional rifle-shots from the Australians. The sun was warming the area which was later to be turned into a bloody ocean.' The small groups of Australians who had pushed across Legge Valley to Third Ridge were now either engulfed or forced to withdraw to 400 Plateau. By 10 a.m. the fighting on this area was developing into a major battle. A Turkish battery behind Gaba Tepe began to shell Anzac Cove, where the congestion was already becoming serious.

The fact that the landing beach was only a few hundred yards long instead of a mile threw out every plan. When the main Anzac force, following hot on the heels of the covering force, began to land, the delays in getting them ashore and re-grouping them were immensely greater than had ever been anticipated. The naval and military beach parties did not land until 10

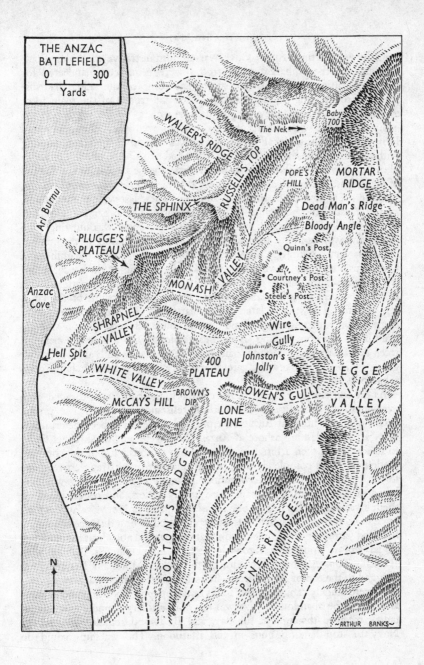

THE ANZAC
BATTLEFIELD
0   300
Yards

Ari Burnu

WALKER'S RIDGE

The Nek →

Baby
700

POPE'S
HILL

MORTAR
RIDGE

RUSSELL'S TOP

THE SPHINX

Dead Man's Ridge

Bloody Angle

PLUGGE'S
PLATEAU

• Quinn's Post

MONASH VALLEY

• Courtney's Post

Anzac
Cove

Steele's Post

SHRAPNEL
VALLEY

Wire
Gully

Hell Spit

Johnston's
Jolly

400
PLATEAU

WHITE VALLEY

LEGGE

OWEN'S GULLY

BROWN'S
DIP

VALLEY

McCAY'S HILL

LONE
PINE

BOLTON'S RIDGE

PINE RIDGE

N

~ARTHUR BANKS~

a.m., by which time Anzac Cove was an administrative shambles. Boats intended for the embarkation of troops were being commandeered for taking casualties back to the transports, and some of the sailors had disappeared to join the fighting inland. When the troops of the main force eventually got ashore, they had no definite orders, no knowledge of the ground or of the whereabouts of other units, or even where the enemy was. From the sea, the scene off Anzac Cove was deceptive. Brereton, landing with the main force, has written that 'it looked like a huge boating picnic in ideal picnic weather; ship's boats and all sorts of vessels going to and fro full of men; those going towards shore perfectly quiet, those coming out waving hats and cheering each passing boat and ship. These last were the wounded, mostly Australians, returning to the transports. The otherwise cloudless sky was flecked and ringed with white where shrapnel was bursting. The enemy fire was rapid but wild, and no doubt they were finding the number of targets very confusing.' 'Shrapnel was bursting above us in the gullies and beyond us out at sea, but very little was actually landing on the beach, which was strewn with wounded and dead, while the stones were bespattered with blood', a young New Zealand sergeant wrote in his account of the landing, written a few days later in his diary. '. . . Wounded soldiers were coming in, some limping, some carried on stretchers. There was no grumbling nor complaining. A man came along with a blood-bespattered face, bound up in a bloody bandage. Yet he was still able to swear gently while he smoked a cigarette and his disengaged hand clung to his tobacco.'

As the sun climbed higher in the clear sky, the battle inland raged with ever-increasing intensity as the Turkish resistance mounted. The precise details of the fighting at Anzac on April 25th have never been determined. New arrivals splashing ashore at Anzac Cove were sent to Shrapnel Gully to re-form, and then arbitrarily dispatched to various parts of the confused battlefield. Units completely disappeared; in some cases, stragglers returned to the beach, to add to the confusion; in many others, nothing was ever heard of them again. The maps were utterly useless, and orders based on them invariably collapsed; on one occasion, a party of New Zealanders took over an hour to move what on the map appeared to be a distance of under a hundred yards, for the simple reason that the map did not admit the existence of an almost impassable razor-edge which links Plugge's Plateau with Russell's Top. Although six guns of the Indian Mountain Battery were dragged to the top of 400 Plateau—in itself an extraordinary achievement—they were quickly caught by the Turks in their exposed position and eventually had to be abandoned. This was the only artillery support that the infantry received throughout the day, and Birdwood actually ordered the Navy to stop landing guns in the afternoon. The warships could do little to help, and it was not until 5 p.m. that a definite report of the position of a Turkish battery near Anderson's Knoll was received and the guns of the Fleet could intervene. No one had any reasonably precise knowledge of what was happening. By 2 p.m. the Anzacs had landed over 12,000 men, and were opposed by under 4,000 Turks, but the nature of the ground, the confusion caused by landing in the wrong place, and the inter-mixing of units, reduced this advantage considerably. By 5 p.m. the Anzacs were fighting for their lives, and were being driven back to the sea.

The critical section of the front was on the extreme left. From the southern end of Anzac Cove one moves left up Shrapnel Gully, leaving the almost sheer side of Plugge's to the left, swings to the right past the final fingers of Russell's Top, and then left again up a deep cleft known as Monash Valley. The sides of Monash Valley are steep and in places precipitous, and are scrub-covered and rocky. The head of the valley is dominated by an insignificant hill known to the British as Baby 700, which is in fact a lower ridge of Chunuk Bair; above it is another gentle ridge, subsequently known as Battleship Hill. At the top of Monash Valley the ground rises steeply to right and left, with a small promontory of rock in the middle. In winter, Monash Valley is a fierce washaway, sweeping from Baby 700 to the sea; in summer, it is an arid valley, with no exit save an almost perpendicular climb up what in winter are waterfalls. On the western side Russell's Top narrows to a promontory known to the Anzacs as The Nek, barely a hundred yards wide, and with a sheer drop on either side; on the eastern side there is an almost equally narrow ridge which links 400 Plateau with Baby 700. It was around and above this plunging ravine that the most bitter and important of the fighting raged.

A party of Australians, led by two Captains, Tulloch and Lalor, had reached The Nek by 8 a.m. The Turks on Russell's Top had melted away as soon as the Australians scaled the cliff, and had now vanished entirely. To the right, spasmodic firing could be heard in invisible ravines, but the morning was generally peaceful. It was decided that Lalor should establish himself at The Nek, while Tulloch took his men over Baby 700. Tulloch's party trudged up the gentle slopes of Baby 700 and advanced inland. At one point a party of Turks opened fire, but when the Australians sank into the scrub and returned the fire, the Turks disappeared over the next crest and the advance continued. By this time the Australians were moving across the south-eastern slopes of Battleship Hill.

Mustafa Kemal, commanding the 19th Division at Boghali, had been awakened by the sound of gunfire from the general direction of Gaba Tepe, and had at once ordered the division to be mustered. His own account continues:

> I spoke on the telephone to . . . Essad Pasha,* at Gallipoli. He said that no clear information about what was going on had yet been obtained. It was at 0630 hours that from a report which arrived from Halil Sami Bey it was learnt that a force of enemy had climbed the heights of Ari Burnu and that I was required to send a battalion against them. Both from this report and as a result of the personal observation I had carried out at Mal Tepe, my firm opinion was, just as I had previously judged, that an enemy attempt to land in strength in the neighbourhood of Gaba Tepe was now taking place. Therefore I appreciated that it was impossible to carry [out] my task with a battalion, but that as I had reckoned before, my whole division would be required to deal with the enemy.

Outside Turkey, no one had heard of Kemal by 1915, and even in Turkey he was generally unknown. Although he had been one of the earliest of the Young Turk officers to turn against the régime in Salonika in 1907, he had been completely eclipsed by Enver, Talaat, Djaved and Djemal, and had remained an able but not particularly outstanding soldier. He was a strange young man, with cold light-blue eyes, and an air of half-controlled smouldering tension. He had seen action in the Balkan wars and Tripoli, but had gradually fallen away from Enver, with the result that his military career had suffered; while Enver marched into the Caucasus and Djemal made his spectacular dash to the Suez Canal, Kemal, after a period as military attaché in Sofia, went to Maidos to command the 19th Division. Now, his moment had come. Before he had even left Boghali, he had taken the vital step of ordering his entire division to prepare to march to the coast.

He rode at the head of the 57th Regiment to Koja Chemen Tepe, the highest of the three summits of the Sari Bair crest. The going was difficult, the sun was hot, and the soldiers soon began to become badly strung out. Having reached Koja Chemen Tepe, Kemal ordered the officers with him to close the men up and give them a short rest, while he, accompanied by his A.D.C., his chief medical officer, an orderly, and the commander of a mountain battery which had come with the 57th Regiment, walked along the ridge to the Chunuk Bair crest. From this magnificent vantage-point they could see some warships and transport off Ari Burnu, but no signs of fighting as they scanned the ground which fell away gently from Battleship Hill towards Gaba Tepe, jutting out into the Aegean some five miles away. Kemal's account continues:

> The scene which met our eyes was a most interesting one. To my mind it was the most vital moment of the occurrence.
> Just then I saw men of a detachment who had been placed on hill Point 261 [Battleship

---

* Essad was in command of the Turkish III Corps at Gallipoli; at about 7.30 a.m. von Sanders ordered him to take command in the south, which until then had been divided between Sami Bey, commanding the 9th Division, and Kemal.

Hill] to the south of Chunuk Bair to observe and cover the shore from there, running back towards, in fact fleeing towards, Chunuk Bair. . . . Confronting these men myself, I said, 'Why are you running away?' 'Sir, the enemy', they said. 'Where?' 'Over there', they said, pointing out hill 261.

In fact a line of skirmishers of the enemy approached hill 261 and was advancing completely unopposed. Now just consider the situation. I had left my troops, so as to give the men ten minutes' rest. The enemy had come to this hill. It meant that the enemy were nearer to me than my troops were, and if the enemy came to where I was my troops would find themselves in a very difficult position. Then, I still do not know what it was, whether a logical appreciation or an instinctive action, I do not know. I said to the men who were running away, 'You cannot run away from the enemy.' 'We have got no ammunition', they said. 'If you haven't got any ammunition, you have your bayonets', I said, and shouting to them, I made them fix their bayonets and lie down on the ground. At the same time I sent the orderly officer beside me off to the rear to bring up to where I was at the double those men of the infantry regiment who were advancing on Chunuk Bair who could reach it in time. When the men fixed their bayonets and lay down on the ground the enemy also lay down. The moment of time that we gained was this one. . . . It was about 10.00 hours when the 57th Regiment began its attack.

It seems clear that it was Tulloch's small party which Kemal checked. Tulloch noticed that the fire from Battleship Hill, although not heavy, was increasing, and he particularly noticed a Turkish officer calmly standing beside a tree near the summit of Battleship Hill, which was on his left, obviously giving orders. He was under 1,000 yards away, and Tulloch opened fire at him; the officer did not move, and the fire which came in reply made Tulloch desist. Although he could see no large numbers of the enemy, the fire from Battleship Hill and the lower slopes of Chunuk Bair was increasing, and his small party was clearly isolated; he gave the order to withdraw, and his party finished up on the slopes of Baby 700, which had been secured by another party of Australians under a Lieutenant Margetts on Lalor's orders. In fact, the two parties were now barely 1,000 yards apart, but were unaware of the fact.

Up to this point—about 10 a.m.—events in this part of the front at least had been somewhat desultory, although, further to the south, enemy resistance was growing. Kemal now brought up the 57th Regiment, and before long Margetts decided to withdraw his party to the summit of Baby 700. The Turks were beginning to establish themselves not only on Battleship Hill but were trickling round the seaward flanks of Baby 700. Lalor sent a party to negotiate this flank, but it was forced to fall back. A scout returned from the fighting which was now developing to The Nek to find a group of Australians ordered by Lalor to entrench in case of a counter-attack sitting in the sunshine, 'smoking and eating as if on a picnic'. When the scout indignantly told an officer that the Turks were coming on 'in thousands', he replied in amazement, 'I didn't dream they'd come back.' Within a few minutes, the Turks were on them.

Colonel Sinclair-MacLagan, commanding the covering force, was a horrified witness of the deteriorating situation on his left flank, which he thought was absolutely secure. Margetts' men had been forced off Baby 700 and the Australians were now grouped just above The Nek, under heavy pressure from the Turks, who 'seemed to roll up in black clouds, fiercely silhouetted against the flame and glare of the rising sun', as one survivor has related. Two companies were hurriedly sent up to reinforce them, but it was not until 11 a.m. that they arrived. Joining up with Lalor's men, they charged the summit of Baby 700; the Turks fell back, and Margetts found himself back in the position he had occupied an hour earlier. The Australians were being virtually led by Lalor, a colourful personality even by Anzac standards; a deserter from the Royal Navy, he had served with the Foreign Legion and had then got himself involved in a South American revolution before returning to Australia to enlist in the army; clutching an old family sword firmly in his right hand, he was directing all operations from just above The Nek. Above him and a few hundred yards away, Kemal was marshalling his men for a major assault on the Australians, which continued throughout the afternoon. Kemal, with Essad's approval, had now called up the whole of the 19th Division. The summit of Baby 700 changed hands no less than five times, reinforcements were rushed from Anzac Cove as quickly as possible, but by 3 p.m. the Australian and New Zealand troops fighting with increasing desperation for the vital high ground above Monash Valley were reduced to fragments of seven battalions, all intermixed, and without their known officers.

Between 4.30 and 5 p.m. a Turkish counter-attack developed all along the front, mainly across Legge Valley on 400 Plateau and down the slopes of Baby 700. The Anzacs began to fall back. Baby 700 was lost, for the last time, and the remnants took up positions on either side of Monash Valley and at The Nek. Lalor was dead,* and no reinforcements came. A thin drizzle began to fall. The Turks came on again and again, with their patchwork uniforms, old-fashioned rifles and screams of 'Allah!' Cut down in swathes, the second and third waves would come on over the bodies of the dead and dying. Units were cut off and killed to a man; neither side was taking prisoners, and the fighting was frenzied and savage. By dusk, with the fearful racket of musketry increasing, the Anzacs were clinging to a series of detached positions at the end of Russell's Top, along the eastern side of Monash Valley, and just inland of the crest of 400 Plateau. A party of New

* A clue to Lalor's death is contained in one Turkish account of the Anzac fighting. 'An Australian officer with a sword in his hand was seen ordering a party of about 30 soldiers to attack a group of 20 to 25 Turks who had got very close to them. Noting this, the Turkish troops stood up and charged the attacking Australians. This fight lasted one minute only; a large number of the enemy and a few Turks were killed. The rest of the Turkish troops followed up this first by firing at the retreating enemy and then running after them.'

Zealanders, led by an Australian Colonel, Braund, hung on dauntlessly to a vital position just to the south of The Nek, which had by now been abandoned; to their right, Colonel Pope had occupied the small promontory of rock at the head of Monash Valley, which henceforward was known as Pope's Hill; to Pope's right, along the eastern crest of the Valley, detachments of men were clinging on to exposed positions subsequently known as Quinn's, Courtney's and Steele's Posts; to the south, the Anzacs had been driven almost to the seaward edge of 400 Plateau.

The confidence of the dawn and early morning had gone; on the beach the confusion was growing; men were coming down from the firing-lines, no one knew what was happening. 'There was no rest, no lull, while the rotting dead lay all around us, never a pause in the whole of that long day that started at the crack of dawn', an Australian soldier has recorded. 'How we longed for nightfall! How we prayed for this ghastly day to end! How we yearned for the sight of the first dark shadow!'

Shortly before 4 a.m., just after the Anzacs went ashore at Ari Burnu, the British battleships and 'tows' carrying the men of the 29th Division stood in towards the black-grey silhouette of the Helles coast. 'The formless clouds were grey,' a naval surgeon on *Euryalus* records; 'a darker streak of grey three miles away where grey sea and sky met, was Cape Helles, and three grey patches still were *Swiftsure*, *Cornwallis* and *Albion* close inshore, waiting to commence the bombardment.' As the uncertain light improved, colour began to creep across the Peninsula, which seemed to float eerily across the limpid calm water towards the invaders. Mists swirled gently about the beaches, making identification difficult. A French doctor, en route from Kum Kale on the liner *Savoie*, converted into an auxiliary cruiser, wrote in his diary at 4 a.m.: 'On deck it is hardly light, and the weather is cool. One can just distinguish to the right the Asiatic coast, and in front the Gallipoli Peninsula and the Pointe d'Europe. There are ships everywhere—battleships, cruisers, torpedo-boats, dredgers: a whole fleet surrounds the Peninsula. A light mist covers everything, and white flaky clouds cling to the valleys of the coast. The Turkish spur appears formidable and very beautiful.' 'We are now at the last lap, waiting our turn', a British subaltern hurriedly wrote in his diary. 'Our ship is anchored in a glassy, sunlit sea—enemy coast on every side—not a breath of air, not a sign of movement. It is still a sheer impossibility to believe that we are at war.'

The absolute stillness of the morning was abruptly shattered by the thunderclap of the opening of the naval bombardment. It is not clear from Turkish accounts if the fleet of ships had been spotted, as the mists clinging to the shore made visibility from their positions almost impossible. For many of them, the first intimation of the opening of battle was the scream and crump of heavy naval shells. No other alarum was necessary.

From the sea, the scene was one of unforgettable grandeur. 'The allied fleet was moving about in a cluster off the southern end of the Peninsula,' Brereton—on his way to Anzac with the main force—has written, 'showing vivid light-coloured flashes from the guns, and rolling clouds of smoke and dust on the ridges accompanied by the heavy sound of the bombardment'; 'the sight was worth all the fatigue, all the work, all the peril and the misery that came after', a major of the Royal Scots subsequently wrote. 'The sun pierces the early mist,' the French doctor on *Savoie* wrote in his diary; 'it emerges above the Gallipoli hills like an enormous globe of blood-red fire.' Thousands of stunned fish rose to the surface.

The British attack was falling upon under 1,000 Turks who constituted the 3rd Battalion of the Turkish 26th Regiment, which had taken over the Helles defences on April 23rd.* The troops had not slept properly for three nights; during the previous day a heavy naval bombardment and frequent patrols by British aircraft—themselves a wonder—had convinced them that an attack was imminent. After the moon had set on the night of April 24th–25th 'there was a feeling of danger'; first light had revealed the sea filled with warships and transports, and then came the bombardment, an awful nightmare of tumult and fear. They had no artillery, and only four Maxim guns at Sedd-el-Bahr.† As the smoke cleared, the survivors could see that the enemy armada was almost upon them.

As the 'tows' for V and S Beaches made to the east, those for X and W Beaches crept towards the silent Peninsula. The naval barrage had ended, the sailors bent to their oars, and the little boats glided towards the beaches. 'To see those boats going in towards the beach, which we knew was so strongly fortified, like a sort of parade as the day broke, is a sight I shall never forget', Wemyss has related.

Further to the north, at Y Beach, 2,000 British troops of the King's Own Scottish Borderers, one company of South Wales Borderers, and the Plymouth Battalion of Marines, were landing without any resistance of any kind. By 6 a.m. they were comfortably established; scouting parties were sent inland to reconnoitre the empty countryside; lines of men carrying ammunition and glittering kerosene cans of water up the zig-zag track from the beach constituted the only activity visible at Y Beach when *Queen Elizabeth* steamed past from Anzac to Helles.

At X Beach, a picquet of 12 hapless Turks had been stupefied by the bom-

* The First Battalion was holding the coast to the north-west of Krithia; the Second Batalion was in reserve south-east of Krithia, making a total of about 2,000 men in the immediate vicinity of the main British landings at Helles.

† The British state that the Turks also had two Maxims at W Beach, which the Turks have denied.

bardment laid down by *Implacable*, and had offered no resistance; by 6.30 a.m. the covering force of two companies of the Royal Fusiliers had scaled the cliffs without suffering a single casualty, and the boats were hastening back to the transports to pick up the main force. 'I recollect a bright sunny morning, a dead calm sea, not a shot fired', an officer later wrote. 'I had a bag in one hand, a coat over my arm, and was assisted down a plank from the boat by an obliging sailor, so that I should not wet my boots. The only thing missing was the hotel.' Had the X Beach detachment looked to the east, they might have seen the three companies of the South Wales Borderers encamped on the further extremity of Morto Bay, having landed successfully at S Beach.

This had been another admirably efficient landing. Covered by the guns of *Cornwallis*, two companies had been rowed ashore under a brisk but erratic fire while the third company was landed at the foot of the cliff under De Tott's Battery. The defending platoon on the crest was quickly overcome by this third company, which had scrambled up the cliff in shirt-sleeves, and the tip of Morto Bay was firmly in the hands of the Borderers. One of the captured Turks told the commanding officer that there were about 1,000 troops in the area; this was literally true,* but the Colonel assumed that they were in his immediate vicinity, and started to dig in. This was warmly supported by Hunter-Weston in *Euryalus*, who sent a message of congratulation and encouragement, and told the Borderers to hold on to their position.

A mile to the south of X Beach, the Lancashire Fusiliers were engaged on a very different kind of battle at W Beach. The Turks, although very few in number, had not been dislodged by the naval bombardment, which indeed on account of its very horror had created in them a kind of desperate determination. From the accounts of the very few survivors it is evident that they had no illusions about their chances, and were surprised to find themselves alive at all. Their trenches were mainly undamaged, the wire on the beach was untouched, and the boats toiling towards the gleaming sand made a perfect target. They had strict orders not to open fire until the enemy was 100 metres away.

Just before the first boat grounded, the shooting began. 'Not a sign of life was to be seen on the peninsula in front of us,' Major Willis of the Fusiliers, destined to win one of the regiment's six V.C.s on that beach, has related; 'it might have been a deserted land we were nearing in our little boats. Then, crack! The stroke oar of my boat fell forward, to the angry astonishment of his mates.' The soldiers jumped from the boats and started

---

* Turkish prisoners at Anzac accurately described their forces south of Gaba Tepe as consisting of only two regiments; this important information was sent to *Queen Elizabeth* at 12.40 p.m., and repeated at 5 p.m. and 10.50 p.m. The British refused to believe it, and it was not until some ten years later that the very small size of the Turkish force at Helles was realised.

hacking furiously at the wire, while the water boiled. Some jumped too soon, and sank like stones, their khaki bodies plainly visible in the clear water; others were hit as they sat helplessly in the boats; more were shot down as they battled, waist-deep in the water, with the accursed wire. To the amazement and relief of the onlookers from the warships, a party tore its way through the wire at one point and raced across the beach; more gaps were cut, and more drenched, grim Lancastrians streamed through. One participant in this wild charge, a Captain Clayton, who was killed six weeks later, wrote shortly afterwards:

> There was tremendously strong barbed wire where my boat landed. Men were being hit in the boats and as they splashed ashore. I got up to my waist in water, tripped over a rock and went under, got up and made for the shore and lay down by the barbed wire. There was a man there before me shouting for wire-cutters. I got mine out, but could not make the slightest impression. The front of the wire by now was a thick mass of men, the majority of whom never moved again. . . . The noise was ghastly and the sights horrible. I eventually crawled through the wire with great difficulty, as my pack kept catching on the wire, and got under a small mound which actually gave us protection. The weight of our packs tired us, so that we could only gasp for breath. After a little time we fixed bayonets and started up the cliffs right and left. On the right several were blown up by a mine.* When we started up the cliff the enemy went, but when we got to the top they were ready and poured shots on us.

A Major Shaw, also not destined to survive the campaign, wrote of the landing:

> About 100 yards from the beach the enemy opened fire, and bullets came thick all around, splashing up the water. I didn't see anyone actually hit in the boats, though several were; e.g. my Quartermaster-Sergeant and Sergeant-Major sitting next to me; but we were so jammed together that you couldn't have moved, so that they must have been sitting there, dead. As soon as I felt the boat touch, I dashed over the side into three feet of water and rushed for the barbed wire entanglements on the beach; it must have been only three feet high or so, because I got over it amidst a perfect storm of lead and made for cover, sand dunes on the other side, and got good cover. I then found Maunsell and only two men had followed me. On the right of me on the cliff was a line of Turks in a trench taking pot shots at us, ditto on the left. I looked back. There was one soldier between me and the wire, and a whole line in a row on the edge of the sands. The sea behind was absolutely crimson, and you could hear the groans through the rattle of musketry. A few were firing. I signalled to them to advance. I shouted to the soldier behind me to signal, but he shouted back 'I am shot through the chest'. I then perceived they were all hit.

In the face of this fierce assault the Turkish fire began to falter, but in spite of the valour and spirit of the Fusiliers, things might have gone badly for them had not the commander of the covering force, Brigadier-General Hare, spotted a reasonable landing to the left of the beach under Tekke Burnu, and personally directed his men to this point. The Navy had appreciated the importance of this beach on the 23rd and had reported to this effect

* It was in fact a British naval shell.

to G.H.Q., but Hare had never been told. The troops who landed under the cliff were sheltered from the fire of the defenders, and scrambled up to the summit to take the defences from the left flank. Firing began to die down, the British were landing in greater numbers, and the landing had been made good. But the three Turkish platoons in the vicinity of W Beach had inflicted over 500 casualties on the 950 officers and men who had left *Euryalus*,* and the survivors were falling back with great skill, making excellent use of cover. Behind them, just over the brow of the ridge, the battalion commander was dispatching his only reserves to meet the threats from X Beach and V Beach and had none to spare for the sorely pressed remnants of the W Beach contingent. The way to what both the British and Turkish commanders regarded as the vital eminence, Hill 138, was virtually open.

At this critical moment, Hare, while leading a party of signallers with reckless gallantry to link up with the X Beach detachment, was severely wounded. By the time that this fact was realised, the situation around W Beach had become extremely confused. Compasses, field-glasses and watches had been ruined by immersion in the sea, and the sodden maps were so vague and inaccurate that there was considerable confusion in determining where Hill 138 was. Hare's successor in command was killed shortly after he had taken over while reconnoitring to the east, where heavy firing could be heard from the direction of V Beach. Heavy casualties among officers and the unexpected fierceness of the enemy resistance, when combined with an understandable bewilderment and inertia among the men, combined tragically to hold up the advance so brilliantly begun.

For the troops of the main body, which were now arriving off the Peninsula, the journey from Lemnos had been delightful. 'It was a pleasant morning,' one officer wrote shortly afterwards, 'calm as to the sea and warm overhead. Dark wisps of smoke above the horizon ahead of us told of transports and warships on the move. And ever the angry mutterings in the air grew louder.' There were some delays in ferrying the men ashore as so many boats had been damaged in the landing, but within an hour of the first assault a number of troops of the main body were ashore at X and W Beaches. Abruptly transferred from the safety and comfort of the transports, the new arrivals were considerably startled by the wild scene when they landed. 'One hundred corpses lay in rows in the sand,' an army chaplain later recorded of the scene, 'some of them so badly mauled as to be beyond recognition. All over the strip of sand, and on ledges of rock, wherever any cover could be got, men lay about wounded, cut, bleeding and dying.

---

* The Lancashire Fusiliers lost in the W Beach landing 6 officers and 183 men killed, 4 officers and 279 men wounded, and 61 men missing, a total of 533 casualties. The regiment won 6 V.C.s, 2 D.S.O.s, 2 M.C.s, and 1 D.C.M.

Some of the Lancashires lay dead half-way up the cliffs, still holding their rifles in their cold, clenched hands. Dead and wounded lay about, mixed up together.' 'A blazing sun, a continuous bombardment from the Navy, incessant musketry-fire ashore, bullets still pattering on to the sand and splashing in the water, a party of stolid Turkish prisoners building the first small stone pier, and the long sad rows of eternally silent figures, their drenched and blood-stained khaki drying in the sun—such were the most vivid impressions of W Beach as we leaped ashore', a subaltern wrote soon after. Midshipman Tate of *Implacable*, who had spent the night in a cutter at the end of a long 'tow' en route for X Beach, was disagreeably struck by the very different scenes on W Beach when he landed troops there at 10 a.m. 'A derelict cutter full of dead and water-logged, formed a basis for a temporary pier. About 50 Turks suddenly appeared overhead, fired at us and then surrendered. 4 of our men found a sniper hidden in the cliff and bayoneted him and chucked him over the cliff. All his insides came out. A subaltern and 3 men tried to locate some other snipers who were firing at us, but each in turn gave little starts and fell down dead. One was wounded and staggered towards us, crying'.

But in spite of the confusion around W Beach which so disconcerted the new arrivals, the situation facing the Turks was in fact far worse. The X Beach force had beaten off a last counter-attack, reinforcements were coming ashore at X and W, and the Turkish commander had absolutely no reserves left. At about 11.30 a.m. men of the Essex Regiment had joined up with a detachment of the Royal Fusiliers from X. The Turks in the area were now outflanked and outnumbered by over ten to one.

Although heavy fire could be heard from V Beach, Hunter-Weston had no information until early in the afternoon of the progress of events there. It would have taken barely five minutes for *Euryalus* to steam to V to enable the divisional commander to see for himself, but the cruiser remained off W all day. It was not until about 12.30 p.m. that a brave officer, Captain Farmar, climbed to a position on the right from where he could see V Beach; his report did not reach the Colonel who had taken over the W Beach operations until 1.10 p.m., and was not received on *Euryalus* until about 1.30 p.m. And thus it was that Hunter-Weston received the news of the action being fought at V Beach, only a few minutes' sailing away, seven hours too late.

The V Beach landing, on which everything hinged, had been delayed by the strong current which had held up the 'tows', and *River Clyde* had run gently ashore under Sedd-el-Bahr castle at 6.20 a.m. at the same time that the flotilla of ship's boats carrying the 1st Battalion, the Royal Dublin Fusiliers, reached the beach. V Beach was a natural amphitheatre. On the right the battered castle; in the middle, ground sloping gently up towards a ridge; on the left, the sheer slopes of Cape Helles. Complete silence reigned.

A staff officer on *River Clyde* wrote in a notebook as she came to a stop: '6.22 a.m. Ran smoothly ashore without a tremor. No opposition. We shall land unopposed.' To his right, but out of sight, two more platoons of the Dublin Fusiliers were going ashore at the Camber landing.

As at W Beach, the Turks had been shaken but not crushed by the naval bombardment, and the long interval which elapsed between the shelling and the actual landing enabled them to return to their trenches and take up their positions. A total of three platoons and four old machine-guns constituted the sum total of the defenders of V Beach. They held their fire until the boats grounded, and then, with a terrible crash, the awful fusillade began.

The scenes which followed have been often described. The shattered cutters, now full only of the dead and dying, drifting away from the beach; the floundering, screaming troops; the ugly crimson stain which spread rapidly over the placid water; the piles of corpses at the edge of the beach and in front of the barbed wire; the spume from the hail of bullets drifting lazily across the water. One survivor, of the Dublins, has related that when all the sailors in his boat were killed or wounded, the soldiers grabbed the oars, and the boat drifted broadside on to the shore. 'Just before we grounded, the boat was hit once or twice with incendiary shells, and commenced to go on fire. She was also half-full of water from the many holes in her by this time. Several of the men who had been wounded fell to the bottom of the boat, and were either drowned there or suffocated by other men falling on top of them; many, to add to their death agonies, were burnt as well. We then grounded, and I jumped out of the bows of the boat and got hit in the head, other bullets going into a pack that I was carrying on my shoulders. I went under water and came up again, and tried to encourage the men to get to the shore and under cover as fast as they could as it was their only chance. I then went under again. Someone caught hold of me and began pulling me ashore. . . . Looking back out to sea I saw the remnants of my platoon trying to get to the shore, but they were shot down one after another, and their bodies drifted out to sea or lay immersed a few feet from the shore.'

Major David French, also of the Dublins, wrote of the scene in a letter he sent to his family a few days later:

I was in the last boat of my 'tow' and did not realise they had started at my boat until one of the men close to me fell back dead—shot. I realised immediately that having practically wiped out those in the three boats ahead they were now concentrating their fire on us. I jumped out at once into the sea (up to my chest) yelling at the men to make a rush for it and to follow me. But the poor devils—packed like sardines in a tin and carrying this damnable weight on their backs—could scarcely clamber over the sides of the boat and only two reached the shore un-hit. . . .

I had to run about 100–150 yards in the water and being the first away from the cutter escaped the fire a bit to start with. But as soon as a few followed me the water around seemed to be alive—the bullets striking the sea all round us. Heaven alone knows how I got thro'. . . . When I was about 50 yards from the water's edge I felt one bullet go thro' the pack on my back and then thought I had got through safely when they put one through my left arm. . . .

I could find only 30 or 40 men intact and we commenced to dig ourselves into the low cliff. Why the Turks with their vast preparations did not level this bank of earth down I cannot imagine. Had they done so, none of us would have escaped.

Meanwhile, Unwin was struggling to create the bridge of lighters from *River Clyde* to the beach, as the steam hopper which had been meant to do this task had been swept away and was useless. Unwin dived into the sea with a rope, followed by an able-seaman called Williams whom Unwin had told to stay beside him throughout the day. Together, they managed to lash some of the lighters together, and, holding one of them in position himself, Unwin yelled to *River Clyde* for the landing to begin.

The men of the Munster Fusiliers and the Hampshire Regiment, pouring eagerly out of the sally-ports and down the gangways, entered the scene just after the first fury of the killing had ended; they met the full blast of the Turkish fire, now concentrated on *River Clyde*. The gangways and lighters were quickly choked with the dead and wounded; only a handful of men, dodging, leaping and slithering across the lighters and through the red water, managed to reach the shore, where they joined the survivors of the Dublins taking cover under a ridge of sand about four feet high at the water's-edge. Williams was then mortally wounded,* Unwin grabbed him, and the lighters swung away again, severing the link between *River Clyde* and the beach.

Hunter-Weston, five minutes' sailing away, knew nothing of all this, and took no steps to discover the situation. The first report he received was that 'troops from collier appear to be getting ashore well'; at 7.50 a.m. he was told that British troops could be seen in Sedd-el-Bahr, and at 8.30 a.m. he ordered the main body to land.

The boats which had taken the original covering force were now either riddled with bullets or were littered around the bay. 'The shore became full of enemy corpses, like a shoal of fish', the Turkish commander reported. The sufferings of the wounded were terrible; as Josiah Wedgwood, a flamboyant Liberal M.P. commanding the machine-guns mounted at the bows of *River Clyde*, related a few days later in a letter to Churchill: 'The wounded cried out all day—in every boat, lighter, hopper and all along the shore. It was horrible, and all within 200 yards of our guns'.

There was only room for General Napier, commanding the main force, his staff and a few soldiers, in the few watertight boats. As they approached the beach the officers on *River Clyde* frantically shouted that it was impossible

* He and Unwin were awarded the V.C.

to land; 'I'll have a damned good try', Napier shouted back, but he and most of those with him were dead long before they reached the shore.

Hamilton, de Robeck and Keyes, who had arrived in *Queen Elizabeth*, were horrified witnesses of this dreadful scene. 'V Beach was a heartbreaking and infuriating spectacle', Brodie has written. '. . . Further west, boats were aground, apparently empty, and abreast of them dark litter spread up the sand. Glasses revealed the litter as dead men, and what had looked like old clothes hanging over lines farther inland, as the bodies of our gallant wire-cutters.' As soon as de Robeck discovered that there had been no advance, *Queen Elizabeth* opened fire. If this second bombardment had been in concert with another attempt to land it might well have succeeded, but no move was made until the clouds of smoke and dust had cleared, and as soon as the men behind the ridge tried to move, in Keyes' words, 'that dreadful tat-tat-tat of machine-gun fire burst out afresh'. 'Sedd-el-Bahr was a perfect inferno,' an eye-witness on *Cornwallis* has written, 'and the dark silhouette of *Queen Elizabeth* loomed through a fog of green, black and yellow smoke as she fired her broadsides at a terrific rate.' It was all to no avail; beyond covering the survivors under the precious ledge of sand, the warships were powerless.

There was an immediate and hurried discussion on the battleship. Hamilton was becoming aware of the grave disadvantages of having no direct control over the movements of ships in an amphibious operation and of trying to conduct land operations from the decks of a warship which had its own functions to perform; his miserable General Staff officers, packed into gun-turrets and various clanging recesses of the great battleship, might as well have stayed at Lemnos. The Administrative Staff, of course, was miles away, incarcerated on *Arcadian*. Hunter-Weston was still firmly stationed off W beach in *Euryalus*, supremely ignorant of the developments of the battle in which his division was engaged. When Hamilton suggested that the troops destined for V Beach might land at Y Beach, Braithwaite was doubtful 'as to whether it was sound for G.H.Q. to barge into Hunter-Weston's plans, seeing he was executive Commander of the whole of this southern invasion.' Ever since the creation of a General Staff on German lines after the Boer War, it had been axiomatic that a commander-in-chief should not interfere once battle was joined; to this philosophy Hamilton strictly adhered. 'It was not for me to force his hands,' he later wrote; 'there was no question of that.' Eventually Hamilton sent a message to Hunter-Weston at 9.15 a.m. which read, 'Would you like to get some more men ashore on Y Beach? If so trawlers are available.' No reply came, and when Hamilton eventually repeated the message, Hunter-Weston replied at 11 a.m. that he was advised by Wemyss that 'to interfere with present arrangements and try to land men at Y Beach would delay disembarkation.' With this Hamilton had to be content, and the troops of the Worcestershire Regiment intended for

123

V Beach were diverted to W, where the congestion and confusion were alike becoming acute.

The situation around the south-west tip of the Peninsula was extraordinary. The Turkish battalion commander had committed his last reserves to X and V Beaches, and those sent to X had been roughly handled; the Turkish resistance in the sector was now reduced to a handful of desperate men. Not until 9 p.m. did units of the 25th Regiment reach the Helles area, by which time the two battalions of the 26th Regiment had almost ceased to exist.

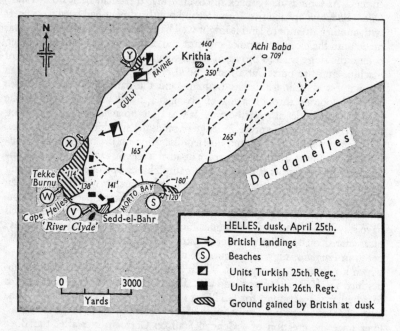

HELLES, dusk, April 25th.
⇒ British Landings
Ⓢ Beaches
◪ Units Turkish 25th. Regt.
■ Units Turkish 26th. Regt.
▨ Ground gained by British at dusk

0 — 3000 Yards

But it was not until after 3 p.m. that the British at last captured Hill 138, and not until evening that the X and W Beach forces were properly linked up. The hard-pressed Turkish commander appealed for reinforcements—'if no reinforcements are sent there will be no prospect of defence or of driving the enemy back'—but got no reply until the evening, when he was peremptorily ordered to 'drive the enemy into the sea'. Meanwhile, Hunter-Weston was ordering his men to entrench and consolidate the position they had occupied virtually without change since 11 a.m. A last attempt to come to the assistance of the V Beach force from W Beach by an attack up towards a well-wired and entrenched position on Cape Helles was beaten back.

Meanwhile, an even more strange situation had developed at Y Beach. The detachment had spent an undisturbed morning. There had been a lamentable failure to give positive orders to the commander, and indeed there was some confusion as to who was the senior officer. Lt.-Col. Koe of the Scottish Borderers thought that he was in command, but at a divisional conference on April 21st it had been discovered that Lt.-Col. Matthews of the Marines was in fact the senior, and had been put in command. Koe had not attended the conference as he was in poor health, and no one had thought of telling him of the decision. Matthews' orders from Hunter-Weston were verbal and imprecise; he was 'to advance some little distance inland, capture a Turkish gun thought to have been located in the vicinity, and, by attracting the Turkish reserves towards himself, to interfere with the reinforcement of Helles and Sedd-el-Bahr.' Almost as an afterthought, he was also instructed to get in touch with the X Beach force, and when the main advance developed, to join the rest of the division in the march to the north.

A scouting party of Marines had been promptly sent inland, and had found only four startled Turks; two companies of the Borderers had penetrated as far as an unexpected deep ravine—later called Gully Ravine—that debouched into the sea a mile or so to the south of the Y Beach position. This formidable obstacle was barely marked on the inaccurate and misleading beautifully printed, multi-coloured, linen-backed maps issued to the officers. More scouting parties were sent out, and Matthews, with his adjutant, walked across to the deserted village of Krithia before returning to the camp which sprawled along the cliff-top. Koe, still under the impression that he was in command, appealed to divisional headquarters for information and advice, but received no reply. The officers began to feel uncomfortably isolated. From the south they could hear the sound of fighting but could get no information as to what was happening; it was a delicious day, and the green country-side was devoid of any enemy troops.

In fact, the landing had been reported by a platoon on the coast, and orders had been issued at once by the divisional commander for the 25th Regiment to march south; the 3rd battalion set off at 11.30 p.m., reached Krithia at about 2.30 p.m., and was dispatched to Y Beach at once while the other two battalions still on the march were ordered to continue to the Helles area, where they arrived at about 9 p.m. Until the 3rd battalion came into action near Y Beach, the total Turkish forces in the area consisted of one company of infantry. By 3 p.m. the British decided to entrench, but it was too late, and at a quarter to six a series of Turkish attacks, most gallantly led and delivered, began to develop. By nightfall the Y Beach force was in a state of siege, and was appealing for reinforcements; again, no reply came. When Hamilton asked Hunter-Weston in the evening for news of the Y Beach force, the divisional commander merely retorted that he had heard it was being hard-pressed, 'but as he had heard nothing more since then he assumed that they were all right.'

In marked contrast with the remarkable efficiency of the Anzac and British landings, the French landing at Kum Kale had been something less than the glittering triumph sometimes claimed for it.* Although the bombardment laid down by the Russian cruiser *Askold* and the *Prince George* had opened promptly at 5.15 a.m., it was not until nearly five hours later that the troops actually got ashore. Kum Kale itself was only defended by one platoon of infantry, which slowly retired as the French came ashore, eventually finishing up in a cemetery in the outskirts of the town, where another platoon reinforced it. The Turkish troops in the vicinity were far greater in number than those south of Achi Baba on the Peninsula, but they fought with an entirely different spirit. The Turkish commander of the 3rd Division was no Kemal or Essad; in the words of the official Turkish account, he 'had issued many orders in great anxiety, had made many arrangements without much meaning and had sent his troops to Kum Kale [to attack] without a commander. In the end Army Corps Headquarters had to warn him and ordered him to move forward.' The ground is flat and marshy, and the naval bombardment had been deadly; demoralised and leaderless, the Turks retreated to a safe distance beyond the Mendere River, and the French—under 3,000 in number—landed without any opposition to occupy the village of Kum Kale, shattered by the British bombardments of the past two months. 'On each side of the main street, which opened on the east gate of the castle, houses—perhaps some hundred—stand gutted, with only fragments of wall, desolate and in ruins,' wrote the French doctor to his wife. 'Some had preserved signs of their former occupation. A watchmaker's shop still had its signboard flapping in the wind, and a display of cuckoo-clocks.'

Partly, but not entirely, due to the strong Dardanelles current, it was not until 5.30 p.m. that the French were properly ashore, and ready to begin to move in the general direction of Yeni Shehr. The Turks had recovered some of their nerve in the face of this dilatoriness; as dusk began to fall and resistance increased, the French were halted and forced to entrench in a position roughly half-way between Kum Kale and Yeni Shehr. The commander of the 3rd Division, under peremptory orders to attack, gave no indication of where and when this was to occur beyond ordering the men to attack the enemy with the bayonet; although some field artillery was now available, it was almost completely ignored; 'in most cases,' the Turkish account states, 'the orders were delivered verbally to companies and battalions as they were met on the way.' In spite of these confusing conditions the Turks now displayed the same valour as their compatriots at Sedd-el-Bahr, and increasingly bitter fighting developed on the outskirts of Kum Kale. The smoke from

* See, for example, Moorehead: *Gallipoli*, 150.

burning houses rose several hundred feet into the still evening air. 'In the scintillating blue sky, where glaucous greens and incandescent golds mingle, an enormous cloud rises over Kum Kale,' the French doctor wrote. 'It remains there till dark, continually changing its shape.'

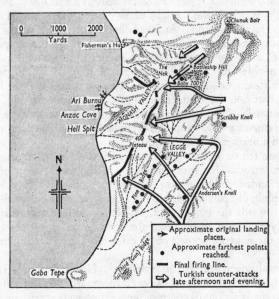

Anzac, April 25th, 1915

And so night fell on the separate battlefields. Far to the north Bernard Freyberg swam ashore near Bulair to light flares, with the object of distracting the local Turkish troops. He swam for over two hours in the freezing water to get ashore, lit his flares, and then swam back. The ships were showing no lights, the stars were hidden by the clouds, and the guns—whose flashes might have helped him—were silent; it was miraculous that he was seen after swimming for more than two hours.

At Anzac, a thin drizzle was falling on the parties of exhausted men clinging to their precarious positions in the scrub, subjected to an unending roar of rifle-fire. At Y Beach a frantic battle was raging in the darkness. At X and W Beaches the men were digging in, and there was a great deal of wild firing at bushes and shadows. At V Beach, as Aspinall has written, 'night closed in on that unforgettable scene with the thin line of tired troops still clinging to their precarious position, the sombre silhouette of ridge and fort still barring their advance, and the burning village reddening sea and sky.' 'The rattle of musketry', a subaltern wrote, 'became more pronounced as the evening wore on, sharper, quicker, more distraught, as if thousands of death-dice were being tossed feverishly by the nervous hands of a multitude of professional gamblers.' *Queen Elizabeth* delivered a final bombardment of Sedd-el-Bahr which, it was thought, must destroy those dogged defenders. 'Not so', as Hamilton wrote. 'Amidst falling ruins; under smoke clouds of yellow, black, green and white; the beach, the cliffs and the ramparts of the castle began, in the oncoming dusk, to sparkle all over with hundreds of tiny flecks of rifle-fire.' The gallant 3rd battalion of the Turkish 26th Regiment had virtually ceased to exist; 'on receiving reports from his subordinates the battalion commander could give moral support only,' the terse Turkish chronicle of the fortunes of this sacrificial battalion states. '. . . But the reinforcements and ammunition for which he had asked did not come, and his own ammunition was exhausted.'

As darkness fell on V Beach, men could lift their heads at last, and for a time movement was almost unrestricted. The thousand or so men in *River Clyde* were landed, and the piteously crying wounded had to wait until this was accomplished; many crawled to the end of the rock spit which stretched invitingly towards the collier, and, as Wedgwood bitterly related, 'there they slowly sank and died'. Soon the moon rose, the firing broke out again from the sinister blackness of the castle and the village, and movement ceased.

Hamilton, although gravely concerned about Helles, had no fears for Anzac when he retired to bed on board *Queen Elizabeth*. But the situation there had become extremely serious. Reports of the fighting were extremely vague and difficult to piece together; a major error had been made of seeking information from the wounded and stragglers who were constantly drifting back to the beach. Not surprisingly, the picture which their reports presented was sombre, if not desperate. The shambles in Anzac Cove itself had now assumed grim proportions, a chilling drizzle was falling, the sea was rising ominously, the men had all the signs of a beaten and demoralised army, and a massive counter-attack at dawn was regarded as inevitable. The rows of the wounded awaiting evacuation now covered the beach to an extent that, as the naval beachmaster reported, 'it was with difficulty that in the darkness one could pick one's way between the stretchers covering the whole width of the beach, at one time for 100 yards or so.' Bridges and Godley, the Australian and New Zealand divisional commanders, decided to ask Birdwood to come ashore.

Birdwood landed soon after 10 o'clock, and met Bridges and Godley in the former's dug-out, which was nothing more than a rudimentary hole in the hill-side, covered with a tarpaulin, and illuminated by two guttering candles. Outside the rumble of the firing could be plainly heard above the shouts of the beach personnel, the cries of the wounded, the crash of the waves, and the uproar of an army in apparent confusion and disorder. All were dead-tired, although Birdwood was the freshest. Bridges was a Scottish emigrant to Australia, dour and cautious almost to a fault, and not a man likely to be easily rattled. Godley, in spite of a certain insensitiveness that did not make him popular with his New Zealanders, was a determined officer with a streak of rashness. Both had been astounded when their officers had proposed withdrawal, but after trying to discover what the exact situation was,* had come to the conclusion that the crisis was such to merit such a desperate proposal. Birdwood was taken aback by the very suggestion of evacuation, but Bridges and Godley were so emphatic that he eventually agreed, with considerable reluctance,† to dictate the following letter to Hamilton which Godley wrote out on an ordinary message form:

> Both my divisional generals and brigadiers have represented to me that they fear their men are thoroughly demoralised by shrapnel-fire to which they have been subjected all day after exhaustion and gallant work in morning. Numbers have dribbled back from firing-line and cannot be collected in this difficult country. Even New Zealand brigade which has been only recently engaged has lost heavily and is to some extent demoralised. If troops are subjected to shell fire again to-morrow morning there is likely to be a fiasco as I have no fresh troops with which to replace those in firing line. I know my representation is most serious but if we are to re-embark it must be at once.

It was by pure chance that this message ever reached Hamilton. In the general confusion it was not addressed to anyone, and eventually reached Admiral Thursby at 11 p.m. He was understandably disconcerted. 'The night had turned dark and stormy,' he subsequently wrote, 'our men were tired and disorganised, the confusion in any attempt to re-embark would have been indescribable and our losses must have been appalling.' He was setting out to put these facts before Birdwood when his launch was hailed by the officer of the watch; *Queen Elizabeth* had returned from Helles, and Thursby at once ordered the launch to the flagship.

Hamilton was in a deep sleep when he was awakened by Braithwaite, and, hastily pulling on a British warm over his pyjamas, he crossed into de Robeck's dining saloon, where he found de Robeck, Thursby, Keyes, Braithwaite—'chewing his big moustache', as one present has related, 'but making no comment or suggestion'—and two of the senior Anzac officers (one of whom was Cunliffe-Owen, now commanding the Anzac artillery).

* It was the opinion of Birdwood's Chief of Staff, the fire-eating Brig.-General H. B. Walker, that these attempts had been inadequate, and he is said to have addressed Bridges in terms which could have jeopardised his career.

† In his account of the events on April 25th in his diary, Birdwood wrote: 'I let Sir Ian on *Queen Elizabeth* know their [Godley's and Bridges'] feelings in [the] matter but decided to remain on.'

As Hamilton entered the room, 'a cold hand clutched my heart as I scanned their faces.' Brodie was also present: 'Sir Ian, roused from sleep after a long and fateful day, looked only a trifle less immaculate and nearer his age than usual, and was his calm and courteous self. De Robeck, as ever, a figure of quiet strength at Sir Ian's side; the rest looked glum and anxious.' Brodie left before the conference began.

After reading Birdwood's message, Hamilton asked for Thursby's views; he was emphatically against evacuation, and Keyes warmly supported him. Hamilton sat down at the table and began a reply to Birdwood. Brodie then re-entered the room. He had just received a message from AE2 that she had passed through the Narrows and had sunk an enemy ship,* and considered that Keyes should know at once; 'the atmosphere was tense,' he relates, '. . . and Keyes was furious at my intrusion, but I refused to be shooed out until he came with me to read it. Then, of course, he instantly recognised its import, darted back delightedly into the cabin, and in two minutes was out again, beaming, to say, "It's done the trick".' In fact, Hamilton had reached his decision as soon as he heard Thursby's opinion that evacuation was administratively impossible, and he only nodded when Keyes burst in with the news of AE2's exploit.

> Your news is indeed serious. But there is nothing for it but to dig yourselves right in and stick it out. It would take at least two days to re-embark you as Admiral Thursby will explain to you. Meanwhile, the Australian submarine has got up through the Narrows and has torpedoed a gun-boat at Chunuk (sic) at Chunuk. Hunter-Weston despite his heavy losses will be advancing tomorrow which should divert pressure from you. Make a personal appeal to your men and Godley's to make a supreme effort to hold their ground.
>
> Ian Hamilton.
>
> P.S. You have got through the difficult business, now you have only to dig, dig, dig, until you are safe. Ian H.

Thursby at once left for Anzac with this resolute message. The night was so dark and the sea so rough that he began to wonder if he would ever deliver it. His account of the events of that critical night continues:

> It was pitch dark, so we stood in until we could see the white breakers and hear the noise of the surf. It looked as if it would be impossible to land in the steam-boat, when, fortunately, we saw a small merchant ship's boat rowed by two naval seamen and called them alongside. They said they had just landed two officers and were returning to their ship. They were just as unconcerned as if they had been coming off from a routine trip after dinner in peacetime, although bullets were coming over our lines and dropping all around them. We got into their boat and after several attempts and getting very wet, we got on shore.
>
> We found ourselves on the right of our position in what was afterwards known as

* AE2 operated in the Marmara until April 30th, when she was sunk, after a two hours' fight, by a Turkish torpedo-boat. It was not for many months, however, that her fate was known. Lt.-Commander Stoker's account of AE2's exploits, *Straws in the Wind*, is one of the classics of submarine warfare.

Anzac Cove. Rows of wounded men were laid out in front of us under the shelter of some rising ground. The doctors in charge, who evidently expected that the beach might be rushed at any moment, implored me to have them taken off as it was murder to leave them there. I promised to do my best for them and went off to find Birdwood who, I was told, was on the beach, a little further along. The beach was crowded with men; some, exhausted after the strenuous day, had just thrown themselves down and slept like logs; some were getting food and drink for the first time for many hours, others were being collected by officers and N.C.O.s and being formed into organised units, being sent either to reinforce the fighting line or to prepare positions to fall back on in case of necessity. I found General Birdwood sitting down with his Divisional Generals and Staff. Birdwood, whom nothing could daunt and who is never so happy as when in the fighting line, and for preference in a tight spot, was cheerful but not very hopeful. I gave him Sir Ian's letter and said I hoped he would be able to hold out till the morning, when we could take stock of the situation, and I thought when daylight came, many of the isolated positions we had seen holding on before dark would be able to join hands and form a continuous line on which they could consolidate and dig themselves in.

It is probable that too much has been made of the effect of Hamilton's message by numerous historians of the campaign. Both Bridges and Godley by now had had second thoughts, and regretted that the first message had ever been sent. Birdwood and Walker would not hear of evacuation, and the thought had hardly occurred to any of the troops. Digging* of new positions to defend the beach had already begun, in anticipation of the expected counter-attack in the morning, and although Hamilton's message undoubtedly relieved Birdwood and his divisional commanders, it is hardly accurate to describe its effect as 'electrical', which is the adjective selected by the official historian. It is perhaps unfair to remove from Hamilton the credit for the only intervention he had attempted in the conduct of operations throughout the day, but the evidence is that by the time Birdwood's message reached him the Anzac commanders had already decided to dig in and hang on.

'I spent an awful night on the beach,' Birdwood wrote in his diary, 'with the thought that morning might bring disaster.' Above him, the drenched and exhausted troops lay in the scrub and fired incessantly into the wet darkness in front of them. 'Never shall I forget that night', Major French of the Dublins, at V Beach, wrote shortly afterwards: 'Heavy rifle fire incessantly. Drizzling with rain. Wounded groaning on all sides and surrounded by dead, I admit I thought it was all up.' 'The beaches were covered with the bodies of the dead, and the slopes with limbs, heads and bodies', a Turkish survivor of the Sedd-el-Bahr fighting has written: 'The small dried-up streams were flowing with blood.'

In the tumult of that terrible night the armies of both sides hung on grimly for what perils the morrow might bring.

* Contrary to a popular misapprehension, the Australian soldiers did not acquire the nickname of 'Diggers' until considerably later in the war, in France.

6

The Battle for Achi Baba

April 26th was another day of triumph and frustration for the British at Helles. There had been heavy firing during the night, and at midnight a staff officer on *Euryalus* wrote: 'Position appeared serious. There is no doubt that our men, whose nerves were naturally shaken by their day's work, were firing away an unnecessary quantity of ammunition, but all managed to hang on to the ground gained.' In fact, the Turks in the immediate Helles vicinity amounted to barely a thousand men. As soon as the light was good enough the warships again pounded at Sedd-el-Bahr, but the troops on V Beach were so exhausted and over-wrought that their officers had considerable difficulty in rousing them. There was a misunderstanding over the bombardment, which had been directed at Sedd-el-Bahr village rather than the fort, but eventually the troops grouped on the right of V Beach advanced to storm the fort, which was cleared comparatively quickly. Severe hand-to-hand fighting developed in the village, and for a time no progress was made. Colonel Doughty-Wylie, realising the critical importance of clearing the village quickly, came ashore from *River Clyde* with two other staff officers, Colonel Williams and Captain Walford, and took command of the troops still taking shelter on the beach. Supported by the spluttering machine-guns of *River Clyde*, the troops rose from behind their sandbanks and rushed across the rising ground into Sedd-el-Bahr village. Major Mure, a spectator from the sea, subsequently recorded that:

> It was a glorious and a terrible sight, and I felt as it looked—fearful and exultant. The infantry pushed and tore through the village of Sedd-el-Bahr up to the fort belching fire and death from the cliff beyond. The blood danced in our veins, as we leaned and looked, our souls fighting with those men struggling in the thick of the carnage. Their bayonets flashed in the dancing eastern sunlight, and as the men rattled on, bleeding, dying, yet persisting, conquering, the glittering sheen they threw before them and about

them scintillated like a sea of liquid, burnished steel, more alive than the molten sun-light it mocked and outshone, throwing great swathes of terrible searchlight for yards in front of our straining, suffering infantry, and for yards on either side of them. It was a field of the cloth of living silver. And we could hear the men shouting, 'Go on, lads: go on you devils! Give them hell!' and cries much more vitriolic, less episcopal.

The Turkish resistance in the village was fierce, and it was not until three o'clock that it was at last overcome; the survivors streamed north across the lush plain which lay beyond the coastal ridge towards the olive-groves on the lower slopes of Achi Baba.

Hunter-Weston, still obsessed by the Helles battles, had no time to cope with the agitated messages being received from Matthews at Y Beach. At 7 a.m. the news was received on *Euryalus* that the situation at Y was desperate, but Hunter-Weston merely passed on the message to Hamilton with the comment that he had no reserves to spare. Nevertheless, at 7.45 a.m. he ordered six battalions of French infantry to land at W Beach. Hunter-Weston seems to have been completely uninterested in the fate of the Y Beach force. Hamilton, whose anxieties were now almost entirely centred on it, still felt that he could not interfere with Hunter-Weston's command. Although Y Beach is only some 20 minutes' steaming from Tekke Burnu, Matthews had now received no messages from his divisional headquarters for 29 hours. At last Hamilton ordered a French brigade to Y on his own initiative, but when he arrived off the beach in *Queen Elizabeth* at 9.30 a.m. it was extremely difficult to discover what was going on. 'The *Sapphire*, *Dublin* and *Goliath* were lying close inshore', he has related, 'and we could see a trickle of our men coming down the steep cliff and parties being ferried off to the *Goliath*; the wounded, no doubt, but we did not see a single soul going *up* the cliff whereas there were many loose groups hanging about on the beach. I disliked and mistrusted the look of these aimless dawdlers by the sea. There was no fighting; a rifle-shot now and then from the crests where we saw our fellows clearly. The little crowd and the boats on the beach were right under them and no one paid any attention or seemed to be in a hurry. Our naval and military signallers were at sixes and sevens. The *Goliath* wouldn't answer; the *Dublin* said that the force was coming off, and we could not get into touch with the soldiers at all.'

Hamilton was in fact witnessing the unauthorised evacuation of the Y Beach force. The Turks, although heavily outnumbered, had pressed forward their attacks throughout the night with great determination, and a confused battle had raged for several hours. By dawn the British had suffered heavy casualties, Colonel Koe was dead, and many of the men had shot away almost all their ammunition; the fact that the Marines used different rifles and ammunition from the rest of the force increased the confusion. The Turks had also suffered heavily, and sensibly withdrew at dawn out of respect for the

133

guns of the warships;* as soon as the Navy realised what was going on, ammunition was ferried to the shore.

Some men had drifted down to the beach, and when a young officer asked for assistance his detachment was at once re-embarked by the Navy. Other officers, thinking that a withdrawal had been ordered, told their men to evacuate. By 7 a.m. several hundred men were either back on the warships or were waiting to be ferried out to them, while on the cliffs Colonel Matthews—whose courage and bearing had been exemplary throughout the fighting—and the rest of the force were beating-off a last Turkish attack. Something like panic began to spread among the ever-growing crowd of men on the beach, and frantic messages sped across to the bewildered and anxious sailors. 'Send all boats at once', one message ran; 'We are outnumbered. Hurry.' 'Send boats to Y beach. Situation desperate', another read, while one officer signalled; 'We are driven on to beach. I will give you the order when we are clear of the crest.'

When it was apparent that the Turks had withdrawn, Matthews inspected his contingent's position, and was amazed to discover that a considerable portion of it had gone, abandoning its equipment. By now the evacuation was proceeding rapidly, and he naturally assumed that it had been ordered from divisional headquarters, which was also Hamilton's assumption. The contingent re-embarked without any intervention from the Turks, but piles of equipment and precious ammunition were left on the cliffs. Later in the afternoon Roger Keyes' younger brother, Adrian, was sent ashore to make sure that no one had been left behind. The battlefield was utterly deserted; there was no sign of the enemy. Not until the evacuation was over had the Turks realised what had occurred; the remnants of the battalion which had delivered the attacks were ordered to Krithia, to help in the menacing situation at Helles. Hamilton, who had desperately wanted to intervene, was again dissuaded by Braithwaite. 'To see a part of my scheme, from which I hoped so much, go wrong before my eyes, is maddening!' Hamilton wrote. Meanwhile, oblivious and indifferent to developments elsewhere, Hunter-Weston was still in *Euryalus*, still off W Beach.

A similar confusion had arisen over the battle at Kum Kale. Throughout the 26th, d'Amade urged Hamilton to permit him to re-embark his force, and at length Hamilton reluctantly agreed.† Both were ignorant of the surprising

* Moorehead (*Gallipoli*, 148) states that 'the Turks, on their side, decided that they had been beaten, and they too withdrew.' Turkish accounts say that their troops fell back a short distance, to be out of sight of the warships and remained in their positions until they discovered that the withdrawal had taken place; they were then ordered south, to join the main battle.

† Moorehead's account of the Kum Kale operations (*Gallipoli*, 150) is brief and somewhat misleading; he also gives the misleading impression that Hamilton was considering delaying the embarkation of the Kum Kale force on April 25th when in fact the decision only came up on the following day.

developments in Asia. The Turks had attacked throughout the night, and some fierce fighting had developed on the outskirts of Kum Kale. But the French had managed to lay barbed wire in front of their positions—'As we have no poles,' the doctor wrote, 'we make use of the hundreds of dead bodies lying in front of us'—when the light was good enough the warships renewed their bombardment, and the Turks began to surrender to a force considerably smaller than their own. 'Almost all the Turkish officers had been killed', the Turkish account states. 'The units were in complete confusion. Touch between [headquarters] and units no longer existed. The surrender and acceptance of arms and prisoners took place in the same confusion.'* One large group which appeared to want to surrender killed the French officer who had gone to parley with them, and in the general confusion some Turks got into Kum Kale village, and severe street-fighting ensued for several hours before the Turks were overwhelmed. The furious French summarily executed the Turk officer in command and eight of his men. Throughout the afternoon the Turks gave themselves up in hundreds; a whole battalion took to its heels when the warships opened fire on them, and by evening the French were in undisputed possession of the area, with over 500 prisoners meekly awaiting removal. The French suffered nearly 800 casualties in the operation, of whom about 300 were killed or severely wounded; the Turks later admitted to over 2,200 men killed, wounded, or taken prisoner.

Both de Robeck and Braithwaite had urged Hamilton not to accede to d'Amade's request to abandon the Kum Kale position, and when Guépratte arrived on board Queen Elizabeth in the evening to report the true state of affairs, Hamilton at once ordered the French to maintain their position for at least another 24 hours. But d'Amade had already given the order for re-embarkation, and without any opposition from the crushed Turks, the evacuation was already in full swing.

Meanwhile, the news from Anzac was more encouraging. The troops had succeeded in digging themselves in to some extent, the expected Turkish counter-attacks had not materialised, four mountain guns had been placed on Plugge's Plateau, and the warships had shelled the Turkish troops whenever they were visible with such demoralising effect that the Turks had abandoned all plans for grand assaults in daylight. The deafening roar of musketry never ceased, and in the midst of this fearful racket, overlooked at almost every point by the enemy, units still intermixed with no real knowledge of the whereabouts of the enemy, the Anzacs dug for their lives and endeavoured to create some order out of the chaos of the previous day.

* One Turkish account also puts blame on some Christian Turk troops, who surrendered willingly to the French.

For the time being, there was absolutely no question of a renewal of the advance towards Maidos.

At Helles, although Sedd-el-Bahr had fallen at last, the British did not make any move to take advantage of their decisive victory. The Turkish defences south of Achi Baba only consisted of scattered detachments hurriedly trying to prepare new defences in front of Krithia and on the high ground above Kereves Dere. Only a handful of outpost detachments were in touch with the British, and, apart from the gallantry of a few suicidal snipers, all Turkish resistance had effectively collapsed by the afternoon of April 26th.

The British, however, were in no condition for an extended advance. They had no idea that the Turks had been routed, for intelligence reports all agreed that there was at least another division in the vicinity. Turkish prisoners, who had given this information, had stated truthfully on April 25th that there were 'only covering troops of one division south-east of Krithia', but this was misinterpreted to mean that there was another division apart from the troops which the British had been fighting; the accurate reports from Anzac of Turkish dispositions south of Achi Baba were discounted. The troops, most of whom had had no sleep for three days and nights, were completely spent; everyone was badly shaken by the fierceness of the Turkish resistance; casualties among officers—including the gallant Doughty-Wylie and Watford, both killed in the moment of victory at Sedd-el-Bahr and both subsequently awarded the Victoria Cross—had been heavy; the problem of landing and allocating food, water and ammunition was becoming acute.

Merely to record the fact that the arrangements for evacuating the wounded had broken down gives no indication of the scenes on the beaches, in the crowded lighters, and on the transports which had been converted into temporary hospital ships. The Adjutant-General and Quartermaster-General, who had not been called in at any stage in the formulation of the plans until a few days before the landings, were marooned on *Arcadian* with their staffs until April 28th. No one had dreamed of casualties such as had been suffered, and the arrangements hurriedly made at Lemnos since April 18th by Surgeon-General Birrell, the Director of Medical Services, were completely inadequate. The situation was worst at Anzac, where the scenes on April 25-26th scarred the memory of all who witnessed them. Wounded men were rowed in small boats in a rising sea from ship to ship, suffering terribly, until they found a ship which could accommodate them. There were isolated cases of the masters of merchant ships refusing to accept wounded men, and one lighter with several hundred wounded was found at 3 a.m. on the morning of April 26th drifting in the ugly swell after having been turned away by seven transports.

The conditions on the transports once the wounded got on board, which in itself was a difficult and hazardous operation as few of the ships had proper tackle, were execrable. On one transport, an Army surgeon found 'mules on the foredeck, the ship had been left dirty, the latrines were choked, the food bad, ventilation very imperfect; actual hospital accommodation was unprovided.' The unskilled orderlies refused to lift badly wounded cases from the stretchers, with the result that stretchers were in desperately short supply on shore. On the 28th a doctor summoned to one of the transports found 'chaos; 200 wounded, all varieties; ship's doctor and a naval medical officer with 2 orderlies trying to cope with cases; wounded lying all over the decks. No arrangements for feeding or bedding. Many of the cases had been hit on the 25th.' At this point the Purser stepped up to say that the food had run out.

This was all entirely unnecessary. A well-equipped hospital ship, the *Hindoo*, was available but received no orders; on April 29th it was 'discovered' off Helles and sent to Anzac. Meanwhile, on Lemnos, there was an Australian hospital, capable of accommodating 400 seriously wounded men, with surgeons, orderlies, an operating theatre and X-ray equipment, while the filthy transports set out on the long, slow journey to Alexandria. Some ships which had been properly equipped for dealing with casualties were permitted to leave the Peninsula on the 25th and 26th barely half-full of slightly wounded men, while many thousands of seriously wounded had to wait for days off the coast without adequate treatment in appalling conditions until the ship was allowed to leave for Egypt. 'Serious cases, if lucky, had [had] their wounds re-dressed once', an Australian medical officer reported of one typical consignment of wounded from the Peninsula on its arrival at Alexandria; '. . . fractured legs without splints—septic legs a bag of pus—arms gangrenous to the shoulder; cases requiring urgent surgical intervention which could not be obtained till arrival in hospital.' Another doctor reported that one ship-load of wounded arrived in Egypt 'covered with filth and muck'. One ship arrived at Alexandria with 1,600 wounded, of whom some 300 were stretcher cases; there were 4 doctors on board. The prodigies of devoted work carried out by the handful of Army and Navy surgeons could not cope with the problem. When the men reached Egypt, the hospital accommodation for this number of casualties simply did not exist, and it was only by seizing accommodation wherever available and by the work of volunteer nurses that the crisis was overcome.

Surgeon-General Birrell, who had been astounded when informed that G.H.Q. anticipated casualties of 3,000, had stated bluntly that 10,000 was a more realistic figure, and had arranged for three hospital ships with a total capacity of 2,000 and for seven transports who could accommodate a further 7,300. The whole of Birrell's necessarily hastily-concocted plan was based on the assumption that the 'stationary hospitals' would be installed on the Peninsula at an early stage to handle serious cases; the transports which were allocated hospital staff were not equipped for the treatment of anything except minor injuries. After the administrative officers were released from their incarceration on the *Arcadian* on the 28th things began to improve, although not before many lives had been unnecessarily lost and a great amount of needless suffering had been endured by the remarkably uncomplaining wounded. To take one example out of hundreds; on the first voyage of the transport *Lutzow* from Anzac to Alexandria with several hundred seriously wounded men, the only qualified doctor on board was a veterinary surgeon, and his staff consisted of grooms and clerks; the ship had been used for transporting mules; 'it was like nothing so much as a scene from the Inferno', the New Zealand official historian has written. 'I cannot help thinking,' Wemyss wrote at the end of a harsh official report on April 28th, 'that had a little less red tape and a little more common sense been used, much misery and suffering might have been averted.'

The night of April 26–27th passed peacefully at Helles, except for occasional bursts of firing when overwrought soldiers blazed away at shadows, shrubs and olive-trees. Hunter-Weston ordered the 29th Division to dig in 'and make all preparations for repelling a Turkish attack.... There will be no retiring. Every man will die at his post rather than retire.' Some three miles to the north, the small detachments of equally exhausted Turks were receiving almost identically-phrased instructions. The commander of the 9th Division proposed a withdrawal to the Achi Baba ridge, but Essad—strongly supported by von Sanders—ordered a more forward line to be held. Reinforcements from Asia were being marched to Chanak from the Besika Bay area, but could not be deployed in any strength until the 29th at the earliest. Until they arrived, the remnants of the 9th Division in the southern Peninsula would just have to hold on as best they could.

The British sent out patrols, which, after walking through deserted countryside, returned to report that the Turks seemed to have vanished. There were now over 20,000 British troops in the Helles area, opposed by about 6,300 Turks, but the British, after their original triumph in getting ashore, seem to have been afflicted with a kind of collective paralysis. The inexperience of the troops was being seen in many curious and unexpected ways. One officer related how his men seemed to be obsessed with the novelty of corpses lying around the beaches; they would drop whatever they were doing, wander over to the bodies, stare uncomprehendingly at them, and return to inform their friends 'in a surprised tone of voice, "Say, mate, that 'un's gone west!" Then the mate would give over his work, go and have a long look, come slowly back, and say, "So he has, Bill."' The shrapnel was a surprising novelty to many. 'One hears a bang, a long drawn out scream, then a sharp "Pah!" and a lot of little thuds as the bullets come down', a midshipman recorded wonderingly in his diary on April 27th.

By the afternoon of April 27th the British and French were ready, and in brilliant evening sunshine they advanced without opposition across the apparently deserted Peninsula until dusk fell and night stopped the advance. Darkness and fatigue were virtually the only opposition the Allies faced, as the Turks were still in considerable disarray, and reinforcements had only just begun to trickle into the Helles sector from Asia. But the supply situation for the British was still critical; only 28 guns had been brought ashore since the landing, and so few mules and horses had been disembarked that the already weary troops were having to carry everything themselves, and distribution of the mounds of equipment heaped on to W and V Beaches was proving laborious and difficult.

Hunter-Weston's orders for the advance on April 28th were, inevitably, somewhat imprecise. The Allied line ran from the western coast about a mile north of X Beach across to the eastern shore just north of S Beach. The British sector covered three-quarters of the line from west to east; the French contingent took over the line on the extreme right. In the middle of the Peninsula there was an uncomfortable bend in the British line which Hunter-Weston was anxious to straighten out. He contemplated an advance on the left flank to a point north of Krithia, while the British in the centre and the French on the right remained at first comparatively static, then moving forward at a considerably slower rate. A complicated wheeling movement of this nature against unlocated enemy positions and across unknown terrain with exhausted infantry and virtually no artillery support was audacious indeed.

Many units did not receive their orders until a few hours before the advance. One adjutant was woken at 2 a.m. to be told that his brigade would advance in six hours' time. 'Of course I had to go round and explain things to company officers,' he later reported, 'and they, poor fellows, being dead with lack of sleep and exhaustion, were in no condition to take much interest. . . . It was not till 7.40 a.m. that I got battalion orders out.' Another officer subsequently recalled that 'We did not receive our orders till just before the time for the advance to commence, and it was practically impossible for everyone to understand in a hurry from the map the exact position we were to reach.' But Hunter-Weston's insistence on an early advance in spite of all the hazards was fully justified. No one could reasonably have foreseen that the lines of dispirited Turks trekking northward on the previous day would be capable of offering serious resistance, and there was a strong feeling at divisional headquarters that the really hard work was over provided that the Allied advance did not lose its momentum.

The First Battle of Krithia opened at 8 a.m. on April 28th with a desultory bombardment by the fleet and the few guns which the Army had brought into position—Hamilton, off Cape Helles in *Queen Elizabeth*, compared the bombardment to 'the rumble of an express train running over fog signals'— and the British on the left flank clambered wearily out of their trenches and walked in the general direction of Krithia. They met little or no opposition, the Turks bolted from their shallow trenches, and by 9 o'clock the bloodless capture of Krithia seemed imminent. In the centre, however, the advance soon lost cohesion, divisional orders were either misunderstood or forgotten, and units advanced as and where they could. By 11 o'clock the Turks were on the run and their commander had ordered a general withdrawal to the top of the Achi Baba ridge, which he countermanded when a fresh battalion fortuitously arrived.

But by midday the Allied advance had lost its early impetus. The centre was hopelessly disorganised; no one knew what was happening on his flanks, or where the Turks were; some units advanced unhindered up the gentle slope towards Achi Baba, while others were being badly held up by isolated machine-guns and snipers. On the left, the wide, profound, tortuous, precipitously-sided Gully Ravine was proving to be almost ideal for defence, while the bare spur between this agonizing defile and the sea—Gully Spur— is so bare and rocky that all movement was clearly visible to the Turks on the slightly higher ground. The British advanced, but at heavy cost, and with increasing lack of cohesion. On the right, the French had tried to cross the deep and rocky Kereves Dere, which was in fact the only part of the Turkish defences which was adequately entrenched and manned, and had been badly held up.

As the day progressed Hunter-Weston lost all control over the battle. A detachment of troops reached Krithia, only to discover that a general withdrawal had been ordered, and were obliged to fall back. On the extreme left, on Gully Spur, the Turkish resistance had become more spirited throughout the day, and the Border Regiment actually broke and fled under a fierce counter-attack with the bayonet. Fortunately, *Queen Elizabeth* was lying offshore, and with one fabulous shrapnel blast destroyed the pursuing Turks, about a company strong, led by an officer brandishing a sword. Aspinall was sent by Hamilton from *Queen Elizabeth* to rally the stragglers and lead them back up the cliffs to their previous position, and the situation was partially restored. The situation near Krithia became critical, and a Colonel of the Royal Engineers, supervising the repair of a bridge and the road on the Krithia Road, took command of a small force of engineers and infantry stragglers, marched them back to the front line, and ordered them to dig themselves in. The engineers remained in their positions all night, without food, water, or equipment of any kind except arms and ammunition, but were safely relieved after over 24 hours. 'This delayed the work on the road and bridge', the gallant Colonel's report apologetically concluded.

At 6 o'clock in the evening the battle was called off, after the Allies had suffered nearly 3,000 casualties out of the 14,000 men engaged. In its effects, the First Battle of Krithia had been one of the decisive battles of modern history. The front line now stretched from just south of Y Beach south-east across the Peninsula to a point just to the south of Kereves Dere, and there was no question of any further advance for several days. The Allied troops were dead-tired, obeyed orders dumbly, some staggered around as though drugged, others just collapsed and slept where they fell. The night of April 28-29th was cold, with a steady drizzle of rain, and the exhausted 29th Division tried to straighten itself out, bury its dead, tend its wounded, dig its trenches, carry up its supplies from the beaches. The landing of stores was imperilled by a storm which arose on the evening of April 28th, and which severely battered the flimsy piers and jetties which were still under construction. De Robeck and Hamilton were faced with a situation of the utmost seriousness, for if the seas did not quickly subside the Army would be literally in danger of starvation, as no reserves had yet been accumulated on the beaches. 'Even the remote possibility of the Army being imprisoned on the Peninsula with but little ammunition and no reserves of rations caused me grave preoccupation', Wemyss has written. 'Two days' storm would go very near starving us', Hamilton wrote; 'Until we work up some weeks' reserve of water, food and cartridges, I shan't sleep sound.' Apart from the serious delay caused by this storm, which fortunately died down on the morning of the 29th, the shelling of the beaches from Asia was becoming a matter for concern. In these early days the Turks were extremely short of ammunition, their firing was inaccurate, and many of their shells did not explode, but the possibility of the precious stores being destroyed on the beaches was a very real one. For two days the British were incapable of anything except occasional patrols.

The excitement and enthusiasm which had gripped the Army as it left Mudros what seemed an eternity ago had gone. Shocked battalions discovered that they had hardly any officers left; others had dwindled so rapidly that they were battalions only on paper. Since dawn on April 25th, the British and Dominion troops had lost nearly 400 officers and over 8,500 men; of these, some 150 officers and 2,500 men had been killed. No one had dreamed of anything like this, and the effect on morale was proportionately far greater than it would have been if such conditions and losses had been anticipated; the shock was almost palpable. Confidently expecting a walk-over, the Army was numbed by the reality. The Allied artillery seemed to the infantry to be virtually non-existent, while the Turkish guns grew daily more numerous and troublesome. No solution had been found to the problem of effective liaison between the Army and the fleet, with the result that the naval bombardments of enemy trenches, even on the extreme left and right flanks, were not as effective as they might have been. 'Movements of our own troops', the captain of *Vengeance* subsequently wrote, 'were as unexpected and unannounced as those of the enemy. In fact, we often had more warning of the latter.' Fresh troops were startled by the haggard look of men who had been fighting for less than a week. Hamilton, with a lifetime's experience of fighting, and his deep sympathetic insight into the mentality of the soldier, was already extremely concerned about the morale of his troops. 'Any violent struggle for life always lowers the will to fight even of the most cut-and-come-again,' he wrote on the 29th. '. . . Yesterday morning, I saw our men scatter right and left before an enemy they would have gone for with a cheer on the 25th or 26th.'

The newcomers to the Peninsula were quickly sobered by their new environment. The nocturnal transition from a warm and comfortable transport —frequently an old passenger liner—on to the sombre desolation of the Peninsula was sharp, painful and immediate. At the two beaches engineers had built some makeshift piers and jetties from the wreckage of lighters, ships' boats and any other material that came to hand; on the beaches themselves mounds of stores were piling up in apparently inextricable confusion; perched wherever they could, the administrative officers of the Army were establishing themselves; the long lines of stretchers with their grim burdens, the evidence of the recent fighting scattered everywhere, the purposeful movement of the beach parties, the flashes from the none-too-distant guns, the roar of the rifle-fire from the front, the flashing sweeps of the Turk searchlights in the Dardanelles, the winking lights of the ships; all these imposed an immediate tenseness and bewilderment in the newcomer. 'No wonder that, at the first glance, the narrow beach seemed the embodiment of desolation,' Douglas Jerrold has written, 'a strange wilderness peopled by flitting figures stumbling against each other sometimes in the darkness, but more usually moving about with the precision of ghosts in a world of shades. And this was no idle fancy, for under the sand and up the sides of the gully many men were buried, and an impalpable atmosphere of death and decay was in the very air men breathed.' Sometimes this new mood of exhausted cynicism had its amusing side; Arthur Behrend has recorded that when his regiment approached Sedd-el-Bahr at the beginning of May they passed an improvised hospital ship leaving the Peninsula, 'Our men roared out in unison, "Are we downhearted?" There was no answer for a moment, and then a single hoarse croak came across the water, "You bloody soon will be!"'

The ramshackle, forgotten, but immensely significant First Battle of

Krithia had signified the collapse of Hamilton's strategy. There was no question now of a *coup de main*. His army was spent, for the moment; Achi Baba, ablaze with brilliant poppies, was as far away as ever; Turk reinforcements were being transported across from Chanak and being marched along the coast road from Kilid Bahr, across behind Achi Baba along the deep Soghanli Dere, and deployed on the slopes of the mountain, with a marvellous view of the Allied lines straggling across the still green countryside. But while the Turks were rushing every available soldier in the area to the Peninsula, Hamilton was still clinging to the hope that he could take Achi Baba without asking Kitchener for reinforcements, and his reports contained no indication of the serious position of the M.E.F.

'Thanks to the weather and the wonderfully fine spirit of our troops,' he wrote to Kitchener on April 27th, 'all continues to go well.' Indeed it was Guépratte who was the first to urge reinforcements for the Army, and it was his first report that alerted Kitchener. Meanwhile, Hamilton was tentatively asking for the 42nd (East Lancashire) Territorial Division in Egypt 'in case I should need them. You may be sure I shall not call up a man unless I really need him'. Kitchener ordered the 42nd Division to move to Gallipoli, overruling Maxwell's vehement protests; Kitchener, with a firmness he had not shown three weeks earlier, told Maxwell that 'unless you have cause for serious alarm in Egypt unknown to me, I think you are sufficiently strong there until we have more troops available. Therefore you should do the best with the troops at your disposal.' The French agreed to send another division, but it would be several weeks before they could arrive on the Peninsula.

Although Hamilton's attention was almost entirely centred on Helles, the Anzacs were still in a state of siege. Kemal launched a series of attacks which were intended as a full-scale assault but which perished in the face of the resolute Anzac fire. Kemal's tactics were ferocious and unsubtle: 'There is no need to scheme much to make the enemy run', one of his orders ran; 'I do not expect that any of us would not rather die than repeat the shameful story of the Balkan War. But if there are such men among us, we should at once lay hands upon them, and set them up in line to be shot.' Even after these attacks had collapsed with terrible losses, the 18 battalions of Turks in the Anzac sector tenaciously contested every yard of ground. They still held the initiative and the high ground, and except in some areas where the steepness of the cliffs afforded cover, every part of the Anzac position was constantly thrashed with bullets. There were no 'rest areas'; the men unloading stores in Anzac Cove were as vulnerable as those in the front lines; the only salvation was to dig, and dig deep; as the days passed with their incessant uproar of firing, the piles of spoil from the trenches began to scar the hillsides, while a small city of dug-outs was conjured out of the cliffs at Anzac Cove and in Shrapnel Gully. There was a tension at Anzac in those early days which was never equalled later in the campaign; under almost impossible conditions, the Australians and New Zealanders could only cling on to their precarious foothold and await developments.

It was at this moment that the long-awaited Turkish counter-attack at Helles materialised. Von Sanders had been peremptorily ordered by Enver to 'drive the invaders into the sea', but his artillery and ammunition was so limited, and the respect for the guns of the British warships so profound, that a night attack was the only practicable method open to him. 'Any attempt at movement, any sign of life during the day was impossible,' Kannengiesser has written, 'because whoever showed himself was immediately shelled from the ships. With frowning muzzles the frightful armoured colossi surrounded the small, barren Peninsula.' On the evening of April 30th Colonel von Sodenstern, the German commander of the Turkish forces south of Achi Baba, was ordered to assault the Allied forces on the following night with every man he could muster, which amounted to 21 infantry battalions. Rifles were not to be loaded, and special units were charged with the duty of burning the boats when the beaches were reached.

'Soldiers! You must drive into the sea the enemy who are in Sedd-el-Bahr', von Sodenstern exhorted his troops in a special order of the day. 'The enemy is afraid of you; he dare not come out of his trenches and attack you. He can do nothing more than wait for you with his guns and machine-guns. You are not afraid of his fire. You must believe that the greatest happiness awaits him who gives up his life in this Holy War. Attack the enemy with the bayonet and utterly destroy him! We shall not retire one step back; for if we do our religion, our country and our nation will perish! Soldiers! The world is looking at you! Your only hope of salvation is to bring this battle to a successful issue or gloriously to give up your life in the attempt.'

Another order of von Sodenstern's, not read out to the troops, went to regimental commanders: 'Let it be clearly understood that those who remain stationary at the moment of attack, or who try to escape, will be shot. For this purpose machine-guns will be placed behind the troops to oblige such people to advance and at the same time to fire on the enemy's reserves.'

Throughout May 1st the Allies were completing their reorganisation and little notice was taken of a desultory artillery bombardment which lasted during the day. The morale of the British and French troops had greatly improved after nearly three days and nights of rest and proper food. The weather was exquisite, the enemy was comparatively quiescent, and the lines of troops marching up to the trenches, the vast quantities of stores being dumped on the beaches, the lines of patient mules, the tents of the dressing-stations dotted along the shores, the sight and sound of guns being laboriously moved up, and, above all, the hundreds of ships anchored off the coast, partially restored the optimism and confidence which had been so severely eroded by the events of the past week. Wemyss stood on the cliffs above W and V Beaches on April 30th and was awed by the intense activity. 'At one and the same time piers were under construction, roads being made, dug-outs excavated, stores and ammunition landed and stowed away in such small space as might be considered clear of shell-fire, whilst horses and mules were being coaxed or shoved from the water's edge to the shelter of the cliffs. Looking down upon this teeming hive from the cliffs above produced the impression of perpetual motion, for nothing in the crowded space was ever still for one moment, except that line of stretchers bearing wounded men awaiting their turn of [sic] embarkation.' 'What a scene!' Hamilton wrote after visiting W Beach. 'An ant's nest in revolution. Five hundred of our fighting men are running to and fro between cliffs and sea carrying stones wherewith to improve our pier. On to this pier, picket boats, launches, dinghies, barges, all converge through the heavy swell with shouts and curses, bumps and hair's-breadth escapes. Other swarms of half-naked soldiers are sweating, hauling, unloading, loading, road-marking; dragging mules up the cliff, pushing mules down the cliff; hundreds more are bathing, and through this pandemonium pass the quiet stretchers bearing pale, blood-stained, smiling burdens.' 'The mouth of the Straits looks glorious', a British officer at Helles wrote in his diary at the beginning of May. 'The intense blue of the sea, with the warships and transports with their motley collection of lighters, picket boats, etc. all standing out strongly against the steely blue of the sky. Farther off, the lovely Isle of Imbros shimmers like a perfect gem set in a sapphire sea. One can just make out the lovely violet tints of her glorious vales, tempered by the pearly grey mists that lightly swathe her mountain crests, as she stands out sharp against the sky. A beautiful sight and not easily forgotten. Looking landward, the trees are all bursting into leaf, the country is wrapped about in a cloak of flowers and flowering grasses, with Achi Baba as a grim and rugged sentry, its sides sloping away to the sea on either hand.' 'So back to the *Arcadian*, glad to rest', Williams' diary for April 30th reads. 'A perfect summer's day with cool breeze. . . . The sun sinks magnificently behind the jagged sierra of Imbros, turning the hills dark purple. A great moon rises behind Eren Keui lighting up the beaches, battleships and transports as darkness falls. The lights of the ships, the incessant winking of signal lamps, and the revolving glare of the Chanak searchlight make the night a wonder.'

At 10 o'clock on the evening of May 1st the Turkish artillery opened with a crash, abruptly sundering the exquisite peace of the early night. 'About 10 p.m. I was on the bridge [of *Arcadian*] thinking how dark it was and how preternaturally still,' Hamilton later wrote; 'I felt all alone in the world; nothing stirred; even the French 75's had ceased their nerve-wracking bark, and then, suddenly, in one instant, hell was let loose upon earth.' With screams of 'Allah!' the Turkish hordes swept across the ground towards the Allied trenches, where the troops were bundling out of their bivouacs and shallow dug-outs and hurriedly jumping on to their rudimentary fire-steps. It was the most confused and savage of battles; reinforcements lost their way in the dark; no one was sure where friend or foe was; the hysterical clatter of the machine-guns, the frenzied screams of the attackers, the agonized crying of the wounded, the bark of the field-guns, the shouted orders of the officers, the screams of terrified horses and mules, all contrived towards a hideous cacophony.

In many places the Turks had to cross several hundred yards of open ground, and only at two points did they succeed in breaking the Allied line. The Munster and Dublin Fusiliers, who had suffered terribly at the landing, were dislodged from their trenches, but units of the Royal Fusiliers and the Royal Scots met the exultant Turks head-on as they poured through the line, and after a brief but fierce struggle, the trenches were recaptured with the bayonet. The front was now illuminated with the dazzling yellow searing flashes of bursting shells and bombs, while from the Turk lines, witnessed by Hamilton, 'there rose in beautiful parabolas all along our front coloured balls of fire, green, red or white; signals to their own artillery from the pistols of the officers of the enemy.'

On the right, the French broke under the artillery bombardment, the Senegalese detachments fleeing almost *en masse*, and for a time the situation was critical. Two battalions of the Royal Naval Division were flung into the battle, followed by a small party of gunners who seized rifles and fought with the infantry, and a company of the Worcesters. Eventually, after heavy losses, the trenches were re-taken. Elsewhere, the British had impassively mown the Turks down before they got within any measurable distance of their lines, and when day broke No Man's Land was choked with Turk dead and wounded, and the assault had definitely collapsed.

After a necessary interval for synchronisation, the whole Allied line moved forward at 10 o'clock, but the Turks had recovered themselves, and only on Kereves Spur and on Gully Spur—where the 87th Brigade advanced 500 yards and captured the Turk front-line trenches—was any real progress made. After the strain and exertions of the terrible night battle the soldiers were so exhausted that when a man tripped and fell he usually had hardly the strength to raise himself up again. Isolated machine-guns caused severe casualties in the middle of the line, and by evening the Allies were back in their old trenches, even the intrepid 87th Brigade being obliged to fall back to straighten the line.

Although the Turks had suffered cruel losses, the events of May 1st–2nd gave little cause for satisfaction to the Allies. The French had suffered over

2,000 casualties, and although the British had fared better, the 29th Division once again had lost a disproportionate number of officers, including five battalion commanders, four adjutants and the commander of an artillery brigade. It did not require great statistical ability to calculate the probable average life of an officer—particularly a subaltern—at Helles, and the estimates were sobering. In these early days there was no established front line as such, and isolated Turks penetrated far into the Allied territory by night and sniped by day. In all probability the stories of penetration by snipers were exaggerated, and many men hit by stray bullets were described as victims of sniping; but the men believed the stories, and the tension was accordingly heightened.

On the night of May 3rd/4th the Turks, apparently tireless, mounted another attack on the French lines which was only repulsed after cooks and orderlies had seized rifles and won back the trenches which had again been abandoned by the Senegalese, who had already acquired an unenviable reputation for unreliability. 'The guns grew so hot that their paint coating melted', a French artillery officer, Captain Feuille, relates. 'Two or three actually exploded. . . . The sounds of battle were drawing closer. I was still holding the trench above the village with my men. A time-shrapnel shattered the air overhead and showered its fragments over us. The sharp notes of the bugles rallying the defenders shrilled through the darkness. Were we going to be overrun and thrown back into the sea? . . . The struggle was terrible; bayonets and knives were used, and the Senegalese fought with their *coupe-coupe*.* Blood was flowing all along the line. At last, a gleam of light rose over the horizon, as darkness gave way to a new day. Like night-birds, the Turks withdrew and dug themselves in. It was high time, for only ten shells remained for each gun, and our troops were exhausted.' When daylight came, however, the 75's caught the Turks in the open and caused terrible havoc. Eight Turkish battalions, flung into the battle after a forced march of 20 miles straight from disembarkation after sailing from Constantinople, were so severely cut up that it was over a week before they could be gathered together and reorganised into effective fighting units. Von Sanders, upon receipt of a verbal report from Kannengiesser, ordered an immediate ending of these disastrous attacks and instructed General Weber, who replaced von Sodenstern (who had been injured), to concentrate upon defence.

But these attacks had not been without effect; on the night of May 3rd/4th Hamilton received wild reports of the French breaking and the 29th Division falling back in disorder to the trenches, and on the following morning Hunter-Weston and d'Amade told him that their troops were strained to breaking-point. 'The Turks have given us three bad nights,' Hamilton wrote on the 5th, 'and they ought to be worn out.' But it was improbable that

* A hideous little chopper-knife, not unlike a machette.

the exhaustion of the Turks was any greater than that of the Allies. The sights in the narrow and twisting communication trenches astounded all newcomers. 'We had a long walk, dodging sleeping men, turning sideways to get the pack through', a subaltern wrote home. 'It was an amazing sight. Those narrow ditches filled with dirt-stained men, rifles laid ready on the parapet or with bayonet fixed against the side of the trench, packs put away at the back.' The troops landing at V Beach beheld the chilling spectacle of the victims of the *River Clyde*, still lying in perfect preservation in the clear water, still staring glassily up at the appalled newcomers. These were not the only manifestations of war. 'On the surface of the water, drifting out towards the sea, we noticed the corpses of two Turkish soldiers', Captain Feuille relates. 'One of them was entirely naked. Everywhere one could see traces of the recent assault on the beaches, cork helmets and many pieces of equipment floating to the sea.'

Hamilton decided to make his supreme effort in the Helles sector when Birdwood told him on May 3rd that he considered the Anzac line to be reasonably secure for the moment. Hamilton instructed Birdwood to abstain from any major offensive action for the time being, and to send two infantry brigades to Helles; 20 Australian field-guns and their crews, ear-marked for Anzac, were diverted to Helles. These troops, added to reinforcements arriving in driblets from Egypt, brought the Allied army at Helles to about 25,000 'bayonets'. On May 1st, several vital days late, but nevertheless warmly welcomed, the 29th Indian Brigade had disembarked. The Brigade consisted of the 14th Sikhs, the 69th and 89th Punjabis, and the 1/6th Gurkhas, but the 69th and 89th Punjabis contained two companies of Mahomedan troops, and General Cox declined to accept responsibility for their loyalty against the Turks. The men were accordingly detailed for supply work on the beaches, and the strength of the Indian Brigade was reduced by a quarter. No one seems to have inquired why their commander had not considered the religious factor before his troops had arrived on the Peninsula.*

'I hope the 5th will see you strong enough to press on to Achi Baba', Kitchener wrote to Hamilton on the 3rd. 'Any delay will allow the Turks to bring up more reinforcements and to make unpleasant preparations for your reception.' Hamilton did not have to be prodded by Kitchener to realise how vitally important it was for him to move rapidly. In his plans for the coming battle, Hamilton again wanted to attack before dawn; 'It would be good tactics', he wrote, ' . . . to cross the danger zone by night and overthrow the enemy in the grey dawn'; but Hunter-Weston was so

---

* Hamilton records that on May 2nd Cox told him that 'if we were sweeping on victoriously he would take them on but that, as things are, it would not be fair to them to do so. That is exactly why I asked K. and Fitz for a Brigade of Gurkhas; not a mixed Brigade.' (*Diary*, I, 193.)

obsessed by the losses among officers that he said he could not sanction an opposed advance in the dark, and, once again, Hamilton gave way. Hamilton and his unfortunate staff had been cooped up in *Queen Elizabeth* for six days, and the information which they received was, as Orlo Williams has pithily remarked, 'fragmentary, uncertain and inaccurate'. The staff had to find different places to work in each day, as no fixed arrangements were made, and their work was always subordinate to the naval tasks of the battleship. Williams' diary for April 30th recorded, 'officers continuously sweating up and down ladders and bumping their heads along various flats to find one another. The atmosphere below intolerably hot and stuffy. No fixed place for us to work in.' On the same day, Hamilton and his staff—none of whom had had more than three hours' sleep a night for over a week—had moved to *Arcadian*, off W Beach, but their difficulties were not greatly reduced. The principal difficulty of the whole campaign, the absence of one Commander-in-Chief—which was to dog it throughout, was becoming apparent. As Williams has justly emphasised: 'Mutual gratitude, good feeling and admiration between Navy and Army have had full play, and quite rightly; but it is also right, for the sake of the future, to say—what everybody who was there knows perfectly well—that the dual control of men and shore, sea and ships and boats, was a source of continual trouble and friction, never eliminated during the whole operation.'

Hunter-Weston's plans for May 6th lacked any subtlety. The Allies were to advance punctually at 11 a.m. after a preliminary bombardment, and while the French captured Kereves Dere, the British were to occupy Krithia and the Achi Baba ridge. There was what was becoming a typically Gallipoli failure to give even company commanders adequate notice to prepare their plans. Hunter-Weston's orders vaguely referred to the Turks having suffered serious losses and 'occupying a position on and in front of the Achi Baba ridge, running roughly south-east and north-west, with an advanced line along the Kereves Dere and in front of Krithia.' One battalion of the Lancashire Fusiliers was marched from disembarkation at W Beach—now called Lancashire Landing in honour of the events of April 25th—straight to the front line on the evening of May 5th, took several hours to find its position in the dark, 'were as ignorant of their position as if they had been dropped from a balloon', as one company commander later wrote, and had no idea that a major attack, in which they were to play a vital rôle, was imminent. The 5,000 Australians and New Zealanders were sent to encamp in reserve and were more or less left to their own devices. The divisional orders for the attack were not issued until seven hours before the assault was due to begin, and some units did not receive them until several hours later.

Hamilton, still on board *Arcadian* off Tekke Burnu, could only await the results of the impending collision between the armies. 'His last remaining reserve had been handed over in advance to his subordinate commanders on shore,' Aspinall has drily commented, 'and all that was left to him of the high office of Commander-in-Chief was its load of responsibility.' 'Too near for reflection, too far for intervention; on tenterhooks, in fact; a sort of mental crucifixion', as Hamilton himself put it.

The German and Turk commanders were also in difficulties. Weber had nothing resembling a proper corps staff, there was not a single telephone line from his headquarters to any of his divisional commanders, the language difficulty was constantly causing delays and complications in the preparation of plans and orders, and Kannengiesser writes of 'the complete confusion existing among the troops'. In these depressing circumstances, it was not surprising that the commanders of both sides contemplated the approaching battle with the most profound apprehensions.

The Second Battle of Krithia, which lasted for three days (May 6th–8th), cost the Allies over 6,000 casualties, or nearly 30 per cent of the troops engaged, and resulted in a gain of about 600 yards. After three days of almost incessant fighting the Allies were still half a mile away from the line which Hunter-Weston had prescribed as the initial objective. On every morning at about the same time—11 a.m. on the 6th, 10 a.m. on the 7th, and 10.15 a.m. on the 8th—the Allied line struggled forward in the brilliant sunshine after an ineffective bombardment. The French had a reasonable supply of high-explosive shells, but the British had virtually none.* On each day there were local successes, but any advantage gained was allowed to pass by, while the Turks fought with a skill and resolution which prevented the possibility of any major break-through.

But in spite of the obvious nature of Hunter-Weston's tactics, the courage of the Turks, and the ineffectiveness of the Allied artillery against unlocated machine-guns, the dogged valour of the British very nearly achieved a decisive victory. They were in a numerical superiority of about 5,000 men, and, however tired, they were determined to advance. The moral effect of their bombardments was tremendous, with which the Turkish field batteries, although situated extremely skilfully and fired very accurately, could not hope to compete. Kannengiesser was sent to the Helles sector as the attack opened, and has left a memorable picture of the scene.

> The closer I approached the battlefield the more powerful was the impression on eye and ear. I recognised the continuous flashes from the fleet which lay in a half circle round the Peninsula and bombarded the land with a ceaseless fire, giving an impression of power and might which I can scarcely describe. A frightful thunderstorm which broke with elemental force and with never-ceasing thunder and lightning against the forces concentrated on that small portion of the Peninsula. . . . Even later, in August 1917, in

* The total British ammunition supply on May 5th consisted of 48,000 rounds for the field-guns and 1,800 for the field-howitzers, almost all shrapnel; the Navy's supplies of high-explosive were also running dangerously low.

the battles of Flanders, I did not have the same overwhelming impression of concentrated shelling as during this period. Although in Flanders the effect of the individual shell was much more destructive, due to more sensitive fuses and improved methods of shell manufacture, yet the total moral effect was in this case much greater.

A German lieutenant commanding a naval machine-gun detachment at Helles reported to von Sanders that 'the battlefield presented a grand and awful spectacle. The point of the Peninsula was surrounded by a circle of warships and transports. The ships' guns maintained a terrible fire against the Turkish lines.' Shaken by this fire, and by the dour determination of the British infantry, the Turkish commanders lost their nerve and implored Weber to withdraw behind the Achi Baba ridge. The Turk trenches, which did not yet form a continuous line, were still very shallow and short; their infantry was becoming demoralised by the naval fire, which made all movement on open ground by day impossible, and had lost heavily in their officers. Von Sanders turned down Weber's request out of hand; the ground was to be held at all costs, with no retirement; the best way to get cover from the artillery was to establish a line as near as possible to the Allied trenches.

The perilous condition of the enemy was not suspected by the British and the French. The artillery bombardments appeared to have had no effect, for as soon as they lifted and the infantry clambered out of their trenches the machine-guns started their deadly chatter. The ground which they had to traverse, although still green and apparently gentle, is almost ideal for defence. The three gullies known to the British as Gully Ravine, Krithia Nullah and Achi Baba Nullah (the latter is officially called Kanli Dere) divide the Peninsula into three roughly equal sectors, and, apart from their use as defensive positions, they provided the Turks with communication lines through which troops could pass without detection by the Allied troops or bombardment by the Fleet. The ground between these gullies form almost completely bare spurs, named (from west to east) Gully Spur, Fir Tree Spur, Krithia Spur and Kereves Spur. Thus the Allied infantry had to advance uphill up the spurs and contest the occupancy of the nullahs at the same time as maintaining an approximately straight line. Worn out by their exertions of the past week, inadequately supplied with hand-bombs and other equipment vital for this type of fighting, and almost completely without effective artillery support, the Allied soldiers could make little progress against their hidden enemy. The pitiless sun, already hot enough to cause discomfort, was another burden on the shoulders of the dogged but exhausted infantry.

On May 7th no advance whatever was made, and Hamilton came ashore to direct the last desperate attempt to force the issue. The orders for May 8th were brutally simple, and, again, were not sent out until an hour before the attack was to begin. Four battalions of New Zealanders were to capture

Krithia, defended by nine Turk battalions; the 29th Division was to advance straight up Fir Tree Spur; once again, the French were to try to capture Kereves Dere. As usual, the orders which units received were wholly inadequate. One Colonel told his company commanders: 'The battalion will attack from the front-line trenches at 10.30 a.m. precisely; 12th Company will lead. And I am sorry, gentlemen, that I cannot give you any further information.'

Aspinall came ashore with Hamilton from *Arcadian*, and has recorded the scene on that deliciously warm, tranquil morning before the storm broke.

> The grassy slopes that crown the cliffs are carpeted with flowers. The azure sky is cloudless; the air is fragrant with the scent of wild thyme. In front, beyond a smiling valley studded with cypress and olive and patches of young corn, the ground rises gently to the village of Krithia, standing amidst clumps of mulberry and oak; and thence more steeply to a frowning ridge beyond, its highest point like the hump of a camel's back. Away to the right, edged with a ribbon of silvery sand, lie the sapphire arc of Morto Bay, the glistening Dardanelles, and the golden fields of Troy. On the left, a mile out in the Aegean, a few warships lie motionless, like giants asleep, their gaunt outlines mirrored in a satin sea; while behind them, in the tender haze of the horizon, is the delicately pencilled outline of snow-capped Samothrace. As far as the eye can reach there is no sign of movement; the world seems bathed in sleep. Only high on the shoulder of Achi Baba—the goal of the British troops—a field of scarlet poppies intrudes a restless note. Yet in half an hour that peaceful landscape will again be overrun by waves of flashing bayonets, and these are the last moments of hundreds of precious lives.

Orlo Williams was on the same hill with Aspinall and Hamilton, and wrote in his diary that night: 'The scene dominated by Achi Baba towering over Krithia and the woods below was peaceful enough. A herd of goats was browsing in the foreground, men were exercising mules, and little bodies of men and wagons went from time to time along the dusty roads. The banks on which we sat smelt sweetly of wild thyme. Every now and again shrapnel burst in the centre, a few shots were fired at our aeroplane, and occasionally the vicious pop-pop-pop of a machine-gun broke out.' Brereton, who had come to Helles with the New Zealand Brigade from Anzac, was struck by the charm and peacefulness of the scene. 'Both armies cooked their breakfast at the same time, each with its three distinct lines of smoke where the front, support and reserve troops were, making a curiously homely and peaceful scene.'

By one o'clock reports were coming to G.H.Q. that the artillery had again failed to locate the Turk machine-guns, that ammunition was running seriously low, and that no progress had been made. 'It is a terrible sight in that clear bright sunshine, men going down like ninepins everywhere, falling with a crash with the speed they were going', Brereton has recalled. At almost the same moment Hamilton was handed a War Office telegram on the subject of his appeals for more ammunition. 'The ammunition supply for your force was never calculated on the basis of a prolonged occupation of the Peninsula. It is important to push on.' By half-past three it was confirmed that the New Zealanders and British were back in their old trenches after suffering heavy losses, and that the French had not even moved from theirs.

The battle had now raged with little respite for two and a half days, and both sides were almost at their last gasp. The composite battalions of the survivors of the Dublin and Munster Fusiliers, who had suffered grievously, and were now known as the 'Dubsters', called out to Brereton's New Zealanders as they had moved forward, 'It's no good advancing, sir, you'll all be killed. It's no good, sir.'* Hamilton determined on one last effort, and at four o'clock he ordered the entire Allied line, reinforced by the Australians, to 'fix bayonets, slope arms and move on Krithia precisely at 5.30 p.m.' Executive orders were issued at 4.30; the artillery was to be recklessly prodigal with ammunition; the whole army was to sweep forward with the bayonet.

The Australians, preparing tea in their peaceful bivouac, were given the task which no one had ever yet attempted; they were to attack along the almost bare Krithia Spur, while the New Zealanders on their left were to storm Fir Tree Spur once again. The Australians were informed of their rôle just after five o'clock, and by 5.20 p.m. they were hurrying forward.

The artillery barrage which fell on the Turks at 5.15 p.m. was by far the heaviest yet seen on the Peninsula, but when the tired troops rose from their trenches they were met with a storm of fire. 'Rays of the afternoon sun at my back struck the bayonets as they were fixed, producing the effect of a silver ribbon being drawn right across the Peninsula,' Wemyss wrote; 'but the continuity of this silver line was quickly dissolved into parties of men, surging backwards and forwards as the battle ebbed and flowed.' The South Wales Borderers were shot down in rows on Gully Spur, and the New Zealanders could make no headway. The first fury of the battle had subsided when the Australians were seen moving briskly up Krithia Spur. Long before the Australians reached even the British lines they came under heavy fire. 'The expected result came presently in salvo after salvo of shrapnel,' C. E. W. Bean, up with the troops, wrote; 'bursting in fleecy little clouds over the 7th Battalion and whipping up other clouds of tawny dust close below, where the hissing pellets struck the dry plain, sometimes obscuring with haze the hurrying platoons. Bullets from long range began to whistle past thickly or peck the dust-like scattered drops heralding a thunder-shower. It was, I thought, like walking against a dust storm in Sydney.' After what seemed an age the Australians reached the British front-line trench, paused for a moment, and then, with a tremendous cry of 'Come on,

---

* Brereton himself was seriously wounded in the attack, and was evacuated from the Peninsula four days later.

Australians', hurled themselves forward into the storm. 'Their faces were set,' Bean, left in the front-line trench, wrote in his diary that night, 'their eyebrows bent, they looked into [the fire] for a moment as men would into a dazzling flame. I never saw so many determined faces at once. Then they threw themselves, heads bent, as if into a thunder-storm, here and there one holding a shovel before his head like an umbrella.' A British major was another witness of the Australian attack.

> The enemy's shelling was shifted on to them in one great concentration of hell. The machine-guns bellowed and poured on them sheets of flame and of ragged death, buried them alive. They were disembowelled. Their clothing caught fire, and their flesh hissed and cooked before the burning rags could be torn off or beaten out. But what of it? Why, nothing! They were as devils from a hell bigger and hotter. Nothing could stop them. They were at home in hell-fire, and they caressed it back when it licked and caressed them. They laughed at it; they sang through it. Their pluck was titanic. They were not men, but gods, demons infuriated. We saw them fall by the score. But what of that? Not for one breath did the great line waver or break. On and up it went, up and on, as steady and proud as if on parade. A seasoned staff officer watching choked with his own admiration. Our men tore off their helmets and waved them, and poured cheer after cheer after those wonderful Anzacs.

It was all unavailing; after an advance of over 500 yards the Australians had lost more than a third of the 3,000 men who had been peacefully bivouacking barely an hour before, and the survivors had been forced to the ground. When night came, two companies of British troops marched up to relieve them and consolidate their position without a shot being fired at them. Even in the long catalogue of futile valour in the Great War, the advance of the Australians up Krithia Spur can still inspire an incomprehending wonder. To stand on the Achi Baba ridge and to look down on the spur up which the Australians advanced is to appreciate the folly of the enterprise, the astonishment of the Turks, and the barbaric heroism of the men who had managed to make the only worthwhile advance in the entire battle of Krithia.

There only remained the French. At 6 o'clock, with drums beating and bugles sounding the charge, they surged forward across Kereves Spur, their red and blue uniforms showing up with terrible clarity. 'It was terrifying, astounding and overwhelming', an eyewitness related. For a moment it seemed that they had at last overrun the enemy trenches. 'No living man has ever seen so strange a vision as this', Hamilton wrote; 'In its disarray, in its rushing to and fro; in the martial music, shouts and evolutions. . . . It seemed, it truly seemed as if the tide of blue, grey, scarlet specks was submerging the enemy's strongholds.' At this point the Turks covered the spur with high explosive shell, 'the puppet figures we watched began to waver', and, as 'night slid down into the smoke', as Hamilton wrote, the French were seen to be falling back to their old trenches. One last counter-attack was ordered, the French again went forward, and captured what became known as the Bouchet Redoubt.

At seven o'clock the Allies were ordered to dig in as best they could. Silence enveloped the battlefield as darkness fell, and both armies spent the following days patching up their lines, burying their multitudes of dead, tending the wounded and reorganising their shattered units.

'The killed lay in confused heaps which increased as you advanced', a French doctor wrote on May 9th. 'Some of their attitudes were extraordinary. Some were in postures of attack, others of defence. A little soldier of the 6th had his hands behind him. He had been shot from behind, and his skull was blown to bits. The bodies had swollen, and their uniforms were tight and narrow. It was awful. It might have been a drunken orgy. . . . Shells were scattered everywhere, masses of shining copper.' 'The cries of the wounded were heart-rending', Bean wrote in his diary on the night of May 9th. ' . . . We got a mess-tin and handed a little [water] down to everyone in the trench or under the parapet. Each fellow took about two sips, and then handed it back—really you could have cried to see how unselfish they were.' For the time being, both the Turks and the Allies were played out. As Kannengiesser has written, 'Both sides had fought with a stubborn bravery as if each individual fighter was personally convinced of the world importance of these battles.'

There was no room for optimism as the Allies counted the cost of their defeat in the Second Battle for Krithia. It was no longer a question of when they would occupy Achi Baba but whether they could maintain their precarious foot-hold on the Peninsula. Apart from eight Territorial battalions and the Indian Brigade, there were no reserves left. The survivors of the landings were now haggard and looked aged; young eager subalterns had become grim veterans within ten days. 'The beautiful battalions of the 25th April are wasted skeletons now,' Hamilton wrote; 'shadows of what they had been. The thought of the river of blood, against which I painfully made my way when I met these multitudes of wounded coming down to the shore, was unnerving.' 'We are working more than an army corps with my 2½F[ield] A[mbulance]s,' the A.D.M.S. of the 29th Division reported on May 9th, 'and 1 Cas[ualty] Cl[earing] St[ation]. I greatly fear a break-down but am doing all man can do.'

Between April 26th and May 10th over 10,000 casualties of the 29th Division had been evacuated; between April 25th and May 12th the French had suffered 12,610 casualties out of a total strength of 22,450. On May 11th Hamilton visited several units, and was depressed by the intense weariness of the men, 'caked as they were with mud, haggard with lack of sleep, pale as the dead, many of them slightly wounded and bandaged, hand or head, their clothes blood-stained, their eyes blood-shot'. A battalion of Marines 'were done; they had come to the end of their tether. Not only physical exhaustion but moral exhaustion. They could not raise a smile in the whole battalion. The faces of officers and men had a crushed utterly finished expression; some of the younger officers especially had that true funeral set about their lips.' Slowly, but perceptibly, the enemy shelling was becoming more frequent and more deadly. Later, the men became used to it as a daily feature in their lives, as constant as the ritual of trench-life and the interminable bully-beef

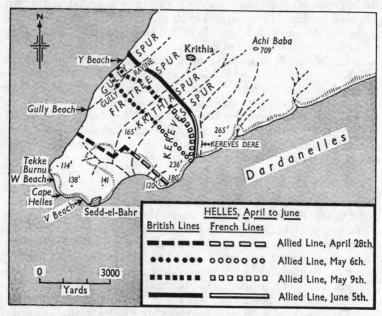

which they ate, but at the beginning it was extremely unpleasant. One officer wrote in his diary:

> The first thing one hears is a noise like the rending of linen, or perhaps the rush of steam describes it better. This gets louder and louder, and then, as the projectile nears the end of its journey, one hears a whine, half-whistle, half-scream, and then the explosion. If it is very near there is an acrid smell in the air. One's feelings are difficult to describe. You duck your head instinctively—you feel absolutely helpless, wondering where the thing will burst, and as you hear the explosion a quick wave of feeling sweeps over you as you murmur, 'Thank Heaven, not this time!'

The bombardment forced the Allied troops into intensive digging. The Hawke Battalion of the R.N.D., like several other units, had received virtually no training in trench-warfare, and had only had one day's training in England in trench-digging. 'However,' one wrote in his diary, 'it is wonderful how a man will work when he knows that his life depends on the result of his labours. . . . Many a man revealed a store of physical energy hitherto undreamed of.' As on the Western Front, the spade was the only effective defence against the shell and the bullet.

Both sides were seriously short of artillery ammunition, and Kannengiesser has related how the Turk artillery officers 'clenched their fists, as I did, when they saw the most wonderful targets and dared not shoot. When ammunition was allowed for a particular shot, it was regarded as a holiday.' On the Allied side, although the French were reasonably well supplied with ammunition, the situation of the British was almost desperate. In the reserve dumps there were only 106 rounds of 4·5-in. howitzer shells; in the whole Helles sector there were no 10-pounder shells, and only 186 for the 60-pounders, while the 6-in. howitzers had only 537 shells left. Kitchener had ordered French to release 22,000 shells, but it would be over two weeks before they reached Gallipoli, and in the meantime the British could only look on helplessly while the Turks feverishly dug lines of trenches that now began to spread across the Peninsula.

The lack of trench-fighting equipment, although not so critical at Helles as it was at Anzac, was already putting the Allied troops in a marked inferiority to the Turks. The only hand-grenades available were Mr. Garland's concoctions—which were not yet available in any quantity—and some bombs manufactured on the beach out of jam-tins filled with snips of barbed wire and Turkish bullets, a small detonator, and a piece of fuse wire. The trouble with this weapon, apart from its notorious unreliability, was that until the troops became more proficient it required two men to operate it; the first man put a match head on the exposed end of the fuse, and held the bomb behind his back to enable the second to pull the side of a match-box against the match head; if the match ignited the fuse, the second man cried 'Ready', and the first flung the spluttering object in the general direction of the enemy lines. Periscopes and other important equipment were almost non-existent in the Allied trenches at this time.

On the evening of May 8th Hamilton wrote to Kitchener: 'The result of the operation has been failure, as my object remains unachieved. The fortifications and their machine-guns were too scientific and too strongly held to be rushed, although I had every available man in today. Our troops have done all that flesh and blood can do against semi-permanent works and they are not able to carry them. More and more munitions will be needed to do so. I fear that this is a very unpalatable conclusion, but I can see no way out of it.' 'I should be glad if you would give me your views as to the future operations that will be necessary', Kitchener telegraphed in reply on May 9th. ' . . . The whole situation naturally gives me some anxiety, particularly as our transport service is much hampered by want of ships. More ammunition is being pushed to you via Marseilles. I hope you and the admiral will be able to devise some means of clearing the way through.' By the time this was received, Hamilton's optimism had returned. 'The only sound procedure', he telegraphed, 'is to hammer away until the enemy gets demoralised. Meanwhile, grand advances are impracticable and we must make short advances during the night and dig in for the day until we get to Achi Baba. I then hope we will be able to make progress without this trench method, but Achi Baba is really a fortress. If two fresh divisions organised as a corps could be spared me I could push on from this end and from Gaba Tepe with good prospects of success, otherwise it will degenerate into trench warfare with its resultant slowness. Everyone is in good spirits and fully confident.' On May 14th, on the instructions of the War Council, Kitchener asked for a definite estimate of the force that Hamilton required, and he took the plunge and asked for four divisions. But before anything could be decided a deep and mysterious silence enveloped London, which lasted for over three weeks, and for that period the Mediterranean Expeditionary Force was obliged to remain comparatively passive while the trenches of the enemy threaded remorselessly across the Peninsula.

Although there was no major attack delivered by either side at Helles from May 8th to June 4th, it was not a pleasant period for the troops. The trenches had to be extended, patrols sent out, and a constant vigilance maintained; the accuracy of the Turk sniping was justly feared. 'Put your head up out of the trench,' Major Shaw of 'Lancashire Landing' fame, wrote at this time, 'whizz goes a bullet from an invisible sniper; walk about outside, and bang goes a shrapnel close to you. The word is, "Get in and get under; dig like mad!"' A young New Zealander, John Allen, wrote home that 'I don't remember even visualising what trench-life was like except that speaking generally it could not be called pleasant. I now know it to be an unimaginable mixture of horror, strain, discomfort and fineness.... Before I came here and fought in a war, I read casualty lists with sympathy but without intense emotion. But nothing can convey to you how dreadful is the sight of the suffering, badly wounded man—nothing can convey it to you. As I write, the word comes down the trench, "Somebody hit". So the thing goes on.'

Occasionally a German aircraft would appear, flying very high, and would hurriedly drop a bomb before being chased away by the British aircraft from Tenedos. The German planes hardly constituted a serious menace to the Allies, but the Turks greatly feared the British aircraft, which were led with tremendous dash and aggressiveness by Commander Samson.

In the early days the planes carried boxes of darts which, it was rashly claimed, could kill a man; in fact, they wobbled so violently in descent that they had no effect whatever, and even bounced harmlessly off tents. The engineers and armourers on *Ark Royal* then experimented with drilling small bombs and inserting an eye-screw at the nose through which a wire was threaded; the pilots or observers, by pulling away the wire, released the bombs. This ingenious device, although crude, worked admirably, and Samson's men ranged deep over the Peninsula, shooting-up lines of troops and bombing camps. The material effects were not spectacular, but the Turks dreaded the British aircraft. Early in the campaign, to the great admiration of the troops, Samson established a rough landing-ground at Helles, but eventually decided that it was more sensible to make his base on Tenedos. He left a dummy aircraft behind, which, to the joy of the troops, the Turks shelled ferociously for several days before it was destroyed.

But for the contending armies, these were merely diversions in the grim realities of the trench-life. The shelling was perhaps the most trying experience, particularly for newcomers. The feeling of utter helplessness under bombardment has been vividly described by C. P. O. Johnston of the Royal Naval Division:

> For quite an hour the huge guns blazed away, whilst we in the trenches lay full length on the ground or stuffed ourselves into small holes cut in the trench side. It was good if two fellows could get together in one of these holes—it meant company. Your feet and legs stuck well out into the trench, but your back and head were safely protected by perhaps two feet of earth which any ordinary size of shell would cut away through in the hundredth part of a second. You are both squeezed together, you don't dare think how easily a piece of shell would penetrate your shelter. You light a cigarette, look at each other, and wait. . . . You press your back harder against the wall and your head harder into the roof. You know you are not safe, but you press harder and that seems to help a bit. You can only see in front of you the opposite side of the sandy trench, at which you gaze in a vacant stare. The shells scream louder and more often, the screeches, whistles and bangs are hopelessly intermingled, and the ground beneath and around you is rocking and trembling.
>
> Thick fumes float into your hole and you cough and your pal coughs. Your knees and legs are covered with pieces of dirt and a layer of dust, and half of the ground that was above your head has gone by way of your neck to the seat of your trousers. You wonder if the bombardment will ever cease . . . .
>
> The crashes suddenly cease, the air becomes clearer at once, and you realise that for the time being at any rate the bombardment is over. You wait a few minutes to make quite sure, and then you struggle out of the hole into the trench. . . . You look over the parapet, and see a stretch of country with no sign of life.

The tension in the front lines was acute. 'The sniping was terrible', writes A. P. Herbert, also of the R.N.D. 'In that first week we lost twelve men each day; they fell without a sound in the early morning as they stood up from their cooking at the brazier, fell shot through the head, and lay snoring horribly in the dust; they were sniped as they came up the communication trench with water, or carelessly raised their heads to look back at the ships in the bay, and in the night there were sudden screams where a sentry had moved his head too often against the moon.'* 'This whole business is too horrible for words,' Lt. Desmond O'Hara of the shattered Dublin Fusiliers wrote to his fiancée; 'I don't expect to come alive through it for an instant—it is a miracle for anyone who does.' 'The war is very cruel,' a New Zealander at Helles wrote in his diary on May 9th, 'and our chaps are much cut up.'

As May progressed, the weather, which had been one of the campaign's saving graces up to that point, became an implacable enemy of the troops. The stench of corpses in No Man's Land, and the perceptible increase in the number of fat, bloated flies turned even the most hardened stomach. 'One gets used to anything in war,' Major Mure wrote at this time, 'but I think that the acrid, pungent odour of the unburied dead, which gets into your very mouth, down your tortured throat, and seems even to taint and taste your food—is really the worst thing you have to face on active service.' The Turks suffered far less from the stench of the unburied dead and the heat. They had abundant supplies of fresh, clear water, and were absolutely untroubled by the revolting scenes in the front lines. Kannengiesser once saw two soldiers sitting on three corpses which they had piled up at the end of their trench as cover from cross-fire, happily eating their bread and olives.

Apart from the gradually increasing heat, the almost incessant sniping and shelling, the absence of any variety in the food, and the arduous chores of humping supplies from the beaches to the front lines, the nights were made hideous for the troops by the innumerable tiny actions, euphemistically called 'straightening the line', or, simply, 'patrolling', to which Hunter-Weston attached great significance. Historians lay great stress on set-piece battles. Yet, for the troops engaged, these minuscule operations, not worthy of mention in the official accounts, provided some of their worst terrors and most abiding memories for the survivors. Trench warfare put a man in a very small world, bounded by a few yards of evil-smelling earth, in which days and nights could pass with interminable slowness. No Man's Land at Helles was not very wide in most places, and was a rocky, shell-pocked, scrubby death-trap. A subaltern, Arthur Behrend, has given an account of one such patrol in May, and his experience was repeated a thousand times.

 . . . . The front was unusually, almost unnaturally, quiet, and in the absolute stillness a single shot rang out loudly. The squelching thud of a bayonet driven right home followed immediately. Then a blood-curdling and despairing wail. 'O-o-o-o-o . . . .'

* A. P. Herbert: *The Secret Battle*, 49–50. Although this book is a novel, Chapter III (from which this quotation is taken) is an exact and detailed account of trench-life at Helles in May 1915. Herbert was in the Royal Naval Division, and it is alleged that he was once heard to address a platoon of dour miners, 'Stay where you are, and regard all Turks with the gravest suspicion.'

Another bayonet thud. 'Oh-oh-oh . . . .' less prolonged and more gasping. Then absolute stillness again.

The rest of the patrol returned with blanched faces. 'Snowball's gone!' said Stancliffe. 'He went right up to the trench and when he got there an officer jumped out and shot him with a revolver. That was him crying'.

Inevitably, and perhaps partly to counteract the prevailing depression, a kind of fatalistic cynicism grew in the trenches. 'When one of our observers was shot through the head and killed the other night,' Colonel Darlington of the Manchesters wrote in his diary, 'a voice from the darkness said, "Has he got his rations on him, sergeant?"' 'Having a good clean-up?' an officer genially enquired of an enormous Anzac washing himself with a mug of evil-looking water. 'Yes, sir,' replied the giant, 'and I only wish I was a mucking canary.' The tenderness of the troops with the wounded and their callous indifference to the dead was a perpetual source of amazement to their officers, and figures largely in their diaries.

The picture was not entirely one of unrelieved gloom, even at Helles, where May was a month of petty attacks, savage encounters in No Man's Land, almost unceasing bombing and sniping, digging and manning the trenches which, by the end of the month, laced the Peninsula. The French found that the shells from Asia were unearthing remarkable treasures from the ancient ground, and there was a kind of archaeological fever in their lines at one time; others were fascinated by the insect-life below ground level, and Shaw-Stewart wrote that 'Besides centipedes and other monsters, this Peninsula is marvellously rich in various species of ants, spiders and beetles, with which, in our troglodytic life, one becomes curiously familiar.'

'We do astonishingly well in our meals here', John Allen wrote on the eve of his death. 'The inside of a two-foot-long trench does excellently for a table. Figure us sitting down to dinner under a yellow deepening sunset sky, tin plates with roast beef and potatoes before us, a whisky-bottle and syphon on the table. Save for shells it is perfectly still; figures in grey shirts and khaki drill with light mud-stains pass by; smoke goes up from the little fires where the men are cooking their food in the trench hard by. We are between two and three miles from the enemy, and you needn't bend to avoid rifle-fire when you get up. The C.O. is in Tommy's clothes and an eye-glass. A case of fever is brought to the doctor as he dines. He prescribes twenty grains of quinine, tells the patient to keep warm if he can, and goes on with his dinner. It is dark when we rise and stroll back to our dug-out.' 'The Gallipoli Peninsula is really lovely just now—you never saw such a carpet of wild flowers,' Dawnay wrote to his wife. 'Very many of them are quite new to me, but there's a lovely thing like a small and very dainty winter rose, and a sort of grape hyacinth and hundreds of others. The variety and colour are really astonishing.' Of Gully Ravine a Scottish chaplain wrote: 'What a wonderful and romantic gorge it is—its earthen cliffs cut into all fantastic shapes by rain and stream; tributary ravines breaking down at every angle into the main cleft. Scrub and heather grew wherever a root-hold was possible; and flowers were still blooming in shady nooks. A multitude of khaki-clad men at arms, with their crazy shelters, dug-outs, and open-air kitchens, their transport and water-carts and animals, crowded the bottom.'

The sights and sound of the Army, particularly at night or in the early morning, could be remarkably beautiful. 'As we silently disembarked,' a soldier in the Hawke Battalion of the Royal Naval Division wrote in his diary, 'the shriek of the shrapnel and the roar of the high-explosive mingled with the distant rattle of musketry. It was a weird scene. At last we were in touch with the realities of war, on the fringe maybe, but still quite near enough to bring home to us its awful potentialities. One could distinguish the ruins of the old fort of Sedd-el-Bahr with its dismantled guns, silhouetted against the starry heavens, whilst the Senegalese sentries, motionless as statues, loomed up out of the darkness.' 'It's a most beautiful day', Lt.-Col. Skeen, at Anzac, wrote to his wife: 'There has been a succession of beautiful days ever since we landed—the sea like glass and the hillsides covered with flowers and trees.... Some of the flowers are really beautiful—a thing just like a white wild rose grows all over the hills and in a field in front of the trenches is a mixture of marguerites and poppies which we must imitate in our next garden.' 'The scene on the Krithia road at night is just what I imagined, in past life, war to be', one officer wrote in his diary. 'The wagons trekking up to the trenches, with, of course, no lights, and troops of all kinds moving up and down. In the distance, star shells shooting up and sailing gently down, illuminating the country as light as day, and as one gets nearer to the firing-line the crackle of musketry gets louder and louder, and during the final walk of three hundred yards from Pink Farm to H.Q., the song of bullets flying past makes one feel very much alive.' 'This evening we had a wonderful sight', a British chaplain wrote in his diary. 'Shells bursting all around us and the hospital crammed with wounded. The sea rising and wind blowing hard; the clouds very black and lightning brilliant all night through. It seemed as if the heavens were fighting with us. Out at sea, a torpedo-destroyer or two were flashing their searchlights on the enemy's flank. The flash of the guns among the searchlights and the lightning made a most brilliant picture.' 'It is really very jolly here', a young officer in the Royal Naval Division wrote home on May 30th. ' ... You never saw such a conglomeration of strange troops. You should have seen me and A. P. Herbert the other evening bathing in the Dardanelles near some Frenchmen and Senegalese, with the Turkish lines (or, rather, the place where they were) in sight on a ridge to our left beside some dismantled forts, the plain of Troy before us on the other side, some guns on the Asiatic side sending an occasional shrapnel-shell over on our right, and a French battery immediately behind us having shots at them. . . . I took a bathing party down to the beach yesterday. The scene was a cross between Blackpool in the season and the Ganges.' 'I awoke at six,' Arthur Behrend has related of one early morning walk across the Peninsula on May 26th; ' . . . after swallowing a few mouthfuls of wet bread Reeves and I started back in the sweet freshness of a summer dawn. Heavy dew lay on the earth, the sky was an intense pale blue, Achi Baba was swathed in mist. The gunners were cheerfully beginning another day; officers and men were washing comfortably outside their dug-outs, and fragrant whiffs of bacon scented the crisp air. Their prosperity contrasted sharply with our hand-to-mouth existence, and brought home the pertinence and truth of the only known lines of a favourite marching song;

> Oh why did I join the Infantree when I joined the bloody army?
> Because, because, because, because, BECAUSE I was bloody well barmy.

The Gully dwellers were also stirring, and curling plumes of smoke were rising lazily from crackling fires. Reeves and I, hurrying along, seemed to disturb the prevailing peace and stillness.'

'And now all the air is sickly with the smell of cooking,' A. P. Herbert writes, 'and the dry wood crackles in every corner; little wisps of smoke go straight up in the still air. All the Peninsula is beautiful in the sunlight, and wonderful to look upon against the dark blue of the sea; the dew sparkles on the scrub; over the cypress grove comes the first aeroplane, humming contentedly. Another day has begun; the officer goes down whistling to wash in a bucket.'

Major Mure, then a subaltern charged with the odious but essential task of burying the dead, has left a remarkable picture of what the Peninsula could be like in those early days.

> It was a beautiful day. I think it was the most intensely blue of all the vivid blue days I saw at Gallipoli. The air danced and shimmered as if full of infinitely small dust of blue diamonds. Butterflies swam through it; a thousand wild-flowers perfumed it. Always there in the radiant days of the brief early summer our eyes saw great patches of bloom, except where they beheld only desolation, aridity, death and blood. Achi Baba, ever the most prominent mark in the view, loomed like a lump of awkwardness in the near distance, so shapeless that its very ugliness was picturesque. The sun went down in glory and in rainbows of fire as we worked, and the guns a little farther inland—the never-ceasing guns—belched out a venomous requiem and a reiterated threat.
> And so—we buried our dead.

'What strikes one at once is the entire absence of any troops or firing line at all,' Captain Pawson, a Military Landing Officer at Helles, wrote in his diary; 'with powerful glasses it is impossible to detect a single trench and the only living creatures visible are the supply and ammunition column drivers and horses going quietly along the roads behind the lines and taking no notice of anything except the work in hand. The only indication of one of the bloodiest fights in history was supplied by the guns which fire practically continuously night and day. Every few seconds a tremendous cloud of dust and smoke would show where a shell had burst, varied by shrapnel with a white cloud high in the air, but where they came from you could not see nor what damage they did.' 'The cheerfulness in the trenches is nothing short of marvellous', a subaltern wrote in his diary on May 21st. 'With a more or less continuous hail of shrapnel overhead, and always bullets from every possible angle, with men falling at fairly regular intervals, they go about their day's work with a sangfroid that is itself a tonic.... Jokes everywhere, good spirits everywhere, only the legitimate grousing which a Tommy claims as his own, and which means nothing when a necessity arises.'

'The long line of the tawny Peninsula cliffs on our port side looked so harmless that morning', Compton Mackenzie has related of his first voyage from Imbros to Helles on May 22nd. 'It seemed impossible to fancy that the vessel could not swing lazily in toward them over that limpid blue water and land us in some jolly cove where we might bathe and picnic at our leisure and afterwards explore those green summits and verdurous chines.' After landing, Mackenzie 'found myself on a road that led toward a grey-green expanse of flat empty country, in which the only sound was the singing of the larks overhead and the faint music of the telephone-wires that glittered here and there in the sunlight like strands of gossamer.'

This beauty became steadily less impressive as May passed. Helles was becoming, as Nevinson was to write, 'a wilderness of mounds and pits and trenches, of heaped-up stores and rows of horses stabled in the open, of tarpaulin dressing-stations behind embankments, of carts and wagons continually on the move, of Indian muleteers continually striving to inculcate human reason into mules. Except for a few surviving trees, hardly a green thing remains. Over all this wilderness a cloud of dust sweeps perpetually, and on the remains of war flies multiply with a prosperity unknown to them before.' Aubrey Herbert, paying a brief visit from Anzac, 'was unfavourably impressed with the insecurity of life in this part of the world, and wished for Anzac.'

'Time after time one wonders how Christianity can allow this,' the subaltern who had been enthusing about morale on May 21st wrote three days later. On the 27th he was writing bitterly of senior officers deliberately malingering to get off the Peninsula; 'everything points to an expedition altogether rushed, ill-planned, against a force ill-calculated.' On the 31st he wrote: 'The afternoon was of the usual sweltering variety. One could not sleep for the heat, nor eat for want of sleep.'

On the three sides of the plain which was the Helles battlefield the ground rises slightly towards the coast, and the fourth culminates in the Achi Baba ridge, its once blood-red poppies quickly withered, so that they gave the impression of a smear of rust drawn across the hump-backed hill, its shoulders hunched defiantly across the Peninsula. In this saucer of land the Allies were trapped. 'The plain, for all its openness,' as Douglas Jerrold has written, 'was a prison, which became a tomb.'

7

The Holding of Anzac

I found, in brief, that all great nations learned their truth of word, and strength of thought, in war; that they were nourished in war, and wasted by peace; taught by war, and deceived by peace; trained by war, and betrayed by peace:—in a word, that they were born in war, and expired in peace.

Ruskin: 'Crown of Wild Olive'

Throughout the first weeks of the campaign, while the eyes of Hamilton, the Fleet and London were fixed upon the brown-grey line of the Achi Baba Ridge and the deceptive green slopes and charming olive-groves of the southern Peninsula, on the parched, scrubby cliffs above Anzac Cove the Dominion troops were struggling for survival.

The fighting in the first week after the landings had been continuous and brutal. 'Days and nights passed slowly enough,' writes an Australian of those first few days; 'such sleep as we could get was sauced with wild dreams. But for the continual rifle-fire we might have been living in a dream world. Every hour our men were falling.' Kemal later wrote that 'On the night of the 25th/26th I could not get any clear information from anywhere . . . on the 26th April the situation was at its most difficult.' The numerical superiority of the Australians and New Zealanders was remorselessly whittled down as fresh Turkish reinforcements were hurried to the front, until by the evening of April 27th there was nearly parity between the two sides.

Kemal, obsessed by the urgency of driving the invaders from their positions before they had established themselves, constantly hurled his tired but devoted infantry into desperate assaults. 'There is no going back a single step,' one of his orders read. 'It is our duty to save our country, and we must acquit ourselves honourably and nobly. I must remind all of you that to seek rest or comfort now is to deprive the nation of its rest and comfort for ever.

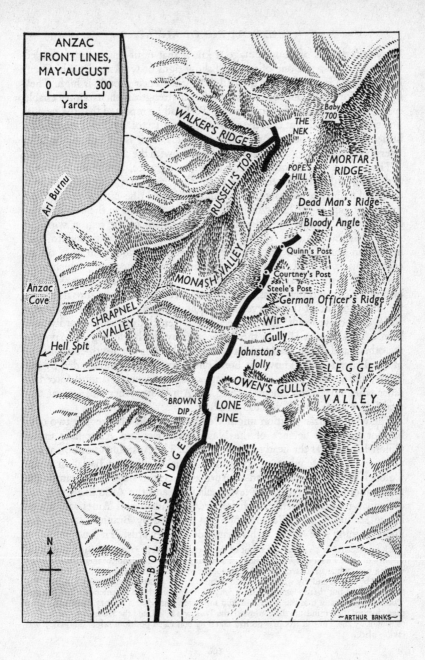

ANZAC
FRONT LINES,
MAY-AUGUST

0   300
Yards

Ari Burnu

WALKER'S RIDGE

THE NEK

Baby 700

RUSSELL'S TOP

POPE'S HILL

MORTAR RIDGE

Dead Man's Ridge

Bloody Angle

Quinn's Post

MONASH VALLEY

Courtney's Post

Steele's Post

German Officer's Ridge

Anzac Cove

SHRAPNEL VALLEY

Wire

Gully

Johnston's

Jolly

Hell Spit

OWEN'S GULLY

LEGGE

BROWN'S DIP

LONE PINE

VALLEY

BOLTON'S RIDGE

N

—ARTHUR BANKS—

I have no doubts of your courage. I know that until the enemy is hurled back into the sea not one of you will show signs of weakness.' Of his men, Kemal wrote in his diary at the end of April: 'Their morale is high. They fight not for glory but for fatherland. Their strength is their unquenchable spirit. It is an astonishing thing to see.' To Essad he reported that the tactical situation was good, but that the most important factor 'was that everybody hurled himself on the enemy to kill and to die. This is no ordinary attack. Everybody was eager to succeed or go forward with the determination to die.'

The Anzacs were equally determined to advance, and countless fierce and unco-ordinated battles raged. In the early days the front lines consisted mainly of shallow trenches and individual rifle-pits, with large and important gaps in the line which it was difficult to locate in the confusion of the fighting. Neither side possessed adequate maps of the region with the result that each missed golden opportunities. Kemal continued to hurl his men in small frenetic groups at separate points without plan, method, or co-ordination, instead of concentrating his forces at one point, which must have broken the Anzac line. 'I persisted in the idea of attacking with the utmost vigour and fierceness,' Kemal later wrote, 'and I was sure that with the throwing in of the reserves and support forces such an attack would achieve a decisive result.' If it had been left to Kemal, there would hardly have been a Turk soldier alive in the Anzac area by the beginning of May. On the other hand, for at least two days after the landing the south-eastern edge of 400 Plateau—later known as Lone Pine—was almost undefended by the Turks, and a small party of Australians actually occupied it until forced to retire when no reinforcements arrived. By April 28th, when this crucial tactical fact was realised, it was too late.*

The whole Anzac position might well have been lost in the first two days but for the dour defence of the New Zealanders and Australians under Colonel Braund at the head of Russell's Top. The Australian position at this point was desperate when 2½ companies of the Wellington Battalion under Colonel W. G. Malone arrived on April 27th. At this stage of the campaign, the relationship between the New Zealanders and the Australians was not dissimilar to that which existed between Canadian and American troops in the Second World War. Malone was appalled by Braund's tactics. 'He knew nothing', he wrote in his diary soon afterwards. 'Had no defensive

* Kemal relates in his dictated account of the operations that he saw Australian troops in the vicinity of Lone Pine on April 27th 'almost as a body come out in front of their trenches, and waving hats, white handkerchiefs and flags, sought to give themselves up. These scenes were watched by myself and my whole staff with the naked eye.' Australian accounts do not confirm this statement, but there seems no reason why Kemal should have invented it. The Turkish official account states that the Australians did surrender, but when a solitary Turk came over they changed their minds; in the confusion, the Turk was killed, and the Australians were killed to a man by the Turkish troops who had taken up concealed positions while the parley was taking place.

position, no plan, nothing but a murderous notion that the only thing to do was to plunge troops out of the neck of the ridge into the jungle beyond.' In their first hour on Russell's Top, Malone's detachment lost 45 men killed and over 100 wounded, and Malone delivered a personal complaint to General Walker, who ordered the Australians to be withdrawn. Malone was so incensed by what had happened that he seriously considered asking for Braund to be court-martialled for incompetence. This violent reaction was understandable, but not at all fair to Braund.* In fact, although at terrible loss, Braund's series of attacks had succeeded in pushing the Anzac line across the head of Russell's Top and had closed the dangerous gap in the line through which Turkish snipers had infiltrated and caused heavy casualties in the outposts clinging to the edge of the eastern side of Monash Valley. By April 28th Malone's men had more or less established themselves in their critical position when a major Turk attack developed at this point, and was repelled with the aid of the guns of the warships.

This attack was part of what Kemal had intended as a simultaneous assault on the whole Anzac line, but owing to the broken ground and poor communications it developed into a series of suicidally heroic headlong charges which were beaten off with heavy loss. Even the shelling of Anzac Cove, which, it had been hoped, would have caused serious casualties to men and stores, was wild and ineffective. 'If only von Sanders had attacked one point of my trenches with his whole force,' Birdwood wrote to his wife on May 15th, 'he must have been nearly certain to get through.' The failure of this attack had one important result; the disintegration of a column advancing over Battleship Hill by the guns of the warships created such a profound impression on the Turks that never again did they attempt a daylight movement on ground exposed to fire from the sea.

But although the Australians and New Zealanders had stood their ground, they had been considerably shaken by the fierceness of the fighting, and many units were physically exhausted after defending their exposed positions for several days and nights. The tumult of the rifle-fire never ceased. 'Whenever it seems on the point of slackening,' Brereton has written, 'it immediately bursts out fiercely again. . . . There were cliff faces all round which echoed and magnified the sounds, until the beating on the ear became almost painful.' 'Eyes were dull and glazed; some spoke heavily like drunken men; others with unnatural vivacity,' Bean related. 'One sign of the strain was the seeing of spies and snipers everywhere. . . . The strain showed in a hundred ways, though without a sign of demoralisation. Men would not run from a shell, though they would turn savagely and curse it as a dog snarls at his

---

* Braund was highly praised in both the Australian and British official histories. The British official historian, Aspinall-Oglander, subsequently regretted this passage in his history after he had read Malone's unpublished account.

tormentors.' This exhaustion and tension resulted in several tragedies; Braund was shot dead by a nervous sentry whose challenge he had not heard, and Malone narrowly escaped sharing his fate a day or so later. A Colonel of the Deal Battalion of the Marines and the Adjutant of the Portsmouth Battalion lost their lives in the same manner.

On the 28th relief came in the form of the Chatham and Portsmouth battalions of Royal Marines, followed by the Deal Battalion on the following day. 'Chatham was in fair shape,' one officer has written frankly; 'Portsmouth had been entirely rebuilt [after Antwerp] from bottom to top. And Deal was entirely composed of recruits and the left-over officers from the Fleet. And none of us had had any battalion training at all.' The delight of the exhausted Anzacs was changed to consternation when they beheld the lines of pith-helmeted, pale and bewildered young men—'children under untrained officers and I feel very sorry for them', Birdwood wrote in his diary—toiling up the ravines, each Marine laden with blankets, waterproof sheets, ammunition and rations as well as his rifle. 'Such *boys* they look,' Malone wrote in his diary; 'still, they must be sturdy.' The Marines had expected to take over a reasonably established trench system, and one officer, it is alleged, enquired about the locality of the officers' mess; the gaunt Australian to whom he addressed the question stared at him in stupefaction and laughed contemptuously in his face. A heavy thunderstorm, which drenched the Marines as they trudged up the slopes to the isolated pot-holes which constituted the Anzac firing line, filled their cup of misery. 'I have now been given some so-called Marines and Naval Battalions,' Birdwood wrote despairingly, 'who are so far as I can see nearly useless. They are special children of Winston Churchill, immature boys with no proper training, and I am quite afraid of them giving me away some day.'

No doubt, the Marines were also unimpressed with the Anzacs. 'Everything was chaos,' writes one, 'and nobody knew where anyone was . . . one met Australians all over the place, wandering round, drinking tea, and having pot shots at anything they saw.' In spite of heavy losses—amounting to nearly 50 per cent—largely due to their own inexperience, the Marines held on with admirable tenacity until the reorganisation of the shattered Anzac battalions was completed.

The reorganisation of the Anzacs provided one of the most moving scenes of the war. The roll of each brigade was called, while the men stood in ragged rows, bearded, dull-eyed, bedraggled and bitter. 'Our clothes were in an extraordinary state of rips and tears', Brereton writes. 'The rents of our pants looked as if we had spent the time sliding downhill. Everyone was in the same state, and senior officers went about with shirt-tails showing.' In six days, the Australian and New Zealand Army Corps had suffered 6,554 casualties, of which 1,252 (or 25 per cent) had been killed. One battalion had gone into action on the afternoon of April 25th with over 30 officers and 900 men; four days later, it had been reduced to nine officers and just over 400 men.

The Turkish losses had been even more heavy, a direct result of Kemal's bloody and unimaginative tactics. In the period April 25th–May 4th the Turkish casualties at Anzac were subsequently estimated by the Turkish General Staff at 14,000, of whom many had been killed or had died of wounds. Although the British medical arrangements almost broke down in the first week, the situation on the Turkish side was far worse, and whereas the Allies' medical facilities subsequently were greatly improved, those of the Turks remained grievously inadequate, with the consequence that there was a much greater percentage of deaths among their wounded. At dawn on May 1st Kemal hurled his troops once again at the Anzac lines in a final head-long attack. 'Our front in comparison with the enemy is not weak,' his order of April 30th read; 'the enemy's morale has been completely broken down. In continually digging trenches he is seeking for a refuge for himself.' The Turks came on in dense masses, and were shot down by the Marines, who emptied their rifles and machine-guns into the screaming hordes. Kannen-giesser, who had arrived at the Anzac front just in time to see this attack, later wrote that 'the first general impression which I received of the conduct of the Turkish troops was not particularly complimentary to them. Quite a number of battalions had failed during the attack.' This was unfair. After fighting for six days and nights, most battalions were below even half strength, there had been heavy losses in the ranks of officers and N.C.O.s, and, for the moment, even the stolid and heroic Anatolian infantry were incapable of anything except stumbling blindly forward into the awful storm of the rifle-fire. Even Kemal took this lesson to heart, later writing that 'the battle which had lasted for 24 hours had caused great fatigue to our troops, and so I gave an order for the attack to stop.' Essad peremptorily forbade any more frontal attacks for the present, and the struggle resolved itself into bitter and incessant fighting for the head of the Monash Valley. 'There was no other means of protecting our homeland but to dig in on the line which had been won and to hold on there', Kemal wrote. 'Therefore I gave the necessary orders.' These orders ended:

> . . . . All soldiers fighting here with me must realise that to carry out completely the honourable duty entrusted to us there must not be one step towards the rear. Let me remind you all that your desire to rest does not merely mean that you are being deprived of your rest but may lead to our whole nation being so deprived until eternity. I have no doubt that all our comrades agree on this, and that they will show no signs of fatigue until the enemy are finally hurled into the sea.

Within a week of the landing, the unique and unforgettable atmosphere of Anzac had been created. The troops, although initially inexperienced, learnt very quickly indeed, and the Australians and New Zealanders demonstrated a genius for improvisation which was one of the marvels of the campaign. The area which they occupied was only a mile and a half in length from the extreme north to the south; the front line was only 1,000 yards from the sea at its farthest point inland; in total it comprised barely three-quarters of a mile; but normal statistics are irrelevant in this hopelessly complex and rugged ground. Although the head of Monash Valley is only about 1,000 yards from the sea, the going is so bad that it can take a fit man in peacetime nearly an hour to cover the distance.

On the extreme north of the Anzac position there were two isolated posts near Fisherman's Hut known as Numbers One and Two Outposts, which were held by parties of New Zealanders. Until a deep communicating sap was dug later in May, the only means of reaching these positions was by night, and they were constantly exposed to fire from Baby 700, Battleship Hill and the spurs which dropped dizzily from those forbidding heights. The New Zealanders had already acquired a remarkable reputation. The blaze of publicity which fell on the Australians barely touched the comparatively small detachments of New Zealanders, but on the Peninsula they were regarded with mounting admiration and confidence by Birdwood, since they combined the élan and dash of the Australians with the meticulous professionalism of the British troops. In their outpost positions on the north flank and at Russell's Top they had demonstrated an aggressiveness, skill and determination which had already saved the Anzac position, and from the outposts they were already sending out scouting parties to explore the maze of scraggy ridges which lay between themselves and Chunuk Bair. They had a good conceit of themselves, and related apocryphal stories of panic-stricken Australians being rallied by individual New Zealanders; at Helles on May 7th Malone wrote in his diary that 'it is a relief to get in where war is being waged scientifically and where we are clear of the Australians. They seem to swarm about our line like flies. I keep getting them sent out. They are like masterless men going their own ways.' These rivalries and antipathies quickly disappeared, but to the end the New Zealanders considered themselves as the elite of the Dominion troops—an opinion which was widely shared on the Peninsula.

The main Anzac line then ran up the sharp and narrow Walker's Ridge, which is so rugged and difficult to scale that it is barely conceivable that it could be entrenched, to the head of Russell's Top, where Braund's trenches faced the Turks, 15 yards or so away, at The Nek. The line then hopped over a deep, plunging ravine to Pope's Hill, and thence over another precipitous gully to Quinn's Post, on the eastern side of Monash Valley. The head of the Valley was entirely in Turkish hands; their trenches 'ran like wrinkles on an old man's forehead' across the gentle slope of Baby 700, as Bean has vividly recorded, and the ground immediately above and between Pope's and Quinn's became so criss-crossed with Turk trenches that it was known as The Chessboard. Between Pope's and Quinn's there was a bare spur later known as Dead Man's Ridge, which was mainly unoccupied by either side throughout the campaign, and between this spur and Quinn's the head of the valley ran in a wide loop, known to the Australian troops with good cause as Bloody Angle. The eastern side of Monash Valley was occupied by the Australians, who had established themselves in small posts along the crest of the narrow ridge called Quinn's, Courtney's and Steele's Posts. The ground dropped away so sharply behind these crucial positions that a rope had to be slung down to enable men to haul themselves up, and until communication trenches were dug all movement up these precipitous cliffs by day was virtually suicidal, as some unfortunate Marines had discovered on April 30th, when they massed behind Steele's and were slaughtered by Turk machine-guns at The Nek, firing across the valley. 'Going down the nullah was like running the gauntlet', Major Jerram of the Marines, who was at Quinn's, has related: 'We'd collect behind a bit of cover and then one would volunteer to make a dash and draw fire. Immediately the rifles had cracked out the rest of us would go, and so on from side to side. One was not encouraged much by the dead bodies of those who had run too slow.'

The situation at the head of Monash Valley was extremely complicated, and it was some time before a fire-system was evolved which made the positions tenable. The Turks tried to establish themselves on Dead Man's Ridge, from where they could fire into the backs of the garrison at Quinn's, but were enfiladed and dislodged by the New Zealand machine-guns on Russell's Top. The Australians at Pope's could prevent a Turkish attack from The Nek, The Chessboard or on Quinn's and were protected in turn by the Russell's Top troops and the Quinn's garrison. The Turks, for their part, could prevent any movement from Russell's Top, Pope's, or Quinn's, and could fire down Monash Valley at all supports and reinforcements. It was a desperate, bitter deadlock.*

From the narrow ridge where the Australians and Turks faced each other barely five yards apart in places at Quinn's, Courtney's and Steele's, the lines moved on to 400 Plateau, where there were two important salients, known as Johnston's Jolly—thus called because an artillery officer named Johnston was wont to 'jolly up' the Turks at this point in the early days—and Lone Pine, whose name was derived from a single tree which stood for several months, and whose remains were visible until the mid-1950's.†
Between Steele's and the Pine there was a deep ravine known as Wire

---

* See the photograph of the head of Monash Valley, fig. 38.

† When it eventually fell in the 1950's, a new Lone Pine was planted from one of its seedlings and in 1962 was growing sturdily.

Gully; at the height of the ridge there was a small indentation which was covered by the fire of both sides and was never occupied. Once, a Turkish soldier who had lost his way wandered to the top of the ridge and beheld the teeming life of Monash Valley; after standing for a second in astonishment, he fled to his lines, pursued by a volley of bullets. He was probably the only soldier of either side after April 25th who stood on this bullet-swept 'nick' in the line and lived to tell the story.

From Lone Pine the Australian line swept south-west along a ridge known as Bolton's Ridge down almost to the beach. This part of the line was relatively secure, as the opposing trenches were separated by a comparatively large distance, and in many places the Anzacs were on higher ground. Within a few weeks the trenches on 400 Plateau had developed into major positions, and those on Bolton's Ridge became so deep that only high-explosive shell could have damaged them, and this was in very short supply on the Turkish side.

The scenes behind the front lines, in the unbelievably restricted area captured by the Anzacs, astounded all new arrivals. They landed at Anzac Cove under a hail of shrapnel-bullets, and splashed ashore to discover a small but active ramshackle town perched on beach and cliff, which reminded Orlo Williams of 'the cave dwellings of a large and prosperous tribe of savages who live on the extremely steep slopes of broken sandy bluffs covered with scrub'. On the beach there were mounds of stores, men hanging about waiting for orders, casualties awaiting disembarkation, pyramids of tinned meat and biscuits which also served as shelter from the shrapnel, trains of patient mules standing in rows being loaded with water-cans or ammunition, fatigue parties laying telephone wires or setting off for the front line with supplies, while above, in the cliffs, hundreds of dug-outs were perched crazily like some extraordinary rookery. At night, as Brereton has written, 'the Anzac position looked for all the world like a great foundry, working strenuous overtime, sparks flying everywhere, and where shells were bursting great fiery showers flew in all directions like a heavy blow on red-hot metal. This was accompanied by a clanging and cracking that made the likeness complete.' 'The whole scene on Anzac beach,' the war-correspondent Ellis Ashmead-Bartlett has written, 'reminded one irresistibly of a gigantic shipwreck. It looked as if the whole force and all the guns and material had not been landed, but had been washed ashore.'

'It is difficult to describe the rush of those first few days', Commander Dix wrote. 'It was one long stream of lighters and horse-boats, picket-boats and pulling-boats, carrying every conceivable sort of provisionment for the Army Corps. On every pier was to be found a hopelessly hoarse naval officer, waving boats alongside or otherwise, and shouting, or rather croaking, through a megaphone, and with him a party heaving lines and ropes for securing the boats and lighters, as well as military working parties for unloading and stowing the different classes of stores as directed by perspiring Military Landing Officers. All this under a fairly heavy shell-fire, which, however, coming as it did in those early days from behind, was fairly easy to avoid.'

Slowly the Anzacs created a system out of this shambles. 'My dug-out is quite homely now,' Malone wrote cheerfully in his diary on May 3rd; 'a bank of sandbags, twigs and leaves for a bed, an old sack for a blanket, my great-coat on, a dead Australian soldier's great-coat for a coverlet, a pack full of leaves for a pillow, and I get some sleep. I wash in a pint of water at night; save it and wash all over with a sponge in the morning—or rather half of me one day and the other half the next—in the same water, and then perhaps the water left does to wash a pair of socks! I have a box or two for odds and ends, and 4 bayonets picked up and stuck in my sand-bag wall to hang up all my gear on. I am getting a table; two oil-sheets overhead keep off the sun.' At Anzac this was supreme luxury, but Malone had realistic ideas on personal cleanliness and comfort in warfare which subsequently earned him a unique Anzac reputation at Quinn's Post. 'To a stranger it would probably look like a disturbed ant-heap with everybody running a different way, but the thing is really a triumph of organisation', Colonel Monash, the Australian commander of the 4th Australian Infantry Brigade, wrote to his wife. 'There are orderlies carrying messages, staff officers with orders, lines of ammunition-carriers, water-carriers, bomb-carriers, stretcher-bearers, burial-parties, first-aid men, reserves, supports, signallers, telephonists, engineers, digging-parties, sandbag-parties, periscope-hands, pioneers, quartermaster's parties, and reinforcing troops running about all over the place, apparently in confusion, but yet everything works as smoothly as on a peace parade, although the air is thick with clamour and bullets and bursting shells and bombs and flares.'

The Turk sniping in Monash Valley, which caused many casualties in the early days, was gradually controlled throughout May after Birdwood had ordered a regular system of sniper-spotting and shooting parties. These worked in pairs; one man would spot, and usually wave a hat to attract the sniper's fire. Slowly, this deadly menace was controlled. But nothing could be done about the steady shelling from a Turkish battery south of Gaba Tepe called 'the Olive Grove'. From Gaba Tepe itself the Turks could see every ship going into Anzac Cove, although the Cove itself was hidden from view, and in spite of every effort by the Navy, the Olive-Grove batteries could not be suppressed. Fortunately for the Anzacs the Turk gunnery and ammunition were poor, although the shrapnel caused many casualties.

The administration of Anzac was a wonder of improvisation and ingenuity. Water was severely rationed, and every drop had to be carried to the lines.

The food was plentiful, but of bad quality, although in these early weeks its unvarying monotony had not wearied the men as it did subsequently. It was several weeks before proper sanitary arrangements could be made, even behind the front lines, and even then the latrines in most cases were merely stinking holes in the ground, where the flies bred ceaselessly. Some wooden box latrines were sent to the front trenches, where the conditions in the first days were unspeakable, but wood was in such short supply that they were almost all broken up at once. The shortage of quite ordinary items at Anzac was chronic, and General Godley once wrote to his wife, 'Please send me a new toothbrush, a good solid tin or aluminium soap box, and a box of tin tacks.' 'One hears the praise of politicians in all men's mouths', Aubrey Herbert, a British M.P. attached to the Anzac Corps for intelligence work, drily noted in his diary at this time. In these weeks there were many episodes which entered Australasian folk-lore. Perhaps the most enduring was that of an Australian private known to the Anzac troops as Simpson who commandeered a donkey called 'Duffy' by everyone and ferried wounded men down Monash Valley under fire day after day until he and his donkey were killed on May 19th. 'Simpson and his donkey' had become so much one of the sights of Anzac that the news of his death spread quickly throughout the troops. It was subsequently discovered that his real name was Kirkpatrick, and that he had carried out his self-appointed task entirely on his own initiative.

All accounts of the early fighting at Anzac emphasise the hatred with which the Australians and New Zealanders regarded the Turk. He attacked in dense formation, screaming and savage, and never took prisoners; his snipers lurked in the scrub and shot men in the back; he infiltrated into the Anzac lines and gave false orders in English; his artillery filled the sky with shrapnel; he rained bombs on the front lines, and the Anzacs—having no bombs of their own—could only either throw them back before they burst or smother them with blankets or sandbags. Above all, it was his alleged brutality to the wounded which particularly embittered the Dominion troops against the Turks. 'It makes one bitter to hear how they treated our wounded left behind in our retirement', a subaltern wrote on May 3rd: 'Stories are rife that men known to have been only wounded were afterwards found with their own bayonets stuck into them. Others [were] horribly mutilated, and none are known to be alive in the hands of the enemy at all. . . . God save me from being captured, that's all.' The stories of mutilation of corpses were probably unfounded; the Anzacs had not yet realised the literally shattering effect on a human being of machine-gun fire at close range, and many 'mutilated' Dominion troops had suffered in this way. The allegations of bayoneting prisoners of war were more strongly verified, and it is undeniable that in the early battles the Turks fought with a barbarous fervour.

At Suvla, in August, two British officers who had surrendered were taken back and bayoneted in cold blood, but this type of killing seems to have been very rare in the fighting. In the front lines the stench of the rotting unburied dead putrefying horribly in the sun, the excrement and urine, combined to turn the stomach of all but the most hard-bitten soldiers.

The roar of battle seemed unceasing in those first few weeks, but gradually the Anzac troops learnt to distinguish the different sounds. If one survived, one became an experienced soldier very quickly at Anzac. Monash wrote on May 13th:

> The bullet which passes close by (say within ten or twenty feet) has a gentle purring hum, like a low caressing whistle, long drawn out. The bullet which passes well over-head, especially if fired from a long range, has a sharp sudden crack like a whip, and really feels as if it is very close. Our own rifle-fire, listened to, of course, from behind the firing-line or in it, sounds like a low rumble or growl. Our machine-guns are exactly like the rattle of a kettledrum. The enemy's rifle and machine-gun fire, on the other hand, sounds as if it were directly overhead, in a medley of sharp cracks like the explosions of packets of crackers just overhead, even though the fire is actually coming from the front, a half-mile away. The enemy's shrapnel sounds like a gust of wind in a wintry gale, swishing through the air and ending in a loud bang and a cloud of smoke, when the shell bursts. Unless one gets in the way of the actual fragments of the shell itself, the Turkish shrapnel does very little harm. Our own artillery is the noisiest of all, both the discharge of the guns and the bursting of the shells being ear-splitting, with a reverberat-ing echo that lasts twenty or thirty seconds. . . . . We are all of us certain that we shall no longer be able to sleep amid perfect quiet, and the only way to induce sleep will be to get someone to rattle an empty tin outside one's bedroom door.

Yet in spite of the dangers and discomforts, there was never any defeatism at Anzac. 'As I write this letter in my dugout,' Monash wrote to his wife, 'I am looking out on a hillside which contains the bivouac of the 14th Battalion, where the men have been living for five weeks in squalor and dirt in rain and shine, and most of them in rags; yet they are laughing and singing and joking and indulging in chaff and horse-play until it is their turn again tomorrow to face the awful ordeal of the trenches for a forty-eight hours' relief.' A halo of romanticism subsequently surrounded the Anzacs, largely as a result of Ashmead-Bartlett's dispatches, and fostered by several occasional visitors to Anzac. In reality, the Anzacs were rough, touchy, brave, casual, often coarse-mouthed, and, in the words of one of them, 'mildly cynical, very sceptical, and very critical of what they considered short-comings in the conduct of their own comrades, their officers, senior com-manders and other troops. Their opinions were of course at variance with those of the higher military authorities. . . . They were a most matter-of-fact, hard-shelled and cynical mob, who at no time exerted themselves more violently than they had to.'

But the weather was superb, the bathing exquisite, and the breathtaking sunsets behind Imbros and Samothrace awed even the most cynical. 'At night the battleships throw out two lines of searchlights, and behind them there gleam the fires of Samothrace and Imbros,' Herbert wrote in his diary. 'Up and down the cliffs here, outside the dug-outs, small fires burn. The rifle-fire comes over the hill, echoing in the valleys and back from the ships. Sometimes it is difficult to tell whether it is the sound of ripples on the beach or firing.'

There was an informality about Anzac which frequently disconcerted senior visiting British officers, and saluting was almost entirely ignored. 'You can't treat these fellows like regular soldiers, with barrack square discipline,' Birdwood wrote to his wife, 'but you can get a lot of intelligence out of them by more casual methods.' It is said that Walker, who was hot-tempered and who expected some deference, once turned his formidable scowl upon an Australian in Shrapnel Gully who was smoking a cigarette and had not saluted him. 'Don't you know who I am?' Walker grimly enquired. 'No', replied the soldier without interest. 'Well,' said Walker, jutting forward menacingly, 'take a good look at me. What now?' 'Well,' said the Australian after a moment's unhurried contemplation of the bristling General's shoulders, 'judging by your crossed swords and battle-axes, you are either a butcher or a pioneer.' Dix had no objection to being widely known as 'that f——ing old bastard Neptune', but, as he related with relish, the Anzacs 'had a great respect for my range of language, having only one word themselves, which they greatly overused as noun, adjective and verb.' 'I had a rummy meeting with an Australian today,' Lt.-Col. Skeen wrote to his wife. 'Rolled up to my dugout and said, Have you a piece of string?' I said no, and he said, 'Well, I've got my dead-meat ticket but no string, and when I asked I found he meant his identity disc!! Dead-meat ticket! They are quaint devils.' 'When I think of Anzac,' a British officer relates, 'it is of meeting a man squatting over a fire with a "billy". I had been on a message to try and get ammunition, water and food and was about cooked, "Boy," he said, "you look tired, sit down and have a mug of tea." Black, sweet and hot, it was a life-saver. He was quite unconcerned—I suppose he had a regiment somewhere. It didn't worry him and he probably found it eventually. But if we had been sniped at, he would have picked up his rifle and, equally unconcerned, gone off to hunt up the sniper. I do not suppose anything could be more different than the British soldier and the Australian. But they were both quite unbeatable.'

'So here the Anzacs live,' Henry Nevinson has written, 'practising the whole art of war. Amid dust and innumerable flies, from the mouths of little caves cut in the face of the cliffs, they look over miles of sea to the precipitous peaks of Samothrace and the grey mountains of Imbros. Up and down the steep and narrow paths the Colonials arduously toil, like ants which bear the burdens of their race. Uniforms are seldom of the regulation type.

1. Mudros, April: French troops in foreground

2. *River Clyde* leaving Mudros, April 23rd

3. Helles, April 25th: Troops of the Essex Regiment going ashore at W Beach

4. Anzac, April 25th: Australians, under fire, on Plugge's Plateau

5. Helles, April 25th: Impasse at V Beach

6. Anzac: Walking wounded in Monash Valley

7. Wounded seeking succour

8. Conference on *Queen Elizabeth*, April 25th

9. V Beach and Sedd-el-Bahr from Cape Helles, April 30th

10 . W Beach, April 30th

11 . Ian Hamilton on Imbros

12 . Hunter-Weston at Helles

13 . Anzac, the Armistice: Turkish dead at The Nek

14 . The Fourth of June: Manchesters crossing No Man's Land

15. Birdwood, Lord Kitchener, Godley and Maxwell at Anzac

Usually they consist of bare skin dyed to a deep reddish copper by the sun, tattooed decorations (a girl, a ship, a dragon), and a covering that can hardly be described even as "shorts", being much shorter. Every kind of store and arm has to be dragged or "jumped" up these ant-hills of cliffs, and deposited at the proper hole or gallery. Food, water, cartridges, shells, building timber, guns, medical stores—up all the tracks all must go, and down them the wounded come.

So the practice of the simple life proceeds, with greater simplicity than any Garden Suburb can boast, and the domestic virtues which constitute the whole art of war are exercised with a fortitude rarely maintained upon the domestic hearth.'

Birdwood delivered his last major attack of this period on the night of May 2nd–3rd. It was an excessively ambitious and ill-conceived project to capture Baby 700 by assaults on The Nek and The Chessboard from Russell's Top, Pope's and Quinn's, with more troops scaling the almost precipitous cliffs at the head of Monash. As a result of the congestion in the valleys and the darkness, many of the troops arrived late at their rendezvous, and instead of a concerted assault the attacks were delivered individually. Brereton, from Number One Post, has recorded of the attack on The Nek that 'the attackers had been told to cheer, and suddenly we heard an awful burst of machine-gun fire, and the cheers and yells of our men as they faced it. This went on for half an hour without pause, and then the voices died away, and left only the terrible musketry, which lasted until morning.' Some troops had managed to establish themselves on Dead Man's Ridge and above Pope's, but the positions were untenable by daylight, the Australians were exhausted, the Turkish fire was intense, and, on top of everything, the warships dropped a number of 6-in. shells into the captured trenches; by noon on May 3rd the survivors were streaming back into Monash Valley. With great gallantry the much-criticised Marines scaled and recaptured Dead Man's Ridge, checked the deteriorating situation in Monash Valley, but were shot down when they reached the summit; for several days their dead lay on the ugly bare spur 'like ants shrivelled by a fire', until a Marine climbed up at night and kicked the bodies down into the valley, where they were buried. Thus did the Ridge acquire its sinister name. Brereton came across some of the survivors of that attack on the beach; 'they were deadly tired, with eyes bloodshot and staring from the horror of the night.' All criticisms of the Marines among the Anzacs vanished after this desperate assault up a near-precipitous cliff against entrenched positions in broad daylight.

By May 3rd the Anzac casualties since April 25th amounted to over 8,500, of whom 2,300 had been killed. The fighting on the night of May 2nd–3rd had cost over 2,000 casualties, of whom nearly 1,000 had been killed. Such a rate of slaughter simply could not continue; apart from these severe losses, certain events in the night battle of May 2nd–3rd had brought home to the senior officers the fact that some units were in neither a physical nor mental condition to undertake any similar operations until they had been rested and drastically reorganised. Birdwood was thus compelled to revert to defence. At the beginning of May a small party of Australians had been landed at Gaba Tepe under the covering fire of two destroyers, but, like the British on V Beach on April 25th, could get no further than a high ridge of sand at the edge of the beach, and had to be evacuated. The Australian casualties had been slight, but would have been far greater if the Turks had not withheld their fire when the evacuation began. This minor operation, carried out by a few men in broad daylight with inadequate support from the troops on Bolton's Ridge, was the only attempt made by Birdwood to extend his position to the south by making use of the guns of the warships.

Hamilton, anxious to use some of the Anzac troops at Helles, instructed him to maintain his position and make no further attempts to advance, while at the same time improving his position and holding down as large a Turkish force as possible. On May 9th Hamilton sent Guy Dawnay to discuss with Birdwood the possibility of abandoning the Anzac position, but by then Birdwood was opposed to the suggestion, and declared that he was confident of holding on. On the following day Birdwood went to Helles on a destroyer to discuss the situation with Hamilton and they agreed that the Anzac position should be strengthened and retained if possible. In view of the heavy casualties which the Anzac troops had sustained and the urgent necessity of giving the troops an opportunity to reorganise, there could be no question of an early advance; indeed, it was more a question of hanging on to the fragment of ground won. Both sides took to the spade in earnest, and the opposing lines writhed over the bare ground. On the whole the Anzacs were the more industrious, if only from grim necessity, and a Turkish officer subsequently related that 'I used to watch those heaps and heaps of earth always accumulating and extending, everywhere heaps and more heaps. I used to say to myself, "What *are* they about? These Australians will tunnel to Constantinople!"' The acute tension remained, and one had only to look over a parapet for an instant to be shot. 'Few will forget that first glimpse of No Man's Land and the Turkish trenches through a periscope', an Australian wrote. 'Just in front of our sector [Johnston's Jolly] lay one of the few flat pieces of ground in the whole line. . . . The gullies were piled with Turkish dead, the flat ground from almost our own parapet to that of the enemy was dotted with inanimate forms, and as if in pity the wild everlasting swayed gently in the spring breeze.' On May 15th General Bridges was mortally wounded in Monash Valley, and on the day before

Birdwood had had his scalp grazed by a bullet when looking through a periscope in the front-lines at Quinn's. This episode gave dramatic emphasis to Birdwood's repeated orders to build bullet-proof parapets rather than just to toss the spoil from the trenches over the top, which was the Australian custom. Birdwood also discovered that the Australians neglected night operations, with the consequence that the Turks used the darkness to throw out barbed wire and improve their positions, and this practice had to be abruptly discontinued.

Birdwood was, in Hamilton's phrase, 'the soul of Anzac', and the part he played in the retention of that impossible position was a very great one. His attention to detail on the narrow front was of particular significance, and his regular tours of the trenches had a considerably greater importance than merely the raising of morale, although the latter aspect was by no means immaterial. Birdwood's main problem was to inculcate into his troops an attitude of what might be loosely described as 'cautious aggression'. Any relaxation of vigilance was literally fatal, but any quenching of the Australians' natural aggressiveness would have been equally disastrous. The central problem was to seize and retain the initiative with deliberate professional method, and, although underlining the importance of taking sensible precautions, not to take the emphasis on caution too far. The dual purpose of the Anzac troops at this time was to hold on to their position while at the same time keeping the Turks constantly anxious. This Birdwood grasped very quickly, but it was some time before it was generally understood by the troops. For all this, and for his constant example of indifference to danger, while at the same time not taking unnecessary risks, Birdwood deserves full praise.

His popularity among his Anzacs was something of a newspaper myth. He is often described as having enjoyed the whole-hearted admiration of his men; some accounts speak of their 'devotion' to him. But it is doubtful if he ever really came to terms with his men, particularly with the Australians. 'Talking to the rank and file his attitude was constrained and stiff, and his affability was obviously forced and unnatural', writes an Australian who was in an exceptionally good position to judge. 'His conversation with them was platitudinous and completely uninteresting. He bored the men and they bored him. He gave me the impression that he realised this fact and found it disturbing. . . . although he conscientiously persisted in trying throughout the whole of his command of Australians. As time went by, "Birdie's bull" became more and more a subject of ridicule among the men, and even the officers, of the A.I.F. The general opinion was however that "he was a decent enough bloke".' But it is difficult to imagine any other British officer—with the notable exception of Walker—doing any better than Birdwood did, and few who would have done as well. He may not have been able to get on very happily with the Australians, but he had a shrewd understanding of their qualities and limitations, and had a genuine feeling for them, which comes out very clearly in his personal papers. Malone, a fairly caustic critic of his seniors, admired Birdwood, and was particularly struck by the fact that he invariably refused a drink in the front lines, knowing full well how precious water was when it had to be laboriously carried up by hand at considerable danger.

The critical situation at Quinn's Post was a constant source of anxiety to Birdwood. 'The Post was noisome and pestilential', one of its garrison later recorded. 'Loathsome and terrible vermin crawled about. The winds blew continuously from the Turkish trenches across No Man's Land where lay the unburied dead. The air was poisoned with the stench.' With a deadly fire beating against the parapet from three sides it was impossible to look over for a moment without being shot, and the trenches had to be packed day and night in order to guard against a sudden attack. The Post quickly acquired an awful reputation of its own, and, as Bean has written, 'men passing the fork of Monash Valley, and seeing and hearing the bombs bursting up at Quinn's, used to glance at the place (as one of them said) "as a man looks at a haunted house".' Quinn's had actually been abandoned twice on April 26th, but an Australian colonel was so impressed by the importance of the position that he ordered a small party of Australians and New Zealanders under a Captain Jacobs to conceal themselves in the scrub at the edge of the summit of the ridge and dig a small trench. On the 29th, Captain Quinn arrived with six officers and 200 men to relieve Jacobs, and gradually the shallow trenches were deepened and extended. By sapping forward and joining the ends of the saps a new front line was created, and eventually communication with Courtney's was achieved by means of a tunnel. Sandbag parapets were built at the back to protect the garrison from firing from across the valley—which had killed many of Jacobs' men—but Birdwood's strict order that the front line should be kept shallow so that the men could leap on to the parapet at once if the Turks attacked meant that casualties from enfilade fire were incessant. In this sector the Turks had only to advance ten yards to split the Anzac position in two, and at one point on the extreme left of Quinn's, there was only an earth palisade two feet thick between the Australian and Turk trenches.* Today, the road built by the Commonwealth War Graves Commission along the top of the ridge runs exactly on the line of the old No Man's Land at Courtney's and Quinn's and at some places is only just wide enough for the Commission's Land Rover. The gutters at either side of the track are the old Anzac and Turk front line trenches.

Gradually the situation at Quinn's was improved, and, when one considers

* See fig. 38.

the difficulties and hazards of the operation, it was one of the most remarkable examples of courage and ingenuity in modern warfare. On May 1st Quinn had reported that '350 Turks have just attacked on our left and in gully. They have thrown six bombs over into our trenches. I require a supply [of] hand bombs, *please.* . . . Can I get one periscope?' Periscopes were essential at Quinn's, but it was some time before an adequate supply could be manufactured on the beach from scraps of mirror-glass, and the shortage of bombs was chronic, in spite of the work of the 'jam-tin bomb' factory in Anzac Cove. The Marines who had come on April 28th to take over some parts of the line 'for forty-eight hours' bore much of the brunt of the early fighting at Quinn's. On 2nd May Jerram noted that 'I took off my boots for the first time this day and all the bottom of my feet came off with my socks and I had a job to get my boots on again.'

The most important single factor in the salvation of Quinn's—and consequently of the whole Anzac position—was the invention of the periscope rifle, without which the valour of the garrison might well have been unavailing. This device was the invention of a Lance-Corporal Beech, and consisted originally of a crude wooden structure which enabled the rifle to be placed on the parapet with a piece of mirror-glass lined up on the sights, while the firer, safely concealed in the trench, looked into another piece of mirror-glass. Beech's contraption was spotted by Major Blamey— subsequently a Field Marshal—and Beech was sent back from the front-line to develop it. On May 25th the first improved prototype was reverently conveyed to Quinn's for trials, and was found to be an accurate and deadly weapon at ranges of up to 300 yards, and its general introduction gave the garrison at Quinn's a superiority of fire which they never lost.*

Before the arrival of the periscope rifle, the garrison at Quinn's could not fire a shot except up in the air to make a noise, and the defence of the Post relied upon the cross-fire protection from Russell's Top, Pope's and Courtney's, and the dogged courage of the garrison. So great was the tension at Quinn's that the men were relieved after forty-eight hours' duty; when Malone's Wellingtons relieved a mixed detachment of the Auckland and Canterbury Battalions early in June Malone was struck by the fact that the relieved garrison 'went off as though they were leaving a death trap. They were cowed, and dreaded being in the position.'

Neither Essad nor Kemal had given up their belief that the Anzacs could be driven into the sea, and after Enver had visited the Ari Burnu sector on May 10th a full-scale assault was decided upon. Some 40,000 Turks were assembled on the 18th, with orders to attack at 3.30 a.m. on the morning of the 19th.

---

* To the delight of his mates, Beech formally applied for a patent for his invention. See fig. 36.

Essad had wanted to concentrate his forces at The Nek and the head of Monash, but von Sanders rejected this sensible and realistic proposal and ordered an attack all along the line. 'Had Turks attacked in unity in one place,' Birdwood wrote in his diary for May 19th, 'they must have got through.' The Anzac garrison was now reduced to about 17,000 men of whom about 12,500 were in the front lines. The garrison had been alerted by an eerie fading of the Turkish fire throughout the 18th and by reports from aircraft and the battleship *Triumph* that Turkish reinforcements were moving across the Peninsula from Maidos and Krithia. In spite of a show of confidence, Birdwood was very alarmed indeed by these reports. 'My men are A.1 in attack,' he wrote to Kitchener on May 11th, 'but curiously callow and negligent, and the only thing I fear is a really heavy night attack driven home against one part of my line, as I cannot get the men to bestir themselves and hurry up to repulse an attack *at once*.'

The Turkish plan was for a major surprise assault at dawn without preparatory artillery bombardment on the centre of the Anzac line at Johnston's Jolly and Lone Pine, with subsidiary attacks on the left and right flanks. The troops were quietly assembled in Legge Valley, but it was an exceptionally clear morning, and the sinister gleam from the thousands of bayonets was spotted by Australian outposts just after 3 a.m., and firing broke out at once. The Turks toiled up to the summit of the plateau to be met with a storm of bullets. As the element of surprise had been lost, the Turks were ordered to attack at once, and by 3.30 a.m. an unco-ordinated battle was raging all along 400 Plateau. The Australians and New Zealanders shot down the bewildered enemy at almost point-blank range, and even jumped on to their parapets to get a better aim. As one attack melted away another would begin on another sector of the line, and the awful holocaust would be repeated. Only at Courtney's, where the Turks had managed to assemble behind the ridge without being seen, was the situation critical, but after a fierce struggle in the trenches they were hurled back. At Quinn's the attack was delayed, and when the Turks emerged with yells of 'Allah!' the long-suffering garrison rose as one man with a perfect example of disciplined fire and obliterated the attack, while the machine-guns from Courtney's and Pope's lashed the bare ridge with a fire which made any movement impossible. At The Nek the Turks were equally unfortunate. The New Zealanders had pushed forward a series of saps which it was intended to join up across Russell's Top to make a new front line, and the Turks swept past these in their first rush and were caught in a deadly fire from front and behind. The few survivors were exultantly pursued by the New Zealanders almost up to The Nek before the Turks managed to repel this impromptu counter-attack.

Misled by inaccurate reports that progress was being made, Essad ordered the attacks to be renewed, and the massacre continued throughout the morning, each attack being progressively more feeble, until Essad broke off the action at noon, by when his casualties numbered over 10,000, of whom some 3,000 lay dead, dying or grievously wounded in No Man's Land under the pitiless sun.

Apart from the spirited counter-attack by the New Zealanders at The Nek, no attempt was made to take advantage of the broken Turkish assault until it was too late, and by then the opportunity had been lost. At about 2 p.m. the New Zealanders tried again at The Nek, but by then the Turks had recovered from their confusion, and the attack was immediately cancelled. A kind of ghastly opaque silence fell on the battlefield. The scrub had been virtually destroyed in places by the intensity of the fire, and the bodies of the attackers lay everywhere on the yellow ground. Soon the awful stench of decaying bodies began to sidle into the Anzac trenches, and by the afternoon of May 20th it was becoming unbearable. Towards evening an Australian Colonel, unable to bear the sight of wounded Turks crying out in front of his trenches any longer, hoisted a Red Cross flag preparatory to sending out his stretcher-bearers. It was promptly shot down, but a Turk at once ran across to pant out an apology, Red Crescent flags appeared over the Turk trenches, and stretcher-bearers emerged. All firing stopped at once, and General Walker went into No Man's Land to parley with some Turkish officers. It was agreed that letters should be exchanged on the subject of an armistice at 8 p.m. that evening.

Meanwhile, impressed by the urgings of his officers and doctors, Birdwood had sent Aubrey Herbert to the *Arcadian* to ask Hamilton if he would agree to a truce to bury the dead and succour the wounded. Hamilton guardedly agreed if the Turks made the first overtures. Birdwood, on receiving Walker's report, had ordered that there was to be no armistice that evening, and sent a message to the Turks to the effect that if they wanted a truce an officer should be sent to the Gaba Tepe road on the following morning. The officer appeared, and negotiations were opened. Meanwhile, on Birdwood's orders, parties of Australian and New Zealand troops were surreptitiously collecting as many rifles as possible from the corpses in No Man's Land.

The conduct of these negotiations caused a temporary coolness between Birdwood and Hamilton. Birdwood was perfectly agreeable to the armistice, since the carrion reek of the dead was making the Anzac trenches almost uninhabitable, but Hamilton was not unnaturally worried by the propaganda value which the Turks might have made out of the episode. Birdwood was extremely offended by one letter in particular which he received from Hamilton, but subsequently apologised 'that I should have been so stupid and made such a mess of communications with Essad.' Hamilton sent Braithwaite to conduct the negotiations with a Turkish officer deputed by von Sanders*, and these were satisfactorily concluded on May 22nd. It was agreed that the armistice should last for nine hours on May 24th, and Aubrey Herbert was in charge of the interpreting arrangements; indeed he rapidly assumed responsibility for the conduct of the burying on the 24th, and Compton Mackenzie has recalled that 'Staff Officers of both sides were standing around in little groups, and there was an atmosphere about the scene of local magnates at the annual sports making suggestions about the start of the obstacle race. Aubrey Herbert looked so like the indispensable bachelor that every country neighbourhood retains to take complete control of the proceedings on such occasions'. Herbert's own accounts of the scene cannot be omitted:

> We were at the rendezvous on the beach (near Gaba Tepe) at 6.30 a.m. Heavy rain soaked us to the skin. At 7.30 a.m. we met the Turks, Miralai Izzedin, a pleasant, rather sharp, little man: Arif, the son of Achmet Pashe, who gave me a card, 'Sculpteur et Peintre' and 'Etudiant de Poésie'. . . . We walked from the sea and passed immediately up the hill, through a field of tall corn filled with poppies, then another cornfield; then the fearful smell of death began as we came upon scattered bodies. We mounted over a plateau and down through gullies filled with thyme, where there lay about 4,000 Turkish dead. It was indescribable. One was grateful for the rain and the grey sky. A Turkish Red Crescent man came and gave me some antiseptic wool with scent on it, and this they renewed frequently. . . . The Turkish captain with me said: 'At this spectacle even the most gentle must feel savage, and the most savage must weep.' The dead fill acres of ground, mostly killed in the one big attack, but some recently. They fill the myrtle-grown gullies. One saw the results of machine-gun fire very clearly; entire companies annihilated—not wounded, but killed, their heads doubled under them with the impetus of their rush and both hands clasping their bayonets. . . . I talked to the Turks, one of whom pointed to the graves. 'That's politics,' he said. Then he pointed to the dead bodies and said: 'That's diplomacy. God pity all of us poor soldiers.' . . . .
>
> At 4 o'clock the Turks came to me for orders. I do not believe this could have happened anywhere else. I retired their troops and ours, walking along the line. At 4.7 p.m. I retired the white-flag men, making them shake hands with our men. Then I came to the upper end. About a dozen Turks came out. I chaffed them, and said they would shoot me next day. They said, in a horrified chorus: 'God forbid!' The Albanians laughed and cheered, and said: 'We will never shoot you.' Then the Australians began coming up, and said: 'Good-bye, old chap; good luck!' And the Turks said 'Smiling may you go and smiling come again.' Then I told them all to get into their trenches, and unthinkingly went up to the Turkish trench and got a deep salaam from it. I told them that neither side would fire for twenty-five minutes after they had got into the trenches. One Turk was seen out away on our left, but there was nothing to be done, and I think he was all right. A couple of rifles had gone off about twenty minutes before the end, but Potts and I went hurriedly to and fro seeing it was all right. At last we dropped into our trenches, glad that the strain was over. . . . I got some raw whisky for the infection in my throat, and iodine for where the barbed wire had torn my feet. There was a hush over the Peninsula.

* Although his name was Kemal, it does not appear that he was in fact the commander of the 19th Division, as stated in some accounts,

In view of the proximity of the front lines and the tension which this created, the conduct of both sides throughout the armistice was irreproachable. The Anzacs had probably benefited from it most, as they used some old trenches and craters in No Man's Land which had been causing trouble as graves, and thereby removed much of the cover which had been used by Turk snipers and bombers. Both sides took the opportunity of surveying the other's trenches, and it was not coincidental that the Australians used their tallest men for the grave-digging. It is said that Kemal himself, dressed as a sergeant, worked close to the Anzac lines, but there is no reference to this in his own diaries and dictated memoirs.

The so-called 'Battle of Anzac' was the climacteric of the struggle to retain a foothold in this bleak and forbidding area of the Peninsula. The Turks at last realised not only that the Anzacs were not going to be dislodged but also that their own lines were almost impregnable, and reduced their forces in the area. 'From the third week in May to the third week in June was the kernel of our time at Anzac', Herbert has written. 'We had grown accustomed to think of the place as home, and of the conditions of our life as natural and permanent. The monotony of the details of shelling and the worry of the flies are of interest only to those who endured them. . . . During this month we were not greatly troubled. The men continued to make the trenches impregnable, and were contented. It was in some ways a curiously happy time.' The intense hatred for the enemy which had been felt by the Anzacs faded quickly after the armistice; the fighting was as severe as it had been before, and there was no lessening of the will to win on both sides, but there grew up in place of the barbarity of the earlier fighting a mutual camaraderie and respect which remained one of the most conspicuous features of Anzac. The Anzacs sometimes threw tins of bully-beef into the Turk trenches, and once received the reply; 'Envoyez milk. Bully-beef, non'; on one occasion a tin of cigarettes came flying over from the Turkish trenches, on which was written, 'Prenez avec plesir a notre heros ennemis'. Neither side hesitated to open tins thrown over No Man's Land after the armistice. The fact that the Anzacs could see for themselves the appalling effects of machine-gun and rifle-fire at close range largely dispelled the stories of the Turks mutilating the dead and wounded which had previously been implicitly believed; some months later, a New Zealander wrote that 'I found I bore the Turk no trace of enmity—nor for that matter did any of us; he was to us "Johnny Turk" or "Joe Burke", almost a fellow sufferer', and this was undoubtedly the attitude of almost all the troops on the Peninsula.

On May 29th there was a graphic illustration of what might have happened if Essad had had his way. For some time at Quinn's the Australians had become aware of strange tapping sounds, and a series of hurriedly dug tunnels were pushed into No Man's Land, in which listeners were established. They confirmed that the Turks were tunnelling almost up to the Australian front-line, and one experienced miner, a tough corporal known as 'Old Ganger' Slack, was urgent in his warnings. His prophecies of doom were ignored until May 25th, when one listener reported that the Turks were clearly preparing to blow up one of their mines. *Camouflets*—counter-mines which were not sufficiently powerful to break the surface of the ground, but which could crush an enemy tunnel—were fired, but matters had gone too far.

On the evening of May 28th 'Ganger' Slack informed his officers with glum satisfaction that the blowing up of Quinn's was imminent. At 3.20 a.m. on May 29th the mine, fortunately just short of the Australian front line, erupted, and in the ensuing confusion the Turks, one battalion strong, entered Quinn's. For several hours the fate of the Anzac position depended on the battle which raged in the trenches at the top of that yellow ridge, while reserves crouched anxiously in the scrub on the slopes of the valley. Eventually, after Major Quinn and many of his men had been killed, the trenches were recaptured and the crisis was over.

Quinn was replaced by the sturdy New Zealander Colonel Malone, whose arrival—coincident with the general use of the periscope rifle and a more regular and plentiful supply of bombs—heralded a new situation at the Post. Malone ordered a drastic and indeed draconian régime of cleaning and organising the trenches, and replaced the haphazard bivouacs cut into the reverse slope with series of covered terraces which gave shade to the supporting troops and protection from shrapnel and sniping. Malone had spent a week at Courtney's—'a very higgledy-piggledy show', he contemptuously wrote in his diary on visiting his new command for the first time—and had already worked miracles before arriving at Quinn's. 'Such a dirty, dilapidated, unorganised post,' he wrote in his diary on June 9th, the day he took over; '. . . gave orders that every rifle-shot and bomb from the Turks were to be promptly returned at least twofold.' Airily declaring that he regretted he could not grow roses to complete the picture, Malone stated that the art of warfare lay in the cultivation of the domestic virtues, and rigorously put this admirable precept into tangible form. He even had blankets nailed along the western fronts of the roofed terraces to keep out the sun, to be rolled up at night like blinds. Combined with this sensible attitude was a new aggressiveness against the enemy which completely changed the situation at the head of Monash Valley. Iron loop-holes plates were widely distributed, and holes which had been closed by the previous garrison because the Turks knew their position exactly were re-opened. Sniper-spotting and execution were developed into such a fine art that it was possible to move up and down Monash Valley by day without any danger; at night, on the other hand, the Turks would fire at random down the valley, and thus the conditions of the early weeks were exactly reversed. Screens of wire-netting, sloping on wooden frames, were erected on the parapets as 'bomb-catchers' with excellent results, and the New Zealanders, now well supplied with bombs of their own, rained grenades on the Turk trenches. On several occasions they threw more than 300 grenades a day; the Turks laid logs on top of their trenches to protect them from this rain of death, but hastily discontinued the practice when on two occasions the logs burst into flames. Australian miners, burrowing continuously into the dry, hard ground, fired mines under the Turkish front line which caused serious losses, and conditions in the Turkish trenches exactly resembled those in the Anzac lines at Quinn's early in May. So bad did things become for the Turks that they seriously considered evacuating what their men called Bomba Sirt (Bomb Ridge) to a less precarious position on Mortar Ridge. By the end of May the entire Anzac front line was laced with communication tunnels, protection against shrapnel-fire, and elaborate 'fire-steps' dug in the sides on which the men stood in comparative safety and sniped with their periscope rifles. It would be unwise to picture the Anzac front line at any time as either safe or comfortable, but when compared with the ghastly squalor of the first trenches the improvement was little short of dramatic.

And thus did June and July pass at Anzac. The flies multiplied and became all-pervading. The monotony of each day was occasionally broken by a sharp brief engagement, but now for longer periods than ever before the front lines were comparatively quiet. The tunnellers, at last efficiently organised, burrowed incessantly into No Man's Land, creating new outposts and new front lines with professional method. When all was ready, the surface was carefully opened from beneath, and the lines had stealthily advanced a few more yards. For a short time four Japanese mortars were available, with bombs which whirled eerily in flight before landing with a satisfying crump on the enemy lines, followed by shrill screams from the wounded. The Turks roofed in more of their front trenches, particularly at Lone Pine, but the supply of bombs quickly vanished, and the War Office announced that any replacements would have to be purchased from Japan, and would take several months to arrive. The armies returned to the hand-bomb, the rifle, the machine-gun and the spade. On June 26th Kemal delivered a suicidal night attack from The Nek on the Anzac trenches across Russell's Top. A Turkish officer, Major Zeki, has recorded: 'I heard the cries of our troops as they began to charge, at first enthusiastic—Allah ! Allah ! . . . But the cries later became tragic. One battalion and a half were lost. . . . It was a black night—there were the wounded crying in No Man's

Land, and both sides rolling out flares. . . . If the British had attacked they would have found no one in the trenches opposite them. Kemal brought his headquarters close up to the front line to defend it, and reserves were rushed into the trenches.' These occasional bursts of activity on the front became progressively rarer, and for days on end nothing in particular happened to enter in the Corps War Diary save the infiltration of Turk deserters and the mounting list of men afflicted with dysentery.

'Here we are', Herbert wrote in his diary, 'for an indefinite period without the power of replying effectively, and with the knowledge that we are firmly locked outside the back door of a sideshow.' 'It is the monotony, and the utter absence of anything of human interest, that has contributed to bringing about a condition of debility from which many of our strongest and most athletic men have been laid low', Monash wrote to his wife. 'What at first used to be gorgeous bathing degenerated into an occasional and furtive washing in the sea, and the hundreds of men who at one time used to bathe for hours dwindled into dozens, all of whom kept an eye on "Beachy Bill", and were out of the water and into the traverses at the first sign of activity on his part', Commander Dix has written. 'There was no change of scene in the burnished sky,' Bean wrote; 'the hillsides worn into hundreds of little paths, the figures of men constantly tramping with water tins or other burdens through the glaring white dust. . . . no change in the smells from the distant corpses of the dead, and from the burning metal and fat of bully-beef tins in the nearest incinerator.'

'A real good fight, artillery support and seeing what to do and where to go would be a treat', Malone wrote in his diary on August 4th.

8

Deadlock

The rising unto place is laborious, and by pains men come to
greater pains; and it is sometimes base, and by indignities men
come to dignities. The standing is slippery, and the regress is either
a downfall, or at least an eclipse.

Bacon: 'Of Great Place'

On the morrow of the Second Battle of Krithia the valiant but exhausted
Mediterranean Expeditionary Force had been definitely brought to a halt on
the Achi Baba slopes and the Anzac cliffs. A dispatch by Ashmead-Bartlett
in the *Daily Telegraph* on May 10th warned British readers of the severe setback to the Allies' hopes. 'We are fighting a brave and tenacious enemy, who
is most skilfully led, and who has always proved himself a more formidable
foe when driven into a corner and placed on the defensive. The men our
troops are fighting today are of the same stamp as those who held Plevna
under Osman.' This was a different note from that previously struck in
the British Press about the Turks, and even in very marked contrast with
the official communiqués from G.H.Q.

The complete check that the Allied army had received, their undreamed-of
casualties, and their inspiring though unavailing valour, had created a profound and painful impression in the Fleet. Keyes in particular—and there
were many senior officers who warmly agreed with him—was shocked and
humiliated by the relative inactivity of the Navy while the Army was
brought to a standstill. Most depressing of all, there was the feeling that the
Navy had not fully carried out its part of the arrangements. De Robeck's
orders for the April 25th landing had said clearly that 'the efforts of the Navy
will primarily be directed to landing the Army and supporting it till its
position is secure, after which the Navy will attack the forts at the Narrows,
assisted by the Army.'

DEADLOCK

On May 9th there was a critical conference on *Queen Elizabeth* attended by de Robeck, Wemyss, Thursby and Keyes, at which Keyes vehemently urged an immediate resumption of the naval attack. Significantly, not one soldier was present, and Hamilton only knew of the results of the conference privately from Keyes.

De Robeck was plainly hesitant to embark upon an attack which, if unsuccessful, would leave the Army stranded on the Peninsula, but his arguments on this score lost some of their convincing nature by the absence of any representatives from the Army. It would no doubt have been wiser if Keyes had confined himself to the proposition of a joint attack along the eastern shore of the Peninsula towards Kilid Bahr, but Keyes was never one for half-measures, and he advocated nothing less than a more efficient and determined renewal of the attack of March 18th. With considerable reluctance, de Robeck agreed to put the matter before the Admiralty, but his telegram reflected more his indecision than Keyes' resolution. 'From the vigour of the enemy's resistance,' the vital passage ran, 'it is improbable that the passage of the Fleet into the Marmara will be decisive, and therefore it is equally probable that the Straits will be closed behind the Fleet. . . . The temper of the Turkish army in the Peninsula indicates that the forcing of the Dardanelles and subsequent appearance of the Fleet off Constantinople would not of itself prove decisive.'

In spite of the unconfident tone of this message, Keyes—and possibly de Robeck as well—thought that it would be sufficient to enable Churchill to carry the matter through. He did not realise the precariousness of the First Lord's position, nor the strength of the forces which were darkly gathering for his overthrow.

Fisher's irritation with Churchill's methods of conducting Admiralty business, the stream of imperious memoranda which flowed from the First Lord, his habit of consulting others on matters which Fisher considered were solely within his jurisdiction, were no less significant than his apprehensions about the Dardanelles operations. In the Admiralty itself, at least three of the Sea Lords had privately informed Fisher as early as April 8th that their support was at his disposal if he should care to make use of it, and outside the Admiralty Churchill's reputation had suffered a comparable decline. 'His attitude from August 1914 was a noble one, too noble to be wise', Lord Beaverbrook has written. 'He cared for the success of the British arms, especially in so far as they could be achieved by the Admiralty, and for nothing else. His passion for this aim was pure, self-devoted and all-devouring. He failed to remember that he was a politician and as such treading a slippery path; he forgot his political tactics. . . . As he worked devotedly at his own job, the currents of political opinion slipped by him unnoticed.'

This insouciance was remarkable, and fatal. The Conservative Opposition

DEADLOCK

regarded Churchill with deeply ingrained hostility and suspicion. When Bonar Law, feeling that it was only fair to warn Churchill of the mounting impatience and mistrust in the Opposition ranks, approached him, Churchill was furious, and told Beaverbrook—then Sir Max Aitken, Conservative M.P. for Ashton-under-Lyme, and very close to Bonar Law—that Law had rated him 'like an angry Prime Minister rebuking an unruly subordinate'. This is an unlikely account of the interview. Law was the least imperious of men, and although he found Churchill personally uncongenial, it is probable that he delivered his warning firmly but moderately. Churchill's violent reaction to the hint demonstrated the less attractive side of his character which his admirers consistently tend to ignore. The 'Churchill magic' was so powerful, and the magnetism of his personality so great, that it is too often forgotten that it could provoke strong antipathy as well as adulation. Too much has been written by those who fell completely under the spell, too little by those who did not. Bonar Law was not a man instinctively prejudiced against flamboyance, and he was a shrewd judge of a man's capacities; although personally shy and reserved, he numbered Lloyd George, F. E. Smith and Aitken—all close friends of Churchill—among his personal friends. Nor was he a political bigot, in spite of the harshness of British domestic politics from 1911 to the outbreak of war. Nevertheless, while he freely admitted that Churchill's abilities and qualities of character were outstanding, there was something about the 'Churchill magic' which Law found repugnant. He had come to the careful, measured conclusion that Churchill was too fertile of unsound and dangerous plans, too quick to resent criticism, too obstinate to admit the possibility of fallibility in his schemes; in short, too irresponsible to occupy an important position in a time of crisis. For his part, Churchill made little attempt to conceal his dislike of Law and consistently underrated his capacities and position. As Beaverbrook has commented with justice on Law's attempt to warn Churchill of the mood of the Opposition, the First Lord 'took the hint in bad part, oblivious of the shadows of doom now creeping upon the Government and his own administration, and sublimely ignorant that he was the principal object which was casting that shadow.'

De Robeck's telegram precipitated the crisis which had been smouldering for so long. Churchill wanted at least a limited attack on the Narrows forts to cover the clearance of the Kephez minefield. Fisher was obdurate. On May 11th, after a long conversation with Churchill, he wrote to the First Lord:

..... Our deliberations on the subject of these operations have been conducted either in personal conference or by the interchange of informal notes, and there is therefore no official record of the views that I have from time to time expressed. Although I have acquiesced in each stage of the operations up to the present, largely on account of considerations of political expediency and the political advantage which those whose

193

business it is to judge of these matters have assured me will accrue from success, or even partial success, I have clearly expressed my opinion that I did not consider the original attempt to force the Dardanelles with the Fleet alone was a practicable operation. . . . I cannot, under any circumstances, be a party to any order to Admiral de Robeck to make any attempt to pass the Dardanelles until the shores have been effectively occupied. . . .

The news of the sinking of the old battleship *Goliath* in Morto Bay on the night of May 12th–13th seemed to confirm Fisher's apprehensions. Under cover of a thick mist, a Turkish torpedo-boat, the *Muavenet-i-Millet*, had slipped down the Dardanelles and had torpedoed *Goliath* from close range after replying in English to a challenge. 'The night was perfectly still,' Wemyss related, 'and now this stillness was broken by an indistinct noise as of an angry crowd in the distance, a noise which gradually rose and fell and finally subsided, as the men were picked up or drowned, until stillness once again reigned.' 'The sea, for an area of some half-acre, was a mass of struggling, drowning people,' an officer of *Majestic* reported, 'all drifting down towards us with the current.' In terms of casualties, this was the greatest single disaster suffered by the Navy in the whole Dardanelles campaign, over 600 officers and men being lost.

In London, matters were moving rapidly toward a major schism at the Admiralty even before the news of the loss of *Goliath* was received on May 13th. Churchill had appealed to Fisher's loyalty with no effect. 'With reference to your remark that I am absolutely committed,' the old man replied coldly, 'I have only to say that you must know (as the Prime Minister also) that my unwilling acquiescence did not extend to such a further gamble as any repetition of March 18 until the Army had done their part.' Churchill was obliged to agree to the withdrawal of *Queen Elizabeth* from the Dardanelles— to be replaced by 14-in. monitors and old cruisers of the *Edgar* class, fitted with large anti-mine and anti-torpedo 'blisters'—and to abandon the plan for another attempt on the forts. This was conveyed to de Robeck on the 14th. 'The moment for an independent naval attempt to force the Narrows has passed', the Admiralty telegram ran. '. . . The Army is now landed, large reinforcements are being sent, and there can be no doubt that with time and patience the Kilid Bahr Plateau will be taken.' The rôle of the Fleet, it was emphasised, would be to support the Army 'in its costly but sure advance, and to reserve your strength to deal with the situation which will arise when the Army has succeeded with your aid in its task.'

Kitchener was informed of the decision to recall *Queen Elizabeth* on the evening of May 13th, and was exceedingly angry. Fisher flew into a tempest of fury at Kitchener's virtual accusations of treachery, and the War Council met on the following morning in an atmosphere described by Churchill as 'sulphurous' and by Hankey as 'one of almost unrelieved gloom'. Sir John French's assault on Aubers Ridge had been repulsed with terrible loss, the Dardanelles operations were gravely checked, and, on that very morning, *The Times*—fed with information from French's G.H.Q.—had delivered a sensational attack on the Government for the alleged shortage of shells. 'Intense anxiety and extreme bad temper, all suppressed under formal demeanour, characterised the discussion', Churchill has written of the War Council's first meeting for eight weeks.

Kitchener was despondent and bitter about the withdrawal of *Queen Elizabeth*, and he described the progress of the war in other sectors in gloomy terms. 'When he had finished,' Churchill relates, 'the Council turned to me—almost on me.' He ill-advisedly tried to strike a cheerful and optimistic note about the Dardanelles operations, declaring that the removal of *Queen Elizabeth* was not of outstanding significance and that it was vital to press on. He was listened to with something like impatience, as the accounts of Hankey and others present clearly show. Churchill, however, thought that his arguments 'appeared to produce a definite impression upon the Council'. At length, the Council decided to ask Hamilton to state his requirements for victory, 'a question that ought to have been put to him before ever a man was landed', as Hankey has observed.

After the meeting, Churchill and Fisher discussed the new ships to be sent to the Dardanelles and apparently reached full agreement, although Fisher made it clear that he was concerned by this remorseless drain of ships and men. When Fisher reached the Admiralty at 5 a.m. on the following morning, however, he discovered that Churchill had added two 'E'-class submarines to the list, and had also drafted changes in the deployment of the Grand Fleet and proposals for heavy siege artillery at the Dardanelles which would have delayed Fisher's cherished building programme. Churchill subsequently argued that his discussions with Fisher on the 14th 'could not be regarded in the nature of a final bargain or treaty between separate and hostile powers. . . . I cannot therefore feel that I was wrong in wishing to include them (i.e. the submarines) among the proposals sent to the First Sea Lord, not as matters decided upon, but for consideration and discussion as I was careful to make plain in my covering note to the minute.'

Opinions may vary on the merits of Churchill's proposals, but hardly on their tactlessness. To add two brand-new ships to a fleet about which Fisher had complained only a few hours before as being already too large; to make emphatic proposals about the deployment of the Grand Fleet; and then, finally, to propose a course which would at least seriously delay Fisher's building programme on which he had set his heart; to do all this in one paper reveals a surprising insensitiveness. Churchill never seems to have realised where he went wrong, and later came to the quite incorrect conclusions that Fisher was jealous of Kitchener—for which there is absolutely no evidence—and that he was incensed by Churchill's decision to authorise naval assistance to the Italians—who were about to come into the war on the side of the Entente—without Fisher's concurrence. Churchill even described this episode as 'the spark that fired the train', when in fact it had virtually no significance although, as Captain T. Crease—who was close to Fisher and who subsequently challenged Churchill's version of the incident—has admitted, it certainly did not help.

Later that morning, as Churchill was walking across Horse Guards Parade to the Admiralty from the Foreign Office, he was handed a letter from Fisher.

> *First Lord*   *May 15th, 1915*
> After further anxious reflection I have come to the regretted conclusion I am unable to remain any longer as your colleague. It is undesirable in the public interest to go into details—Jowett said, 'Never explain'—but I find it increasingly difficult to adjust myself to the increasingly daily requirements of the Dardanelles to meet your views. As you truly said yesterday, I am in the position of continually vetoing your proposals.
> This is not fair to you besides being extremely distasteful to me.
> I am off to Scotland at once, so as to avoid all questionings.
>
> > Yours truly,
> > Fisher.

At first Churchill and Asquith did not take this letter seriously, but when Fisher was nowhere to be found concern began to be felt. Eventually he was run to earth in the Charing Cross Hotel, where he received a peremptory message from Asquith ordering him to remain at his post in the King's name. Both Asquith and Grey saw Fisher, and both urged him to say and do nothing for several days. Hankey found him lurking at the Athenaeum Club on the evening of May 15th 'to escape from Winston'.

There is something revealingly pathetic about Fisher's refusal to see Churchill in these crucial days. Fisher, the man of so many words, cunning, fierce and disconcertingly articulate, was almost powerless against 'the Churchill magic', with the result that he had acquiesced in decisions which he believed to be wrong and which caused him intense anguish before and after he saw Churchill; but in Churchill's presence his confidence seemed to wither, he found difficulty in combating Churchill's arguments and enthusiasm. This, of course, was part of the difficulty; Fisher genuinely liked and admired Churchill, and could no longer trust himself in his presence. 'YOU ARE BENT ON FORCING THE DARDANELLES AND NOTHING WILL TURN YOU FROM IT—NOTHING. I know you so well!' he wrote in reply to a friendly appeal from Churchill. 'I could give no better proof of my desire to stand by you than my having remained by you in this Dardanelles business to this last moment against the strongest conviction of my life. . . . *You will remain.* I SHALL GO. It is better so.'

Bonar Law had been alerted when he received an envelope addressed in Fisher's unmistakable handwriting containing nothing except a brief cutting from the *Pall Mall Gazette* to the effect that Fisher had had an audience with the King. Law assumed, after pondering this cryptic communication, that Fisher had resigned, and on May 17th he called on Lloyd George to put the question directly to him. On Lloyd George's confirming Law's deduction, the Conservative leader remarked; 'then the situation is impossible.'

The Dardanelles crisis and the first ugly rumblings of what became known as the 'shells scandal' put the Government in a position in which it could not dispense with the active support of the Opposition. On the shells issue Law had his party under control, and the Government's case in any event was a good one, but he knew that if Churchill came down to the House of Commons and announced that Fisher had resigned and he had not, the Tory Party would erupt. Lloyd George took Law to see Asquith at once on May 17th, and the Prime Minister agreed that a major reconstruction of the Government was inevitable. Churchill arrived at Westminster that afternoon armed with a defiant speech and a projected new Board of Admiralty, with, he thought, the support of the Prime Minister, who had refused his resignation on the previous day. Churchill had also got the support of Balfour, but Law was the arbiter of his fate. He saw Lloyd George and Asquith at the Commons, and from them discovered that a far greater reconstruction than that of the Board of Admiralty was under consideration. On the same evening, in company with other Ministers, his formal resignation was requested.

Churchill's removal from the Admiralty was a *sine qua non* in the discussions between Law and Asquith about the formation of a Coalition Government. Churchill himself was stunned by the brutality of his downfall. He played a last desperate card by offering Fisher a seat in the Cabinet if he would withdraw his resignation, but as Hankey, who was with Fisher when Churchill's emissary, the Civil Lord, Lambert, arrived, has written, 'Fisher's reply was to tell Churchill to go to hell.' This episode is not recorded in *The World Crisis.** Churchill was in no position to offer anything to anybody, and in the circumstances was fortunate to be given the sinecure post of Chancellor of the Duchy of Lancaster, with a position on the reconstituted War Council, now to be called the Dardanelles Committee. Arthur Balfour replaced him at the Admiralty. There was a prolonged and undignified argument over offices. 'The Unionist leaders, on coming to the aid of the nation at this juncture, made no conditions as to policy, but stipulated for half the places and patronage,' as Churchill subsequently commented with acerbity.

Fisher, by presenting Asquith with what was virtually an ultimatum on

---

* Indeed, Churchill stated that after May 16th 'it was no use persisting further [with Fisher], and I turned to consider new combinations'. (*World Crisis*, II, 364). The offer to Fisher was in fact made on May 17th.

May 19th, demanding supreme control over naval policy, cut himself off completely from the conduct of the Navy's affairs. Sir Arthur Wilson refused to serve under anyone but Churchill, and Fisher was replaced by Sir Henry Jackson, whose attitude to the Dardanelles operations was at best unenthusiastic. Balfour, although a supporter of the Dardanelles operations, was by temperament and background entirely unsuited to a position in time of war in which energy and imagination were essential. 'In place of two men of driving power, initiative and resource, but occasionally lacking in judgement,' Hankey has commented of the change at the Admiralty, 'there were now in charge two men of philosophic temperament and first-rate judgement, but less dynamic than their predecessors.'

The new Government was a coalition only in name. It never worked together as a team, and its proceedings were marked by a mutual suspicion which made it an even more cumbersome and inefficient body than its predecessors. And while it was in the throes of composition, over three weeks of almost complete inactivity in the conduct of the war passed.

May was a sublime month at Gallipoli, but in the last week it was evident that the climate, which had until then been an ally of the troops, was beginning to become an implacable enemy. The heat was beginning to be uncomfortable, the flies were multiplying rapidly, and already there were isolated cases of dysentery. The long-range shelling of the Helles position from the Asiatic shore became steadily more serious and accurate, and began to get on everybody's nerves. Every now and then a warship would enter the Straits and pound the area where the guns were supposed to be, but never succeeded in silencing them for very long. A new town of dug-outs had to be hurriedly constructed facing west at W Beach, and before long the Helles sector was laced with communication trenches which enabled one to walk for hours without showing one's head above ground. The trenches themselves were narrow and stifling, and there was hardly any shade; the interminable business of carrying up supplies to the front from the beaches was tiring, boring and dangerous. From time to time there would be a burst of firing down the line, here and there a patrol into No Man's Land, and then lassitude would spread over the trenches. The men dug new communication trenches, pushed forward saps into No Man's Land to bring the lines closer together, drew their rations, whiled away the time in a variety of ways, lolled listlessly in the trenches, sniped and were sniped at. Days would pass with nothing in particular happening, even the isolated artillery bombardments having a somewhat half-hearted air. There was some throwing over of propaganda messages into the enemy trenches, which was an occupation widely regarded as dangerous and futile.

The Turks responded by inviting the Moslem Indians to turn on their Christian masters and with a message which contained the ambiguous phrase, 'be convinced that everybody of you who has been taken prisoner will be treated just as well as the international law commands'. At Anzac, Aubrey Herbert would crawl into the nearest saps to the Turk trenches and talk to them, a practice which did not endear him to the Anzacs, as the reply usually took the form of a cloud of bombs. Attempts to improve morale by the distribution among the troops of glowing reports of great victories had rather the opposite effect. In such a close-knit world as the Peninsula it was stupid and useless to claim triumphs when everyone knew exactly what was happening. 'We get chits here every day telling us that the Turkish morale is gone', Colonel Darlington of the Manchesters drily wrote in his diary; 'we haven't noticed it in the trenches.'

The junior officers, struggling with a host of problems for which they had received little training, became pink-eyed with lack of sleep, and imbued with a certain fatalistic cynicism which abruptly sobered the new arrivals from Egypt. 'The men have been twelve days in the trenches, and are shaken in morale', John Allen wrote to his family on May 31st, a week before his death. 'A groaning, tortured man lying below you in a trench is not pleasant company. Twelve days and nights we have been at work almost continuously. Yesterday we had a quiet day after we left the fire-trench. The men talked about wounds and dead men all day. It was getting on their nerves— remember Wellington's observation that every man in uniform is not a hero.' 'There is very little noise on the beach in the way of talk and laughter,' Aubrey Herbert wrote in his diary; 'the men never expected to be up against this.' Corporal Alec Riley, a signaller in the 42nd (East Lancashire) Division which arrived at Helles in May, has written:

> When we landed on the Peninsula we had a new kind of life in a strange country before us, with a freshness, and an interest in the unknown. Now, we had reached the end of this period of discovery. Routine was becoming monotonous, and we were becoming irritable. We had learnt many things without effort, for new experiences just happened in the natural course of our duties. We had learnt that bullets can turn corners, that lice thrive on Keating's and cleanliness, that our own cooking had failed to give us indigestion, that the sun's heat was becoming greater every day, that the large green flies were more numerous, that the smell from the dead was always with us, that we could read the same newspapers several times, and that war is made of blood, smell, lice, filth, shells, noise, weariness and death.

A young subaltern in the same Division was startled by the low level of morale at Helles, even in the 29th Division. 'Everyone was deeply shocked by the casualties and by the fact that the Turks were such successful killers. The small amount of ground we held—which meant that one was never out of it, even at the furthermost beach—was another powerful factor. Leadership was so bad or so inexperienced, at any rate in our Division (which became a good one in France two or three years later). Somehow or other one felt we hadn't a chance of winning, and I never felt like that in France or Flanders even when things were at their worst during Third Ypres or the March 1918 retreat.' This was almost certainly an exceptionally gloomy picture, but it must be remembered that a great majority of the officers and men had had no previous experience of modern warfare, and many of them were genuinely shocked by the mood of the Army. The standard of many senior officers undoubtedly had a serious effect on morale. 'It is an absolute record here the number of Brigadiers, Colonels and other senior ranks who have only been able to stick it from three days to about a fortnight, and who have then gone home with shattered nerves,' Colonel Darlington wrote in his diary in June. 'Regulars just as much as Territorials. In our division (12 battalions) there is not one single C.O. now commanding who was at Cairo with us.' The system of promoting junior officers temporarily to senior positions on account of their knowledge of the unit and the front rarely operated at Gallipoli, with disastrous results.

The men themselves were very willing to learn, but nothing could fully compensate for the lack of experienced officers. One soldier has written of his regiment that 'we were not better or worse than any other unit. We could march and shoot. We were very fit and had good *esprit de corps*. But we were woefully inexperienced in warfare, and rather amateur campaigners.' It was a description which had a wide application in the Mediterranean Expeditionary Force. The Turks, in spite of their poor equipment and lack of imagination, were tough fighters, dogged and brave in defence, wildly and suicidally heroic in attack, and were led by officers who had the bitter but invaluable experience of the Balkan Wars behind them. The British acquired a deep respect for their enemy, which was reciprocated. It was something more than the camaraderie which often exists between frontline soldiers, and one understands the remark of Brereton that 'there was a flavour about the Gallipoli fighting which made it fiercer and more romantic than on any other front.'

The attitude of the army towards G.H.Q. had also undergone a significant change. General Cox, commanding the Indian Brigade, wrote that 'G.H.Q. became out of touch with the Army. . . . The Army on the spot knew quite well that the ideas and hopes of its Commanders as expressed to them in addresses, orders, etc., were not in accordance with the facts which were being faced by them at the Front. The want of any intimacy between H.Q. staff and the Army had an undesirable effect on the latter.' Orlo Williams referred in his diary at this time to 'the abnormal want of united feeling between troops and staffs, the growing dissensions at G.H.Q.' Braithwaite's genius at getting everybody's back up was largely responsible for this unhappy situation, but it is evident from the private papers of Hamilton's staff that there was a mounting feeling of disillusionment and disappointment among them at his failure to devise and impose a strategy for the campaign. Lt.-Col. Pollen, Hamilton's Military Secretary, expressed himself forcefully as early as May 8th that Hamilton was too afraid of Kitchener, 'and never would run his own show in his own way', while another staff officer wrote in his diary of Hamilton at the same time that 'I fear he is run by the C.G.S. [Braithwaite], who may be a good soldier but is a stupid man, with no ideas.' Orlo Williams' diary records an extraordinary outburst by two senior members of the staff, occasioned by Hamilton refusing to deal with an important telegram to London before he had finished the press telegram. 'That's the worst of having a journalist in command', one exclaimed angrily; 'That's not fair,' the other rejoined; 'all journalists are not mountebanks.'

The real source of the staff's dismay lay in the fact that Hamilton had in effect surrendered all his powers to Hunter-Weston, whose domination was formally established on May 24th when the three British divisions at Helles were grouped under his command into the VIII Corps, General de Lisle being sent for from France to command the 29th Division. Furthermore, Hamilton's buoyant confidence tended gradually to irritate rather than to inspire his subordinates. Nevertheless, they did not fully comprehend the difficulties under which he worked. On May 18th he received a disturbing telegram from Kitchener:

Private and Personal

You will fully realise my serious disappointment that preconceived views as to the conquest of positions necessary to dominate the forts on the Straits, with naval artillery to support our troops on land, and with active help of naval bombardment, were miscalculated. A serious situation is created by the present check, and by call of men and munitions that we can ill spare from France. From the standpoint of an early solution of our difficulties your views are not encouraging. The question whether we can long support two fields of operations draining our resources requires grave consideration. I can rely on you to do your utmost to bring the present state of affairs in the Dardanelles to as early a conclusion as possible, so that any considerations of withdrawal, with all its dangers in the East, may not enter the field of possible solutions. . . .

Hamilton and Braithwaite were naturally puzzled by the tone of this despondent telegram, and eventually decided that Kitchener was warning them not to send information which might be seized upon by opponents of the Dardanelles operations. 'I certainly read that telegram as an appeal to be careful how we worded our telegrams for fear of the evacuationists', Hamilton later stated. It was an understandable but disastrous interpretation. Hamilton's telegrams had rarely veered on the side of pessimism, and their tendency towards prolixity—which never ceased to madden his staff— made them both sanguine and vague; from this time, as a result of this grave misinterpretation of Kitchener's telegram, his reports became even less realistic. Orlo Williams considered that Kitchener 'had been speaking his innermost thoughts. A nature of similar calibre at the Gallipoli end would have seized the opportunity to put before Lord Kitchener, with equal frankness, a searching analysis of the whole position and prospects. . . . It was typical of Sir Ian Hamilton, both now and later, that he would dilute cogently drafted reports with literary palliatives and comforting trimmings that were justified less by facts than his own personal convictions.' The judgement is harsh, but not wholly opposed to the truth. It is only when it is realised that Hamilton thought he had received this hint from Kitchener that it is possible to appreciate the facts behind some of Hamilton's most mystifying telegrams. His reply to Kitchener's telegram of May 18th, accordingly, gave little hint of anything amiss, and so encouraged Kitchener that he made a widely-reported speech in the Lords which gave a wholly inaccurate portrait of the Gallipoli situation.

> All quiet in the French section and the 29th Division section. In the East Lancashire Division section the line has been straightened out and 500 yards of trenches gained during the night, 17th-18th May. The situation on the Australian-New Zealand Army Corps section is satisfactory, and the enemy's shelling has been less heavy than usual. The work of improving the communications, etc., continues. Although I made certain requests for additional troops in my number M.F.234 of 17th instant, I am sure that you will realise that does not imply that I am not doing all I possibly can with the force at my disposal, and every day sees some improvement in our position. The Lancashire Territorials are very keen and doing well.

And so, once again, they were at sixes and sevens. Maxwell begrudges reinforcements for Hamilton, de Robeck refuses to budge until Hamilton has captured the Kilid Bahr Plateau, Hamilton feels he cannot ask for further reinforcements from Kitchener in case he gives the enemies of the campaign their chance to abandon it, and Kitchener is misled by Hamilton's reports. And, at this point, the Fleet disappeared.

Ever since the landings the sea had seemed to be filled with Allied warships and transports. The liners, transports and trawlers lying off the beaches or manoeuvring with calm impunity had given as much confidence to the Army as the great battleships majestically pounding the Turkish positions. On the night of May 12th-13th there had been a brilliant example of what could be done with effective co-ordination between the Navy and the Army when the Gurkhas captured a heavily entrenched promontory which dominated Y Beach and Gully Spur and from where the Turks had not been dislodged in the Second Battle of Krithia. With the cruiser *Talbot* and destroyer *Wolverine* in close support the Indians stormed and captured the position—henceforth known as Gurkha Bluff—with relatively trivial casualties.

On May 17th the ominous news was received that a German submarine had passed through the Straits at Gibraltar. As an immediate precaution, the number of warships lying off the Peninsula was reduced by half, and large transports were no longer allowed to sail between Mudros and the Peninsula. Thus, instead of being taken directly to the beaches in the transports which had brought them from Egypt, all men, animals and stores had to be disembarked at Mudros and then re-embarked on light-draught ferry boats which sailed only at night. The facilities for these operations simply did not exist at Mudros, and the Lines of Communication arrangements virtually broke down within a few days. De Robeck also insisted that *Arcadian*, anchored off W Beach with Hamilton and his staff, should be transferred to Imbros; cables were laid down from the ship to Anzac and Helles, but the situation was so unsatisfactory that the staff landed on Imbros itself on May 31st and established itself in a series of fly-blown tents on a particularly unpleasant part of the beach. Hamilton was now 18 miles from Helles and 15 from Anzac, and the physical separation inevitably reduced what control he exercised over the strategy in the Helles sector, where Hunter-Weston now reigned supreme.

Up to this point the British submarines had become a serious menace to the Turks. The feat of AE2 had fired the imagination of the British and French submariners, eagerly urged forward by Keyes and Guépratte, and at the end of April E14, commanded by Lt.-Commander Boyle, had reached the Marmara and had caused havoc with the troopships and supply transports going to the Peninsula. Then Lt.-Commander Nasmith had taken E11 to Constantinople itself, and sunk a freighter berthed alongside the arsenal, and had lurked in the approaches to the capital until he had completely paralysed all shipping and had reduced the population of the capital to something not far removed from complete panic. Quite apart from the minefields and the Turkish gun-boats and destroyers patrolling the surface, there was an additional natural hazard to the passage of the Dardanelles. The current of fresh water from the Marmara, about ten fathoms deep, caused an abrupt change in the density of the water which made a submarine almost uncontrollable. This freak had caused the loss of the French submarine *Saphir* in January and of E15 in April; in addition to these losses, the French submarine *Joule* had been sunk in the Kephez minefield on May 1st, the *Bernouilli* had been forced to return, and AE2 had been lost. Out of six submarines that had tried to get through, four had been sunk. These facts underline the achievements of Boyle and Nasmith, and of the submariners who came after them.

By the middle of May the Turks had been forced to stop sending troops by sea to the Peninsula, with the result that the men had to travel for nearly a week by train and on foot instead of twelve hours by sea. The supply situation at one stage was so serious that the capacity of the Turks to remain on the Peninsula was jeopardised, and at one point the troops had only

160 rounds of ammunition per man left. But brilliant and daring though the British submariners were, they never quite succeeded in preventing the supply ships getting through. By hugging the shores, and sailing as much as possible by night, the supply ships continued to bring their precious supplies to the improvised harbour of Kilia Liman opposite Nagara, but after Boyle's feat in torpedoing an old White Star liner with over 6,000 troops on board—whose fate is uncertain—all reinforcements had to endure the long and wearying tramp on bad roads to the Peninsula.

The arrival of Commander Hersing and U21, after an epic voyage from Wilhelmshaven since April 25th, dramatically reversed the situation. On May 23rd *Albion* had grounded off Baba Tepe, and had eventually been hauled off by *Canopus* and the recoil of her own guns after enduring a prolonged close-range bombardment from the Turks. Coming so shortly after the loss of *Goliath* and the submarine reports, this episode considerably increased the tension in the Fleet. On May 25th there was a flurry of activity when *Vengeance*, *Canopus* and *Agamemnon* spotted U21 off Helles, and just after noon *Triumph* was torpedoed off Anzac, in the full view of both armies. 'This morning I was talking to Dix,' Aubrey Herbert recorded in his diary, 'asking him if he believed there were submarines. "Yes," he said, and then swore and added, "there's the *Triumph* sinking".' The destroyer *Chelmer* and a swarm of picket-boats were soon at the stricken ship's side, and managed to rescue almost all the crew before the old battleship—'growling like a wounded dog, as the things inside went adrift', as one of her officers wrote—went down. Birdwood, returning in a trawler from a reconnaissance of Suvla, related in a letter to his wife that *Triumph* 'suddenly turned just like a fish diving, pointed her bows to the bottom and went quietly straight to the bottom. It was really rather an awful sight and most solemn.' The cheers of the exultant Turks came echoing down the ravines and across the calm water. 'There was fury, panic and rage on the beach and on the hill', Aubrey Herbert relates. '. . . Men were crying and cursing.' 'It was a nerve-racking sight,' an Australian officer wrote in his diary that night, 'and has done none of us any good to see it.'

De Robeck promptly recalled all the larger warships to Imbros. 'I saw them in full flight,' Compton Mackenzie has written; 'transports and battleships, the *Agamemnon* seeming to lead the van. The air was heavy that evening and, what wind there was being in the south, the smoke of every ship was driven down astern, which gave the effect of a number of dogs running away with their tails between their legs. The sense of abandonment was acute. There was a sudden lull in the noise of the beach, as if every man had paused to stare at the unfamiliar emptiness of the water and then turned to his neighbour with a question in his eyes about their future here. It is certain that the Royal Navy has never executed a more demoralising manoeuvre in the whole of its history.' 'All the ships had disappeared as if God had taken a broom and swept the sea clear', Kannengiesser writes. '. . . The joy of the brave Turks can scarcely be described.'

On the following day de Robeck, acutely conscious of the effect of the undignified withdrawal of the Fleet, ordered *Majestic* to Helles, where she anchored off W Beach with torpedo-nets extended like a Victorian dowager at a ball, surrounded by small craft. Nobody had much confidence in these precautions, and while the soldiers eyed the old battleship with impotent solicitude, the crew resigned themselves to their fate. At 6.40 on the morning of May 27th Hersing struck, firing his torpedo through the crowd of small craft 'like picking a royal stag out of his harem of does', as Hamilton remarked. A Commander Barnes was on deck, supervising the launching of the Admiral's barge when 'happening to look about me, I saw some 350 yards off our port beam a whitish-coloured patch, marked also by an absence of ripple, on the surface of the water. As I looked, I saw emerging from this patch a line of bubbles extending rapidly in our direction: unmistakable the wake of a torpedo coming at us. There was little time to give the alarm. . . . I remember hearing the rush of many people over to the starboard side, and going myself towards that side of the after-bridge when the explosion came. It was terrific. . . . The whole ship seemed to lift, there was a tremendous shock, a column of water, bits of spars, net-shelf, etc., went high up in the air. I remember looking aloft, expecting the main topmast to come down on me, and saw it was moving like the top joint of a trout rod. The ship immediately began listing to port.'

The impression ashore was rather different. An Army chaplain has related that 'At first the ship did not seem even to tremble. About a minute later her spars dipped slightly. There was much excited movement on her deck, and the crew began to spring overboard. Soon the water round her was full of struggling men.'

Ashmead-Bartlett—who had prudently spent the night on deck—had been on board, and has written of the spectacle from a boat to which he had swum;

> *Majestic* presented an extraordinary spectacle. She was lying over on her side, having such a list that it was no longer possible to stand on her deck. About one-third of her crew still seemed to be hanging on to the rails, or clinging to her side, as if hesitating to jump into the water. All around, the sea was full of men, some swimming towards neighbouring ships, others apparently having their work cut out to keep themselves afloat. All the vessels in the neighbourhood were lowering boats, and steam launches were hastening to pick up survivors, but they did not dare to stand in too close for fear of being dragged under in the final plunge.

The cliffs were now packed with silent and shocked soldiers, watching the frantic attempts to rescue the crew as *Majestic* heeled over slowly but inexorably. Suddenly she rolled right over and sank bottom upwards, her final plunge marked by a tremendous roar 'as everything movable, from saucers to turrets, fell from their places.' The swirling water and part of her ram, which remained above water as the bows were lying on a sandbank, were all that remained. It had taken under half an hour, and the only gleam of solace was the fact that the number of fatal casualties was small. Guy Dawnay wrote to his wife that 'I never, never want to see a sight like that again. It was horrible—and somehow intensely pathetic as well. The great ship sorely wounded and then her death!'

Fortunately, this was Hersing's last triumph. On May 30th he sank a transport fitted up with dummy guns and superstructure to represent the battlecruiser *Tiger*, and had the mortifying experience of seeing the wooden superstructure floating away as the ship settled. Chased by Samson, he sailed through the Dardanelles to Constantinople, and the German submarine effort never again achieved anything like the same impact on the campaign, although there were eventually several U-boats in the Eastern Mediterranean. Nevertheless, no Allied ship ever felt safe again, and one practical and important consequence of the withdrawal of the battleships—which only emerged for special occasions after the end of May—was that the Asiatic guns were for a time virtually unmolested, and the shelling of the Helles sector from across the Straits steadily increased.

Although both armies soon realised that the departure of the battleships did not have as great an effect as they had expected, as the cruisers and destroyers became more active than before, and eventually the new monitors supplied any deficiency in heavy naval bombardments, the effect on morale was enormous. 'It is stupefying,' an Australian soldier wrote in his diary; 'those massive ships stricken so suddenly. It is woe to us, for the help of their great guns feels almost like human support.' 'Our return to the Peninsula from Lemnos was a strange experience', Charles Lister, who had been wounded earlier in May, wrote in a letter home. 'When we first anchored off Cape Helles in May there was a huge collection of ships of all kinds, all lit up, making an effect like Brighton Pier illuminated. At present all there is to be seen are a couple of hospital ships, a few destroyers and a green shape protruding from the water, the keel of the *Majestic*.'

'What a change since the War Office sent us packing with a bagful of hallucinations', Hamilton, established in a wretched tin shanty on Imbros, wrote. 'Naval guns sweeping the Turks off the Peninsula; the Ottoman Army legging it from a British submarine waving the Union Jack; Russian help in hand; Greek help on the *tapis*. Now it is our Fleet which has to leg it from the German submarines; there is no ammunition for the guns; no drafts to keep my Divisions up to strength; my Russians have gone to Galicia and the Greeks are lying lower than ever.'

PART THREE

ATTRITION

9

Towards a New Offensive

This is the Fourth of June.
  Think not I never dream
The noise of that infernal noon,
  The stretchers' endless stream,
The tales of triumph won,
  The night that found them lies,
The wounded wailing in the sun,
  The dead, the dust, the flies.

The flies! oh God, the flies
  That soiled the sacred dead.
To see them swarm from dead men's eyes
  And share the soldiers' bread!
Nor think I now forget
  The filth and stench of war,
The corpses on the parapet,
  The maggots in the floor.
    A. P. Herbert: 'Half-Hours at Helles'

While the future of the Gallipoli operations hung in the balance in London for three weeks, Hamilton was confronted with a sombre and difficult decision on the Peninsula. After the check sustained in the Second Battle of Krithia, Hunter-Weston had prescribed a policy of steady pressure on the Helles front throughout May, and the Allied lines had been pushed forward nearly half a mile in some places. More ground had been gained by these stealthy and almost bloodless advances that had been won in the battle of May 6th–8th, and by the beginning of June the opposing front lines were extremely close to each other.

This progress unfortunately aroused an unreasoning optimism at VIII Corps Headquarters. Hunter-Weston was a dogged and resolute soldier, as his record in France had demonstrated, but, as the events of April 25th–May 8th also showed, his reactions to changing situations were not rapid. His Chief of Staff, Brigadier-General Street, shared with Hunter-Weston an intense faith in the carefully organised set-piece battle; more seriously, he was excessively optimistic, and was not adequately acquainted with the actual conditions in the front lines. His over-sanguine reports played an important part in misleading Sir Ian Hamilton as to the true situation at Helles. On May 21st, for example, Hamilton wrote to Asquith that 'I speak by the book then when I say that we have now defeated 3 Turkish armies in succession.' General Egerton, the commander of the 52nd (Lowland) Division, subsequently described Street as 'the evil genius of that bombastic person Hunter-Weston, and encouraged the latter in his extraordinary tactics'. Aspinall, less harshly, has written of Street that 'he could not bring himself to admit the increasing difficulties that confronted the troops at the southern end of the Peninsula.'

But although there is no doubt that Street's unvarying optimism had some effect on Hunter-Weston, it is doubtful if Hunter-Weston required much goading. In many respects, 'Hunter-Bunter' was a preposterous figure; fond of making dramatic entrances at staff conferences, rubicundly gruff, self-important and vain, he was 'something of a classic caricature of a British General at the beginning of the Great War', as one who served under him has commented. Like Keyes and Guépratte, he was a passionate believer in attack. 'Casualties?' he once remarked; 'what do I care about casualties?' A staff officer remembers finding him sitting in the sun above W Beach in the middle of one of the earlier battles, calmly writing some letters at a little table. 'My dispositions are made, my orders delivered', he placidly observed. 'There is nothing for me to do but wait, so I must occupy myself usefully.' Such phlegm may be admirable in a Commander-in-Chief; in a Corps Commander fighting on a narrow front with scanty ammunition and hardly any margin of reserves, it demonstrated a less praiseworthy detachment.

In very broad terms, his policy was the only justifiable course open to him. The Allied army could not afford to remain quiescent, and there were indications that the Turks were suffering heavily from the effects of the submarine campaign on their supplies and reinforcements. An Allied advance of a thousand yards, moreover, would have broken the Turkish line and virtually assured the capture of Achi Baba. The Allied army on the Helles front now consisted of three British divisions (the 29th Division, the 42nd (East Lancashire) Division and the Royal Naval Division) and two French divisions, and the artillery ammunition situation had slightly improved. Another division, the 52nd (Lowland) Division, was due to arrive at the end of the first week in June, its departure having been grievously delayed by the worst railway accident in the history of British railways at Gretna Green, in which 210 officers and men of the Royal Scots had been killed and 224 injured.

The optimism at Hunter-Weston's headquarters was so great that it was decided to launch the next major offensive before the 52nd Division arrived. The preparatory planning of what was officially designated the Third Battle of Krithia, but which is perhaps better known as the Battle of the Fourth of June, was a vast improvement on anything yet seen in the campaign. Excellent aerial photographs of the enemy trenches had enabled the staff to prepare duplicate and distribute accurate and detailed maps of the Turkish positions; over 30,000 men and the biggest artillery concentration of the campaign so far were to be employed; the advance was strictly limited to about 800 yards; instead of lunging into the unknown, with vague objectives and grandiose ambitions, the troops were to undertake a limited, systematic and meticulously prepared destruction of the enemy's front lines. Special digging parties were to follow the assaulting troops to strengthen the captured trenches and dig new communication trenches; independent groups—the forerunners of the 'mopping-up' parties—were to round up snipers and eliminate pockets of resistance; eight armoured cars, the pride and anxiety of the Royal Naval Division, were to be used, and the roads on which they were to move forward were specially levelled.

Morale rose sharply when the general lines of attack were made known. One company commander wrote in his diary that 'it was the first time that I had seen such elaborate orders. Every detail was provided for, and the plan seemed invincible.' Although the plan had little subtlety, a somewhat ponderously conceived attempt was to be made to deceive the enemy by a ruse; when the initial bombardment ended at 11.20 a.m., the troops were to cheer and flourish bayonets above the parapets; as soon as the Turks had anxiously packed their front lines again, the main bombardment was to fall on them; at noon, the infantry would attack. As in all set-piece battles of this kind, success depended almost entirely on the effectiveness of the preliminary bombardment and the immediate capture of all preliminary objectives; if part of the enemy's front line were uncaptured, the advancing units on either side would be in danger of being caught in enfilade.

June 4th opened as an exquisite summer's day, although a firm breeze blew the dust into a choking storm as it progressed. The gunners checked ammunition, ranges, communications and their dully gleaming charges; the blue smoke rose wispily from the field-kitchens, where many hundred men received their last meal; an electric tension reminiscent of April 25th ran through the crammed trenches and communication saps. 'Everyone was excited and impatient,' Corporal Riley prosaically wrote in his journal, 'and we could not eat much breakfast.' 'The greyness of the morning had vanished by now, and the air outside was brilliant after the damp and gloom of the shelter,' Compton Mackenzie has written of the scene; '. . . Out at sea, escorted by destroyers, *Albion* and *Implacable*, their guns spurting vivid yellow from turrets that stood in blackest silhouette against the dazzle of the sea and silver fume of the horizon, were steaming up and down at their slow and stately business and their solemn firing.' To remove any doubts which may have remained in the minds of the Turks that a major battle was imminent, white-hulled Red-Crossed hospital ships assembled off the shore, at once comforting, solicitous and sinister. Long before the British and French troops were assembled in their positions, the Turks were thoroughly alerted. Reserves were aroused from their bivouacs behind the Achi Baba ridge, the dust rose in gentle clouds as the lines of men marched along the Soghanli Dere, officers clattered urgently to and fro, the cool morning air was filled with the myriad clinkings, callings and cursings of an army urgently aroused, soon to be drowned by the shuffling-tramp of the marching troops, the creaking of carts, the thuddings of hooves and whinneyings of horses and mules as the army heaved itself purposefully into action. As the men walked up the valley, the dull rumbling of the guns became ever more menacing and ever more close. By 10 a.m. both sides were ready.

The Allied ruse at 11.20 was only partially successful in deceiving the Turks, and when the infantry clambered out to the attack at noon they were met with a furious fire. Dense clouds of dust and smoke were already obscuring the Peninsula, and now the spume of earth aroused by the Turk bullets and shells added to their contribution to the choking dust-storm which clutched at the soldiers' throats as they stumbled into what one has described as 'hell heaped up, running over, multiplied a thousandfold'.

On the right of the British line the Royal Naval Division, their advance preceded by a tremendous bombardment of the Turk trenches by the batteries of French 75's, made immediate progress and occupied the enemy front line. To their right, however, the French had been severely repulsed in an attack on a trench-work known as the Haricot Redoubt. At 12.15 p.m., as if on parade, the Collingwood Battalion moved forward in a long extended line. The battalion had landed on the Peninsula on May 30th, and many of the men were suffering severely from the after-effects of injections given on board. They now marched across the bare ground into the merciless fire from the Haricot Redoubt and oblivion. The trenches captured in the first charge were now untenable, and in the subsequent retirement more heavy casualties were suffered; the Collingwood Battalion had literally ceased to exist.* 'I saw an expanse of burned up grass and the barbed wire

* The battalion lost 16 officers killed and 8 wounded, and suffered over 500 casualties among the men; on June 8th the battalion was broken up, and the survivors posted to other units of the Royal Naval Division.

entanglements', an officer who had travelled to Gallipoli in the same boat as the Collingwood, has written. 'But also there were bodies. Tumbled heaps of khaki everywhere. Scores and scores of them, looking like dead leaves in autumn.' Denis Browne, who had been with Rupert Brooke when he died, 40 other officers and over 600 men of the Royal Naval Division, lay in the choking dust. By the time that the Division had regrouped itself in the trenches it had left so confidently so shortly before, it had lost 55 officers (out of 64) and 1,300 men killed and wounded.

The tragedy of this terrible repulse was that, elsewhere, things had gone remarkably well, although the vaunted armoured cars had proved useless. Chief Petty Officer F. W. Johnston, attached to an armoured car detachment, relates: 'The air was very heavily laden with dust and we could see absolutely nothing but a bank of yellow fog. . . . Presently a shout went up and hands pointed to a rise which formed the skylines across the Nullah. Plainly we could see a string of armoured cars jolting and swaying over the rough and shell-torn ground. As they got nearer the firing line the cheering increased and puffs of shrapnel played around the cars or high explosives fell near and hid them by a cloud of dust from our view. We noticed one car topple on its side—its two off-wheels had skidded into a trench and immediately it became the target of the enemy guns. One car turned and made its way rearward, another suddenly dropped into a depression suffering a shock which caused the turret to become detached and toppled off with the gun, leaving the car useless. Dust rose in huge clouds and hid the remainder from our sight.'

In the centre, however, the Manchesters of the 42nd Division had burst clear through the enemy lines and were within half a mile from Krithia. Kannengiesser, trying to move a battalion from another part of the line to deal with this crisis, was forced to abandon the idea when a senior Turk officer shouted, 'For God's sake, Colonel, don't order a single man to retire. If the others see that, they will all retire and run as far as Constantinople.' By early afternoon the Turkish situation was critical, and Kannengiesser and his fellow-officers were almost in despair. On the extreme left, near Gully Ravine, the Worcesters had gained almost all their objectives in their first rush, and, although the line was being held elsewhere, in most places the Turks were almost on the point of breaking.

Although unaware of the extent to which the Turks were demoralised by the fury of the British assault, Hunter-Weston at Corps headquarters was fully seized of the situation. Communications were far better than in any previous battle on the Peninsula, and the position on each sector of the front was accurately reported. Hunter-Weston's problem was whether to use his reserve of 12 British and six French battalions, and, if so, at what point. To use them all would have been a desperate gamble, and in the event—urged by Hamilton in an uncharacteristic personal intervention—Hunter-Weston decided to use only nine battalions, and to deploy them against the uncaptured Turk trenches facing the French and the remnants of the Royal Naval Division rather than to exploit the large gap cut by the Lancashire Territorials in the centre. It was a hard decision, and the wrong one. In spite of personal appeals from Hamilton, General Gouraud—who had replaced d'Amade—decided that he could not renew the offensive, and so the battle faded away. The Lancashire Territorials, without reinforcements, and uncomfortably isolated, were obliged to withdraw and consolidate new positions some 500 yards in front of those they had left at noon.

The painful contrast with the high hopes of the morning plunged the Allied troops into bitter despair. 'A pitiless sun beat down on the trenches and the afternoon heat was parching,' Arthur Behrend has written; 'many had emptied their water-bottles earlier in the day and no refilling points had yet been established. Men of different regiments were now hopelessly mixed, and messages passed continuously in both directions. . . . Everyone was in an impressionable mood, and the wildest reports of success and failure surged to and fro. Yet over all it was clear, even to soldiers as inexperienced in battle as ourselves, that the big advance had failed.'

'As I made my way along the trench I passed many heaps of dead upon which the great ugly flies were feasting', C. P. O. Johnston records in his diary. 'Wounded by the dozen were huddled in side trenches waiting for the time when it would be possible to get stretchers along to convey them to the base.'

For Hamilton, established in a dug-out on the left flank, with a commanding view of the battlefield—although not of the battle itself, because of the swirling dust-clouds—it had been an agonising day of exaltation and depression, culminating in the decision to order the Manchesters to fall back from Krithia. 'A black depression fell,' Compton Mackenzie relates. 'I stood aside for Sir Ian Hamilton to pass back along the trench. Then with one glance over my shoulder at that accursed hill of Achi Baba which still stood with hunched defiant shoulders between us and Constantinople, I followed the single file procession down the trench. Nobody spoke a word. Birds were twittering in their flight through the radiant air, and beyond them three biplanes went winging homeward to Tenedos, one behind the other, as birds fly across the sunset to roost. The sixty-pounder was still moaning on its way to the enemy's lines; but neither gunshot nor gloomy thoughts could quite destroy the amber peace of that evening of the Fourth of June . . . when we stepped ashore on the soft beach of Kephalo I felt that a long century lay between the flushed twilight in which we came back and the grey morning when we started.'

It took several days for the Allies to bury their dead and reorganise units.

The stench of death from No Man's Land was awful, and the flies were eagerly multiplying. The disposal of the remains was a ghastly business; 'the flies crawled in their millions over the dead and rose in clouds when a corpse was lifted to the grave and then descended to their feast before the spadeful of earth was placed', a sickened Johnston wrote in his diary of the scene in Gully Ravine.

The Turks had fared even worse than the Allies, but the line had held. The British casualties were over 4,500, those of the French more than 2,000; the Turks subsequently admitted to a casualty total of about 9,000, and regarded the situation at dusk as still critical. Kannengiesser has written that 'I felt that another energetic attack by the English would have the worst results', and a Turk officer wrote that 'had the British continued their attack the next day with the same violence, all would have been lost.' If Hamilton and Hunter-Weston had not been so dominated by unreasoning optimism and had delayed the attack for even a few days, they would have been able to use the 52nd Division, and its intervention might well have been decisive. But the Allies once again had been fought to a standstill, and it was only by a heroic defence that the Lancashire Territorials were able to retain their hard-won positions in the face of fierce counter-attacks over the next few days.

Five weeks had now elapsed since the operations began. In that period the British and Dominion troops had suffered nearly 40,000 casualties, while the French losses amounted to a further 20,000. The hospitals in Egypt, Malta and England were crammed with Gallipoli casualties. The stream of wounded seemed endless, and the Assistant Director of Medical Services in Alexandria has written that these weeks were 'a nightmare'; 'I used to wake in the morning and see the ships waiting to enter the harbour, and wonder where we could put all the people.' By June 10th the medical resources of Mudros, Malta and Egypt, in spite of urgently dispatched medical staff and supplies, and much devoted work by civilian volunteers, were utterly exhausted.

Three days after the Battle of the Fourth of June, the newly created Dardanelles Committee—consisting of Asquith, Grey, Lloyd George, Balfour, Bonar Law, McKenna, Churchill, Kitchener, Lansdowne, Crewe, Selborne and Curzon*—met for the first time. They were faced with three courses of action; they could abandon the Gallipoli enterprise; they could send Hamilton large reinforcements; or they could make good Hamilton's losses and leave him to make what progress he could. Kitchener, in a memorandum circulated on May 28th, favoured the third course. He considered that Hamilton's recent telegrams and letters had not inferred that massive reinforcements were required, and if only his existing divisions could be brought up to

* Sir Edward Carson joined in August.

full strength and more ammunition pushed out as quickly as possible, all would be well; this was his understanding of Hamilton's messages. Kitchener's memorandum was an eloquent commentary on the unhappy interpretation Hamilton had put upon his letter of May 18th.

Ministers had also before them a far more eloquent and persuasive memorandum submitted by Churchill, urging a vigorous effort in Gallipoli. In a much-publicised speech in his constituency (Dundee) on June 5th he had boldly declared that 'there never was a great subsidiary operation of war in which a more complete harmony of strategic, political and economic advantages has combined, or which stood in truer relation to the main decision which is in the central theatre. Through the Narrows of the Dardanelles and across the ridges of the Gallipoli Peninsula lie some of the shortest paths to a triumphant peace.' In spite of the shadow which had fallen across his career, the Dardanelles Committee members were profoundly impressed by Churchill's arguments; no supporters were to be found for a policy of evacuation, although Bonar Law was clearly uneasy about the whole enterprise, and Lloyd George still tended to favour Salonika; everyone was deeply disillusioned by the failures in Flanders and the heavy casualties suffered for no discernible object.

In addition to these important factors, there had been a significant adjustment in public opinion. Partly as a result of the enormous excitement and pride of Australia and New Zealand at the performance of the Anzacs and partly as a consequence of a belated realisation of the feat of the British landings, public interest in the Gallipoli operations was intense. Churchill's speeches, the trickle of photographs from the front, Ashmead-Bartlett's reports, and the excitement engendered by the whole enterprise, all combined to capture the public imagination. In April and May, public interest had been absorbed by the introduction of gas warfare by the Germans at Ypres, the sinking of the *Lusitania*, and the great Allied offensive in France; from now onwards it was increasingly centred upon the Dardanelles. The new Government could not fail to take notice of this changed mood, and the fervour and speed with which the Australian and New Zealand Governments were raising new divisions and transporting them to Egypt both embarrassed and spurred forward the Dardanelles Committee. For a period, enthusiasm for the Gallipoli operations reached unparalleled heights in London, and the dispatch of three divisions of the New Army (the 10th (Irish) Division and the 11th and 13th Divisions) was authorised, to arrive at the Peninsula not later than the first fortnight in July. Two light cruisers fitted with anti-torpedo 'bulges', 14 monitors, six submarines and four sloops were to join the Fleet. The liners *Aquitania*, *Mauretania* and *Olympic*, each of which could hold six or seven battalions of infantry, were to be chartered.

The Cabinet, with some reluctance, sanctioned these measures on June 9th, and on June 17th the Dardanelles Committee agreed to send more troops if ships could be found to convey them. Kitchener telegraphed Hamilton to ask if he wanted another division, to which Hamilton replied that he did not feel justified in refusing the offer. A few days later Kitchener offered another, and on July 5th the dispatch of these two further divisions (the 53rd and 54th Divisions) was ordered, to arrive before the middle of August.

In spite of this enormous increase in his force, Hamilton remained profoundly concerned about the artillery situation. By June 9th the British batteries were reduced to a daily expenditure of not more than eight rounds *per battery*, 'except in cases of emergency', and the reserves were dangerously low. Hamilton's protests and appeals met with so little practical response that he telegraphed in exasperation to the War Office on June 16th that 'we realise for our part that in the matter of guns and ammunition it is no good crying for the moon, and for your part you must recognise that until howitzers and ammunition arrive it is no good crying for the Crescent'. On July 13th he specifically requested 15,000 rounds of high-explosive shells, and a monthly consignment of about 400,000 rounds. This was quite out of the question and although Hamilton received some high-explosive ammunition and two batteries of 4·5-in. howitzers, the artillery capacity of the British was still inadequate.

Unfortunately, Hamilton's private letters to Kitchener were not really consistent with his formal appeals for more ammunition. On June 27th, for example, he wrote apologetically to Kitchener: 'You won't, I know, think I am nagging away about the H.E. ammunition by telling you this story [about the French supplies of ammunition]. I would indeed be a rotten fellow if I were doing anything of that sort, for you have been more than generous and more than kind to us in all these matters.' This ambivalent attitude undoubtedly misled Kitchener in the sense that he was not sufficiently personally impressed by the urgency of the ammunition situation; so long as the War Office revolved around his sense of priorities and whims, this was of great significance. On July 15th it was calculated that the entire British artillery ammunition at Helles amounted to 5,000 shrapnel-shells and no high-explosive. If the artillery weakness became something of an obsession with the British commanders it was not surprising.

Knowing that massive reinforcements were on their way, it is difficult to comprehend why Hamilton persisted in the Helles offensives throughout June and July. Writing to Kitchener on June 7th, he said clearly that 'anything like a general advance and general attack cannot be entertained at present as, apart from munitions, the men are not equal to it'. 'While steadily pressing the enemy,' Kitchener telegraphed on the 8th, 'there seems no reason for running any premature risks in the meantime.' Hamilton was writing a week later that 'if we are to remain [here] we must keep on attacking here and there to maintain ourselves. But to expect us to attack without giving us our fair share—on Western standards—of high-explosives and howitzers shows lack of military imagination.' Kitchener did not expect Hamilton to attack until his reinforcements had arrived, and had no inkling from Hamilton that he proposed to renew the Helles offensive; Hamilton's letter to him of June 7th had seemed to rule out the possibility of any major attacks for the present.

The main pressure on Hamilton came from Hunter-Weston, urged on by the enthusiastic Street. If, as Hamilton's letters of this time and his subsequent statements clearly indicate, he saw no future in frontal attacks against prepared positions with inadequate artillery, he took no action to dissuade Hunter-Weston from following such a policy. VIII Corps Headquarters, and particularly Street, now saw the events of June 4th as almost a brilliant victory; 'next time' all would be well.

General de Lisle, now commanding the 29th Division, and Egerton, commanding the 52nd Division, took a different view. De Lisle had landed on the afternoon of June 4th to take command of the 29th Division and his first experience of the Peninsula could hardly have been less inspiring. It was always something of a shock to men coming straight from England or France to land at Helles or Anzac by way of a rickety pier under sporadic shell-fire and to find their way up the beach past lines of mules and mounds of supplies, then to discover that the front line was only a couple of miles away. De Lisle, in addition, had had to pick his way to Corps Headquarters through the lines of wounded men lying in the scorching sun or being carried down to the beaches through over-crowded communication trenches. It is not surprising that he later wrote that 'on my arrival at Cape Helles on 4th June, 1915, my first impression was that our situation there was hopeless, and even critical had the Turks had more artillery'. Hamilton, himself perpetually optimistic—on June 7th he wrote disparagingly of the Turks to Kitchener that 'good as the Turks undoubtedly are, they are not fighting for any cause they clearly understand', a statement which can only be explained by the fact that he had fallen prey to his own propaganda—saw no reason to interfere with Hunter-Weston, whose plans for a renewal of the Helles offensive were therefore permitted to go forward.

At this point, with the New Army divisions being embarked in England for Gallipoli and the weary Helles troops preparing for another series of battles for Achi Baba, it is necessary to turn to Anzac, where several highly significant events had occurred in May, and which had turned the eyes of many at G.H.Q. away from Helles.

The New Zealanders on the north flank of the Anzac sector in their two dangerous, rocky and isolated outposts* had undertaken regular scouting operations after they had established themselves satisfactorily. On the night of May 15th Major Overton of the New Zealand Mounted Rifles, accompanied by a Corporal Denton, set out from Number One Outpost to find out if there was a practicable route to Chunuk Bair. They returned with a report of supreme importance. The first part of the climb was difficult, involving the scaling of a steep cliff to a plateau known as Table Top. Number Two Outpost and Table Top are connected by an unclimbable razor-back ridge,

*North Anzac: New Zealand
Mounted Rifles
Reconnaissances*

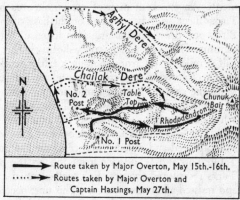

but Overton and Denton found that it was possible to reach the foot of Table Top by dropping into the Sazli Dere and skirting the connecting ridge. From Table Top it was possible to climb up to a long spur—known to the troops as Rhododendron Ridge on account of the red flowers† which blazed along its length in the early weeks of the campaign—which led directly to the summit of Chunuk Bair. About 1,000 yards from the summit itself there were two minor elevations on Rhododendron—subsequently called The Apex and The Pinnacle—and Overton and Denton reached The Apex before deciding to return. They had seen no Turks, and only three old, shallow and unoccupied trenches could be seen on Chunuk Bair itself.

The importance of this information was immediately realised by Birdwood. Overton's reconnaissance had proved that although many of these dizzy yellow ridges dropping down from the Chunuk Bair to the beach

* No. 1 and No. 2 Posts had been established on April 30th by the Nelson Company of the Canterbury Battalion under Brereton; after this unit went to Helles, the posts were taken over by the Deal Battalion of the Marines; the N.Z. Mounted Rifles took over on May 13th.

† Most accounts refer to these flowers as red oleanders, but Mr. R. J. Alexander of the War Graves Commission, then in charge of the Gallipoli cemeteries, told the author in 1962 that he had never seen oleanders on the Peninsula, and considered that the flowers were almost certainly a small bright red flower which grows in profusion early in the summer.

were unclimbable, the valleys were passable, Rhododendron Ridge was relatively easy to scale, and that the area was practically undefended. Refugees
and deserters, who were now coming into the Anzac line in a fairly steady
stream, all confirmed that there were hardly any Turks on the Sari Bair Ridge
or Suvla Plain. Further reconnaissances were made on May 27th into the Sazli,
Chailak and Aghyl Deres, which confirmed that the valleys were relatively
lightly picqueted. A party of New Zealanders was landed at Nibrunesi Point
and crossed Suvla Plain without meeting any Turks or any signs of emplacements. An excellent map of the whole area had been taken from a dead
Turk officer on May 19th, and on the basis of the information at his disposal,
Birdwood drew up a daring plan to seize Chunuk Bair and the adjoining
summit of Hill Q—which is only slightly higher than Chunuk Bair and about
half a mile distant from it along a fairly gentle ridge—by a surprise night
march, following Overton's route via Table Top and Rhododendron.
With the summit in their hands, it would be a relatively simple matter to
drive the Turks off Battleship Hill, and the possibilities once this had been
achieved were unimaginable. At this point the plan suffered a grievous setback. On May 28th a new Turk outpost between No. 2 Post and Table Top
was captured and called Number Three Outpost; it was overlooked from
Table Top and Rhododendron, and on the night on May 29th–30th the
Turks recaptured the post in a well-planned and bravely conducted attack
and resisted all counter-attacks. This unexpected blow seriously jeopardised
the whole operation, as the Outpost stood directly in the way of an advance
on Rhododendron and overlooked both the Sazli and Chailak Deres;
Overton was so dismayed that he urged the abandonment of the whole plan,
'as the element of surprise will be lacking'.

Although the chance of a stealthy *coup de main* on Chunuk Bair had gone,
both Birdwood and Hamilton were keen to incorporate the plan as a vital
part of a far larger operation, and by the middle of June Hamilton had
definitely endorsed it. To Hamilton, this bold and adventurous plan made an
immediate appeal. 'We are becoming tied-up—knotted up, I might say—
into this accursed trench warfare', he wrote to Kitchener on June 7th.
'. . . Every day I see the growth of the system. Machine-guns; barbed wire,
redoubts. . . . Had the conditions between us and the Turks been at all
equal we should long ago have got them on the run. But, so far, the conditions have not been equal.' The new plan, if successfully carried out, would
reverse the position. 'The whole scheme hinges on these crests of Sari Bair
which dominate Anzac and Maidos, the Dardanelles and the Aegean', he
wrote soon after, and on 13th June he telegraphed to Kitchener that 'I only
await the promised reinforcements to take the next step in prosecution of my
main plan from Anzac.' At this stage, the plans were somewhat vague, and
consisted of a break-out to the north from Anzac by two divisions, to be

quickly followed by two more, to be landed as soon as possible afterwards. The decision to go for Sari Bair rather than Achi Baba was of great significance, but, for the moment, all that could be done was to concentrate activity at the south of the Anzac position to distract the Turks' attention while Overton and his men continued to collect information about the incredibly twisted and complicated ravines and precipices which lay between the shore and Chunuk Bair.

At Helles, the attacks went on.

By now the heat was becoming almost unbearable. The trenches were like ovens; the grass had long since withered and vanished, and the hot wind stirred up the dust, which drifted across the Peninsula, covering everything, and horribly pungent with the stench of war and death. On the limpid sea the corpses of horses and mules floated stiffly. The Navy towed them out and tried to puncture them with bayonets tied to broom handles; if that failed, the corpses were churned up in the propellers; if they still refused to sink they were left to their own devices, and the hideously mangled carcasses often found their way back to the beaches.

Ashore, the bloated loathsome green flies—'corpse flies' the men called them—were becoming literally pestilential. Feasting on the corpses in No Man's Land, swarming hideously in the latrines, filling every trench and dug-out and covering the food, they were directly responsible for a virulent form of dysenteric diarrhoea—generally known as 'the Gallipoli Trots' or the 'Gallipoli Gallop'—which spread rapidly through the army in July. It was particularly serious at Anzac, where the closely packed trenches and dug-outs provided perfect conditions for the spread of disease. By the end of July Birdwood was losing as many men in a fortnight through sickness as would be expected in a major attack; in one week alone (July 21st–27th) 1,221 cases of acute dysentery were reported at Anzac, or nearly 5 per cent of the garrison, but these figures give no adequate indication of the extent of the epidemic. Hardly anyone escaped it, and Bean has written of the Australians that 'the great frames which had impressed beholders in Egypt now stood out gauntly, faces became lined, cheeks sunken.' 'Men who were merely walking skeletons from continual diarrhoea could be found, if off duty, sleeping nightly alongside a foul latrine pit,' one Australian wrote. The Standing Orders of the M.E.F. stated that 'all food must, as far as possible, be protected from flies and dust. Uncooked fruit should be sparingly eaten.' It proved quite impossible to protect any food from the swarms of flies, and uncooked food—apart from bully-beef—was virtually unknown to the Gallipoli troops. Latrines were usually holes in the ground with a pole to hang on to; box latrines with seats were regarded as a supreme luxury;

disinfectants were inadequate, and the men were adjured, in the words of an actual notice at the W Beach latrine,

Cover with earth just after you rise,
To keep down disease and lessen the flies.

The attitude of the senior medical officers at Imbros in the face of this situation is difficult to explain. Surgeon-General Birrell, when appealed to by the sorely-pressed Anzac doctors for advice, replied that the breeding grounds of the flies should be destroyed by incineration and fly-papers hung on bushes. Incineration at Anzac was virtually impossible, although some incinerators were constructed on the beach, and the reference to 'hanging fly-papers on bushes' not unreasonably convinced the medical staff at Anzac that little practical assistance could be looked for from G.H.Q. Birrell did not even visit Anzac until August 1st, when he wrote under the heading 'sickness': 'A good deal of diarrhoea among the Australians, possibly due to sea bathing.' When the War Office, alarmed by independent reports of the condition of the army, asked G.H.Q. for information, the reply was sent that the causes were 'mainly diarrhoea, mild dysentery and debility caused by the prolonged occupation of trenches under fire, also by war diet to which men are unaccustomed'. In August, when it was at last conclusively proved by a team of Australian doctors that most of the men were suffering from dysentery and diarrhoea, and some from a virulent form of paratyphoid, Birrell issued circulars on 'The Prevention of Flies in Camps and Billets' and 'The Prevention of Typhoid'. As an embittered Australian doctor remarked, 'you might as well have spat on a bushfire'. By then, the Anzac force was melting away at the appalling rate of 10 per cent *per week*, and it was calculated that nearly 80 per cent of the Allied troops on the Peninsula were suffering to some extent from the disease.

All the blame did not rest on G.H.Q. Many of the senior officers on the Peninsula did not awake to the gravity of the situation until it was far too late. Birdwood in particular did not realise the serious effect the dysentery was having on his men until the end of July, and was unsympathetic to many practical suggestions for improving the troops' diet. Monash, when reporting the unhappy condition of his 4th Australian Brigade, perhaps the worst affected unit on the Peninsula, did not accurately assess the consequences of the debility and lassitude on his men. The consequences of this general failure to appreciate the effects on the army of the dysenteric epidemic were to prove catastrophic. The dogged determination of the men to 'carry on' was a contributory cause to this failure; an Anzac doctor saw a private in September who had been wounded on April 25th; he was having 'a little trouble' and would be grateful if the doctor 'could advise a little treatment'. Apart from dysentery, the man had a compound fracture of the arm, two bullets through his thigh, and another through his diaphragm, liver and side.

The situation was slightly better at Helles, partly because the army was not nearly as congested as at Anzac, but partly also—it must be admitted—because of the professionalism of the 29th Division, who had brought their sanitary detachments with them, and had quickly established rules of hygiene whose importance was not then fully appreciated at Anzac. It was not until far too late that matters such as the provision of fly-proof latrine-boxes and the methodical destruction of excreta received sufficient attention at Anzac or in the French sector at Helles, where the situation was almost as bad.

The heat, the flies and the dysentery were only part of the trouble. The food, although ample, was utterly unsuitable for the climate in which the men were living. Bully-beef, sizzling hot in the sun, greasy and unappetising, formed the staple diet; fresh meat was a rarity, and when it did arrive it was often permitted to lie for hours in the sun and exposed to the flies, so that it constituted an additional threat to health; fresh vegetables and fruit were almost unknown. There was no opportunity for the troops to buy extra rations from canteens, although a few stalls, run by Greeks, were available at Helles early in the campaign. Plum and apple jam became as nauseating as the bully-beef. Fresh bread, which the French had almost from the beginning, was not available for the British and Dominion troops until a few mobile bakeries were set up. Hard biscuits, which often broke a man's teeth, were no recompense. The British army medical service included no qualified dentists, and the Australians—modelling their system rigidly on the British one—found that they only possessed a few dental instruments in the general field ambulance equipment. When the seriousness of the situation was at last realised, all that could be done was to scour the ranks for enlisted dentists, who did their best with the few crude instruments which were available; C.P.O. Johnston had to suffer the amateur attentions of a blacksmith, who first pulled out the wrong tooth, then removed the other in sections, leaving 'a great jagged prong'; not surprisingly, a man had to be in a bad way before he submitted himself to the somewhat rough-and-ready dental facilities. By the end of July, 600 men from the 1st Australian Division alone had been evacuated with dental disease. In its way, the raging toothache from which many men suffered was almost as serious in its effects on the fighting capacity of the army as the dysentery.

The lice were another source of misery. 'They were beasts of prey and of a most voracious and ferocious nature,' wrote a New Zealander. 'They did not haste and they did not rest. They moved slowly, deliberately, surely. They could not jump or fly, but they could crawl, and they moved with a certain cold, passionless persistence in quest of blood. They throve on Keating's powder. They would not drown. They refused to die—except under great pressure—and they multiplied with amazing rapidity. One generation perished in the morning offensive, but at midday their descendants were foraging fiercely. They also died, but their children were there to be massacred at the time of the 'evening hate'. At midnight a new generation was in readiness to carry on the good fight.' 'We itched and scratched until we were tired with scratching', Riley wrote on June 15th. 'We turned our clothes inside out, and ran the burning ends of cigarettes up the seams. The crack of a frizzled louse was one of the sweetest sounds we knew.' The filthy maggots on the trench-floors were in a way more nauseating than the corpse-flies. 'We lived in a headquarters of maggots,' Riley wrote; 'pale, wriggling, stinking, blasted things. As we sat on our ledge we watched the sandy trench floor heaving with them.'

All these things combined to increase the widespread feeling of disillusionment which so struck newcomers to the Peninsula. The men felt that they had been forgotten and were being neglected, an emotion which all who fought in the Burma campaign in the Second World War will instantly recognise. 'It was a pretty hopeless fiasco of course,' Lt. O'Hara wrote of the Battle of June 4th to his fiancée; '. . . I don't think my nerves will stand it much longer.' 'When I say that the troops are discontented,' Captain Hawkes of the 2nd Hampshires wrote in his diary early in June,' 'I know from personal conversation with the officers that they have the same feeling about affairs as the men. As one officer put it to me the other day, "We have been properly let in".'

Criticism of G.H.Q. became widespread. Hamilton laid great insistence on staff officers going to the front as often as possible, and he himself visited the Peninsula. But in spite of these visits, he was regarded by the troops as a somewhat remote figure, and Braithwaite acquired an unenviable reputation among the officers and men for which it is impossible at this length of time to give an explanation. Many Anzacs had a good opinion of Birdwood—although the New Zealanders increasingly resented Godley—and Hunter-Weston, for all his faults, never fully lost the affection of his men; his breezy and at times bombastic manner, which infuriated many of his officers, did not greatly trouble VIII Corps. A strong community spirit had grown up at Anzac and Helles, and the fact that general and private alike were exposed to the same dangers created a close bond between them. The staff officers, coming over for the day from Imbros, were regarded almost as strangers, and an altogether false and unfair—but undoubtedly very real—opinion was held that they left as soon as they decently could for the comfort and safety of their island. In a way, this feeling of comradeship on the Peninsula made the senior commanders increasingly disinclined to accept advice from G.H.Q., and sensibly added to Hamilton's difficulties. Hamilton, for his part, remained as reluctant as ever to appear to interfere in the work of his subordinates. G.H.Q. did not improve matters by continuing to issue false reports to the troops designed to raise their spirits but which had absolutely the opposite effect. Lord Slim recalls one such document which described the Turks opposed to him as 'the riff-raff of Constantinople' and relating how their German masters drove them to their slaughter at a safe distance from the actual fighting; to emphasise the absurdity of this document an enormous German officer, festooned with grenades, was killed on the British parapet on the following morning, suicidally leading a ferocious and enthusiastic attack by 'the riff-raff of Constantinople'.

But the most intense resentment in the army was reserved for the Lines of Communication staff at Mudros, now established in some comfort in the liner *Aragon*. Hamilton's unfortunate tendency to ignore his administrative staff—which occasioned a memorable and distressing outburst before the Dardanelles Commission by the Adjutant-General, Woodward—had its logical consequence in the downright inefficiency which reigned at Mudros at this time.

Kitchener had peremptorily rejected the sensible advice of General Cowans —Quarter-Master General to the Forces—at the very beginning of the campaign that the M.E.F. should be properly equipped with adequate staff to form a Lines of Communication organisation. This unconsidered decision had put the expedition at a serious disadvantage from the very beginning, but with more common sense the situation need not have become so grave. The French had been quick to realise that it was an absurdity to have their main base at Alexandria, and by the middle of May had established it at Mudros; they had also appointed a competent officer to administer the Lines of Communication, had given him precise instructions, an adequate staff, and ships specifically allocated to him. The problem facing the French was of course far less large than that with which the British had to contend, but it was quickly evident that theirs were the only arrangements which had any hope of success. Wemyss had quickly seen the merits of the French system, but Hamilton obstinately refused to consider the establishment of an advanced base at Mudros. Wemyss's regular warnings that the Lines of Communication arrangements were bound to break down unless there was a drastic revision of the organisation were as regularly met with the reply from G.H.Q. that there would soon be room to establish advanced bases on the Peninsula, and that the present situation whereby the supplies were held in depot ships in Mudros harbour, replenished from Alexandria, was only a temporary inconvenience.

By the beginning of June Wemyss' most gloomy expectations were close to complete fulfilment. The Lines of Communication arrangements were a shambles; relations between the naval officers of the Naval Transport Branch and the merchant masters of the transports were strained to breaking point;* the process of loading and unloading the depot ships was slow, in-efficient, and, in the blazing sun, exhausting for the men; the very small staff was either incompetent or grossly overworked; the hospitals were in a lament-able condition; undisciplined troops were to be found slouching around; there was a general atmosphere of apathy, bad-temper and surliness. As an ex-ample of what was expected of the staff, the Deputy Director of Medical Services, Lines of Communication, was dispatched to Mudros by G.H.Q. with orders to administer the temporary hospital ships, the sweeper ferry service from Mudros to the Peninsula, the return of recovered casualties to their units, the dispatch of medical supplies to the Peninsula, and the shore hospitals at Lemnos; his total staff consisted of one staff sergeant.

Matters were further complicated by the physical separation of the G.H.Q. administrative staff on Imbros from the Lines of Communication staff on Lemnos. There was not even a Lines of Communication headquarters organisation. The ramshackle organisation only worked at all because of the very hard work undertaken by a very small minority of the staff officers. When Kitchener did decide to appoint an officer to take over the military side of the organisation he chose an elderly retired Indian Army officer in poor health, who had no experience whatever of administration and who had just been relieved of his command in Egypt by Maxwell; in his in-adequate hands the system very nearly collapsed completely, and would probably have done so had he not been served by an exceptionally competent Chief of Staff, a Lt.-Col. Armstrong of the Royal Marines. Although the main responsibility for the disastrous state of affairs was that of Hamilton and Braithwaite, rather than that of the few officers running the Lines of Com-munication, it must be stated that although the tasks placed on these officers were enormous and novel, the attitude of many of them did not help. On this subject the evidence is overwhelming and painful. 'Certainly, to anyone coming fresh from the dug-outs, dust-storms, monotonous rations and per-petual risks of the Peninsula, the *Aragon* was like an Enchanted Isle', Nevinson has written. '. . . Perhaps it was the arbitrary exclusion of many passing officers from the delights of a real dinner and other pleasurable contrasts to life at the front which made the *Aragon* a byword, as though she were "a sink of iniquity"; and from the same contrasts arose the report that at the end of the campaign she was discovered to be aground upon empty bottles, as upon a coral reef.' Lest it might be thought that Nevinson was guilty of journalistic excess in this account, an examination of the diaries and recol-lections of many soldiers fully confirms it. Major Davidson of the R.A.M.C. wrote angrily in his diary that 'these men have no intention themselves of going nearer the Front, they are all fat and sleek and live on the fat of the

* According to at least one observer, the faults were by no means all on one side, and many of the officers of the N.T.B. were of a very low calibre.

land, are faultlessly dressed, and strut about with their monocles, looking with contempt on all the poor devils who are doing the dirty work.' A New Zealand corporal, curtly rebuffed when he went on board to ask for medical equipment, wrote in his diary: 'I heard one officer breathe a sigh of thankfulness. "That's good news", he said. I asked what. "Twenty cases of soda-water have come safely for the top-dogs".' Samson has recorded of *Aragon* that 'I certainly had the feeling that I was considered a beastly nuisance, rather untidy in appearance, and generally undesirable.' When Davidson eventually managed to get on board he was astounded by the quality of the food, 'excellent cider with ice, and comfortable lounges in which to smoke'.

At the beginning of July Hamilton was driven to a drastic reorganisation of the Lines of Communication arrangements, and General Sir Edward Altham was sent out from England to handle them. His first reports spoke of the 'appalling confusion' which reigned at Mudros, and one of his staff has described the 'miscellaneous, half-organised camps, foul, undisciplined and disorderly. It was very hot, and our men . . . had the morale of a beaten army.'* Altham and his staff set to work to sort out the Augean Stables at Lemnos, and their achievements showed clearly what could have been done if G.H.Q. had emulated the French; nevertheless, even Altham could not obtain Hamilton's approval for the construction of longer jetties at Mudros, and the troops on the Peninsula still spoke of 'Imbros, Mudros and Chaos'. Before Altham arrived, Major Allanson, commanding the 1/6th Gurkhas, wrote in his diary at Mudros in the middle of July that 'I fear there are a terrible lot of self-seekers about, and they tend to eat into the guts of the military administration. . . . One cannot but fail to be struck with the lack of organisation everywhere.' In September Monash was writing; 'here at Lemnos the watchwords for everything and everyone are "inefficiency" and "muddle" and red tape run mad'. 'There seemed to be no system, no central control or direction,' the Director of Works subsequently wrote; 'we were sheep without a shepherd.'

The troops felt almost as keenly about the postal arrangements as anything else. The arrival of the mail boat was one of the great events of life on the Peninsula, and when it was realised that letters were often weeks in transit—and parcels months—feelings in the army were bitter. General Cox described the postal arrangements as 'beneath contempt', protests were made, but little improvement resulted. There was now no laughter at the stern admonition in the M.E.F.'s Standing Orders that 'the sending of topical picture postcards is prohibited'.

In their defence, the Lines of Communication staff could claim with

* See Sir George MacMunn: 'The Lines of Communication in the Dardanelles' (*The Army Quarterly*, April 1930).

justice that the army never went short of food, that all available ammunition was dispatched and disembarked under conditions of great difficulty and danger and that, in view of the size and novelty of the whole operation, the army on the Peninsula had much to be grateful for. This was all true, and much would have been forgiven had it not been for the self-esteem and incompetence of many of the Lines of Communications staff, naval as well as military.

After the arrival of the 52nd Division on June 6th, it was at last possible to send some of the troops who had been on the Peninsula since the end of April to Lemnos and Imbros to rest. In spite of the wonderful respite from the incessant strain and danger of the front, there was little other difference between the torrid treeless islands and the Peninsula. The flies still fought for every morsel of food, the heat was equally stifling, the camps were dirty, hot and badly run; until Altham took stern measures to stamp out indiscipline in the camps the contrast between the vigorous and freely accepted battle discipline on the Peninsula and the groups of morose bloody-minded soldiers on Lemnos did very real harm to morale. In short, Lemnos was ghastly, and one understands the emotions of an officer who wrote in his diary on Lemnos: 'we soon wished ourselves back in Gallipoli with its shells'.

Conditions at G.H.Q. on Imbros were only marginally better. Hamilton believed strongly that staff officers should live under similar conditions to the troops, and thus, in a dust-encased set of tents pitched on a particularly dreary part of the coast, suffering from poor food, the flies, the heat and 'the prevalent complaint', the staff struggled with its heavy responsibilities. Inevitably, tensions increased, and the diaries and letters of the staff constantly allude to petty animosities and incompatibilities which at times made life almost unbearable. On one occasion there was a major flare-up at dinner when an unpopular officer suggested that the stewards should be tipped, and there were countless trivial incidents of this kind, the result of strained nerves and bad living conditions. Hamilton suffered particularly severely from the dysentery, and, like many of the troops, did not shake off its effects for several years. 'It fills me with a desperate longing to lie down and do nothing but rest', he wrote.

Braithwaite, who had always tended to protect Hamilton too enthusiastically from what he regarded as unimportant matters or importunate junior officers, now became more protective than ever. Hamilton was the most accessible of men, he could act swiftly and decisively when a problem was put before him, but his own views on leaving senior commanders to conduct their own operations, when combined with the virtual isolation which Braithwaite forced on him, and now exacerbated by the crippling enervating dysentery, all resulted in an excessive physical and mental detachment from the realities of the situation on the Peninsula. The disillusionment of his staff rapidly increased; 'the General strikes me as a weak and too highly strung man', one wrote on May 8th, and one of the most able of them burst out towards the end of July that 'Hamilton really does nothing at all, never has a scheme, has a shallow, at times obstinate mind, no grasp of detail. . . . He doesn't for a moment realise how serious and extraordinary the situation is.' This was wholly unfair, but its significance lies in the exasperation which this outburst occasioned. 'When I look round,' George Lloyd, a Member of Parliament* engaged on intelligence work at G.H.Q. wrote to his wife at this time, 'the one thing that hits one in the face the whole time is the very small number of men who are efficient. What is the cause of it? Is it our system of education, is it something in the character that we are breeding? This is the one thing—*the one thing*—that has struck me over and over again.'

Offensive operations continued on the Helles front throughout June and July. 'Day after day we watched the P.B.I. going up and down the nullah to and from the trenches', Corporal Riley relates. 'Some of them looked like old, tottering men, bowed stooping, and most of their faces were colourless, except that they were grey or dirty. Now and then we heard some odd remark, but there was very little talking and less laughing. There was so little to laugh about, now. . . . We were all gossips and scandal-mongers in those days. Most of us had sick minds in sick bodies. We were becoming mentally dulled, living for the day and the hour, for food and sleep, and for very little else. It seemed impossible that a day would come when we should leave this place of torment.' 'Nothing but mountains,' an Australian private at Anzac wrote, 'and barren at that, save for a little scrub here and there, to say nothing of the flies with which we had to contend. These pests would be on your face, hands, down your throat, and if you were eating biscuits with jam on it, it was more like biscuits and flies.'

On June 21st the French delivered a strong and carefully prepared attack on the Turk positions in front of them, which, although not completely successful, secured not only the Haricot Redoubt but the trenches on the crest of the spur overlooking the Kereves Dere. For the first time, the French were on top of the hill, looking down on the enemy. On a front of only some 650 yards the French fired off some 28,000 rounds of field artillery, 2,700 rounds of heavy artillery, and some 700 trench mortar shells, to the envy of the British. Although the operation cost the French some 2,500 casualties, the Turks suffered terribly, and admitted to over 6,000 killed and wounded.

* Aubrey Herbert, Lloyd and Josiah Wedgwood were all Members of the House of Commons while serving on Gallipoli.

On June 28th the British and Indians carried out a similar limited operation on the left flank at Gully Spur on a blisteringly hot day. Hamilton came over from Imbros in a destroyer to see the battle. 'The cliff line and half a mile inland is shrouded in a pall of yellow dust, which, as it twirls, twists and eddies, blots out Achi Baba himself', he records. 'Through this curtain appear, dozens at a time, little balls of white—the shrapnel searching out the communication trenches and cutting the wire entanglements. At other times spouts of green or black vapour rise, mix and lose themselves in the yellow cloud. The noise is like the rumbling of an express train.'

The battle followed what was now becoming a grimly familiar pattern. Where the artillery ammunition was sufficient the enemy trenches were easily captured in the first rush, but elsewhere no progress was made and heavy casualties suffered. Hamilton subsequently declared that this battle was 'the most brilliant affair. . . . We had the Turks beaten then. . . . We felt victory in the air.' At the time he wrote: 'The tide of war is indeed racing full in our favour.' The men had small metal triangles sewn on their backs to assist identification, and, as the bombardment lifted, the ground was suddenly filled with thousands of sparkles of glittering metallic light, 'as if someone had quite suddenly thrown a big handful of diamonds on to the landscape', as Hamilton relates. A closer view was less dramatic. 'We could see some of the 29th advancing on a slight rise to our left front', Riley recorded in his journal. 'At times a long line of men in extended order, at others a handful, holding their rifles with bayonets fixed in the most useful position. . . . Here and there a man stumbled, or sank down and lay still. For an instant the smoke thinned, and we saw our men reach the chalky parapet of the Turkish trench. They stood along the top, and they disappeared, except for lonely figures apparently lost in the smoke.' By evening, when the British had suffered nearly 4,000 casualties and—with the notable exception of the positions on Gully Spur, where the line had been pushed forward nearly half a mile—no progress had been made, a blood-red sunset fell over the Peninsula, where the scrub was burning fiercely. 'Everything was red', Riley wrote. 'A bloody sunset, closing a day of bloodiness.' 'The survivors of us,' Lt. O'Hara wrote hurriedly to his fiancée after the battle, 'were in a condition bordering on lunacy when it was all over.' The battle— hailed by Hunter-Weston and G.H.Q. as a great victory—had confirmed the lesson that, as Hamilton admitted in 1925, 'trench warfare without artillery munitions is rough on the troops.'

It was a lesson which the Turks quickly learnt again. The loss of five lines of trenches on Gully Spur stung them into a series of desperate counter-attacks in the Gully Ravine area, and between June 28th and July 5th they suffered the staggering number of over 16,000 casualties. Hamilton refused a Turk request for an armistice to bury their dead, as the local commanders considered that the Turks were more worried by the effect on the morale of their troops attacking over the bodies of their comrades than by any humanitarian considerations. Over 10,000 Turks had been killed in the area, and nothing at Anzac compared with the dreadful scenes on either side of Gully Ravine. Piles of grinning skulls are still everywhere to be found on the Spur and in the Ravine; in the scrub one only has to kick the ground to send a cloud of bones scuffling through the dust. 'The mangled bodies of the dead, unburied, half-buried, or partially dug up by shells, under the fierce heat, with loathsome clouds of flies, could only be dealt with by fire', a chaplain attached to the 52nd Division has written. 'The valley with its heaps of rotting refuse, its burning pyres and sickening stench, was a veritable Gehenna.'

The morale of the Turks was shaken by this dreadful and futile slaughter. Reinforcements were now arriving in a steady stream, but although the losses were soon made up, the effect on both survivors and newcomers of the massacre at Gully Ravine, which was infinitely greater than that in the much-vaunted 'Battle of Anzac', was profound. For the moment the Turks in this sector were incapable of attack, and divisional orders stressed the importance of preparing new positions and desisting from all aggressive operations. Officers were told that they would be held personally responsible with their lives for the loss of any more trenches, and were to shoot any man who tried to leave the trench 'on any pretext whatever'.

The elation of G.H.Q. and VIII Corps H.Q. was not shared by their divisional commanders. De Lisle was now more than ever convinced of the futility of frontal attacks in broad daylight until the ammunition situation was drastically improved, and had a formidable ally in General Egerton, whose 52nd Division had endured such a terrible baptism. Egerton was particularly enraged by Hunter-Weston's bland remark to the Brigade Major of the shattered 156th Scottish Brigade that he had been glad to have had the opportunity of 'blooding the pups', and when he took Hamilton around the 52nd Division introduced each unit as 'the *remains* of the –th Battalion' with such bitter persistence that Hamilton formally rebuked him. Hunter-Weston began to agitate for Egerton's removal, but Hamilton, although he sympathised, and passed on the complaints to Kitchener— describing Egerton as 'highly strung and apt to be excitable under stress' —did nothing. Egerton eventually collapsed from strain and was evacuated; his subsequent bitterness against Hamilton, Hunter-Weston and Street became almost obsessional, but it is not every man who can see his magnificent division savaged by a series of apparently futile attacks with equanimity.

In spite of these manifestations of doubt on the wisdom of their tactics, Hunter-Weston and Street were not now to be gainsaid, and Hamilton approved their plans for an attack on July 12th–13th on the centre of the line to bring it parallel with the gains on the right and left flanks, officially designated the Action of Achi Baba Nullah, and described by Egerton as 'positively wicked in conception and cruel and wasteful in execution'. Hunter-Weston had unthinkingly decided to entrust this battle to the Royal Naval Division, but a series of urgent medical reports reluctantly forced him to recognise the fact that the division was on the verge of complete exhaustion. It had been fighting almost without respite for over two months and many officers and men had long passed the limits of human endurance. The fact that the proposal had even been made dramatically illuminated the ignorance of the condition of individual units which reigned at Corps Headquarters; on so narrow and small a front, this was inexcusable. The 52nd Division, although it had been in action for barely a month, had also been roughly handled.

The heat and flies were becoming worse every day. 'July stole upon us in a blister of heat', a subaltern wrote. 'Only the early hours of morning, between 5 and 7 a.m., were humanly comfortable, and for the rest of the day till late afternoon, if no attack threatened and you were not on fatigues, you sat about in shirt and shorts, trying not to remember personal discomfort and always being horridly reminded of it as soon as you moved by the great black swarm of pestering flies that hung or settled about you all day long. Officers and men went through a trial of endurance that brought to the top their best and their worst. . . . The amazing thing was that so many preserved their good humour. It was accomplished only by making fun of the life as it steadily grew worse.' The shelling from Asia was now extremely serious, and the daily drain of killed and injured caused by 'Asiatic Annie'— particularly on the French—made everyone jumpy. General Gourand was blown over a wall in Sed-el-Bahr and severely wounded; he was replaced by General Bailloud, of whom Hankey wrote with justice on July 28th that he was 'the most confirmed pessimist I have met since the war began. . . . He is a stupid old man and ought to be superseded.' Very unfairly, the British had lost all confidence in the French, and Hamilton in particular never seems to have appreciated the fact that they had been up against the most formidable part of the Turkish defences since the end of April, and had lost heavily from the Asiatic shelling.

In one of the hottest days yet experienced on the Peninsula, after a stifling night, the British and French attacked at 7.35 a.m. on July 12th. The British were still wearing their thick khaki serge uniforms, and were heavily weighed down with ammunition and equipment. The enemy's front lines, as usual, were quickly occupied; then, as usual, the attack was badly held up, the Turk reserves were briskly pushed in, and everywhere the attack was brought to a standstill after heavy losses. By the evening the troops were utterly exhausted, and, for almost the first time in the campaign, British troops in one sector 'could not be induced to go forward',* in the sober report of their commanding officer.

The battle raged throughout the following day and Hunter-Weston even ordered up the haggard but undaunted Naval Division to make a last desperate assault, but although some progress was made, the battle had to be broken off by evening, by which time the Allies had suffered over three thousand casualties. The troops occupying the newly captured Turkish trenches found themselves in conditions which turned the stomach of even the sturdiest professional. 'The bottom of the trench was choked with dead bodies,' a young soldier wrote in his diary, 'friend and foe, and slippery with their life blood. Corpses had been built into the parapet, the dead thus affording protection for the living. Wherever one looked there was death in some ghastly form, arms and legs and decapitated bodies sprawling around in all manner of horribly grotesque postures. To me that scene was the personification of stark, naked horror.' 'Some of the worst scenes ever experienced on the battlefields of France or Mesopotamia were crowded into this narrow front of half a mile, over which fighting had been continuous for nearly forty-eight hours,' Douglas Jerrold has written, 'where many hundreds of men lay dead or dying, where a burning sun had turned the bodies of the slain to a premature corruption, where there was no resting-place free from physical contamination, where the air, the surface of the ground, and the soil beneath the surface were alike poisonous, fetid, corrupt.'

C.P.O. Johnston was sent forward with other men of the Royal Naval Division to reinforce the Royal Scots, who 'were in a thoroughly exhausted state, and seemed to be without a drop of water, for every man I passed craved some from me but mine, alas, had long since been finished. There seemed to be an amazing number of wounded, and these, poor fellows, were trampled on and kicked as they lay helpless in the bottom of the trench.' After dark, these men were counter-attacked. 'All along our line the exhausted troops—now super-human—blazed away at the indistinct but rapidly approaching Turks. The trench was one great sheet of flame which lighted up the night . . . drawing my revolver I crouched beneath the trench side and waited for the first figure to show itself above. My hand ran over the cold face of a corpse as I felt the thing I was kneeling on and with a piercing shriek the man next to me came crashing to the ground. They were very near now, only a few yards. . . . There was a clash and clatter of rifles to my left, a scream, the flash of a bomb and I knew the Turks were in our trench.' This particular attack was repulsed with heavy losses, and Johnston

* A month earlier a young subaltern had been awarded the M.C. by Hunter-Weston for summarily executing three men for alleged cowardice on the battlefield, and there had been one or two similar—but very isolated—episodes.

survived to relate his experiences in his diary; his fears were shared by many more that night, who did not survive.

Hunter-Weston's confidence was undimmed by this repulse. Major Davidson met him on the evening of July 13th and relates in his diary that 'the progress of the day had greatly satisfied him I could see, and he was in great glee.' Since the beginning of June the Allies had advanced some 500 yards in the Helles front at a loss of over 17,000 casualties, but this time the effort was final. The Turks had lost over 40,000 men in the same period, but reinforcements arrived steadily. Within a week of the action of Achi Baba Nullah they had completely made good their losses and had consolidated themselves in their new front line. This is not to say that they were not severely shaken by the British attacks, and there had been several critical moments when they had nearly broken. The nerve and confidence of their commanders had been subjected to an almost unendurable strain, and advocates for withdrawal still existed until von Sanders heard of them, when they were promptly removed from their commands and bundled unceremoniously back to Constantinople.

At this point, Hunter-Weston collapsed from overstrain and sunstroke, and left the Peninsula for ever, leaving the still optimistic Street in virtual command of VIII Corps until his replacement, General Davies, arrived from England.

Hunter-Weston left the Helles army in a condition of almost complete exhaustion. The bitter anti-climax of every battle, the daily struggle against the flies, the dreadful lassitude of the dysentery, the heat, the strain, and the grim drain of casualties, had combined to reduce the once-magnificent divisions to pitiful shadows of their former selves. 'All the old campaigners are thin, hollow-eyed and haggard', Davidson noted in his diary. The Royal Naval Division, which had lost 79 officers and over 2,000 men in the July battles, was now reduced to 129 officers and 5,038 men, of whom, as Jerrold has written, 'not 10 per cent would have been considered fit in France for duty in the quietest part of the line. In Gallipoli at this time all officers and men who could actually walk to the trenches were reckoned as fit.' By the evening of July 13th the 52nd Division, which had landed on June 6th with 10,900 officers and men, was reduced to a total of just over 6,500: in five weeks it had lost 169 irreplaceable officers. The French were now definitely broken, and incapable of further effort. Only the 29th Division was in any condition to renew the offensive.

Helles, as Corporal Riley wrote, 'looked like a midden and smelt like an opened cemetery'.

10

The August Plan

The old battle tactics have clean vanished, I have only quite lately
realised the new conditions. Whether your entrenchments are on
top of a hill or at the bottom of a valley matters precious little:
whether you are outflanked matters precious little: you may hold
one half of a straight trench and the enemy may hold the other
half, and this situation may endure for weeks. The only thing is by
cunning or surprise, or skill, or tremendous expenditure of high
explosive, or great expenditure of good troops, to win some
small tactical position which the enemy may be bound, perhaps
for military or perhaps for political reasons, to attack. Then you
can begin to kill them pretty fast. To attack all along the line is
perfect nonsense—madness!

Sir Ian Hamilton to Lord Kitchener, 2nd July, 1915

The development of the plan for the capture of the Sari Bair Ridge falls into
two distinct phases. The first phase—already briefly described—consisted of
a bold secret night march from the north of the Anzac position, the scaling
of the ridges to Rhododendron, and the march upon Chunuk Bair. This
was an Anzac plan, conceived at Birdwood's headquarters, and the brain-
child of Lt.-Colonel Skeen, a quiet Scotsman with a scholastic air who had
been a lecturer at the Quetta Staff College before the war, and who had been
hand-picked by Birdwood for his staff.

Skeen's plan, which was formally laid before Hamilton on May 30th,
was an extremely good one. It had been proved by Overton that the
heart of the Turk position, Chunuk Bair, was accessible and undefended;*
the loss of Old Number Three Outpost was unfortunate, but Skeen had

* Moorehead, in an account of the August plan which is open to controversy, refers to
Chunuk Bair as 'the enemy's strongest point.' He also condemns the plan on the ground

235

already prepared a draft plan for its recapture. Every night for three weeks before the operation a destroyer was to fix her searchlight on the Post promptly at 9 p.m. and open fire for exactly 30 minutes, at the end of which the searchlight would be switched off and the destroyer would withdraw. On the night of the operation the ritual would be repeated, except that as soon as the firing ceased a party of New Zealanders, who would creep up while the garrison was blinded by the searchlights, would leap into the Post before the Turks had emerged from their shelters.

It was the extension of this plan which was its eventual undoing. Birdwood asked for one new division and a brigade and suggested a date early in July, when the moon had passed the full. Hamilton had already decided to approve the plan when the news of the three New Army divisions came, and the massive increase in strength which this new acquisition gave him made him

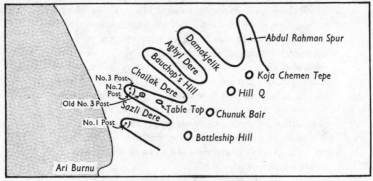

North Anzac: the principal ridges and valleys

decide to postpone the attack until August. Towards the end of June he asked Birdwood how he could use three reinforcing divisions if available. Equipped with their new maps, the Anzac staff now proposed a much more ambitious operation. While one column of troops made for Chunuk Bair by way of Table Top and Rhododendron, another would march two miles north along the beach, and turn right into the deep and scraggy Aghyl Dere. It would then divide itself into two parties; one would climb up the Aghyl Dere to the summit of Hill Q, while the other would advance on Koja Chemen Tepe—the third of the Sari Bair summits—by way of a long spur called Abdul Rahman Spur. There was no chance of reconnoitring this route, and even Overton had only got half way up the Aghyl Dere. Both

_____

that 'except for the Suvla landing it did not force the Turks to react to the British, it was the British who were reacting to the Turks.' (*Gallipoli*, 253.) This is a somewhat baffling criticism of an encircling movement against a thinly defended position.

Birdwood and Skeen, furthermore, were justly apprehensive of arousing Turk suspicions in the area, and the capture of any of the New Zealand scouts—particularly of Overton—would jeopardise the entire operation.

On the maps, and from the air, the route up the Aghyl Dere seemed rather easier than the climb on Table Top, and local guides were recruited who claimed to know the area well. In an attempt to simplify the extremely complicated ground over which the assaulting columns were to advance, Bean has compared it to a left hand laid on a table, palm downwards, the fingers representing the spurs, the tips their seaward edges, and the metacarpal prominences the heights of the main range.* Roughly speaking, the task of the covering force was to capture the 'finger-tips' at Old Number Three, Bauchop's, and Damakjelik Bair, to allow the assaulting columns to advance up the four gullies to the main ridge. In addition, the covering force was to seize Table Top to clear the way for the advance on Rhododendron Ridge.

The extreme difficulty of the ground which the Left Assaulting Column was to traverse can hardly be exaggerated. It is a mad country. Watercourses change direction, seemingly gentle slopes conceal a precipitous and treacherous surface under the scrub, there is no method in anything. It is very easy to lose one's way, and even with accurate maps on a clear day one gets easily confused. One ravine is very much like another, the levels are all wrong, and without a compass or the summits to guide one, it is surprisingly easy to scale a tortuous ravine only to find oneself farther away from the summit than when one began. All these things were completely unknown to the staff. The maps were clear and precise, and the guides were confident. And, above all, there would be very few Turks in the way. Overton estimated that the climb to Chunuk Bair would take six hours, and that to Koja Chemen Tepe not much longer.

The project also took no account of the health of the Australian and New Zealand troops. In particular, the decision to use the 4th Australian Brigade for the march to Koja Chemen Tepe is difficult to understand. The 4th Brigade, through no fault of its own, was unquestionably in the worst state of all the Anzac brigades; as one battalion commander wrote, 'our physical condition was very poor.... We had too many untrained reinforcements who, though keen and willing, had not the unit *esprit de corps*.... Most of our men were very weak.' The combination of weary troops who had been fighting without respite and ravaged by dysentery for over three months and inexperienced drafts was one which boded ill for the success of the enterprise.†

* *The Story of Anzac*, Vol. II, p. 567–8. See map on page 236.
† Moorehead's description of the Anzac troops (*Gallipoli*, 253–4) as 'the most aggressive fighters in the whole peninsula' is difficult to substantiate. He states, truly, that the Anzac

It was clear that there would not be sufficient room at Anzac for more than one of the new divisions coming from England, and the problem was where these could be most profitably used. Now that Hunter-Weston had gone, Hamilton was setting his face firmly against further offensives at Helles, and so the staff were reduced to considering new landings either at Suvla Bay or Gaba Tepe. Gaba Tepe was heavily defended, whereas Suvla Plain was virtually deserted, and the fateful decision was taken to land at Suvla. When Birdwood submitted his detailed plans on July 1st, they had included a proposal that as these divisions could not be accommodated at Anzac, one should be landed either in Suvla Bay or on the beach near Fisherman's Hut, with the object of capturing a particularly troublesome Turk battery, as well as the main heights. This suggestion was the germ of the Suvla Plan. It was essentially an afterthought to the main Anzac attack, and consequently never really received the full attention at G.H.Q. which it merited. Already, the errors of April, of which the most serious had been the random *ad hoc* additions to the main plan at a relatively late stage, were being repeated.

The Suvla Plan, however, had much to commend it. For months the Anzac troops had looked across the Suvla Plain, surrounded on three sides by formidable hills, like an enormous amphitheatre, the salt lake glistening harshly, and the yellow aridity of the ground, which looks deceptively flat and uncomplicated, broken here and there by a few stunted olive trees. The feeling of desolation is almost tangible. There is hardly any shade, the glare from the Salt Lake assails the eyes, the ground is coarse and thirsty-looking, and the sentinel hills sweep in a great arc from north to south, grim, aloof, and hostile, quivering in the heat. Towards the hills, as the ground begins to rise, there are belts of scrub, thickening at the foot-hills, and here and there one can detect a patch of greenish cultivation among the dreary dusty brown of the Plain. As the ground begins to rise sharply towards the heights of the Kiretch Tepe and Tekke Tepe ridges, the going becomes steadily more difficult, and progress is virtually confined to a number of narrow goat-tracks winding through the harsh, thick scrub.

From north to south, the main lines of hills are the Kiretch Tepe Ridge running along the north edge, the Tekke Tepe Ridge on the east, and the Sari Bair range on the south. Running from the Tekke Tepe Ridge due west is a spur, about 300 feet high and about a mile in length, culminating in a series of low but rugged eminences known to the Anzacs as the W Hills (so-called because of the shape of a particular cluster of stunted trees) and Scimitar Hill, a low, rounded spur which juts into the Plain. Rising from

---

troops 'had not been heavily engaged through June and July like the British and the French,' but this underestimates the great strain of maintaining the Anzac position and the effects of disease on the troops. In any event, the description certainly did not apply to the sorely-tried 4th Brigade.

the Plain, midway between the W Hills and the low hump of Lala Baba, are two small isolated hillocks known as Chocolate Hill and Green Hill from their prevailing colours. To the north-east of the Salt Lake is another, lower, hillock known as Hill 10. The Plain is so flat that the importance of these small eminences is out of all proportion to their actual height. On the south of the plain another hillock, known as Hill 60, should also be noted. It is a kind of last gasp of the ridges plunging down from Sari Bair, yet it dominates the ground between the W Hills and Lala Baba. Dried watercourses copiously score the Plain, and it is not easy ground to traverse, although by Gallipoli standards it could not be described as exceptionally difficult. The Salt Lake does not dry out completely every year, but by the July of 1915 there were indications that it was hardening daily.*

Hamilton now called in de Robeck and Keyes to discuss the feasibility of landing two of the New Army divisions at Suvla. Both were enthusiastic, and recommended a landing immediately to the south of Nibrunesi Point, as the waters in the bay itself were uncharted. A new torpedo-net about a mile long had recently arrived, so that Suvla could be cordoned off from sub-marine attack. Most important of all, the Navy now had several of Fisher's motor-lighters for which Hamilton had appealed unsuccessfully in March. They were bullet-proof, could carry 500 men each, and had long ramps at the bows down which the troops could disembark in a matter of minutes when the boats grounded. This removed the nightmare of April 25th; this time there would be no pathetic gaggles of rowing-boats toiling ashore under fire, but fast, armoured landing-craft, capable of landing a division in a few hours. The arrival of the lighters at Mudros in July—at once called 'beetles' by the sailors on account of the long projecting arms of the landing ramps, which resembled antennae, and their black paint—removed G.H.Q.'s greatest anxiety about a new landing.

The question of which units were to make the landing caused Hamilton and his staff considerable difficulty. The New Army divisions now on their way from England were unblooded and inexperienced, but as the Suvla landings were regarded as the easiest part of the whole operation, it was eventually decided to use them, grouped into an army corps numbered IX Corps. Hamilton had seriously thought of using the 29th Division, but it was considered that even that indomitable division might quail at the prospect of another landing on a hostile shore. Furthermore, the plan now embraced a major holding operation at Helles to prevent the Turks from bringing up troops to Anzac, and it was clear that this would be a difficult business, which should not be given to fresh untried troops.

* This fact gives a good indication of how exceptionally hot the summer of 1915 was. In 1962, regarded as a particularly hot summer, no rain fell between the end of April and the beginning of October, but the Salt Lake did not fully dry out.

When it was decided in June to group the three New Army divisions into an army corps, Hamilton had telegraphed to Kitchener on June 15th on the subject of the corps commander that 'only men of good stiff constitution and nerve will be able to do any good. Everything is at such close quarters that many men would be useless in the somewhat exposed headquarters they would have to occupy on this limited terrain, though they would do quite good work if moderately comfortable and away from constant shell-fire. I can think of only two men, Byng and Rawlinson. Both possess the requisite qualities and seniority.'

This was asking for a lot. Byng and Rawlinson were senior commanders on the Western Front, where they were doing excellently; Gallipoli, further-more, was not the only front on which good senior officers were at a premium. Kitchener, not unreasonably, told Hamilton somewhat perempt-orily that this would be impossible. Even if Byng and Rawlinson were available, both were junior to General Sir Bryan Mahon, who had raised and now commanded the 10th Division.* Hamilton, for reasons which are not clear, would not hear of Mahon as a corps commander—'he would be quite hopeless,' he wrote to Kitchener on June 9th—so that the choice lay between the only two available generals senior to Mahon, Sir Frederick Stopford, who had taken over Hamilton's previous command of the Central Force in England, and General Ewart. Kitchener favoured Ewart, though not enthusiastically—'Ewart, who is very fit and well, would, I think, do', he wrote to Hamilton on June 15th—but Hamilton considered that his height and girth were too large for trench-warfare. As trench-warfare was not envisaged at Suvla, the force of this argument is somewhat difficult to appreciate. A more formidable objection was that Hamilton considered that Ewart lacked the common touch with his men and did not get on well with his staffs. And so, in the end, only Stopford was left. Hamilton's subsequent protests that Stopford was forced on him were understandable but were not wholly justified; furthermore, events were to throw considerable doubt on his low estimate of Mahon's capacities.

Stopford was 61, and not in good health. He had served as an A.D.C. in Egypt and the Sudan in the 1880's, and had been Military Secretary to the hapless Buller in the early disastrous months of the Boer War. When Buller was relieved of his command Stopford came home with him, and had been living in retirement since 1909, until the war uprooted him, like so many other officers, from placid oblivion into a senior command. Once again, an important command at the Dardanelles had gone to a man whose active career was, to all intents and purposes, over. Although a man of considerable personal charm and a keen and respected student of military history, he had

* The fact that Mahon was a close personal friend of Carson, and that the 10th Division was Ireland's first major contribution to the New Army, may not have been without their effect.

never commanded troops in battle, and his experience of actual fighting, through no fault of his own, was minimal. Stopford arrived on July 11th, and was sent to Helles to gain some battle experience. He had been strongly briefed by Kitchener on the supreme importance of surprise and imagination in operations, and when he was given a very general indication of the forthcoming operations he seemed well pleased.

Stopford was of course to be in charge of what was regarded as a complementary operation to the main attack from Anzac. The appointment of General Godley to command the main attack has passed without comment in every account of the campaign, but it was to prove a far more serious error. Godley's standing with his New Zealanders had never been high, and he was known to some as 'make 'em run Alex', this being an allegedly strident admonition by Lady Godley at a review of the New Zealanders in Egypt.* In appearance and attitude, as well as in capacity, he was the Hunter-Weston of Anzac, without the prototype's inexplicable popularity. His decision to establish his battle H.Q. at No. 2 Outpost was reasonable enough; what was not reasonable was his refusal to leave it throughout the operations except to embark on a destroyer to view the battle from the sea.

The plan was now rapidly gathering momentum. August 6th was fixed as the day of the offensive, as the waning moon, then in its last quarter, would not rise until about 10.30 p.m., and Hamilton and his staff were insistent that IX Corps must be landed at Suvla that night before the moon rose, to make the surprise complete. This date meant that only three of five divisions of the New Army on their way could be used, but it was considered that these should be sufficient. The 10th and 11th Divisions would be used at Suvla, and most of the 13th Division smuggled ashore at Anzac and concealed there until the break-out.

This was in many ways the most difficult administrative feature of the entire operation. When one visits the Anzac position it is almost inconceivable that this tiny area of mountainous country could ever have accommodated more than 20,000 men, their supplies, ammunitions, dressing stations, artillery and animals. On top of this, it was now proposed to dribble ashore a further 20,000-odd men on the three nights before August 6th and conceal them from the enemy. The operation required meticulous organisation and timing by the staffs, and much hard work by the already heavily occupied Anzac garrison. New terraces and dug-outs, tunnels, and paths had to be hacked out of the cliffs, and elaborate arrangements made for the landing and storage of greatly increased water supplies.

On the whole the planning of this great operation went reasonably

---

* Lady Godley's other claim to notoriety was her alleged complaint that the wounded were not lying at attention in their beds when she visited a military hospital in Egypt.

smoothly, but there was a serious dispute at Anzac on one aspect of it. To create a major diversion, Birdwood proposed to launch the magnificent 1st Australian Division, commanded by the aggressive General Walker, in a frontal attack on the formidable Turk trenches at Lone Pine early in the afternoon of August 6th. Walker was probably the best senior commander which the campaign produced; originally Birdwood's Chief of Staff, it was soon clear that his abilities did not lie in this direction, but in command in the field; this fact was largely responsible for Monash being preferred over him as Corps Commander later in the war. In almost every respect, Walker's qualities were in complete contrast with those of Monash. Monash had a genius for organisation; Walker was an outstanding 'fighting General'. The Australian Prime Minister, W. M. Hughes, considered for a very long time whether Walker should command the Australian Corps in France in preference to Monash, and subsequently stated that if the British Government had not accepted Monash he would have insisted on Walker.

Walker was appalled by the prospect of a headlong charge on the Lone Pine position, and begged that his men could be given another task; he proposed that they should march out of Anzac with the columns heading for Chunuk Bair and Koja Chemen Tepe and should go north to attack and secure Chocolate Hill and the W Hills. Walker was outspoken almost to a fault with senior officers when he thought their plans were bad. His remarks to Bridges on April 25th when the latter proposed evacuation had not been recorded, but Major Blamey, who was present, later remarked that no one ever spoke to Bridges in such terms before or after. Walker did not give a damn for anyone except his troops; he was ruthless in getting rid of inefficient or even exhausted officers, and his gentleness and tact when dealing with the men was in marked contrast to the outspoken bluntness with which he often addressed his superiors. He liked and respected Birdwood, but there were several furious exchanges between them before he eventually submitted to the Lone Pine attack.

Birdwood was surprisingly obstinate about the attack, for not only Walker but most of the members of the Anzac staff were dead against it. After heavy pressure he agreed to put back the time of the attack from 3 p.m. to 5 p.m., and eventually to 5.30 p.m. With this the staff had to be content, as their principal objection to the scheme—the length of time between the launching of the Lone Pine attack and the break-out to the north—had been partially met. Walker and most of the Anzac staff considered that the Lone Pine attack, in itself a desperate business, would alert the whole Turk line and bring up the reserves; Birdwood believed that it would draw those reserves to the Lone Pine area, and thus help to clear the way for the advancing columns of Sari Bair. It was largely a matter of guesswork, of judging how the Turks would react. Everything depended on the attack being made as ferociously and successfully as possible, and Walker and his staff, with heavy hearts, began to lay their plans.

This, then, was the plan. On the nights of August 3rd–4th, 4th–5th and 5th–6th, the 13th Division was to be smuggled ashore at Anzac and hidden until the evening of August 6th. On the afternoon of the 6th the British at Helles were to conduct a holding operation in the centre of the line, at a point called The Vineyard where the Turk line bulged invitingly. At 5.30 p.m. the assault on Lone Pine was to begin. As soon as night fell, parties of New Zealanders were to steal out of Anzac to clear the foothills to the north, beginning with Old Number Three Outpost. When the foothills were cleared, the two assaulting columns, totalling 10,000 men, were to leave Anzac along the beach road. The Right Assaulting Column, consisting entirely of New Zealanders, was split up into two groups, one of which would advance to Table Top by way of the Chailak Dere and the other up the Sazli Dere, before joining up on Rhododendron for the march on Chunuk Bair. Once established on the summit, they were to attack the enemy positions on Battleship Hill from the rear at dawn on August 7th. To synchronise with this attack, the Australians at The Nek, Pope's, and Quinn's, assisted by British troops, were to assault the Turk trenches opposite them at first light on the 7th. Meanwhile, the Left Assaulting Column, under General Cox, was to pick its way via the Aghyl Dere to the summits of Hill Q and Koja Chemen Tepe. This column was principally composed of Australian and Indian troops, and was to be guided by Overton and his trained local guides. By dawn on August 7th it was hoped that the Sari Bair summit would be captured and that the Turk positions on Battleship Hill would be under attack from front and rear. If the Lone Pine attack were successful, the Turkish line would have been completely broken.

Meanwhile, at 9 p.m. on the evening of the 6th, some 13,000 men of the 11th Division, under General Hammersley, were to disembark at Nibrunesi Point, capture Lala Baba and Hill 10, and then advance across Suvla Plain to capture Kiretch Tepe, Chocolate Hill and the W Hills by daybreak.* Mahon's 10th Division would land at first light on August 7th with the task of continuing the advance along Kiretch Tepe, while the 11th Division captured Tekke Tepe, so that early on August 7th the line would stretch from Ejelmer Bay to Chunuk Bair. Some 63,000 Anzac, British and Indian troops would be fighting in the Anzac-Suvla area, mainly in country lightly held by the enemy. Including all troops stretched along the coast between Gaba Tepe and the Helles front, the Turks could muster barely 30,000 men in the

---

* For some reason which is not entirely clear, G.H.Q. did not accept a proposal by the Navy to land some troops on the northern shore of the Kiretch Tepe ridge. This had actually been done on June 20th, when a party of New Zealanders had scaled the cliffs without difficulty and walked across the Plain before returning.

vicinity of the British thrust, and many of them were several hours' march away.

At this point what appeared to be a minor irritation occurred. Stopford had asked Hamilton for some reasonably precise information on the rôle of IX Corps when he had arrived at Mudros on July 11th, but Hamilton had mysteriously told him that it was still highly secret. On July 22nd the plan was revealed to him first by Hamilton and then by Aspinall, who described the tasks of the corps in considerable detail. Almost the entire burden of planning the Suvla operation had fallen on Aspinall, Dawnay and Deedes—the architects of the April landings—and Aspinall explained the situation clearly.

Stopford's instructions were explicit. The capture of Chocolate Hill and the W Hills before daybreak on August 7th was 'of first importance'. 'Your subsequent moves', the instructions continued, 'will depend on circumstances which cannot at present be gauged, but it is hoped that the remainder of your force will be available on the morning of 7th August to advance on Biyuk Anafarta with the object of moving up the eastern slopes of Hill 305 [Koja Chemen Tepe] so as to assist General Birdwood's attack.' This was clear enough; having secured all the heights on the north and eastern sides of the Plain, Stopford's corps was to swing to the right and move up the Sari Bair slopes to relieve pressure on Birdwood. Aspinall told Stopford that the total Turkish force in the Suvla area was estimated at five battalions (in fact there were only three).

Stopford expressed himself well satisfied with the plan. His Chief of Staff, Brig.-Gen. H. L. Reed, V.C., took a different view. Reed brought from France a profound hatred of undertaking offensive operations without adequate artillery support, and he considered the artillery allocated to IX Corps wholly inadequate. Indeed, it was virtually non-existent. Hamilton had been unhappy when he had heard that Reed was joining Stopford, as Reed had been his own Chief of Staff once, and he knew his limitations. Stopford was charming, intellectual, and pliant; he was also conscious of his own battle inexperience and was eager to learn, a rare attribute in a senior officer in his sixties. Reed was four-square, professional, brave, and dogmatic. His personal courage, as his memorable V.C. in South Africa demonstrated, was beyond question, and he had what Stopford lacked, a recent and personal experience of modern warfare. Furthermore—and this is a point not generally appreciated by his critics—he had been attached to the Turkish army during the Turco-Bulgarian war, and had been deeply impressed by the courage and discipline of the Turk infantry, particularly in defence. Reed did not think well of operations whose basis was hope and guess-work, and, when it was reduced to its essentials, this was exactly the foundation of the whole Suvla enterprise. A surprise attack rests upon a certain element of hazard, as adequate reconnaissance invariably alerts the enemy, but Reed at once put his finger on the weakness of the Suvla Plan. How did G.H.Q. *know* there were only five battalions in the area? What about artillery?

To these questions there was no really convincing reply. Guns *had* been seen on Suvla Plain, and it was possible that there were others concealed in the scrub and ravines. The reconnaissance aircraft had not flown low enough, for fear of arousing Turk suspicions. All the available information pointed to the fact that there were few guns and few infantry in the area, but this was not good enough for Reed. Reed later vehemently denied that he had been pessimistic, and said that he had only been realistic, which was his job. De Lisle subsequently described him as an exceptionally capable Chief of Staff. Furthermore, in his defence—although he did not cite them—were the *Field Service Regulations*, which stated flatly that 'a thorough reconnaissance is an essential prelude to a night advance or to a night assault. . . . Every commander who orders a night operation which is not preceded by a complete reconnaissance increases the risk of failure and incurs a heavy responsibility. Reconnaisance from a distance is insufficient.' Reed, it should be noted, was not alone in his apprehensions. Mahon, when he eventually saw the plans, described them as 'far too intricate and complicated to have a reasonable chance of success. . . . I told Sir F. Stopford my opinion.' Most of the senior officers were aghast when the plans were unfolded to them.

As Aspinall subsequently admitted, G.H.Q. was so obsessed by the Anzac operation that little serious attention was given to Reed's rumblings. As Hamilton wrote in his dispatch, 'Anzac was to deliver the knock-out blow. *Helles and Suvla were complementary operations.*'* They were also afterthoughts, and both Street at Helles and Stopford at Suvla were to some extent left to their own devices.

On July 26th Stopford asked Hamilton to revise his instructions. He wanted a third of the first landing force landed in Suvla Bay itself, and the sailors, although still uneasy about the depth of water, eventually agreed. Instead of some 10,000 men going ashore south of Nibrunesi Point, 3,000 were to be landed in Suvla Bay itself, nearly two miles away. This was trivial when compared to what then happened to Stopford's instructions. Reed was now in full cry, and did not attempt to conceal from everybody his gloomy expectations. Stopford's confidence withered away completely in the face of Reed's arguments and exhortations, and Hamilton and his staff were so preoccupied with Anzac that little heed was given to the implications of amending Stopford's instructions as he wished. When they were revised and agreed to by Hamilton, they read as follows:

*Your primary objective will be to secure Suvla Bay as a base for all the forces operating in the northern zone.** Owing to the difficult nature of the terrain, it is possible that the attain-

* My italics.

ment of this objective will, in the first instance, require the use of the whole of the troops at your disposal. Should, however, you find it possible to achieve this object with only a portion of your force, your next step will be to give as much assistance as is in your power to the G.O.C. Anzac in his attack on Hill 305 [Koja Chemen Tepe], by an advance on Biyuk Anafarta, with the object of moving up the eastern spurs of that hill. Subject only to his final approval, the General Commanding gives you an entirely free hand in the selection of your plan of operations.

Tekke Tepe was now not mentioned at all, and as for Chocolate Hill, Stopford's instructions now read: 'If it is possible, *without prejudice to the attainment of your primary objective*,* to gain possession of these hills at an early period of your attack, it will greatly facilitate the capture and retention of Hill 305.'

This was a fundamental and disastrous change in the nature and tone of Stopford's orders. Hamilton had a clear warning of Stopford's attitude, as he wrote to Hamilton on August 3rd that 'I fear that it is likely that the attainment of the security of Suvla Bay will so absorb the force under my command as to render it improbable that I shall be able to give direct assistance to the G.O.C. Anzac in his attack on Hill 305.'

If anything ought to have alerted Hamilton, this should. Quite apart from the indication it gave to Stopford's frame of mind, it clearly demonstrated his failure to understand the real purpose of the Suvla landing which, as the first instructions had made clear, was to help Birdwood. The Suvla landing, by itself, was an irrelevancy. Even if Kiretch Tepe and Tekke Tepe were captured, the Sari Bair heights—which dominate both—remained the key to the Peninsula. Tekke Tepe is three miles from Sari Bair, and, although it dominates Suvla, is not otherwise of commanding importance.

Thus, instead of a great co-ordinated battle waged on three fronts, there were now to be three independent battles fought on three fronts by three independent commanders—a very different thing. By failing to keep Stopford to his first instructions and by not seeing where his new instructions were leading him, Hamilton had made perhaps the greatest—and least excusable—error of the whole campaign. The muddled thinking which existed in his own staff is demonstrated by an interesting episode at this time. As well as writing to Sir Ian on the subject of his inability to help Birdwood, Stopford saw an unspecified senior member of G.H.Q.—almost certainly Braithwaite—who told him that 'I might take it from him that it was the wish of the G.O.C.-in-C. that the security of the harbour should be my first consideration, and that this security was not to be forfeited by an advance to Biyuk Anafarta to General Birdwood's assistance'. Stopford subsequently complained that Hamilton never really took him into his confidence, although they had worked together closely in the past in Southern Command in England, and that he was never properly consulted. He was told what to do, and when he proposed revision of his instructions, no particular interest

* My italics.

was taken by Hamilton or his staff in the alterations. Hamilton, in reply, pointed out that Stopford could have come to see him any time he wanted.

But there was some justice in Stopford's complaints. In a letter to Kitchener on August 11th, Hamilton wrote: 'The vital importance of time had been impressed over and over again on the higher command.' This was simply not true, and Stopford was not the only senior officer to be kept at arm's length; Mahon lunched with Hamilton at G.H.Q. a few days before the operations were due to begin, but Hamilton made no reference whatever to the military situation, even in general terms. 'I know nothing of the situation here,' Mahon wrote to Sir Edward Carson in London, 'but all I can gather is unsatisfactory.' Braithwaite's protectiveness of Hamilton probably also played its part. When even senior officers are discouraged from 'troubling the C.-in-C.' by his Chief of Staff it requires some strength of mind to insist, and Stopford was not a strong man. The blame for the fatal imprecision of the orders finally given to Stopford must be laid firmly at Hamilton's door. One consequence of this vagueness was that Hammersley was under the impression that Birdwood's attack at Anzac was partly to distract the Turks' attention from the Suvla landings, and said as much in his divisional orders.* Of far greater significance, he told his brigade commanders that they were to reach the W Hills only 'if possible'.

One of the principal causes of this confusion was a mania for secrecy which had gripped Hamilton and his staff, and which had been evident for several weeks even before the conception of the Suvla operation. On June 28th, for example, it was planned that a diversion should be made at Anzac to distract attention from Helles, but Birdwood was not told until 8.30 a.m. on the morning of the 28th, and the resultant operation, hurriedly conceived and carried out, cost the Australians over 300 officers and men. This was exactly the sort of hastily organised, costly and futile operation which caused much of the bitterness subsequently felt by the Gallipoli troops towards G.H.Q., particularly among the Anzacs. The two senior officers in charge of the 'demonstration' never recovered their position among the troops. Previously, the men had been glad to see them in the trenches, and had spoken freely to them; now, they only replied, curtly, to questions directly put to them. For weeks, the atmosphere was sulphurous.

Even at G.H.Q. itself, the majority of the staff was kept in ignorance of the impending operations, and all officers of the New Army divisions arriving at Mudros were ordered not to discuss the probable operations, even among themselves, in case, by chance, they guessed right, and were overheard by an enemy agent. Maps of the Asiatic coast were printed in Egypt and widely distributed to the 10th, 11th and 13th Divisions. Hamilton

* This was a very strange misconception, as Hammersley had discussed the operations with Birdwood at considerable length on July 28th.

even rebuked Birdwood for discussing the operations with Godley and Walker in the middle of July, and ordered him to tell them that the operations had been abandoned. Skeen, who had originated the Anzac plan, was not consulted at all about the Suvla operation. Stopford, as has been related, was not told until July 22nd.

Other senior officers were not briefed until July 30th, and many of them never saw a map of the Suvla area before the landing. A few were rushed past in a destroyer, which was not informative. The senior naval officers were prohibited from mentioning dates, times and places of the landing even at staff conferences. Reconnaissance flights were forbidden over the Suvla area except at a considerable height, and Hamilton was extremely angry when a destroyer fired a shell into the Salt Lake to test its hardness. General Cox, commanding the Indian Brigade, who was to command the operations of the Left Assaulting Column, only arrived at Anzac at the beginning of August, and when he urged reconnaissance scouting parties to find the best route to the summit was peremptorily told this was impossible. 'I find there is an idea in some high places that you have only to show a Gurkha (officer or man) a bit of country, however difficult, and he can *at once* say the best way to tackle any proposition regarding it,' he had complained to Birdwood from Imbros, where his troops were training in night operations, on July 19th; 'I am sure you do not share this idea, and know that to get the real value out of their special knowledge they must have time to look about them and to study the lay of the land.' He now discovered that the Gurkhas were to land at Anzac on the night before the attack, were to be hidden all day in caves, and were to be given no opportunity whatever of reconnaissance.

The unfortunate Adjutant-General, Woodward, was once again kept completely in the dark. 'Everything was so secret and they would not admit me into their confidence at all.' he subsequently complained. 'It is really difficult to force the running in these circumstances.' On Braithwaite's attitude he said: 'If I went to see him I would get an answer to one particular question, but he always seemed anxious for me to go. He did not want to confer with me.'

One incidental by-product of the secrecy which enveloped the entire operation was the fact that very few officers knew that Godley was commanding the Sari Bair attack; most of the British officers had never even heard of him. The challenge and response passwords for the night of August 6th–7th were 'Success' and 'Godley'; it was not until several years later that many of them discovered that the response was a reference to the name of the General Officer Commanding.

Again, there was trouble over the medical arrangements. Birrell, when aware of the scale of the forthcoming operations, drew up plans for handling 30,000 casualties in the first three days, an estimate which proved almost exactly right. Hamilton himself reduced this estimate by one-third. 'Our first landing found out a number of chinks in our arrangements,' he wrote, 'and now my Director of Medical Services is (quite naturally) inclined to open his mouth as wide as if ships were drugs in the market. So I have tried very hard, without too much help, to hit the mean between extravagance and sufficiency.' Unfortunately the principal lesson of the April landings was not yet fully appreciated at G.H.Q. The actual landing of the troops was a relatively simple operation so far as the naval side of the operation was concerned; the handling of casualties, the landing of stores and water, put a strain upon the available ships which had proved too great in April. Birrell's figures showed only too clearly that exactly the same problem was to occur if casualties were to occur on the scale that experience of Gallipoli fighting suggested.

Matters were now rendered even more complicated by the unwelcome arrival of Surgeon-Admiral Sir James Porter in a hospital yacht on July 28th with the post of Principal Hospital Transport Officer. Both the War Office and the Admiralty had been extremely concerned by the reports of the treatment of the wounded in the April landings and since, and Porter had been forced on Hamilton, charged 'to direct the movements of all sick and wounded by all Services by sea in the Mediterranean'. This merely provided another link in an already absurdly long and complicated chain of command. There was now a Principal Director of Medical Services (General Babtie), who had arrived in June with general responsibilities for the whole of the Mediterranean, the hapless Birrell, and now Porter, whose responsibilities were defined as starting at high-water mark, with complete control over the dispositions of all hospital ships and troop transports allocated for the embarkation of casualties—known as 'black ships', as they did not fly the Red Cross—without any responsibility to the military command. Birrell and Babtie had already been at loggerheads over the plans for the handling of casualties, and now came Porter, on the eve of the operations, with an entirely new scheme of his own.

Porter was not the only unwelcome arrival at the Dardanelles. Churchill was eager to come out, and at one stage this was agreed by the Cabinet, to the dismay of Hamilton, who was personally devoted to Churchill, but had no wish to have him prowling restlessly about Imbros; experience suggested, furthermore, that Churchill would not confine his prowlings to Imbros. In the end, Churchill's proposed visit was vetoed by his critics in the Cabinet, and Hankey was sent instead. The presence of such a distinguished personage at Imbros, with the ear of the Prime Minister, could have caused difficulties, but Hankey soon dispelled any suspicions.

As the medical episode and the story of Stopford's instructions demonstrated, the operation had grown to such proportions that it had swamped

Hamilton and his staff. The scale of it was enormous, involving the deployment of nearly 100,000 men on three separate fronts, the landing of 20,000 men on a hostile shore, the secret disembarkation of another 20,000 at Anzac on three nights, and the subsequent supplying of these three armies from the sea. Both Street at Helles and Stopford and his senior officers had some justification in their subsequent complaints that they were never adequately informed or taken into the confidence of G.H.Q. Almost all the mistakes made in the planning of the operations were a direct result of their very scale. More seriously, almost all of the mistakes made in the original landings, particularly on the administrative side, were repeated. The plan had grown and grown from a limited attack to a breathtakingly ambitious operation involving intricate and complicated preparations in a short time. Amendments to the original plan—most conspicuously, the Anzac landing—had been 'tacked on' in much the same way as they had been in April. The importance of close liaison between the Anzac and Suvla commanders was not considered; once again, G.H.Q. was to take little or no part on the execution of the operations. To make these mistakes once was excusable; to repeat them faithfully, within three months, was not.

Thus the Generals and the Admirals laid their plans, while their staffs wrestled with their complicated tables, charts and logistic calculations in their stifling dug-outs and tents. The tension at G.H.Q. was almost unbearable. 'The signs of nervous strain were most apparent', Mackenzie has written. ' . . . Even the indomitable optimism of Sir Ian was having its bad moments.'

The New Army divisions, now arriving at Lemnos, had been the first to enlist in response to Kitchener's first call for recruits in the previous August, and had been training for ten months. They were fit, enthusiastic, and well equipped, and G.H.Q. derived great comfort from the fact that they were led by experienced regular Army officers. But to the hard-bitten Gallipoli veterans the new arrivals did not inspire confidence. They had no experience of active service, and although the junior officers were of a high calibre, the senior officers were old, and brought with them what many regarded as an excessive amount of pomp and pageantry. 'Generals seem to spring up like mushrooms in the night,' Wemyss wrote on July 23rd, 'and each one's Staff seems to be more glittering than the last; I *hope* their usefulness is in like proportion.' Some units of the 13th Division were sent to Helles to gain battle experience. 'I hope these K's lot are good,' Darlington wrote doubtfully in his diary; 'they *look* pretty mixed'.

The rest of the New Army divisions were not so fortunate as the 13th Division. They arrived at Mudros after a long voyage from England, and the first impressions of that awful transit camp—the fly-blown tents and huts, the swirling dust, the cruel glare from the parched earth, the dreary food, the administrative shambles and universal bad temper—confirmed their most gloomy expectations.

Those who had spent a short time in Egypt had found the atmosphere there equally dispiriting. Allanson wrote in his diary that 'there seemed to be a good deal of cross-pulling. Canal defences want things out of India, India wants to stick to its own, Alexandria, the base of the Dardanelles Expeditionary Force, wants officers and men out of the Canal defence force, who are not keen on giving them, and so the game goes on'. This clash of interest between Egypt, India, and Gallipoli had been tormenting Hamilton for months, and relations between him and Maxwell were now extremely strained; their divergencies of views had long since spread throughout the army, to the point where they were immediately noted by the new arrivals. 'I cannot say one is cheered passing up the Lines of Communication,' Allanson wrote.

On the voyage the officers had studied Hamilton's dispatches of the April landings which, although wonderfully written, were not the most encouraging reading for young men about to undertake a similar operation. Hamilton's determination to bring his army's achievements to the attention of the world had resulted in a highly-coloured and dramatic account which struck a chill into the hearts of the newcomers. Gallipoli had by now acquired a reputation as a death-trap, and Mudros was a grim introduction. An officer of the 13th Division has described his arrival at Mudros. 'The arrangements for our reception were distinctly primitive. On going aboard the *Aragon* I was taken on deck by a staff officer, who, with a sweep of his arm indicated the foreshore and foothills of East Mudros and told me that a portion of this landscape was to be the temporary home of the 13th Division. I asked how I could get ashore, and he said this was very difficult as there was a shortage of small craft!' Allanson was disagreeably struck by the 'general lack of confidence' which was his dominating impression of Mudros. The low morale of the veterans of the old divisions 'resting' on Lemnos had a particularly bad effect on the new arrivals. Davidson wrote in his diary of the departure of some units of the 29th Division from Mudros on August 2nd: 'As we passed through the shipping the old familiar cry of 'Are we downhearted?' came from some of the shiploads of fresh troops. There was but a feeble reply from our men, very unlike their shouts as we passed through Malta on the way out. We could not raise a cheer now-a-days, we are still too tired in spite of our rest.' Allanson, as did most of the officers and men now arriving at Lemnos, sought information about the Peninsula from the veterans; as he related in his diary, they 'tell one a great tale of how formidable our task is, and how appalling the loss of life has been'. The heat and the dysentery affected the new arrivals at once. And thus, utterly unaware of the nature of the operations they were to undertake, depressed by their dreary surroundings and the unhappy atmosphere of Mudros no less than by their forebodings of what the future held in store for them, the New Army assembled.

By the beginning of August everything was ready. Elaborate steps had been taken to deceive the Turks by assembling six battalions of the 10th Division at Mytilene, and Hamilton had gone down to inspect the men with little attempt at concealment. Unfortunately, among those deceived was General Hill, commanding the battalions on Mytilene, who had no idea of his part—if any— in the forthcoming operations. His divisional commander,

August Offensive
PLAN OF PROPOSED
OPERATIONS AND
TURKISH
DISPOSITIONS

General Mahon, was at Imbros, and even when he had been let into the secret, he was unable to communicate with Hill. As there was no accommodation on land for Hill's men, they were incarcerated for weeks on board ship.

As soon as the troops on the Peninsula realised that something was up, morale improved dramatically. Almost everyone was suffering to some extent from the dysentery, and over half of the veterans had septic sores which had been officially reported. Of the men who had been at Gallipoli since April, over half were suffering from symptoms of cardiac debility, and a great number were suffering pain as a result of the complete absence of qualified dentists. The marvel was that so much aggressive determination remained. 'It is not war that one admires', a British chaplain noted at this time. 'It is the spirit of the men that is admirable as it is existing among the depressing scenes around them. As one moves about in the lines or the camps, this is the thing that elevates and cheers one. . . . The effect of continued life seems to produce a peculiar sense of cheerfulness.' 'Put all the men under my charge right now (51) together,' Captain Hawkes of the Hampshires wrote in his diary, '[and] I do not think I could find more than three really fit men, yet it is wonderful how they go on with their duty and how little they complain.' 'Dreadful things are all around us,' Malone wrote in his diary, 'yet [there is] no dread. It seems the same with all of us.' A letter from a young officer in the Royal Naval Division later in the campaign probably accurately summarises the general attitude of the men. 'The men know that blunders have been made, are being made, and will be made, and they seem to regard their superiors in proportion increasing, according to rank, with a tolerant scepticism. It never enters their heads that they will not ultimately beat the Turks or Germans, staff or no staff.' But the mood was very different from that of April. A young New Zealand sergeant, E. G. Pilling, was one of many who kept a diary. Pilling had an almost mystical conception of the British Empire as God's chosen instrument, and, like so many others, had dreamed of glory. On July 21st he wrote in his diary that 'one's old ambitions and childish visions of winning a V.C. or some other distinction fade away . . . we put little value on decorations now, and will be satisfied if we do our work and get back home alive.'

In spite of Hamilton's excessive security precautions, the Turks were fully aware that something was about to happen. On July 27th officers at Anzac were warned that 'the enemy seems to be preparing for an attack, and important reinforcements have arrived. Our Division must, therefore, take all necessary steps to be on the defensive'. Von Sanders was again apprehensive of Bulair and Asia, and the commanders in these areas were ordered to 'henceforth be vigilant and ready to fight at any moment, above all after midnight and at dawn'. It was again a question of guessing where the British were to make their main effort, and the reports of 50,000 new troops in the islands and the assembling of another armada of transports, warships and lighters clearly indicated a new landing. Von Sanders' dispositions were as cautious and practical as they had been in April. His main force, of over 40,000 men, was at Helles, a remarkable tribute in itself to the fierceness of the British effort in that sector; 30,000 were at Anzac and defending the coast between Anzac and Helles; 20,000 were at Bulair, and a further 20,000 in Asia. Thus, of the total Turkish forces at the Dardanelles, only some 28 per cent were in the vicinity of the main thrust, and of this, one whole division (under Kannengiesser) was stretched along the coast south of Gaba Tepe; north of Battleship Hill, the Turks were well under 3,000 strong in all, or 2·5 per cent of the total Turkish forces at the Dardanelles.

By the end of July the Turkish situation was in many ways even worse than that of the Allies. Losses, particularly in officers and N.C.O.s, had been far heavier, and some 80,000 men had been evacuated with disease. Desertions were common, and whenever men were brought out of the Peninsula for leave they tended to disappear for good. The war was now extremely unpopular in Constantinople, food prices were high, fuel was almost unobtainable, and there seemed to be no end to it all. The British submarines, even though they never managed to obtain a complete stranglehold on the Marmara, were seriously delaying the arrival of reinforcements and supplies. Maidos and Chanak were in ruins, the Turco-German fleet was strangely inactive, while the Allied air supremacy, in spite of the arrival of a few German aircraft, was still unchallenged. Von Sanders was acutely aware of the limitations of the Turk conscripts and the majority of their officers; magnificent in defence, they had not shown up well in attack, and since June there had been many instances of even the stolid Anatolians protesting at being ordered into hopeless frontal assaults. There was nothing for it but to hold on.

Von Sanders' own position was in jeopardy, as a result of continued friction with Enver. On July 8th he was ordered to return to Constantinople, but refused, as 'I realised at once what this return from a hot battle to a far distant headquarters meant.' On July 26th he was told to hand over his command to von der Goltz, but managed to postpone a final decision. He had a staff officer forced on him, who, according to a long and confidential report he made in 1919 to the British in Malta, tried to poison him. After being seriously ill for a few days he recovered, and thereafter insisted that all his food be cooked and served by his devoted personal staff. When one remembers Enver, the story is not improbable.*

Von Sanders says that he was alarmed by the reports of increasing British activity at the north of the Anzac position, but that Essad did not share his apprehensions. There is no firm evidence to confirm this statement, and the dispositions of the Turkish forces at the beginning of August show that his main fears were for Bulair, the Asiatic coast, and the western coast-line of the Gallipoli Peninsula south of Gaba Tepe.

Kemal, however, was extremely concerned by the possibility of the British attacking to the north of the Anzac position, and so pestered Essad with warnings to this effect that he came to Chunuk Bair to see for himself. Kemal was convinced that the British would advance up the almost undefended Sazli Dere, and tried to convince Essad of the necessity for making some senior officer responsible for what Essad somewhat peremptorily dismissed as 'a little valley'. Kemal also thought it likely that the British would advance up the other valleys to the north of the Sazli Dere to attack the Sari Bair summit, but Essad and his staff were incredulous. The Sazli Dere was overlooked from the Turkish positions on Baby 700 and Battleship Hill, and was precipitously steep in places; it was not altogether surprising that Essad was unimpressed by this threat, as Kemal never dreamed of a night attack.

* The episode is not related in von Sanders' memoirs.

It is not difficult to picture that critical conference on the bare summit of Chunuk Bair. There were no trenches in the vicinity, and the scrub was untouched by the battle. To the north-west, the great sweep of Suvla Bay and the flash of light on the Salt Lake; to the south-west, the intermittent sounds of firing from the hidden Anzac lines; to the south, the Gaba Tepe promontory, jutting out into the Aegean, and the grey outline of Achi Baba on the horizon; and, to the west, immediately before them, the confusion of cliffs, ridges, precipitous water-courses and ravines dropping sharply away down to the sea. Understandably, Essad and his staff were unimpressed by Kemal's warnings of the threat from this impossible country; Essad agreed to strengthen the garrison at the head of Sazli Dere, but that was all, and it remained, as Kemal bitterly wrote, 'the most important point in our defences and the most inadequately manned'.

The commander at Suvla was Major Willmer, a Bavarian officer who had been appointed in mid-June to command what was called the Anafarta Detachment, with orders 'to prevent a landing by the enemy, or any extension of his existing front, to the north of Ari Burnu'. His force had never consisted of more than six battalions of infantry, and by the beginning of August it had dwindled to four. He had no machine-guns and hardly any barbed wire, and his few artillery pieces had perforce to be scattered rather thinly over the plain, although by using dummy guns and constantly changing the positions of the real ones he hoped that he could conceal their exact location. His tactical plans were based on the assumption that he would have to hold on for at least 36 hours before reinforcements arrived from Bulair, as he realised that a landing at Suvla or a break-out from Anzac would be accompanied by a strong assault on the other Anzac positions which would strain Essad's resources to the full. He accordingly established three strong-points on the summit of the Kiretch Tepe, on Hill 10, and Chocolate Hill; Lala Baba was entrenched and picqueted by a small party, whose task was primarily as a look-out post. Willmer's main force was positioned in a line running about a mile north of the W Hills, parallel with the sea, and barring the way to Tekke Tepe. With under 2,000 men at his disposal, it was the best he could do, and no one knew better than he how little it was.

Like Kemal, Willmer had been concerned by the signs of activity at the north of Anzac and the single shot fired by the destroyer on to the Salt Lake had increased these apprehensions, but beyond urging his men to be more vigilant than ever, there was little to do but wait.

As July merged into August, and one suffocatingly hot day succeeded another, the component parts of the great enterprise were moved into their allocated positions.

The smuggling ashore of the reinforcements for the great attack at Anzac was one of the major administrative achievements of the campaign. Over 20,000 men with their attendant supplies and 40 guns were disembarked on the three successive nights and hidden away in the labyrinths of new caves, trenches and dug-outs. By dawn the sea was empty again.

The period of waiting for the new arrivals, in their cramped and broiling-hot holes, was extremely trying. To be landed at dead of night on a strange beach and then herded in fetid caves for two days and nights, with only the knowledge that some kind of new attack was imminent, was a particularly depressing experience for the New Army men. Most were suffering from the dysentery, and the water-problem—which had been haunting Birdwood and his staff for weeks—became acute when a promised water-boat failed to arrive and the only pump broke down; another water-boat was discovered and sent to Anzac, but there was barely enough to go round. The heat was getting worse than ever. Allanson's 1/6th Gurkhas were ferried over on the night of August 5th–6th, arrived exhausted from the effects of a bad crossing, and were disposed of in what Allanson described as 'little rabbit holes in a steep cliff'. Twenty of his men were killed or wounded in the course of August 6th by enemy shelling, and their one precious water-tank was destroyed.

The officers who were to lead the march on Koja Chemen Tepe and Hill Q had been taken in a destroyer to survey the ground, and on the evening of August 2nd the plans were at last divulged to them. The general reaction seems to have been one of stupefaction. 'I felt what one would have done to a subaltern at a promotion examination who made any such proposition', Allanson wrote in his diary after the conference. 'The more the plan was detailed as the time got nearer the less I liked it, especially as in my own regiment there were *four* officers out of *seven* who had never done a night march in their lives.' The Indian Brigade, which was to form part of the Left Assaulting Column, had been brought up to strength by the addition of British officers who had no experience of working with Indian troops and no knowledge of their language; this had already caused difficulties, and was bound to cause more when the fighting began.

On the last night of the disembarkation at Anzac the first serious hitch occurred when men of the Indian Brigade were still landing when day broke. The Turks opened fire at once, and 200 men had to be taken back to Imbros. To add to the tension, the Turks launched a fierce attack on a new Australian position known as Leane's Trench half a mile to the south of Lone Pine, and although it was beaten off, the fighting did not die down until after 10 a.m., by which time the Australians had suffered 150 casualties. The rest of the morning and early afternoon of August 6th passed quietly enough at Anzac, and it became clear that the Turk activity had had nothing to do with the impending attack. 'The very air seemed charged with some peculiarly mysterious feeling,' Sergeant Pilling wrote in his diary a few days later of August 6th. '. . . It was a fine, quiet day, but for the restless questionings within.' At Helles, also, the tension was great. 'Another hot, depressing monotonous and nervy day', a British major wrote in his diary.

At Imbros, Mudros and Mytilene the fleet of 'beetles', transports, hospital-ships and men-of-war assembled, and the men of the 10th and 11th Divisions began to embark. The long rows of pith-helmeted soldiers seemed to stretch interminably across the shimmering wharves. Many of them had been up since dawn to attend instructional parades, and a high proportion had only been recently inoculated against cholera. Company commanders had not been told of the imminent departure until nearly noon, and were not issued with maps until 2.30 p.m. The men, many of whom had now been on their feet for ten hours and were suffering from tiredness, dysentery, and, on top of all, the harsh effects of the inoculations, were marched down to the quays in the blazing afternoon sun, with no idea whatever of where they were going or what they were meant to do when they got there.

The contrast with the great departure of the April 23rd was as complete as it could be. An elderly petty officer, recalled from retirement to work in trawlers ferrying men and equipment from the islands to the Peninsula, wrote in his diary: 'Hope it is going to be a success, but I have my doubts. The troops are nervy; have not the same view as [at] the landing on April 25th. Most of them I have spoken to say they will get slaughtered.'

'The sea was like glass—melted,' Hamilton wrote, 'blue green with a dull red glow on it; the air seems to have been boiled. Officers and men gave me the "feel" of being "for it" though over-serious for British soldiers who always, in my previous experience, have been extraordinarily animated and gay when they were advancing "on a Kopje day". These new men seemed subdued when I recall the blaze of enthusiasm in which the old lot started out of Mudros harbour on that April afternoon.' By early evening the embarka-tion was complete. The rumble of the guns at Helles could be clearly heard; the sea was glassy, the evening remarkably clear, and, in Mackenzie's account, 'the smoke of many funnels belching into the clear air and making turbid a sky slashed with the crimson of a long slow sunset suggested the glimpse of a manufacturing town in a hollow of the Black Country beheld from some Staffordshire height'.

At about 8.30, in the gathering dusk, the armada began to slip out of Mudros. 'The empty harbour frightens me', Hamilton wrote. 'Nothing in legend stranger or more terrible than the silent departure of this silent army.' 'The metallic blues and greens and blood-reds in the water had turned to a cold dull grey', Mackenzie wrote. 'Eastward the ever increasing surge and thunder of the guns: here an almost horrible quiet.'

At Suvla, Willmer had spent the afternoon peering apprehensively out on the empty sea. He remained at Lala Baba until well after sunset, and then rode back across the empty and peaceful plain towards his headquarters at Anafarta Sagir.

PART FOUR

CULMINATION

Was it hard, Achilles,
  So very hard to die?
Thou knowest, and I know not—
  So much the happier I.

I will go back this morning
  From Imbros, over the sea;
Stand in the trench, Achilles,
  Flame-capped, and shout for me.

Patrick Shaw-Stewart

11

The Fight for Sari Bair

Thus . . . the war was rekindled. Greeks and Trojans rose from
the ground on which they had stretched themselves, and soon the
battle was again surging tumultuously over the plain, now in one
direction, and now in another.

Witt: 'The Trojan War' (Francis Younghusband's translation, 1884)

The August Battles began at Helles at 2.20 p.m. on the afternoon of August
6th. Out of a nominal establishment of 46,000 men, the four British divisions
could only muster some 26,000 'rifles', and the French a further 13,000.
Artillery ammunition, as always, was extremely limited. Opposed to them
were over 40,000 Turks, well established in good positions, and themselves
preparing for an attack. In Aspinall's bleak words, 'the problem resolved
itself into a crude calculation as to the best value that could be obtained for a
battle-expenditure of not more than 4,000 men'. The attack was to be delivered in two distinct stages; on August 6th units of the 29th Division were to
attack the enemy positions north of Krithia Nullah supported by every
available gun; on the morning of the 7th August the full artillery fire was to
fall on the trenches to the south of the Nullah, which were to be attacked by
units of the 42nd Division. The Navy was to provide a cruiser, five monitors
and five destroyers to support the field artillery. As in the case of the
proposed IX Corps operations at Suvla, G.H.Q. exercised little or no control
over what the over-optimistic Street was up to. His corps orders spoke
grandiloquently of the capture of Krithia and Achi Baba, and so great was
the optimism that plans were prepared for subsequent operations. In fact, he
was attacking one of the strongest parts of the whole Turkish line with
insufficient ammunition for even a brief limited action.

At 2.20 on another cloudless, blazing day, the Allied artillery opened a slow
bombardment of the enemy lines. The Turk artillery, recently strengthened

in anticipation of their pending attack, replied at once, and long before the men of the 29th Division scrambled over their parapets at 3.50 they had suffered heavy casualties in the front and communication trenches. The Military Landing Officer at W Beach, Captain Pawson, witnessed the battle from the top of Hill 114 above the beach. 'It was a truly awful sight,' he wrote in his diary; 'the whole Peninsula shook with the roar, and the slope of Achi Baba seemed torn away and blown to pieces. At first you could distinguish individual shells and judge of their weight by the size of the volcano produced, then gradually one volcano merged with the next, till the landscape was blotted out in smoke and dust, in the midst of which the shells flashed as they burst and white puffs of shrapnel showed like tiny clouds.' Telephone wires had been cut, the communication trenches were choked with wounded, and after the first wave of troops vanished into the cloud and fog of the battle it was impossible to retain any control over the operations.

As dusk fell the confusion increased, contradictory orders sped to and fro, trenches were stormed, lost and then abandoned, wild hand-to-hand fighting raged around The Vineyard, and absolutely no progress was being made. Ordered to renew the attack, one senior officer angrily replied: 'The chaos is indescribable. I have only 50 men of my battalion with me. I cannot state when I shall be ready to attack. The firing line is subjected to heavy rifle and machine-gun fire.' The 88th Brigade engaged in this murderous operation lost nearly 2,000 officers and men out of 3,000. Corps headquarters told 29th Divisional headquarters that the Turkish front line was definitely captured, as their observation officers could see the metal discs on the soldiers' backs in the enemy trenches; their wearers, however, were all dead.

The attack was renewed on the following morning by the 127th Brigade of the 42nd Division, and only a tiny portion of The Vineyard was captured, which changed hands twice again in the following days. In less than twenty-four hours, in a limited attack on a front of less than a mile, three brigades of VIII Corps lost nearly 3,500 officers and men. It was all in vain. At dawn on August 7th the Turkish commander at Helles, Wehib Pasha, was peremptorily ordered to send his reserve division north to help Essad; Wehib protested, but von Sanders was adamant. Kannengiesser, at the head of two regiments of the 9th Division, had already been ordered north from his position south of Gaba Tepe two hours after the Helles attack had begun. In spite of all the endeavours and sacrifices of the British troops at Helles, von Sanders had already discerned where the real threat lay.

'Once more the long procession of wounded, dirty, ragged, torn and bloody men came down to the dressing-station,' Corporal Riley wrote; 'once more those who were deafened, shaken and quivering, sat still on the trench-seats, their eyes fixed vacantly; once more the M.O. worked as hard as he could; once more shells burst about us and the dressing station, filling the trench with yellow, stinking fumes, while dust and earth dropped on all of us; once more our heads ached with the strain and noise, and we were lucky to get away with that. Some of the 7th Manchesters were lying, wounded, about 25 yards in front of their trench; and they lay there all day, in the hot sun, not daring to move until night, when some of them might be able to crawl slowly and painfully back to our lines. . . . The trenches were crowded with dirty, ragged, worn-out officers and men. They sprawled everywhere, many of them asleep, and we trod carefully so as not to disturb them. It is impossible to describe how these men were living. Tall men slouched, thin, round-shouldered, bandaged over their septic sores, dirty, unshaven, unwashed. Men were living like swine, or worse than swine. About those crowded trenches there hung the smells of latrines and the dead. Flies and lice tormented men who had hardly enough strength left to scratch or fan the flies off for a few seconds. The August sun scorched us, for there was no shade. No photograph could show the misery of those trenches that Saturday afternoon.'

The plans for attacking the Turkish trenches at Lone Pine had been laid with a thoroughness, skill and imagination unusual in the Gallipoli fighting, remarkable also when it is remembered that Walker and his staff had been so violently opposed to the operation. On the face of it, the attack was madness. No Man's Land at this point was a wide, flat and bare stretch of ground, nearly a hundred yards wide, completely commanded by the fire of both sides. The Turks justifiably considered the Lone Pine position one of the strongest of their whole line, and had shown considerable ingenuity in making it almost impregnable. The front trenches were covered with baulks of timber to protect the troops from bomb and shrapnel-fire, and a series of deep support-trenches and communicating saps ran back from, and parallel to, the front line, leading to Owen's Gully and Legge Valley, where reinforcements could bivouac or move up in complete safety. Barbed wire entanglements, thrown out earlier in the campaign before the Australians realised the importance of night operations, were an additional hazard.

Walker and his staff eventually resolved to deliver a massive frontal assault, to be preceded by a slow barrage lasting three days to destroy the wire. An elaborate system of underground tunnels had been pushed out into No Man's Land, from which the first wave of assaulting troops was to emerge at the moment the barrage ended, so that the troops would be only briefly in the open; if this period of greatest danger could be passed without serious loss, the capture of the enemy front line was inevitable. As soon as the attack was launched, another tunnel, which almost reached the Turk front trenches, was to be opened from underneath to provide a safe communicating trench from the Australian to the Turkish trenches. Walker, at least, had learnt from the bitter lessons of Gallipoli. Most other commanders, not only on Gallipoli but in France, would have used the long tunnel to the enemy front line for mining, leaving the second and third waves of troops to cross the open ground under enfilade fire.

With the aid of excellent aerial photographs, the Australians had prepared a detailed and accurate map of the enemy position. Unfortunately the science of interpreting aerial photographs was so much in its infancy that two vital features were overlooked. In the first place, although it was clearly visible in the photographs, the timber cover of the front trenches was not detected; in the second, the existence of a steep gully branching off from Owen's Gully, and subsequently known as The Cup, was not appreciated. It was in this ravine that the enemy reserves and headquarters were bivouacked, and which formed the main line of communication with the front trenches on the left of the Lone Pine position. Because of the nature of the ground, the Turks had not entrenched the reverse slopes of The Cup as they had done elsewhere, and if the Australians were to break through at this point they would be fighting again in open country.

The slow barrage continued in an apparently desultory manner throughout August 4th, 5th, and 6th. The first day's shooting did little damage, but on the next day shrapnel, set to burst upon percussion against the ground, systematically destroyed much of the wire entanglements. On the third day, heavy howitzer shells began to fall on the front lines. The Turks were completely deceived, had no idea that this preceded an attack, and indeed thought that the bombardment was in retaliation for placards they had hoisted over the trenches announcing the capture of Warsaw by the Germans. The howitzer shells inflicted considerable damage on the front lines, as the heavy timbers crashed down on the troops packed in the dark and stifling trenches, causing heavy casualties. Major Zeki visited the Lone Pine position on the 6th and was shocked by the fearful damage made by the howitzers. 'There was the head-cover blown in, and the men lying smashed up and dead. I was very frightened.'

At 2 p.m. on the afternoon of August 6th three mines were blown in No Man's Land to give more cover to the attackers on the bare ground, and at 2.30 the men of the 1st Australian Brigade were assembled. To the south, they saw the dense yellow clouds over Achi Baba, and clearly heard the thunder of the Helles cannonade. More warships began to gather off Anzac, and the soldiers disappeared into the fetid tunnels which led into No Man's Land. In Brown's Dip, immediately behind the trenches, the three battalions who were to deliver the attack were marched to their positions. 'The bright sun of a warm summer afternoon shone upon their backs, white calico squares, and broad white armlets.'* Bean has written. 'Behind them, far down on the twinkling sea, lay the warships, firing occasional salvoes. The three columns steadily disappearing into the dusty rabbit-warren of trenches reminded onlookers of the regulated traffic of a metropolis.'

The bombardment now increased in intensity as the Australians in the underground trenches, who constituted the first line of assault, lay in their tunnels, sweating in the dreadful heat. Just before 5.30 the last sandbags were removed from the tunnels, and the leading officers looked up at the bright sky, watches in hand, whistles in mouths. In the trenches, the men of the second line, on the fire-steps, crouched higher against the trench-wall; the men of the third line, on the trench floor, prepared to spring on the fire-steps as soon as the second line had gone. At exactly 5.30 the bombardment stopped, the whistles shrilled, the Australians erupted into the sunlight from the forward tunnels and trenches, anguished screams of 'the English are coming!' arose from the Turk outposts, and the Turk positions were lashed with a fierce fire from the adjoining Australian trenches.

The surprise, in spite of the bombardment, was complete. The Australians swept across the broken scrub, suffering surprisingly few casualties. But when they arrived at the enemy's front-line they were checked, nonplussed by the unexpected head-cover. Bean, watching from the old front-line trench, could not make out what was happening. 'Instead of disappearing into the trench,' he wrote, 'they could be seen standing by its nearer edge, until there was strung along it a crowd not unlike that lining the rope around a cricket field.' Some men went on until they reached the uncovered communication saps, and leaped down; others tugged at the logs, fired through holes, or jumped through gaps made by the howitzers. The engineers had quickly opened up the long sap across No Man's Land, and the reinforcements were scurrying forward. The anxious onlookers, baffled by the apparent hesitation of the troops when they reached the enemy front line, could see bayonets flashing in the Turk communication trenches.

In the dark stinking trenches which honeycombed the Pine, a ferocious struggle was taking place. Men grappled on the ground, bayonets flashed, screams, curses and shots echoed hideously down the tunnels. The Australians quickly realised that to advance round corners with the rifle held horizontally was fatal; the only practical method was to hold the rifle upright and run round the corner, and then drop it to fire from the hip. Nevertheless, one brave Turk concealed around a sharp corner could account for several Australians before being overwhelmed. There were several instances of Turks killing Turks and Australians killing Australians in that terrible mêlée. Countless stories of great heroism have emerged from the fighting at Lone Pine, and indeed both sides fought with equal desperation and

* Used for identification purposes.

valour. No quarter was given by either side. The second and third waves of Australians found themselves trampling over the dead and wounded lying in ghastly heaps. 'The dead lay so thick,' Bean relates, 'that the only respect which could be paid to them was to avoid treading on their faces.'

Major Zeki had just withdrawn the 1st Battalion of the 57th Regiment from German Officer's Trench after holding it for 45 consecutive days when the Australian attack on Lone Pine began. He heard the rifle-fire after the bombardment 'like after thunder you hear the rain beginning; and the observers beside us said, "The English are getting into our trenches".' Zeki at once ordered his men to put on the equipment they had just thankfully taken off and to move down Legge Valley at the double to Lone Pine, fixing their bayonets as they ran. They arrived to find the entrance of Owen's Gully filled with troops hurriedly moving up into the Pine, and, most disconcerting of all, realised that they were under fire in a place previously absolutely safe. A battalion commander came rushing down the slopes of the gully, crying 'We're lost! We're lost! I have no one left under my command.' Zeki ordered his men to occupy a communication trench at the head of The Cup and to fire wildly in the general direction of the Australians. It was in fact the last line of the Turk defences. Other reserves were arriving, unnerved by the lines of their dead, sprawling four deep in places, the fusillade of bombs and bullets, and, on the skyline, the sinister silhouettes of the Australian periscopes.

Zeki had arrived at the most critical moment of the battle. The bitter fighting in the trenches was continuing, but the Australians were gaining command of the situation. Their officers now realised the significance of The Cup, but in the appalling warren of trenches it was extremely difficult to move men with any speed to the Turks' weakest point. A group of Australians actually burst through Zeki's men and swept down the steep sides of The Cup, reaching the Turk battalion headquarters. They could not be reinforced in time. The rest of Zeki's men held firm. The Australians were killed to a man. This marked the limit of the advance.

Although only a few yards of improvised trenches and a handful of desperate men stood between the Australians and a complete breakthrough at the edge of The Cup, elsewhere in the Pine the fighting continued unabated for two more days. The Turks launched frenzied and, in many cases, successful counter-attacks. 'For God's sake send bombs' ran the last message from a beleagured Australian outpost, almost immediately engulfed. Behind the original Anzac front line, men were bribing each other and actually fighting to get to the battle. Had they been adequately equipped with bombs, they would surely have broken through. By dusk they had seized the whole of the Turk front line and two-thirds of the rest of the trenches, and were resisting all attempts at counter-attacks. The Turks were responding with equal ferocity, and the fighting raged until exhaustion ended it. By then, the Australians had lost over 2,000 men and the Turks nearly 7,000 and almost all their trenches. 9,000 ! Today it takes barely ten minutes to walk over the whole of the Lone Pine position; the Australian war memorial covers much of it, but the majority of those who died in The Pine have no known grave.

The conditions at Lone Pine were unspeakable. 'The dead, Turks and Australians, are lying buried and half-buried in the trench-bottom, in the sides of the trench, and built into the parapet', an Australian wrote in his diary. 'They have made the sand-bags all greasy. The flies hum in a bee-like cloud. . . . Of all the bastards of places, this is the greatest bastard in the world. A dead man's boots have been dripping grease on my overcoat, and the coat will stink for ever.'

But, desperate though the situation was at Lone Pine, the Turks began to be aware of an unpleasant new development. Stray bullets began to sing down Legge Valley, and raise clouds of dust on Mortar Ridge; it was evident they came from Chunuk Bair. 'All these days,' Zeki has related, 'I was looking over my shoulder at the shells bursting on the reverse slope of Chunuk Bair, and, although the situation in Lone Pine was critical, I could scarcely keep my eyes on it. I knew that things must be happening on Chunuk Bair which were more important by far.'

At 8.30, immediately after the fall of darkness, on the evening of August 6th, with the roar of the Lone Pine fighting continuing unabated, 2,000 New Zealanders, comprising the Right Covering Force, crept out of the northern end of the Anzac position to carry out the vital task of seizing the foothills. The first objective, Old Number Three Outpost, had been heavily en-trenched by the Turks; part of the trenches had been roofed over with logs as at Lone Pine; and reserves were bivouacked immediately to the rear in the Chailak Dere. Promptly at nine o'clock the destroyer switched on her searchlight and shelled the outpost, while men of the Auckland Regiment stole up the precipitous south side of the hill; at 9.30 p.m. exactly the bombard-ment stopped and the New Zealanders stormed the outpost with the bayonet before the Turks could emerge from their shelters. Passing swiftly over the trenches, which were held by only about 40 stupefied Turks, they fell on the rest of the garrison in its bivouac. The surprise was complete, the Turks scattered wildly, and, for the loss of 6 men killed and 15 wounded, the New Zealanders had accounted for over 100 Turks killed and many prison-ers;* by 10 p.m. the area had been completely cleared of the enemy.

* Moorehead (*Gallipoli*, 279) writes of the attack on Old Number Three Outpost that 'there developed almost at once some of the most brutal fighting of the campaign along the side of Sazli Dere, but the Turks, as Kemal had predicted, were not strong enough to hold. They fell

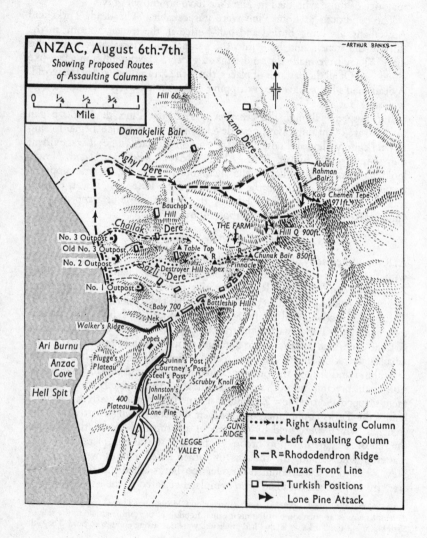

ANZAC, August 6th-7th.
Showing Proposed Routes
of Assaulting Columns

—ARTHUR BANKS—

N

0   ¼   ½   ¾   1
Mile

Hill 60

Damakjelik Bair

Azma Dere

Aghyl Dere

Abdul
Rahman
Bair

Koja Chemen Tepe
971 ft.

Bauchop's
Hill

Chailak   Dere

THE FARM

Hill Q 900 ft.

No. 3 Outpost
Old No. 3 Outpost
No. 2 Outpost

Table Top

Sazli   Dere

Destroyer Hill

R   R   Chunuk Bair 850 ft.

Apex   Pinnacle

No. 1 Outpost

Baby 700   Battleship Hill

Nek

Walker's Ridge

Pope's

Ari Burnu

Plugge's
Plateau

Quinn's Post
Courtney's Post
Steel's Post

Scrubby Knoll

Anzac
Cove

Johnston's
Jolly

Hell Spit

400
Plateau

Lone Pine

GUN
RIDGE

LEGGE
VALLEY

······▶· Right Assaulting Column
── ─▶ Left Assaulting Column
R — R = Rhododendron Ridge
─── Anzac Front Line
▭ ▭ Turkish Positions
▶ Lone Pine Attack

Meanwhile, the Wellington Mounted Rifles had captured a small Turk position on an adjoining hill known as Destroyer Hill, and, after a stiff climb up the almost sheer cliff, captured Table Top shortly after midnight. Further to the north, the Otago and Canterbury regiments met more spirited resistance at Bauchop's Hill,† but captured it shortly after 1 a.m. with the bayonet. Two New Army battalions—the 4th South Wales Borderers and the 5th Wiltshires—had seized Damakjelik Bair by 1.30 p.m. with great dash and skill, and had thus secured the entrance of the Aghyl Dere for the Left Assaulting Column. The way was now open for both Assaulting Columns to advance on the Sari Bair ridge. Brilliantly successful though the operation had been, it had taken over two hours longer than planned, and the precious hours of darkness were relentlessly ebbing away.

The Right Assaulting Column left Anzac 45 minutes late, but made good progress. The northern column, led by the Otago Battalion, advanced steadily up the Chailak Dere and reached Table Top at about 1 a.m. At this point there was a small hitch. When the Wellington Mounted Rifles had captured the hill they had missed a small Turk picquet in the dark; the Turks were very eager to surrender, and greeted the two companies of New Zealanders who toiled up to the summit to discover what was happening with cheering and hand-clapping; nevertheless, this took over an hour, and it was 2.30 a.m. before the column set off again. The moon had risen, progress was quicker, and the Turks had apparently disappeared. One Turk rushed out of the shadows and was shot by Major Temperley, the brigade-major; he was the only Turk seen that night. The column now moved up on to Rhododendron, and halted barely 1,000 yards from the deserted summit of Chunuk Bair. Dawn was beginning to break. Looking down into the Sazli Dere, they could see numbers 'of scared Turks streaming back towards Battleship Hill'.

The halt on Rhododendron was called by Brigadier-General Johnston,* contrary to Birdwood's strict orders that all units were to push on towards their objectives regardless of the progress of other units, to await the arrival

---

back along a ridge known to the British as Rhododendron Spur.' In fact, little fighting took place in the Chailak or Sazli Deres, and no Turks 'fell back along . . . Rhododendron Spur'. Troops in retreat do not normally climb an almost precipitous cliff to escape; the few troops in Sazli Dere seem to have retreated in the opposite direction to Rhododendron, and those in the Aghyl Dere scattered to the north.

† Colonel Bauchop was killed in the attack.

* Doubts as to Johnston's capacities were widespread through the New Zealanders. Malone, who first writes of him on October 2nd, 1914, as 'a fine fellow', had grown progressively disenchanted with him. It was widely believed by the New Zealanders that he drank excessively; it has even been suggested that he was not sober on August 7th. Aspinall subsequently wrote of Johnston in a private letter: 'I did, of course, know the truth, though, as official historian, I could not blurt it out . . . it was nothing but a national calamity that he was allowed to continue in command.'

of the Canterbury Battalion, which had been given the apparently easier task of advancing on Rhododendron up the Sazli Dere. This half of the column had lost itself disastrously, and by the time it was realised that it was scratching away at the most precipitous part of Table Top and new orders had been issued, it was nearly daylight.

The Left Assaulting Column had also left Anzac late. The business of assembling the men in the dark ravines at Anzac had taken far longer than expected, and Allanson relates that it took him nearly an hour and a half to assemble the 1/6th Gurkhas. 'There was a feeling of panic and doubt in the air as to where we were and where we were going', his account continues. 'It was a pitch-black night. Suddenly I heard a rush in front; I thought it was the Turks, and drew my revolver, and was almost at the same moment knocked down. Dallas* behind me fixed bayonets and stopped the rush; it was only a panic of a few men in the regiment in front.' Apart from a few senior officers, hardly anyone knew anything about where they were meant to be going or what they were expected to do. The troops stumbled along in the dark, already tired and apprehensive. Disastrously, one of the native guides persuaded Overton to take a short cut to the Aghyl Dere down a narrow little ravine, a few Turk snipers caused great confusion as the troops groped their way down the valley in the dark, and by 2 a.m., when half of the column should have been on Abdul Rahman Spur and the other half on its way to Hill Q, the head of the column had only reached the Aghyl Dere. When units had been sorted out, Overton and the guides found it extremely difficult to fix their position. The nerves of the men were not improved when the moon began to rise. 'The place was covered with dead and dying,' Allanson relates, 'many in great pain, and throwing themselves about; one began to know again what war was.' In fact, the casualties had been slight, but the sniping had disconcerted the troops, most of whom had never been in a night operation in their lives; in these circumstances, the sight of the dead and wounded in the Aghyl Dere greatly increased the apprehensions of officers and men alike. General Cox arrived in the Aghyl Dere with one Gurkha as escort; his column and headquarters had disappeared; he had been slightly wounded. Monash, understandably but unfortunately, was showing signs of the strain of the night.

Eventually Overton decided on the best practicable routes for the two halves of the column, and a party of Australians was pushed forward in the direction of Abdul Rahman, only to be badly held up by more enemy snipers. As one of their officers reported, 'the resistance, even though small, coming to us after a long and nerve-racking night, tired-out and generally done-in, made it difficult to get the troops on—their natural inclination was to go to ground, and it was hard to get them up and on the move again.'

* Captain J. S. Dallas, 1/6th Gurkha Rifles, killed in action, August 8th.

At daybreak, the Left Assaulting Column, in considerable disarray, exhausted and bewildered, was still entangled in the foothills, and had not begun to move towards the preliminary objectives it should have reached over four hours before. Only Allanson's Gurkhas, as a result of individual initiative and good fortune, had the right idea, and had reached a position 1,000 yards from the summit of Hill Q. On their way up the Aghyl Dere they passed through an abandoned Turk encampment, and enemy resistance to their advance was negligible. 'The great thing now was to push on everyone at all costs', Allanson wrote a few days later. 'Alas! it was not done.' He was peremptorily ordered to stop where he was, 'and to take up a covering position'.

Overton, whose contribution to the success of the operation had been unique, had been killed at dawn in the Aghyl Dere while directing Indian troops towards Abdul Rahman, but by then the momentum of the operations had sagged. Monash had prepared his plans with meticulous attention to detail, but when they were unexpectedly dislocated he did not possess the experience or resources to cope with the new situation. Monash was an Australian Jew, an engineer by profession, who had studied military history and the art of war with deep application and care. He once wrote that 'a perfected modern battle plan is like nothing so much as a score for an orchestral composition, where the various arms and units are the instruments, and the tasks they perform are their respective musical phrases. Every individual unit must make its entry precisely at the proper moment, and play its phase in the general harmony.' He was a brilliant officer of whom it was often said that he could command a division better than a brigade and a corps better than a division. Lloyd George subsequently described Monash as 'the most resourceful general in the British Army', a description warmly echoed by Moorehead.* This is a very debatable judgement; Monash was the organiser *par excellence*, and the battle of Le Hamel in 1918 was his master-piece. But if he lacked anything, it was resource. His sector of the Anzac line was always well administered, but was far from being the most aggressive; Malone noted in his diary early in June that Monash's Brigade—the 4th Australian Infantry Brigade—was regarded as being the least effective of all the Anzac units, and a British officer has written of Monash at the end of April that 'no one at that time could have imagined that Monash would become a Corps Commander. He was a bewildered, tired man, without an idea of what to do or how to do it. No one could blame him; he must have been completely worn out, and those few days of no responsibility [Monash, exhausted, had been persuaded to take a brief rest] probably

* *Gallipoli*, 252–3. Beyond stating that Monash 'was confined to the rôle of taking one of the Anzac columns on a roundabout route up Sari Bair', Moorehead makes no reference to, nor comment upon, the crucial part played by Monash in the failure of the Left Assaulting Column.

saved him'. In the Aghyl Dere, his plans destroyed and his men exhausted, he was lost. In a confidential unpublished account of what occurred in the Aghyl Dere on August 7th, made available to me, Allanson has written:

> When dawn broke on that day [August 7th], we found ourselves after the night march not half way up the Sari Bair, as we should have been, but at the bottom of the foothills not far from the sea.
>
> Fresh orders were clearly necessary, and General Cox made a grievous mistake, which afterwards rectified itself, by splitting up his brigade, and ordering my battalion to support Monash's brigade, which as we turned to face Sari Bair, became the extreme left of the Anzac attack. I, thus, really came under Monash's command.
>
> I left my battalion well under cover, and with a few men went off to try and find Monash; about half a mile ahead I discovered him hopelessly tied up, it seemed to me, in the low hills, a lot of shooting seemed to be going on, and there were some wounded lying about, but what I mostly saw were men hopelessly exhausted lying about everywhere, all movement and attempt to advance seemed to have ceased.
>
> This is not surprising to me now, after passing months in the trenches on the Peninsula, as these men could have had no marching exercise for 3 months (they had been tied up in Anzac); it had been a most exhausting night march, and the sun was terribly powerful.
>
> But what upset me most was that Monash himself seemed to have temporarily lost his head, he was running about saying 'I thought I could command men, I thought I could command men'; those were his exact words; I knew him by sight, as I had been at certainly one conference before the great attack at which he was present.
>
> I went up and told him that my battalion had been placed in reserve at his disposal, but he said to me 'what a hopeless mess has been made of this, you are no use to me at all'.
>
> I said nothing more, but got back to my battalion as soon as I could, wrote a message to General Cox to say that Monash had come up against a dead-end, did not require my battalion, and that I thought that the best thing that I could do was to start up the hill on my own and to place myself again in my own brigade.
>
> It was obviously useless to lie in cover in the low hills, when every minute counted, and I knew the rest of my brigade were on the move forward. I was in reality anxious to get away from Monash as quickly as I could, as I felt thoroughly upset by what I had seen. . . .

Monash was not a young man, being over fifty, and he had been working under exceptionally arduous and dangerous conditions for over three months. Like his men of the 4th Brigade, he was physically and mentally exhausted before the attack began. He was a very competent officer in the wrong place at the wrong time; what was required was a younger fighting general of Walker's capacity. Having come so far, and within barely a mile of their objectives, the chances of the Left Assaulting Column still achieving a spectacular victory were still good at daylight on August 7th, but Monash was adamant for delay until he had sorted things out. Allanson was stopped in his unopposed climb to the top of the Sari Bair Ridge, the Australians were allowed to stay where they were. Cox at first refused to accept Monash's gloomy account of the situation and exhorted him to push on; Monash was a stubborn man, and would not push on; with great misgivings, Cox was forced to agree. Thus 'the most resourceful general in the British Army' let pass a unique opportunity of a spectacular victory. 'Apart from occasional sniping,' Aspinall has written, 'all opposition had ceased'.

Moorehead has categorised the night march on the Sari Bair heights as 'folly'; General J. F. C. Fuller has described it as a 'fiasco'.* The facts were that by about 8 a.m. on August 7th Allanson and his Gurkhas were established within striking distance of Hill Q, the Australians were a mile from Koja Chemen Tepe, held up by a handful of snipers, and Johnston's New Zealanders were well positioned on Rhododendron, about 1,000 yards from the virtually undefended summit of Chunuk Bair, still waiting for the Canterbury Battalion. The Turks had been completely encircled, and the Dominion troops were on the brink of a complete victory.

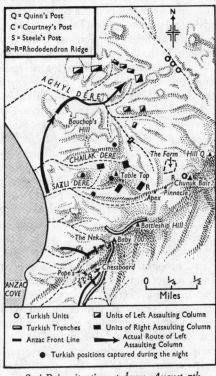

Sari Bair, situation at dawn, August 7th

As has been related, one consequence of the fury of the Lone Pine assault had been the recall of Kannengiesser and two infantry regiments from their coastguard position south of Gaba Tepe to the Anzac Front. On arriving at Lone Pine late in the evening Kannengiesser had been summoned to Essad's headquarters at Scrubby Knoll. Shortly after midnight, ominous but inprecise reports of enemy activity at the north of the Anzac position had begun to trickle in. Belatedly alarmed about the undefended Sari Bair Ridge, Essad had ordered Kannengiesser to take his two regiments and a mountain battery to occupy it. Going on ahead of his men, Kannengiesser

* Moorehead, *Gallipoli*, 280; J F. C. Fuller, *Decisive Battles of the Western World*, III, 249.

had left Essad's headquarters at 4.30 a.m. and arrived on the empty summit of Chunuk Bair at about 6 o'clock.

The view which he beheld was an astounding one. The sun was high and the heat was already becoming uncomfortable. Suvla Bay was filled with ships of all sizes and descriptions. Suvla Plain was 'like a disturbed ant-heap'; some troops could be clearly seen advancing across the Salt Lake, and others could be seen on Lala Baba. Most sinister of all, there was virtually no sound of firing. In front of Chunuk Bair a similar silence reigned, although, to the left, in 'old Anzac', the rattle of musketry was incessant.

While Kannengiesser was trying to discover what was going on in the immediate vicinity, a party of New Zealanders suddenly appeared from behind The Apex on Rhododendron, moving in single file and with disconcerting remorselessness across the scrub towards Chunuk Bair. After waiting in vain for four hours for the Canterbury Battalion to arrive, Johnston had at last pushed his men forward to capture the summit. Kannengiesser ordered the 20 men with him to open fire, but they replied that they required the order of their battalion commander, and it was evident that a panic retreat was imminent. Kannengiesser flung himself into the one shallow trench and opened fire on the New Zealanders, who sank into the scrub. 'They gave me the impression that they were glad to be spared further climbing', Kannengiesser relates. Seeing some more troops nearby, he ordered them to come at once to the summit of Chunuk Bair and form a rough firing line, and some time later the two infantry regiments which he had brought from south of Gaba Tepe arrived. While searching for further reinforcements, Kannengiesser was shot through the chest. 'This was most annoying.' Having ordered his Turkish staff officer to continue the defence 'as much as possible in an offensive fashion', Kannengiesser's crucial part in the defence of Chunuk Bair was concluded. Although the New Zealanders outnumbered the Turks by more than ten to one, and were barely 500 yards from victory, in the grim words of the Official Historian, 'the men were told to take the opportunity to eat a hasty breakfast'. When this was ended, the summit was 'bristling' with Turk rifles.

The price paid for Johnston's dilatoriness was a terrible one. At 4.30 a.m. the Australians and the British were due to attack the Turk trenches at the head of Monash Valley as the bottom half of the 'pincer' while the New Zealanders from Chunuk Bair formed the top half. The success of this operation entirely depended on the New Zealanders attacking simultaneously from Chunuk Bair and upon the suppression of Turkish machine-guns at German Officer's Trench which commanded No Man's Land at The Nek, Pope's, and Quinn's. Neither of these conditions had been fulfilled. During the night the Australians had attacked the trenches at German Officer's from Steele's Post, but, after losing 80 killed and 66 wounded, had been thrown back. The only effect of this bloody repulse had been to make the Turks exceptionally alert when first light broke on the morning of August 7th. The plan was extremely simple. After a heavy bombardment, the Australian 3rd Light Horse Brigade was to charge the Turk trenches at The Nek across a ridge so narrow that only 150 men could advance at a time, in broad daylight, with the sun in their eyes, at point-blank range, and under enfilade fire from the machine-guns at German Officer's. As Birdwood himself had written on July 1st, 'the narrow Nek to be crossed . . . makes an unaided attack in this direction almost hopeless.' Meanwhile, men of the Welch Fusiliers, under the eyes of the Turks, were to march up Monash Valley and attack Bloody Angle up the same virtual precipice which the Marines had so gallantly tried to storm at the beginning of April, before attacking The Chessboard. The 1st and 2nd Light Horsemen at Pope's and Quinn's respectively were to attack the trenches in front of them, a task which had been proved over and over again to be impossible, as the remains of hundreds of Australians and Turks rotting in the withered scrub testified.

Birdwood, however, resolved that the attack should go on as planned. Anything which might reduce pressure on Chunuk Bair and give the Turks anxiety was worth while, and it is probable that he, like everyone else in 'old Anzac', had been fired to exultation by the triumph at Lone Pine. 'It is not the light horse I am anxious about,' Skeen said; 'I think they will be all right. What I hope is that they will help the New Zealanders.' The troops themselves were more than willing to try. The Light Horsemen were undismayed by the appalling task before them. They had been at Anzac for eleven weeks, and had spent the entire time either digging trenches or carrying supplies up the bullet-swept ravines; they were young, enthusiastic, aggressive and bored with the inactivity of the past three months. They had seen the wonderful spectacle of the Lone Pine attack, and had no doubt that they would burst through the trenches at The Nek and would be then fighting in open country; 'the prospect filled them with a longing akin to home-sickness', as Bean has written. Lt.-Col. White was to lead the first wave himself, and his second-in-command the second. As dawn broke, they heard from the left 'a sound as of the bubbling of water in a cauldron. It was the rifle-fire at Suvla'.

At 4 a.m. the heaviest concentrated barrage ever laid at Anzac crashed down on the Turk trenches. For 20 minutes the side of Baby 700 leaped and twisted in the sunlight but then, at 4.23, seven minutes too soon, the bombardment ended, 'cut short as if by a knife' as one puzzled observer later wrote. A chilling silence spread over the hills. The clouds of dust gently moved away. For seven minutes utter silence reigned.*

At 4.30 the Light Horsemen bounded from their trenches. Within 30

* It was subsequently discovered that the synchronisation of watches had been overlooked.

seconds Lt.-Col. White and the first wave had been obliterated; the men at Pope's saw the Australian line leap forward across the sky-line, falter and sink to the ground 'as though', one said, 'their limbs had become string'. At 4.32 the second line hurled themselves into the dazzling sunlight and swept across the open ground. An officer found himself some 15 yards from the enemy line, looked round, and found he was alone; he flung himself to the ground, and later managed to crawl back to the Australian trench. One Australian actually did reach the enemy trench and waved a red and yellow flag, which disappeared almost at once.

In spite of the frenzied appeals of the officer in charge of the third wave, the order to continue the attack was given, and by 4.45 the ridge was choked with fresh dead and wounded. As a result of a misunderstanding another charge was made; only those who were hit at once and fell back into the trench had any chance. Out of the 600 officers and men who had made the attack, 372 had been killed or wounded, and of these, 234 had been killed almost at once. In 1919 an Australian mission counted the bodies of over 300 Australians at The Nek in an area smaller than a tennis court, most of whom had fallen in the one attack. The survivors looked across a few yards of scrub filled with bodies.

The Fusiliers had been repulsed by the Turks with the simple expedient of rolling bombs down the slopes and after they had suffered 65 casualties the attack was cancelled. The attack at Quinn's was abandoned by the officer on the spot when the first wave was destroyed before it had gone more than a few yards; at Pope's some ground had been gained at heavy loss, but had to be abandoned after savage hand-to-hand fighting; out of the 200 officers and men who made the attack, 60 were killed and 94 wounded. By 6 a.m. it was all over. 1,250 officers and men had taken part; 650 had been killed or wounded. 'At first here and there a man raised his arm to the sky, or tried to drink from his waterbottle,' Bean has written. 'But as the sun of that burning day climbed higher, such movement ceased. Over the whole summit the figures lay still in the quivering heat.'

At 10.30, five hours too late, in response to peremptory orders from Godley, Johnston again ordered the New Zealanders forward on Chunuk Bair, but could not advance beyond the Pinnacle. Johnston at once ordered them to dig in after 250 men had been lost, and Godley had to endorse the decision. Kemal's headquarters were behind Battleship Hill, only 1,000 yards or so away from Chunuk Bair, and when he had heard that British troops were advancing up Rhododendron he had immediately dispatched his only reserve battalion. They had been spotted from the Anzac positions and suffered heavy casualties from artillery fire which made movement on the reverse side of the Sari Bair slopes extremely hazardous for the Turks, but enough had reached the summit to repel the belated New Zealand attack. Cox, rightly obsessed by the urgency of the situation, obtained Birdwood's permission to call on a brigade of Godley's reserve to capture Hill Q and Chunuk Bair, but, after hours of exhausting marching and counter-marching in the maze of ravines between the Chailak Dere and the Aghyl Dere, only the 7th Gloucesters actually joined up with the New Zealanders and it was dusk before the rest were reassembled in some kind of order.

We left Major Willmer riding back to Anafarta on the evening of August 6th across the silent Suvla Plain. On reaching his headquarters he was told that reports were coming in of a landing at Nibrunesi Point. He had just ridden through his only reserve battalion marching towards the Sari Bair foothills, and he telephoned von Sanders to beg for its return. Essad now realised that he had a desperate battle on his hands, and Willmer's appeal was turned down. All von Sanders could promise was that three battalions at Bulair, some 30 miles away, would be ordered to Suvla at once. By 6 a.m. on the morning of August 7th von Sanders was convinced that his position at Anzac-Suvla was perilous, and ordered Feizi Pasha at Bulair to march two divisions south at once; all troops on the Asiatic shore were ordered to proceed to Chanak for conveyance to the Peninsula with all possible speed; in the middle of the morning Wehib at Helles was told to dispatch another division to the northern zone, and two regiments left at once. Although he had been completely deceived about Hamilton's intentions, von Sanders' reactions were swift and decisive. Every available soldier was on the march from north, east and south towards the threatened area. But, until they arrived, the Sari Bair ridge would be held by only a fragment of troops, and Willmer at Suvla had to face an army of over 15,000 men with about 1,500.

The British had landed just south of Nibrunesi Point shortly after 9.30 p.m. with remarkable precision and efficiency, and within half an hour four battalions were ashore without a single casualty (except for one naval rating, killed by a chance single shot from the shore) and the Beetles were chugging back to pick up their second loads. But things quickly began to go wrong. Lala Baba was stormed and captured, but not before relatively heavy casualties had been sustained. Many of the men had been on their feet for 17 hours, many were suffering from the after-effects of the cholera inoculations they had been given only the day before, the night was pitch-black, and there was considerable confusion on and around the beach. One of those present has commented that 'our first introduction to casualties was too great a shock, and led to a crop of absurd alarmist rumours that had no basis in fact. . . . To the raw soldier a foe lurks in every bush and shadows become enemies, and both are magnified tenfold. Add a few casualties, and the whole venture is in the melting pot. This is precisely what happened, and what knocked us off our balance.' Their training in England had never envisaged this kind of confused groping in the dark on a strange beach; as one officer said, 'an energetic offensive movement, pushed for all it's worth, was a thing which probably they had never practised or even dreamt of.'

It had been planned that the troops at Lala Baba should march north to join those landing in Suvla Bay itself to attack Hill 10, but there was a great deal of wild firing going on, the men were bewildered and tired, no one had any idea of the situation, and runners were either killed or lost their way in the dark. The officer who had captured Lala Baba sent off a message to his brigadier reporting his position; the runner was killed, and when his body was discovered after daylight, the message was unintelligible; in the excitement, the officer had given the runner a page of rough notes jotted down at the conference on the previous afternoon. This was an extreme, but not untypical, example of the confusion which existed that night.

The landing of Sitwell's 34th Brigade in Suvla Bay itself had confirmed the Navy's fears. The first three Beetles came under a scattered fire as they approached the shore, and two of them struck a reef about 50 yards from the beach. The men had to struggle ashore up to their necks in water, holding their rifles over their heads, in pitch darkness only lightened by the flash of fire from the shore. Eric Bush, one of the young midshipmen in the lighters, who had distinguished himself in the Anzac landings, has written that the troops 'made a poor showing—no dash and a certain amount of talking. Finally, a handful of men, who obviously had the wind up, looked as if they were afraid to land.' When the men got ashore, it was soon apparent that they had landed in the wrong place. The destroyers carrying the covering force had anchored in the wrong order* nearly 1,000 yards south of the intended position, and the troops were landed nearly a quarter of a mile south of the proper place. To add to the confusion, the lighters themselves had landed in the wrong order, and by the time the occupants of the two stranded boats had arrived, soaked and shivering, on the beach, units were badly mixed up; the Lancashire Fusiliers, for example, found themselves on the left of the landing force, and not on the right. Not everyone was confused, however, and one battalion of the Manchesters, admirably led, climbed the Kiretch Tepe ridge and by 3 a.m. was established in a commanding position nearly two miles inland.

Elsewhere, everything was going wrong. Hill 10 had not even been located, let alone captured. The moonlight aided the defenders more than the attackers, particularly as the British were wearing white armlets, and heavy losses were suffered in the officer and N.C.O. ranks; one battalion

---

* It was subsequently discovered that the only written naval order on the subject was so vague as to be almost incomprehensible.

of the Lancashire Fusiliers lost 60 per cent of its officers and 20 per cent of its rank and file before noon on August 7th. The disembarkation proceeded slowly, and the confusion on the beaches got steadily worse. It transpired that many of the naval officers were as ignorant of the whole operation as the soldiers; one officer in charge of two drifters towing spare cutters, for example, had been told nothing until he was about to leave Imbros, when he was ordered to 'follow the destroyers'. His drifters could not keep up with the destroyers, and he soon found himself in an empty sea, with only a small chart of the eastern Mediterranean, which fortunately marked Suvla Point; with commendable initiative he made for the Point, but, after arriving, it was several hours before the drifters and the urgently required cutters were discovered.

By daybreak on August 7th the British had not advanced far beyond the beaches, which were under a spasmodic fire. When Stopford and his staff had arrived on H.M.S. *Jonquil* shortly after midnight everything seemed quiet, and Stopford had gone to sleep on deck. No news came from the land, no officer was sent ashore to discover the situation, and no reports were sent to G.H.Q. on Imbros. Hamilton had intended that Stopford should remain on Imbros for the night of the 6th–7th, and should land at Suvla at dawn, but Stopford was anxious to be close to his troops from the start, and took his General Staff with him on the small sloop *Jonquil*. The administrative staff came over in the liner *Minneapolis*, and it was hoped that the whole of corps headquarters would be established on shore early on the 7th. One weakness of this arrangement was that *Jonquil* was not equipped or staffed to receive and transmit military messages.

At G.H.Q. on Imbros, the long hours passed with agonising slowness. A telegram arrived from the military attaché at Sofia inquiring about the situation at Gallipoli; Aspinall remarked with a curt laugh that he would very much like to tell him. Dawnay and Mackenzie walked to the shore and peered anxiously to the east. 'Over the Peninsula the blood-red horn of the waning moon just risen was clawing up at the sky', Mackenzie writes. 'A rocket flamed on the horizon. A ship was hooting mournfully while it waited to be allowed in through the Kephalo boom. At half-past two somebody in the O tent produced a bottle of Horlick's Malted Milk Lozenges, and we all sat sucking them in a melancholy.' It was not until 2 a.m. that a chance message to his mate from a Suvla wireless operator gave the impression that all was well.

Throughout August 7th the confusion at Suvla grew. Dawn was breathtakingly exquisite; 'the sullen horseshoe of hills, as nameless to us as the mountains of the moon, came unstuck from the slow-lifting mother o'pearl buoyancy of the sky', a sergeant of the 32nd Field Ambulance has written. 'The white leprous patch of the Salt Lake unfolded from the scumbled darkness of rock and scrub.' The six battalions of the 10th Division under Hill arrived from Mytilene at daybreak, and were considerably surprised to find themselves sailing into an unknown bay under shrapnel fire; it was only after the Salt Lake had been spotted and the staff had examined their maps that they realised where they were. Hill went to see Stopford on *Jonquil*, who told him to go to Nibrunesi and place himself under Hammersley; if he could not be found, he was to go north and 'complete the capture of the Kiretch Tepe ridge'. Keyes was very anxious that they should be landed further north and join the Manchesters on Kiretch Tepe, but after some coming and going this was decided against. No one seems to have thought of consulting Mahon, the divisional commander, who subsequently

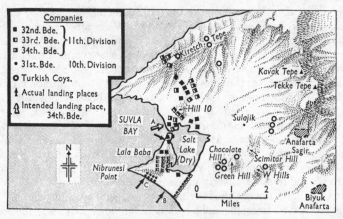

Suvla, 8 a.m., August 7th

found himself with only three battalions, the divisional pioneers, and three field companies out of the division he had raised and led. Mahon was sent to the Kiretch Tepe ridge with three battalions, while Hill and his six bewildered battalions eventually found themselves attacking Chocolate Hill, three and a half miles away.

Believing that he could communicate more easily with the divisional commanders from the deck of *Jonquil*, Stopford decided not to go ashore, and in fact remained on board with his General Staff until the evening of the 8th. If *Jonquil* had been intended for such a rôle this change of plan might not have mattered very much, but she was not. Furthermore, the General Staff and the administrative staff were—as on April 25th—separated at a moment when close co-operation was essential. IX Corps' principal administrative staff officer could not get ashore from *Minneapolis* until nearly noon on

August 7th, owing to the confusion in Suvla Bay and the shortage of small boats; although he realised that the army was being badly held up through delays in the disembarkation of animals and supplies, it was not until evening that he could get another boat to take him out to *Jonquil* to report this serious matter.

Disorganised and bewildered though the army was, spirits had risen with daylight, there were some 20,000 men safely ashore, resistance was negligble, and a single act of resolute leadership would have secured the capture, on very easy terms, of the whole of Kiretch Tepe and at least the Tekke Tepe foothills. None was forthcoming. The stream of conflicting orders which passed between commanders and units have been set out in Aspinall's official account, and give a graphic picture of the confusion at Suvla on August 7th. But it was the scene itself which was so extraordinary. The army was bunched around the beaches, under a persistent but hardly serious fire. 'I was struck by the restfulness of all around', an artillery officer wrote in his diary. 'There appeared to be little going on, a good many infantrymen sitting about or having a bathe. The impression conveyed to my mind was that of a "stand fast" at some field day.' The bay was crowded with warships, transports and hospital ships. The sun burnt down relentlessly. The Turks lurked in the scrub and sniped. Here and there a small group of British troops would set off in the general direction of the foothills, falter, and disappear into the scrub. Willmer reported to von Sanders that the British soldiers moved 'bolt upright, as if on parade', bunched together, and 'made no use of the available cover'. It was mainly because of this that the British suffered more casualties on August 7th than the total Turk forces opposed to them. Hammersley—whose health was poor—had been badly shaken by a near-miss and was feeling the heat. Sitwell, commanding the 34th Brigade, who had been the most gloomy of all the senior officers before the landings and had sworn that he had seen Turk carrier-pigeons winging over to the Peninsula from Imbros and regular lamp signalling to the mainland, lived up to his name. Attacks were ordered and countermanded at the last moment. It was not until dusk that the British started to make a belated and hesitant move forward, and succeeded in capturing Chocolate Hill and Green Hill just as darkness was falling.

The blistering heat and the shortage of water were proving far more serious enemies than the Turks. By the afternoon many of the men had emptied their water bottles and some were nearly mad with thirst. The inevitable bully-beef was the main item of food available for the troops, and, as Aspinall has written, was 'a wretched diet for a thirsty man when the temperature stands at over 90° in the shade, and the beach was littered with tins which the men had thrown away.' The Navy had never expected to have to supply water to so many men, and although de Lotbiniere had arranged for four water-lighters at Imbros, they had been left behind. 'Apparently no interest had been taken at Headquarters nor by any officers concerned in the success of the expedition in seeing that these boats accompanied the troops', he subsequently wrote.* Hamilton said it was Stopford's fault; IX Corps said that it was all G.H.Q.'s fault; meanwhile, until the Navy could bring over the water-ships, the Army was paralysed. The storeship *Prah*, equipped with water-tanks, pumps, hoses, water-troughs and well-digging apparatus, sat quietly behind Suvla Point for nearly a week. The troops on Kiretch Tepe, tormented by the lack of water, vaguely wondered what this transport anchored in the lee of the steep cliffs was doing. The officer responsible for the engineering and water arrangements for IX Corps collapsed on August 9th and had to be evacuated. When a waterboat did arrive and grounded off the beach, some of the troops stripped off their clothes, struggled through the water, and cut the pipe to fill their bottles. The arrangements for the landing of other supplies were also badly dislocated. In this respect the Navy was partly to blame; while making every allowance for the confusion which existed on the shore, the shelling of the beaches and the lack of small craft, the disembarkation of urgently required supplies was not carried out with an adequate appreciation of the importance of speed. No guns were landed throughout the day. Blame was subsequently laid on Rear-Admiral Christian, the officer responsible for superintending the landing of stores and equipment, for the dilatory progress made on August 7th, but much responsibility lay on the staff of IX Corps, and not least on Reed. When one has said that Suvla on August 7th was an unrelieved shambles one has said everything.

The failure of Hamilton to act is difficult to comprehend unless it is remembered that he classified Suvla with Helles as a subsidiary operation to the main attack from Anzac on Sari Bair. A report from Stopford, received at noon on August 7th, revealed that he had not even taken Hill 10; 'as you see,' the message ended, 'we have been able to advance little beyond the edge of the beach.' This alarming message did not perturb G.H.Q., and Braithwaite telegraphed at 4.20:

> Have only received one telegram from you. Chief glad to hear enemy opposition weakening, and knows you will take advantage of this to press on rapidly. Prisoners state landing a surprise, so take every advantage before you are forestalled.

This was hardly a trumpet call, but, as Aspinall subsequently told the Dardanelles Commission, 'the attention of the General Staff throughout

---

* In his extremely interesting evidence before the Dardanelles Commission, de Lotbinière complained of the difficulties he encountered when dealing with the Navy in combined operations. 'They have to refer, refer, refer, so often. . . . It is very difficult for a naval officer to act on his own authority—much more than for an army officer.' Controversy subsequently arose about the availability of water-springs at Suvla. Aspinall told the Dardanelles Commission that on August 8th he saw fresh water trickling down the Kiretch Tepe ridge; General de Lisle

7th August was focussed on Anzac'. 'When we heard at G.H.Q. that the ships with Hill's lot on had sailed into Suvla Bay at dawn,' Braithwaite related, 'and that we had taken Lala Baba during the night, we said: "The thing is done".' There was no contact between Godley's and Stopford's headquarters through the battle. Street carried on with his futile battering at Helles. Meanwhile, G.H.Q. on Imbros, far from giving any central direction to the fighting, hopefully awaited news from the three separate fronts. Hamilton and his staff chafed at the absence of information, but this was an occasion on which chafing was hardly adequate. Guy Dawnay was sent to Suvla to discover what was happening. He returned with an accurate report of the situation, but no notice was taken; 'I returned hot-foot to report to G.H.Q. at Imbros, only to gain the impression that I was looked on as unduly impatient.' Wemyss described the complacency at G.H.Q. on August 7th as 'something awful'.

If it was the nadir of Hamilton's career as a Commander-in-Chief, it was von Sanders' zenith. Turkish and British accounts do not afford him adequate credit for the resolution and skill which he showed as soon as he divined the British plan early on August 7th. His orders to his commanders at Bulair, Helles, Suvla, Anzac and in Asia were clear, urgent and precise. He had now arrived at Suvla. To his delight and surprise he was told by Feizi Bey that the Bulair troops had covered the 30 miles so rapidly that they would arrive that evening. Von Sanders ordered an attack at dawn on August 8th. Everything seemed to be going remarkably well. Willmer's men had withdrawn with small loss from Chocolate Hill, and then abandoned Hill 10, and had already inflicted disproportionate casualties on the British, who seemed to have no plan or aggressiveness. The night of August 7th–8th passed in utter tranquillity at Suvla. 'Only the Suvla spiders—and Feizi Bey's troops coming down from Bulair—had toiled through the night', Sergeant Hargrave of the 32nd Field Ambulance has written. 'It was a cobweb morning, misty-thick, foretelling a steaming-hot day. Every sagebush and wild thyme hassock festooned with spiders' webs heavy with dew.'

The situation at Anzac was extraordinarily complex when Godley made his plans for the resumption of the attack on the 8th. The troops were widely scattered, and it was extremely difficult to obtain accurate information of the exact position of many units. Although losses had not been heavy on the

---

said that between Kiretch Tepe and the Salt Lake 'you had not to go more than 15 feet before you got as much water as you wanted. Inside the area which they [IX Corps] occupied on the first day they only had to scratch the sand to get as much water as they wanted. On the shore, within 100 yards of high-water mark, you had only to dig the sand 4 feet down to get water. All that means bad staff work, because the Royal Engineers could have found that out as easily as I could.'

7th, there had been several cases of senior officers being killed or wounded by snipers. The present Lord Slim, for example, then a subaltern in the Warwickshire Regiment, found himself commanding a company because all his superior officers had been shot, one while standing up to discover his position. The scenes on those bare spurs and deep ravines were pathetic. Every now and then a group of men would try to double forward to better positions, leaving several of their number lying in the dust. 'It was like a fight in fairyland,' Aubrey Herbert wrote: 'they went forward in parties through the beautiful light, with the clouds crimsoning over them. Sometimes a tiny, gallant figure would be in front, a puff would come, and they would be lying still.' Water was becoming scarce, the business of bringing down the wounded to the improvised dressing stations and carrying water and ammunition up to the troops was extremely trying, and the heat was awful. Cox, who had fought in the North-West frontier of India, said that the Gallipoli heat was worse than anything he had ever experienced.

The Gurkhas remained under the summit of Hill Q, patiently awaiting reinforcements and orders. With their invaluable experience of this kind of fighting, they had avoided the literally fatal mistake of bunching together, had kept out of the ravines, and had concealed themselves with great skill. At 1.30 a.m. Allanson received orders to attack at dawn on the 8th. 'We had been heavily shelled that evening,' he wrote in his diary, 'and I had been much frightened. We had no blankets and no coats, and when I got the orders I was so shivering with cold (fright!) that I could with difficulty read them.' As it was impossible to get in touch with the two British regiments with whom he was ordered to attack, Allanson decided to press on with his Gurkhas. Advancing in short bursts, they got to within 300 feet of the crest before coming under a hot fire. This magnificent advance, executed with great skill and enterprise and at relatively minor cost, had been seen by Slim, whose company of Warwicks were occupying a cramped and dangerous position on Allanson's left. Slim had some Gurkhas with him, and led them across with him to a line of men lying in a row in cover; there he found Allanson, with whom he shared a 'dirty envelope of raisins', and discussed the situation, agreeing to act together as far as possible as a single unit.

To Allanson's right, at Chunuk Bair, things had gone even better. Attacking at first light, the Wellington Battalion under the intrepid Malone—he who had gloried in the cultivation of the domestic virtues at Quinn's—had captured the summit. Some accounts make a mystery out of the fact that the summit was only held by a machine-gun crew; Moorehead, for example, refers to an 'inexplicable gap in the Turkish line. . . . One does not know why it was that these exhausted Turks had not been relieved or reinforced, but it was so.'* Turkish accounts state that the heavy naval

* *Gallipoli*, 283.

bombardment preceding the advance had wreaked such havoc in the very shallow trenches—in most cases only a foot or so deep—that the survivors had been forced to run back to positions behind the crest; to state that this constitutes a more likely account than versions which ascribe to the Turks an incredible failure to safeguard what they now regarded as a critical position is to understate the case. The New Zealanders occupied an old Turkish trench on the crest and began to dig in on the forward slope, and a new support trench on the reverse slope of the hill was begun.*

Meanwhile, Monash's Australians, who had made another attempt to reach Koja Chemen Tepe by way of Abdul Rahman Bair, had been shot to pieces by well-concealed machine-guns and, for the first time in the campaign, had broken and run. At 2 p.m. the plans for a renewal of the attacks on Koja Chemen Tepe and Hill Q were abandoned for the day. The situation on Chunuk Bair was engrossing everyone's attention.

Throughout the day the New Zealanders on Chunuk Bair were subjected to a terrible fire from the Turk positions on Hill Q and Battleship Hill. A battalion of the Gloucesters, which had attacked the crest to the north of Chunuk Bair at the same time as the New Zealanders advanced had been very badly shot up and forced to retire, and some were taken prisoner in a Turk counter-attack. The Turks were full of admiration for the courage with which the Gloucesters fought, and Major Prigge writes of their 'young, athletic and spirited officers'; but they were terribly exposed on the almost flat ground and the survivors forced to retire. It was impossible to reinforce the New Zealanders at Chunuk Bair. Time had been too short, and the ground too hard, for the new trenches on the crest and forward slopes to be completed, and before long the Wellingtons were driven off the summit; on the reserve slope, with men of the Gloucesters and the Welch Fusiliers, they held on. The Turks brought up reinforcements which worked their way up to the crest-line, and it was only by means of repeated counter-attacks that the New Zealanders and British were able to retain their two lines of shallow trenches. Before them, the lost summit, and their lost trenches, now occupied by the enemy; from the left and right, a merciless, incessant fire; behind them a hundred yards of exposed ridge, which to cross was to die; and above them, a pitiless sun.

By early afternoon the forward trench was so choked with bodies that it had to be abandoned, and another scratched immediately behind it. 'The Wellingtons seemed to rise up each time from nowhere,' one of the few survivors, Captain Hastings, has related, 'and the Turks were hurled back; in the first of these attacks Colonel Malone's rifle was twisted by a bullet, so after this he kept it with him, as he said it was lucky. Later the Turks began

* Malone's adjutant, Sir Ernest Harston, has most kindly made available to me his detailed unpublished account of the events of August 8th on Chunuk Bair.

hurling bombs, new ones with a longer fuse, so the New Zealanders were catching them and throwing them back.' A New Zealand corporal, Basset, won an epic V.C. by laying and maintaining a field telephone wire to the front line from brigade headquarters.

At about 5 p.m. the long-needed artillery support came. Harston, Malone and a few other officers saw a warship approach the shore 'at a great pace', turn, and open fire. 'Swish! swish! came the shrapnel', Hastings has related, 'and all except two in our little trench were killed or wounded. . . . Colonel Malone collapsed into the adjutant's arms.' By the time Harston had got through to brigade headquarters by field telephone and the bombardment had stopped, Malone was dead, and only Hastings and he remained. Of all the misfortunes of the day, this was the hardest one to bear. The official histories make no reference to it.

When merciful darkness came, reinforcements from the Otago Battalion and the Wellington Mounted Rifles moved up from their positions on Rhododendron. Sergeant Pilling led a platoon, and was appalled by the ranks of dead and wounded, the cries for water. The shattered remnants of Malone's force were withdrawn. Their uniforms were torn and drenched in sweat and blood; they were caked in dust; they could hardly walk; most of them had had no sleep for more than forty-eight hours; none had had any water since dawn; they spoke in whispers and trembled violently; some broke down and wept. Of the 760 New Zealanders who had advanced so confidently at first light, only 70 were unwounded; the 8th Welch Fusiliers had lost 17 officers and 400 men; the 7th Gloucesters had lost every officer and sergeant and over 350 men. But the grip on Chunuk Bair had not been relinquished.

The Turks themselves were hardly in better shape. Although they had about 7,000 men on or near the Sari Bair ridge and had managed to regain the Chunuk Bair crest, their losses had been very heavy, and the senior officers were almost in despair. Throughout the day Kemal had received alarming reports of the confusion in the Turkish units, heavy losses in officers and men, and, most disturbing of all, unmistakable signs of panic. 'An attack has been ordered on Chunuk Bair,' one message ran; 'to whom shall I give this order? I cannot find the battalion commander . . . I do not know what I am supposed to do.' 'There are men here from different regiments, but I cannot find any of their officers', another read. 'The last commander of this regiment has been killed. Most of the officers are dead or wounded. I do not even know the name of the hill I am on. I can see nothing. I know nothing. I implore you for the safety of the nation to appoint someone who knows the land and us.' Kemal met the officer in command of the Chunuk Bair troops, and spoke to him with such confidence and authority that much of his dwindling courage was restored.

After the high promise of the dawn, August 8th had been a day of heavy losses and little progress for the British. It was developing into a nightmare battle. The gunners sweating at their guns, the doctors struggling in a welter of blood and pain, the toiling, slow-moving, dogged stretcher-bearers, the dust-caked runners staggering down the interminable ravines with their precious messages, men in full battle equipment slowly climbing the ravines towards the unseen front lines not knowing or much caring where they were going, troops squatting apathetically by the side of a rough track waiting for orders, officers standing in small groups, clutching grimy maps, lines of mules dustily making their way along rock-paths, and the endless ragged lines of men carrying ammunition, food and water; these were the scenes that etched themselves most indelibly on the memory. The tormenting sun, the everlasting flies, the dust, the glare, the tumult, the physical exhaustion and ever-present tension dominated everything. Men blundered along, some in a stupor of exhaustion; shock, intense weariness and nervous strain manifested itself in a thousand different ways. It seemed incredible that the battle had been raging for only two days and nights, for all sense of time had gone. There was no respite at night, as the wonderful relief from the sun and the shrapnel was more than compensated for by the wearying grind of bringing up supplies. Men suddenly crumpled and fell where they stood through sheer exhaustion. Sleep was something that men snatched in odd moments if they were lucky; the troops high on the hills at grips with the enemy had no sleep at all, very little water and food, but they stuck to their shallow stinking trenches with dumb fortitude.

It was extremely difficult for Birdwood and Godley to determine the exact situation, but certain facts had emerged from the events of August 8th. The Australians under Monash were still trapped in the ravines of the northern foothills, and were almost incapable of further effort. The road to Koja Chemen Tepe was now definitely barred; the grip on Chunuk Bair was tenuous. But Allanson's party of Gurkhas and British troops perched high on the Sari Bair Ridge beneath a point just under the crest half-way between the summits of Hill Q and Chunuk Bair, although only about 450 in number, were in a wonderful position for an assault at dawn if sufficient artillery fire could be laid down by the Fleet and the Anzac artillery. They had had an extremely unpleasant time throughout August 8th. Movement was impossible, and the heat intense. As Allanson has related: 'I lay without moving till 6 p.m. with every conceivable shot flying in the air about me, shrapnel, our own maxims, rifles, and our own high-explosives bursting extremely close, which told me how near we were to the top. I lay between two British soldiers; the man on my left had a Bible, and read it the whole day; the man on my right I found was a corpse. I wondered if I ought to make good resolutions for the future, and did not.'

New plans were hurriedly prepared for the morrow. The main attack was to be made by the New Zealanders on Chunuk Bair and by five comparatively fresh battalions* of British troops under General Baldwin. Godley wanted Baldwin's men to march along Rhododendron and attack from the Pinnacle at 5.15 a.m., and he sent Baldwin to discuss the matter with Johnston. He himself did not attend this critical conference and, inexcusably, did not even send a representative. Neither Godley nor Birdwood, nor a single staff officer, visited The Apex—rightly described by one historian† as 'the nodal point of the whole battle'; stuck fast at No. 2 Post, they had no idea of the country over which they were ordering men to advance; of even greater importance, they were buoyed up by an entirely inappropriate over-confidence and satisfaction at the course of the battle.

Johnston, who was quite exhausted by the long strain of the battle, succeeded in persuading Baldwin not to attack along Rhododendron, but to move up the Chailak Dere and thence in to the Aghyl Dere, and to advance to Chunuk Bair by way of a small plateau about 1,000 yards short of the summit, known to the British as The Farm because of a small white-washed sheepfold at its edge. This disastrous advice, in spite of the urgings of some of Johnston's own staff officers, was accepted. None of Baldwin's officers had any clear idea of their route or objective; even if they had, the darkness was absolute, and they could only follow their guides. The brigade stumbled along the awful ravines, the guides lost their way, the groping column became inextricably entangled with wounded men, other reliefs, and fatigue parties, and daybreak on August 9th found it stretched out in a long, confused and straggling line in the Aghyl Dere.

When the tremendous bombardment died away promptly at 5.15 a.m. on the morning of August 9th, Baldwin's men had not even reached The Farm, and on Chunuk Bair the New Zealanders came under such heavy fire that they were hard put to it to maintain their own precarious position. The naval shells had fallen so near to the New Zealand trenches that, as Sergeant Pilling wrote in his diary a few days later, 'our men were nearly blinded by the flash and almost suffocated by the fumes. No sooner had this stopped than we were furiously bombed from the Turks' trench in front . . . we could not reply with rifle-fire, because whenever we lifted our heads we were sniped. We had no bombs.' Only on the left was there an attempt to assault the Sari Bair ridge.

Allanson had pushed forward another 50 yards towards the crest as soon as darkness fell on the previous evening, and had managed to secure further reinforcements—in addition to Slim's Warwicks—in two companies of the

---

* One was sent to reinforce Johnston on Rhododendron on the 8th, bringing Baldwin's force down to four battalions.

† North: *Gallipoli, The Fading Vision*, 224.

South Lancashire Regiment. There was some confusion at Cox's head-quarters as to exactly where Allanson's party was, although he had given it fairly accurately in a report on the 8th. Cox ordered Allanson to retire and dig in on a better position lower down, but Allanson, pleading the difficulties of moving his men, averted this order. At 10.34 p.m. on the evening of the 8th Allanson sent back an urgent message to brigade headquarters: 'Please note very carefully my position on map, some of the naval high-explosive are coming frightfully close to us tonight and it is important tomorrow 9th support should not catch us.' This message was partly occasioned by one from brigade headquarters sent to Allanson at 9.30 p.m., which ordered him to move his men to assaulting distance of the crest by 5.15 a.m.; this was in fact the position Allanson's men had been occupying all day. His men had now not had any sleep since the night of August 4th–5th, their water-bottles had been refilled only once, and since the 6th they had been existing on the rations issued to them that evening, which were intended for only one day; all Allanson's appeals for food, water and ammunition were met with the reply that all were available if he sent men down to fetch them.

The Gurkhas and the Warwicks thus had to endure another sleepless and waterless night in their eyrie. 'By this time,' Allanson relates, 'the enemy had discovered I was immediately below them, and throughout the night there was a perfectly terrible fire; my wee dug-out was a mass of dust flying about. . . . The men fired over 120 rounds on an average each through-out the night. The roar was incessant. I was rather weak from want of food, and I trembled most of the night. The Navy greatly helped us by keeping their searchlight on the hill, which enabled my fellows to keep the Turks from getting up to rush us.' During the night he received orders to attack at 5.15 a.m., when the naval bombardment ended. A warning message to Lt. Le Marchand, commanding the detachment of Warwicks and South Lancashires in the firing line, was only despatched at 4.45 a.m. His account continues:

At an angle of about 35 degrees, and only 100 yards away, were the Turks . . . I had only fifteen minutes left; the roar of the artillery preparation was enormous; the hill was almost leaping underneath one. I recognised that if we flew up the hill the moment it stopped, we ought to get to the top. I put the three companies into the trenches among my men, and said that the moment they saw me go forward carrying a red flag everyone was to start. I had my watch out, 5.15. I never saw such artillery preparation; the trenches were being torn to pieces; the accuracy was marvellous, as we were only just below. [At] 5.18 it had not stopped, and I wondered if my watch was wrong. 5.20, silence: I waited three minutes to be certain, great as the risk was. Then off we dashed all hand in hand, a most perfect advance, and a wonderful sight. . . . At the top we met the Turks: Le Marchand was down, a bayonet through the heart. I got one through the leg, and then, for about ten minutes, we fought hand to hand, we bit and fisted, and used rifles and pistols as clubs; blood was flying about like spray from a hair-wash bottle. And then the Turks turned and fled, and I felt a very proud man: the key of the whole

Peninsula was ours, and our losses had not been so very great for such a result. Below I saw the Straits, motors and wheeled transport, on the roads leading to Achi Baba.

As I looked round I saw we were not being supported, and thought I could help best by going after those [Turks] who had retreated in front of us. We dashed down towards Maidos, but had only got about 300 feet down when I saw a flash in the bay and suddenly our own Navy put six 12″ monitor shells into us, and all was terrible confusion; it was a deplorable disaster; we were obviously mistaken for Turks, and we had to get back. It was an appalling sight; the first hit a Gurkha in the face; the place was a mass of blood and limbs and screams, and we all flew back to the summit and to our old position just below. I remained on the crest with about 15 men; it was a wonderful view; below were the Straits, reinforcements coming over the Asia Minor side, motor-cars flying. We commanded Kilid Bahr, and the rear of Achi Baba and the communications to all their Army there. . . . I was now left alone much crippled by the pain of my wound, which was now stiffening, and loss of blood. I saw the advance at Suvla Bay had failed . . . I now dropped into the trenches of the night before, and after getting my wound bound up, proceeded to try and find where my regiment was; I got them all back in due course, and awaited support before moving up the hill again. Alas; it was never to come, and we were told to hold our position throughout the night of the 9th–10th.*

Slim had been severely wounded while directing his men to move to the right to help Allanson; of the only two other officers left, one was killed as he bent over Slim, who was bleeding profusely. Slim's batman cut off his equipment and got him down to a field dressing station before returning to the fight and to his death. Slim's wound was roughly bound with a pugaree, and eventually he reached an Australian field ambulance, 'where we lay in the sun and got shelled'.

Considerable controversy later arose over the shells that fell on Allanson's men, and which killed over 100 of them. The Navy pointed out that the shells had fallen on the *reverse* slope of the ridge, out of their sight. Allanson, although he omitted the reference to 'a flash in the bay' in the version he allowed Churchill and Aspinall to publish, emphatically maintained that the shells were naval shells, and came from behind him. From Allanson's own account it is clear that he was on the reverse slope when the shells were fired, and from there could not have seen the British ships, which makes his reference to 'a flash in the bay' all the more mystifying. Bean shared the Navy's scepticism of Allanson's allegation, and unearthed evidence which made it more probable that the shells came from a battery in the old Anzac area, which had been firing at the reverse slopes of the Sari Bair for days,

---

* This graphic account of the attack on Hill Q has been quoted several times in histories of the campaign. The extract quoted above is taken from Allanson's diary, of which 50 copies were printed and privately circulated, and differs in some minor respects from other versions. The most interesting passage, omitted from other published versions, concerns the shells. The words 'I saw a flash in the bay' are not included in those quoted in the Official History, Churchill's *World Crisis* or Moorehead's *Gallipoli*.

Allanson was recommended for the Victoria Cross, but eventually was awarded the D.S.O. Cox said that he would have also recommended Le Marchand 'had he lived'.

and naturally assumed the streams of men running down the hills were Turks.*

But to suggest, as has been done, that this disaster changed the course of the battle is to misinterpret the situation.† As an American military commentator has remarked, 'a few shells, fired fifty-six hours after the attack began, did not decide the fate of that famous hill'. Allanson's exploit, brilliant though it was, could not have been decisive unless Baldwin's men had seized the enemy positions to his right, and Baldwin for his part, would have been in a serious position if the New Zealanders failed—as they did—to seize Chunuk Bair.

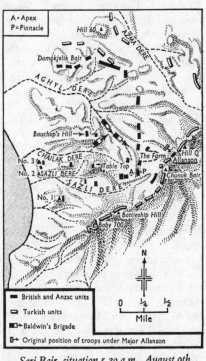

Sari Bair, situation 5.30 a.m., August 9th

By noon on August 9th the British were no further than they had been on the morning of August 7th, except that they had now suffered over 12,000 casualties, the survivors were in a state of utter exhaustion, and the Turks were hurrying every available man to Chunuk Bair. Baldwin's leading battalion had tried to move across the Farm plateau, but had been subjected to such a fierce fire that Baldwin had decided to dig in at the edge of the plateau. A major Turkish attack developed from the north on August 9th against the British and Australians on Damakjelik Bair, which had been most gallantly repulsed with heavy losses inflicted on the enemy. But this was a sombre reminder of the fact, as yet unperceived by Godley in his headquarters

---

* After examining the ground and the official reports of the naval and military staff concerned, this is also the opinion of the present writer. As related on page 289, Allanson was very concerned by the possibility of the naval shells falling on his men, and when they were shelled at 5.25 a.m. may have jumped at once to the conclusion that what he had dreaded had in fact occurred.

† It is interesting that in his first report, written at 6.30 a.m. on the 9th, as soon as he had got back to the trenches, Allanson wrote: 'I do not think that casualties by high explosive should have been sufficient to cause the retirement, but all the troops concerned had an extremely bad night last night, and only just clung on.'

at No. 2 Post, that the balance of numbers and initiative had passed to the enemy.

Godley had long since lost any direction over events; remote from the fighting, receiving only fragmentary information from his scattered outposts, he was fortified with a dangerous false optimism, unfortunately shared by Birdwood. The performances of Stopford and Hammersley at Suvla have obscured the vital fact that there was an equal lack of personal initiative and drive by the commanders at Anzac, with precisely the same consequences. When Hamilton, encouraged by the cheerful atmosphere at Godley's headquarters, offered Birdwood his last remaining reserve, the 54th Division, on August 9th, Birdwood replied that the water situation at Anzac made it impossible to accommodate another division.

Meanwhile, black masses of Turkish reinforcements were gathering behind Sari Bair. British reconnaissance aircraft reported long lines of troops being marched from Bulair and Maidos to the area; on August 8th it was reported that enemy troops were massing behind Chunuk Bair, and on the 9th a pilot reported that the Turk camps at Anzac had increased to fully three times their original size since the 7th. Before the weary troops, in Churchill's vivid phrase, 'the terrible summits flamed unconquered as ever'.

Von Sanders had been up at first light on August 8th to watch Feizi's promised attack at Suvla. The sun rose on a placid scene. Apart from an occasional outburst of firing and some desultory shelling, there was hardly anything to connect the empty plain with war. After waiting with mounting impatience for a considerable time, von Sanders went to see Feizi, who told him that his divisions had not arrived, and that the attack would have to be postponed for 24 hours. Von Sanders peremptorily dismissed Feizi from his command, and Kemal was appointed to command all the troops in the Anafarta section. Von Sanders gives no reason for this decision in his account, except to say that he had full confidence in Kemal's ability and enterprise. Meanwhile, on his horse on the high ground above Suvla, with only Willmer's fragments between himself and Stopford's army, von Sanders passed the day in gnawing anxiety and apprehension.

August 8th was another completely wasted day for the British at Suvla. Inanition, confusion and lethargy combined to keep the army of over 20,000 men glued to the beaches. When Hammersley, encouraged by the inactivity of the enemy, consulted his brigadiers about the possibility of an advance, they replied that they were still sorting out their units. Stopford, still in *Jonquil*, sent his generals a message of congratulation, and informed Hamilton that Hammersley and his men 'deserve great credit for the results obtained against strenuous opposition and great difficulty . . . I must now consolidate the position held, and endeavour to land stores and supplies, which are badly needed.' 'You and your troops have done splendidly', Hamilton replied on the morning of the 8th. 'Please tell Hammersley how much we hope from his able and rapid advance.'

Hamilton, as this telegram shows, was still not yet seriously troubled about Suvla, even though it was now some 36 hours since IX Corps had landed, but he decided to send Aspinall—accompanied by Hankey—to report on the situation. The destroyer put at Hamilton's disposal had developed boiler trouble, and they did not reach Suvla in a trawler until after noon, having been delayed for more than four hours.

Stopford had, that morning, at last ordered an advance on the W Hills. 'It is of the greatest importance to forestall the enemy on the high ground north of Anafarta . . . If you find the ground lightly held by the enemy, push on', he wrote. 'But in view of want of adequate artillery support I do not want you to attack an entrenched position held in strength.' To G.H.Q. he reported: 'Heavy fighting yesterday and unavoidable delay landing artillery make me consider it inadvisable to call on troops to attack a strongly entrenched position without adequate support.' As Aspinall subsequently said of Stopford, 'he had half expected to be held up before he started, and it seems that the casualties made him believe that his fears had been realised, and that he must wait for more guns. He accordingly stopped driving, and if the man on the box stops driving, the horses will not get up the hill.'

Aspinall and Hankey landed to find a holiday atmosphere on the beaches. Men were bathing, there were no signs of any fighting, and they at once assumed that the hills had been captured. 'I thought the operation was over,' Aspinall related, 'and that we were on the hills. I never felt so happy during the whole operation as I did that morning.' 'A peaceful scene greeted us,' Hankey wrote to Asquith a few days later. 'Hardly any shells. No Turks. Very occasional musketry. Bathing parties round the shore. An entire absence of the expected bustle of a great disembarkation. There seems to be no realisation of the overwhelming necessity for a rapid offensive, or the tremendous issues depending on the next few hours. One staff officer told me how splendidly the troops were behaving, and showed me the position where they were entrenching. Another (straight from France this one) abused the policy of the Dardanelles operation. A third remarked sententiously that it was impossible to attack an entrenched position without a strong artillery, and this was not yet available. . . . At the headquarters of the 10th Division I was told that the strength of the enemy in front of them was 800 gendarmes! that they were stout fellows, regular Boers in fact, and that in this rocky, bushy hill-country of the Suvla ridge we really could not turn them out without field artillery (they had a battery of mountain artillery) or colossal losses!'

The next half-hour was a nightmare for Aspinall. He and Dawnay had conceived the whole Suvla operation, had secured Hamilton's approval and that of the Navy, and for the past two months had been working indefatigably on the details of the scheme. He subsequently blamed himself for not keeping Stopford strictly to his original instructions, but although this was strictly more a matter for the C.-in-C. than a junior and over-worked staff officer, Aspinall cannot be wholly exonerated. After a few minutes' walk across the plain he was shocked to be told that he was in the front line. One officer, recognising him, angrily said that 'nothing is being done, and it looks as if nothing is going to be done'. Another, pointing into the scrub said: 'We are being held up by three men. There is one little man with a white beard, one man in a blue coat, and one boy in shirt-sleeves!' Hammersley, when run to ground, said that his men were dead beat, had suffered heavy casualties, and that he hoped to advance next morning. By now thoroughly alarmed, Aspinall went on board *Jonquil* to see Stopford, who had just been ashore and seemed well content with the progress made. Aspinall said that he was sure Hamilton would be greatly disappointed that the hills had not been reached, to which Stopford replied that the men needed rest, and that he was going to order an advance for the next day. Aspinall left to send a despairing telegram to Hamilton—which the latter did not receive—and Stopford, perhaps more impressed by Aspinall's urgency than he showed, left *Jonquil* to order Hammersley to make an immediate advance. Hammersley was not at his headquarters, and when Stopford heard that he was arranging a joint attack on the W Hills for the following morning, abandoned his proposal.

Hamilton arrived at 6 p.m. The faulty boilers in the destroyer which had held up Aspinall and Hankey delayed Hamilton for over six hours, and it was not until 4.15 that he had got a passage in de Robeck's yacht *Triad*. When the Navy had apologised earlier in the day for the 'inconvenience' caused by this delay, Hamilton had sent a reply to the effect that it was less a matter of inconvenience than of preventing the C.-in-C. exercising his proper functions. Unfortunately Braithwaite got hold of the message and drastically watered it down. Hamilton, now obsessed with an intuitive apprehension, chafed at Imbros for over six hours; it never seems to have occurred to him or anyone at G.H.Q. that a message to de Robeck or Keyes could have provided transport almost immediately.

Hamilton arrived in a fever of anxiety, and was met by Keyes and Aspinall, who were distraught at the deplorable turn of events. A short and strained conference took place on *Jonquil*. Stopford said that Hammersley was to undertake a general advance on the following morning; Hamilton said that Tekke Tepe must be taken that night; Stopford said that Hammersley did not consider a night advance feasible; Hamilton said that he would go ashore to see Hammersley himself. According to Hamilton, Stopford asked to be excused, as his knee was hurting badly; but Stopford's account says that he was not invited to accompany the C.-in-C., and professed himself hurt by the slight. Aspinall, in evidence before the Dardanelles Commission, supported Hamilton's version, but admitted under examination that he could not be categorical on the matter; it was only his impression that Stopford had asked to remain on *Jonquil*.

In any event, Stopford was left behind to nurse his knee and his feelings, and Hamilton 'tumbled into Roger Keyes' racing motor boat and with him and Aspinall we simply shot across the water to Lala Baba. Every moment was priceless.'

Hammersley was digesting a warning message from *Jonquil* when Hamilton bounded up. He was insistent that the advance must begin at once, and overruled Hammersley's objections. So critical did he regard the Suvla situation that he decided to remain off the shore in *Triad*. More than ever he was regretting that he had not insisted on moving G.H.Q. to Suvla on the 7th.

Hamilton's intervention was disastrous. Unknown to anyone, an officer and a signaller of the 6th East Yorkshire Regiment had climbed almost to the top of Tekke Tepe and found it unoccupied. This momentous report, like so many others, went astray, and Hamilton himself did not learn of it until 1923. The 32nd Brigade, also unknown to Hammersley, had pressed forward on its own initiative, and two battalions were established on Scimitar Hill and near Abrikjar respectively. Hamilton, on learning that the bulk of the brigade was near Sulajik, ordered it to advance 'and dig themselves in on the crest line'. On receiving this order, the two advanced battalions were recalled and concentrated with the rest of the brigade. Priceless time was lost, there was considerable confusion, and the invaluable position on Scimitar Hill unnecessarily abandoned. By one of the supreme ironies of military history, Hammersley's plan for a concerted advance early on August 9th might well have succeeded, whereas Hamilton's perfectly justifiable, if belated, intervention resulted in a major catastrophe. In spite of his orders for an immediate advance on Tekke Tepe, by the time that the 32nd Brigade had sorted itself out, dawn was nearly breaking, and no time whatever had been saved.

The two Bulair divisions had now arrived at Suvla, and Kemal, after a quick reconnaissance, had confirmed the order to attack at dawn on the 9th from the summit of Tekke Tepe. One division was to climb Tekke Tepe and attack from the summit; the other to advance on Biyuk Anafarta and attack from that direction, von Sanders being convinced that the weight of the British attack would fall in that area; not unreasonably, he assumed that the purpose of the landing had been to advance on Koja Chemen Tepe via

Biyuk Anafarta. The removal of this division meant that Kemal had barely 6,000 men to deliver the attack from Tekke Tepe, but they sufficed.

The British were just half an hour too late on the one hand, and an hour too early on the other. If they had been on the summit of Tekke Tepe or advancing to a proper plan up the lower foothills the tumultuous charge planned by Kemal might have resulted in an overwhelming Turk defeat. As it was, the charge caught the 32nd Brigade at its most vulnerable, spread out on the steepest part of the hill, tired and bewildered. A party of East Yorkshires which had almost reached the summit before being overwhelmed, was

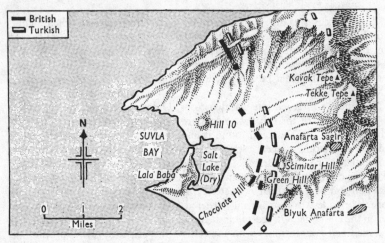

Suvla, evening, August 9th, showing opposing lines

annihilated; only three officers and two men survived to be taken prisoner, and two of the officers were bayoneted after surrendering.

At about 6 a.m. the line broke, 'like a crowd streaming away from a football match', as an officer wrote in his diary, and the British were swept back to the plain. Scimitar Hill had been taken by the enemy, and a British counter-attack thrown back. Under the intense machine-gun fire the dry scrub burst into flames, destroying the wounded as they lay on the ground, and adding a new horror to the Gallipoli fighting. 'I watched the flames approaching and the crawling figures disappear amidst dense clouds of black smoke', Ashmead-Bartlett has written. 'When the fire passed on little mounds of scorched khaki alone marked the spot where another mismanaged soldier of the king had returned to mother earth.'

The Battle of Suvla was determined at that moment. The fighting continued throughout August 9th and 10th, and after the British had suffered nearly 8,000 casualties they occupied positions only marginally different from those held at daybreak on August 7th. 'My heart has grown tough amidst the struggles of the Peninsula,' Hamilton wrote, 'but the misery of this scene well-nigh broke it. What kept me going was the sight of Sari Bair—I could not keep my eyes off the Sari Bair ridge.'

The New Zealanders on Chunuk Bair were relieved after nightfall on August 9th by two battalions of the 6th Loyal North Lancashires and the 5th Wiltshires.* The Otago and Wellington battalions had been fighting the Turks at virtually point-blank range for twenty-four hours and Sergeant Pilling has recorded that out of 200 men in the three shallow trenches near him, only 20 survived. As the front trenches—which hardly merited such a title—could only hold 700 men, when 2½ companies of the Wiltshires arrived from The Farm after a miserable climb, they had to take up their positions in the Sazli Dere. They were so exhausted that they took off their equipment, piled their rifles, and flung themselves on the ground for their first sleep for four days. Including the remnants of the Wellington Battalion at The Apex and the machine-guns of the New Zealand Infantry Brigade, there were about 2,000 British and Dominion troops in the immediate vicinity of Chunuk Bair, all of whom had long passed the normal human physical and mental endurance. In the neighbourhood of The Farm, and occupying a position almost immediately below the plateau, Baldwin commanded a mixed force of Hampshires, Wiltshires, Warwicks and Royal Irish Rifles, amounting to about 3,500 in all. Allanson's men were still perched high to the left,† although Allanson himself had been forced to return to Anzac for medical attention. 'The nullahs on the journey back were too horrible,' he relates, 'full of dead and dying, Maoris, Australians, Sikhs, Gurkhas and British soldiers, blood and bloody clothes, and the smell of the dead now some two days old. . . . I left that battlefield a changed man; all my ambitions to be a successful soldier have gone; knowing all I now know, I feel the responsibility, the murderous responsibility, that rests on the shoulders of an inefficient soldier or one who has passed his prime to command.' Monash's Australians were still pinned down in the foothills farther to the north.

By dawn on August 10th the British, Indian and Colonial troops strung

* The New Zealand Infantry and Mounted Brigade had lost 1,871 officers and men out of a total of about 4,500 since August 6th.

† Moorehead (*Gallipoli*, 293) states incorrectly that 'Allanson and his men had been withdrawn, but other British troops had taken up their positions on the hill' by the afternoon of August 9th.

out on the hills were in a condition of complete exhaustion; most of them had been fighting for three days and four nights under conditions which would have strained the resources of fully fit men to the limit, and few of them had been even half fit when they had started. The scenes on the tracks down to the beaches and in the fly-blown dressing stations were pitiful. 'The condition of the wounded is indescribable', Aubrey Herbert wrote. 'They lie in the sand in rows upon rows, their faces caked with sand and blood; one murmur for water; no shelter from the sun; many of them in saps, with men passing all the time scattering more dust on them. There is hardly any possibility of transporting them. The fire zones are desperate, and the saps are blocked with ammunition transport and mules, also whinnying for water, carrying food, etc. Some unwounded men almost mad from thirst, cursing. We all did what we could, but amongst so many it was almost impossible.'

The Turks were in a similar plight. Their casualties had been even heavier than those of the British, and the prolonged strain of the battle had exhausted officers and men alike. At Helles the Chief of Staff advised a complete abandonment of the south of the Peninsula 'while there is still time', and was promptly dismissed by von Sanders. At Suvla, in spite of the spectacular charge down the Tekke Tepe slopes, the Turks were still heavily outnumbered, and the British were pushing tentatively along Kiretch Tepe towards the main Turkish ammunition dumps (of whose existence they were not aware). Kemal, when he arrived at Chunuk Bair late in the evening of August 9th, having satisfied himself that Suvla was safe for the moment, found all the officers asleep. 'They appeared to have left the battle to the will of God', Kemal brutally remarked. The commander of the 8th Division, Ali Riza, was almost in despair. Throughout the day he had delivered a series of attacks on the New Zealanders at Chunuk Bair which had been repulsed with heavy casualties. The 23rd Regiment was literally the last remaining Turkish reserve on the Peninsula, and if it were to be cut up as the 24th Regiment had been, there was nothing left. Kemal, although haggard with exhaustion and nervous strain, remained calm and confident, and his demeanour had some effect in restoring the confidence of his officers.

Including the 23rd Regiment, there were six battalions available on the reverse slopes of Chunuk Bair, and Kemal ordered them to prepare for an attack at first light over the crest towards The Farm and Rhododendron. He did not even know if the side of the hill above The Farm was precipitous, but decided that the risk must be taken. 'I had come to the conclusion', Kemal later wrote in his diary, 'that we could defeat the enemy by means of a sudden, surprise assault.' It was a desperate gamble. The warships had the range of Chunuk Bair to a yard, and during the day it was impossible to live on the crest; the New Zealand machine-guns at The Apex swept the slopes down which Kemal proposed to attack. All the bitter experience of the campaign had proved over and over again that a frontal attack in daylight against machine-guns, artillery and entrenched troops was madness. If the attack failed, as so many of Kemal's attacks had failed in the past, there was nothing left; the British would have been able to capture the summit of Chunuk Bair, occupy the whole of the Sari Bair ridge, dominate Tekke Tepe, Anzac and the Narrows, and the campaign was over. His senior officers begged him not to imperil everything in this reckless manner. Kemal later commented: 'As a matter of fact, they were right, but I was sure that success for us depended not only on the amount of men but also on their quality and using them to the best advantage. To wait would have given greater advantage to the enemy. Therefore, in spite of all their objections, I had to attack.'

Kemal's description of the events of August 10th has never been given in full in English accounts:

> The blanket of night had lifted. Now was the hour for the attack. I looked at my watch. It was nearly 4.30 a.m. After a few minutes it would become quite light and the enemy would be able to see our troops. Should the enemy infantry open fire with his machine-guns and should the land and naval guns open fire on our troops in our close packed formation I didn't doubt the impossibility of the attack. I ran forward at once. I encountered the Divisional Commander. Together and with those accompanying us we passed in front of the assault line. I made a short, rapid inspection. Passing in front I greeted the men and addressed them:
>
> 'Soldiers! There is no doubt that we shall defeat the enemy opposing us. But don't you hurry, let me get in front first. When you see me wave my whip all of you rush forward together!'
>
> I told my commanders and officers to get the troops to watch for my signal. Then I went to a point forward of the assault line, and, raising my whip, gave the signal for the assault.

The Turkish attack was an awesome spectacle. The astounded British suddenly beheld dim, dense masses of Turks pouring over the sky-line, not firing a shot, and advancing with the bayonet. The trenches on Chunuk Bair and at The Pinnacle were overwhelmed almost at once, and none of the British troops—over 1,000—survived. The Wiltshires in Sazli Dere, unarmed and unequipped, scattered wildly.

The New Zealand machine-guns at The Apex roared into life, and the warships sent shell after shell screaming into the Turkish hordes rampaging across the slopes in the weak morning light. The Turks were cut down in swathes as they stormed down towards The Farm, but they moved so rapidly, and were visible so briefly, that the survivors reached the plateau in great numbers, exultant and fanatical. Baldwin's men rose in desperation to meet them. Accurate details of what ensued have never come to light.

Sergeant Hargrave, watching the amazing scene through binoculars at Suvla, relates that 'below the oncoming shoulder-to-shoulder mass we saw little groups of men scattering, breaking down the gully-forks, taking cover behind crook-backed knolls, crossing scrub-dotted architraves from one gully-fork to another, crawling forward, firing uphill'. The British on Rhododendron, themselves desperately pressed, saw the Turks close with Baldwin's men on the edge of The Farm, and then all was fearful confusion. By 10 a.m., with the sun high in the sky, Baldwin and almost all his officers had been killed, and the remnants were falling back into the shelter of the ravines, leaving over 1,000 officers and men dead or dying on the tiny plateau. Many of those who fled were lost in the ravines and never heard of again. Even in the 1960's their bones are still being found. When Bean visited the Peninsula in 1919 he wrote that 'the number that must have been trapped, and the hopelessness of their situation on those steep ridges ... did not bear thinking of'. The Turks were also fought to a standstill, and their survivors dragged themselves back to the summit, leaving The Farm to the dead and dying.

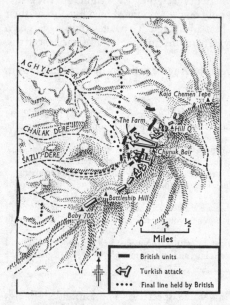

Sari Bair. Turkish attack, dawn, August 10th

On Rhododendron itself, the Turk attack had been halted by the New Zealand machine-guns at The Apex, but not only Chunuk Bair but The Pinnacle had been lost. Later in the day the British recaptured The Farm without difficulty, but it was now under fire from the new Turkish position at The Pinnacle, and had to be abandoned at nightfall. Allanson's Gurkhas had not been attacked, but were now so isolated and vulnerable that they had to withdraw. After Allanson had been wounded, Captain Phipson, a medical officer, clambered to the Gurkhas' position to take command, only to be informed by a redoubtable Subadar-Major, Gambirsing, that he had succeeded Allanson. The Gurkhas would probably have remained indefinitely on the mountain, as Gambirsing did not speak or read English, and took no notice of the frantic heliograph messages winking from head-quarters.* When persuaded by Phipson that withdrawal had indeed been ordered, all equipment which could not be carried was destroyed under Gambirsing's stern inspection; 'the Battalion then retired in good order, and reported at Brigade Headquarters'. Gambirsing received the M.C., which, in the circumstances, seems as inadequate as Allanson's D.S.O.†

At Helles the fighting had gradually subsided, and even at Lone Pine the battle in the dark suppurating trenches began to lose its ferocity. At Suvla, IX Corps relapsed into its previous lethargy. The fate of the 1st Battalion, the Herefordshire Regiment, was fairly characteristic. Landed at Suvla at dawn on August 9th, it was ordered to march to Azmak Dere. 'No information as to the operations and plan of action was mentioned,' Lt.-Col. Drage later reported, 'and no information was given as to what our side was trying to do.' Having reached the position with some difficulty, Drage relates that 'I was in a quandary, and confess I did not know what to do.' Eventually a lone horseman arrived, with orders for the battalion to return to Lala Baba; on arriving there, it was sent back to the Azmak Dere; having arrived back—Drage by now having been wounded—orders were received for it to fall back to the trenches south of the Salt Lake; this occupied two days, during which the battalion never saw a Turk, suffered casualties from shrapnel and sniping, and exhausted itself in futile marching and counter-marching across the plain.

Major Hore Ruthven, V.C., a staff officer from G.H.Q., visited Suvla on the 14th and found almost complete peace reigning. 'There were no Turkish trenches or Turks to be seen in front, and the only sign of the enemy was some desultory shelling and sniping. The officers in command of this part of the line were often unaware of the position of troops on their fronts, and while I was there it was discovered that what for some days had been supposed to be Turks in Turkish trenches in the bushes on our left front were in reality our own men.'

Out of about 50,000 men engaged in the Suvla and Anzac fighting, over 18,000 casualties had been suffered in three days; between August 6th and 13th nearly 22,000 sick and wounded had been evacuated from the Peninsula; the hospitals in Egypt and Malta were full by August 13th, and the *Aquitania* and other transports had to be used to ferry the wounded direct to England. Paralysed by their tremendous exertions, both sides rested in their positions.

* Allanson considered—and told Slim as much on the 8th—that far more extensive use should have been made of the heliograph during the fighting to flash messages from head-quarters to the troops in the hills. It often took several hours for messages to be brought up on foot, and frequently the bearers were killed or lost their way.

† He was subsequently severely wounded in the head at Suvla; after appearing to recover completely, he suffered a relapse and died some four years later.

As Prigge has written: 'On the evening of August 10th all the heights, with the exception of the insignificant elevation of Chocolate Hill, were firmly in the hands of the Turks.' 'On the hills we are the eyebrows,' Aubrey Herbert wrote in his diary, 'and the Turks are the forehead.'

12

The Darkening Scene

Every British General knew that without powerful interest his
future prospects and reputation for past services would wither
together under the first blight of misfortune; that a selfish government would offer him up a victim to a misjudging public and a
ribald press with whom success is the only criterion of merit.

*Quotation from Napier's History of the Peninsular War, sent to
Sir Ian Hamilton by Lt.-Col. Hankey, July 14th, 1916*

With his armies at Helles and Anzac completely played out by their prodigious exertions of the past four days, Hamilton could only look to IX
Corps for a successful continuation of the battle. 'Going over all our trenches
up on the hillsides yesterday,' Birdwood wrote to his wife on August 18th,
'they would say, "Yes, Sir, we are quite ready to go on killing Turks whenever you call on us—but we are weak as cats and I don't think we could
march a couple of miles." *That* is the awful thing that really worries and
frightens me. . . . I often feel it is all I can do to drag my legs after me when I
have had a long day in the trenches—but seeing and talking to the men makes
it well worth it.' 'It is hard to get any men to work', Godley wrote to his
wife on September 5th. 'They are all quite worn out, and from my Division
alone are going sick at the rate of 100 a day.' 'The Turks . . . knew they were
done unless they could quickly knock us off our Chunuk Bair', Hamilton
wrote wearily. 'So they have done it. Never mind: never say die.'

Hamilton reasoned that the Turks must be equally exhausted, and he
now had at his disposal two fresh New Army divisions. The 53rd Division
landed on August 8th–9th. Its efficiency was hampered by the fact that it
had no artillery, only one field company (without stores) and one field
ambulance; the divisional signal company arrived five days late, and was
attached to another division. The 54th Division landed on August 10th; it

had no artillery, no signal company, no field ambulances, no mules and no ammunition.

Hamilton now envisaged a bold sweeping attack by IX Corps supported by Birdwood round the northern flank of Sari Bair, but he had reckoned without what Aspinall has described as 'a miasma of defeat . . . rising from the Suvla Plain.' 'The usual scenes of a battlefield added to the distress and alarm', Nevinson writes of Suvla on August 9th. 'The dead were lying about in great numbers; the wounded were crying aloud for help; the hands and faces of hastily buried men protruded from the ground, and as I walked I felt at intervals the squelching softness of a man's body, scarcely covered beneath the soil.' 'Every visit to Suvla', Hore-Ruthven reported, 'discloses confusion, inertia and magnification of difficulties, due to the pessimistic attitude of higher commanders and staffs, which filters down to the troops.' Stopford, ordered to seize the Tekke Tepe ridge, replied with a long letter complaining of the lack of training and pusillanimity of the 53rd Division. Hamilton again sped over to urge Stopford forward, but Stopford, describing the new divisions as 'sucked oranges', was equally adamant for inaction. The best Hamilton could secure was a promise that the attack would take place at dawn on the 13th.

The relations between Hamilton and Stopford were by now very strained indeed, and Hamilton's intervention, although again absolutely justified, had unfortunate consequences. Stopford's lack of confidence in his new divisions was not without foundation, and the objections he put forward to Hamilton's plans, as Aspinall admits, 'were very far from frivolous'. Braithwaite was sent over to discuss the matter with Stopford, was more impressed than Hamilton had been by the hazards of a major attack until the corps was properly ready for it, and consented to a further postponement. A brigade had been ordered to push forward to the Tekke Tepe foothills on the afternoon of the 12th, and this advance, over unreconnoitred ground, with inadequate artillery support, was completely repulsed. Stopford saw this as a clear indication of the perils of undertaking a major attack, and was now exhibiting clear signs of panic. The 53rd Division, he said, was exhausted and incapable even of defence, the Turks were 'inclined to be aggressive', and the situation was perilous. Hamilton once again came over to Suvla, but could not move Stopford, who was now ordered to reorganise the units, consolidate his line, and to 'take every opportunity to make as forward a line as possible and make that line impregnable'.

Stopford's reaction to this order was somewhat unexpected, for, without any reference to G.H.Q., he ordered Mahon to push forward along the Kiretch Tepe Ridge on August 15th. The three battalions of the 10th (Irish) Division had now been on the bare Kiretch Tepe for a week, and had suffered terribly from the heat and the acute shortage of water. 'The drawn faces and haggard look told of that dreadful week into which more privation and suffering had been compressed than fell to the lot of most men in a lifetime', one eye-witness writes. 'Their faces were begrimed with smoke and sweat. The clay of the trenches showed on their hands and through the unshaven beard and close-cropped head.' Although the attack was conducted with great resolution, little real progress was made, and casualties amounted to nearly 2,000. If the attack had taken place only 24 hours earlier it might well have succeeded, but by the time Mahon attacked the Turks had managed to create some kind of defensive position on the rocky crest and steep sides of the ridge and had brought up reinforcements. Not until long after the war was it realised that this attack gave von Sanders considerable concern, and he refers to August 15th in his memoirs as a day of crisis.

The Suvla fighting had already acquired a hellish quality all its own. To acquire some realisation of this, it is instructive to follow the account of a young subaltern in the 5th Inniskillings, ordered to lead his platoon across the southern side of Kiretch Tepe on August 15th.

> My platoon deployed on either side of me, and we began our advance, stumbling over the rough ground. As we proceeded, it became impossible to keep a perfect line. Now and then a clump of bush or a hollow in the ground hid the men from their neighbours. Some places were so exposed that it was necessary to race across them at full speed, others so thorny and rocky as to be impassable. . . . Orders by word of mouth were impossible in the din of the guns and the bursting shells, the incessant and voluminous roar of rifle-fire and the whole orchestra of bullets and ricochets and shell splinters that streamed past us or danced at our feet. Orders by signal were equally and utterly futile, seeing that one could rarely be visible to more than four of one's men at once. . . . The bullets from rifles and machine-guns were descending in a curtain over the ground that we were covering, the sand was dancing up about our feet, dust and smoke were leaping up in little clouds, shrapnel was bursting overhead, and a great deal of small shell was falling innocuously enough, but with a terrifying trumpeting, in every direction.

The subaltern was wounded first in the shoulder, then in the head, and finally in the hip. He crawled to a small hollow, and laboriously built a small pile of stones as cover.

> With my free hand I took off my puttees at my leisure and bound them round my head. This would serve as a bandage, turban and pillow. Next came the ampule of iodine, which I broke and poured into my shoulder through the torn shirt. It seemed to attract the flies, who came, green- and blue-bottles, in dozens to the feast. I began to stink horribly in the sun. . . . Once a few puffs of blue smoke and the scent of burning thyme drifted into my nostrils. The scene of the burning plain flashed into my mind. I turned my head to watch. The tiny flames in the wild thyme met a little patch of sand and died away: there was luckily no wind that day. . . .
> Occasionally a straggler would come and ask where such and such a company was, and I would send him on ahead. At length, at dusk, not far off, I heard the shouts and screams of a bayonet charge confusedly above me, and a little later, the rattle of entrenching tools. The fire dies down. I heard a little rustle in the bush behind me. It was

the water-carrier. A real boy with real water came and knelt beside me, giving me drink and talking to me, and putting a haversack for my pillow.

After a while I sent him off because I was stinking so vilely, telling him to let someone know where I was in case the wounded could be moved that night. My shoulder was by this time full of maggots.

Though there was no other wounded man in sight, the whole valley was resounding with that ghastly cry, 'Stretcher-bearers! Stretcher-bearers!' and awful curses. All day when the din of firing sank a little I had heard it. It went on all night until the dawn. The valley was full of groaning. No stretcher-bearers came: there were not enough, and they were not allowed. I began to give up hope of leaving the spot where I lay, being sure that another day's sun would be too much; besides, it was really No Man's Land, and had been under fire for a week by day. I turned over and lay on my face in the sand.

The subaltern was fortunately discovered, and carried down to the shore, where he lay in the sun for hours, awaiting attention from one of the few exhausted doctors. 'The heat was very nearly unendurable, and the stench of wounds and the swarm of flies quite indescribable ... every foot of space between the tideless sea and the low cliffs was covered with laden stretchers. Being midday there was no shade—nothing but flies and stretchers, with here and there an orderly with cigarettes.'

The subaltern eventually left for Mudros on a hospital ship, and was disembarked that night, to be taken to a collection of tents bearing the red cross equipped to handle a maximum of 400 casualties; that night alone, over 1,000 casualties arrived. In the congested, stinking tents on Lemnos the scenes were almost as bad as anything seen in the Crimean War. Deliverance only came by death—as it came to many—or in the shape of a hospital ship sailing to Egypt, Malta, or England.

Hamilton had not yet brought himself to the point of asking for Stopford's recall, even though his telegrams to Kitchener had put all the blame for the failure of the Suvla operations firmly on the shoulders of his generals. On the 15th Kitchener gave Hamilton the lead he had been waiting for:

> If you deem it necessary to replace Stopford, Mahon and Hammersley, have you any competent generals to take their places? From your report I think Stopford should come home. This is a young man's war, and we must have commanding officers who will take full advantage of opportunities which occur but seldom. If, therefore, any generals fail, do not hesitate to act promptly. . . . Any generals I have available I will send you.

Shortly afterwards, Kitchener telegraphed Hamilton to say that French had been ordered to supply a corps commander and two divisional commanders; 'I hope', he added, 'that Stopford has been relieved by you already.'

De Lisle replaced Stopford in the command of IX Corps on August 15th, pending the arrival of General Byng from France. 'It gave me a heavy heart to have to do the business,' Hamilton wrote to Kitchener, 'but there was absolutely nothing else for it. He had got into that sort of state when he could not make up his mind whether he would sit down or stand up, or go into his tent or get out of it.' Mahon was asked to waive his seniority and serve under de Lisle, but he refused to do so, and was temporarily replaced by Hill. Mahon, seething with rage, and suffering from the strain of a terrible week on the Kiretch Tepe, left Suvla while his brave Irishmen were locked in their desperate battle on the craggy and exposed ridge. Mahon hated de Lisle, and made it clear that he would have willingly served under anyone else; after a few days' reflection he cooled off, and returned to command his severely mauled division. The gloomy and cautious Sitwell and General Lindley (commanding the 53rd Division) also went—the latter at his own request—but Hammersley was recalled not by Hamilton but by Kitchener on the 23rd. Stopford and Reed left Suvla on August 16th.

De Lisle—'a real thruster', as Birdwood described him in a letter to his wife; 'everyone hates him as he is a brute, with no thoughts for others, rude to everyone and has no principles, but I believe him to be the right man in the right place, and by his brutality I hope he will see things through'— had not been at Suvla for 24 hours before he came to the conclusion that Hamilton had greatly under-estimated the seriousness of the situation; he found a disorganised, exhausted, leaderless and disillusioned army scattered across the Suvla plain, entirely exposed to the enemy, apparently barely capable of hanging on to the fragment of ground it occupied. His black report jolted G.H.Q. into a sudden realisation of the gravity of IX Corps' position. On August 17th Hamilton at last admitted that his 'coup had failed', and asked Kitchener for 45,000 reinforcements to bring existing units up to strength and new formations amounting to another 50,000 men. This addition of 95,000 men would double the Allied force on the Peninsula.

In the Navy, also, it was definitely realised that a crisis had been reached. Keyes—now supported by Wemyss, a valuable new ally—proposed that the Fleet should make another supreme effort to break the deadlock, and de Robeck, although again unconvinced, asked for a definite plan to be prepared for his consideration.

The British submariners had demonstrated what could be done with aggression, skill and courage. By late July the Turks had stretched an anti-submarine net across the Narrows, a mesh of wire two-and-a-half inches thick, reaching 220 feet to the floor of the channel. Motor-boats with bombs patrolled the surface, and guns were set up on both shores. The submariners had now realised that the fierce current of fresh water coming down from the Marmara, about ten fathoms deep, was responsible for the abrupt changes in the density of the water which had made earlier passages so hazardous. They had in fact learned to use the shift in density to great advantage, lying for hours at a time with engines stopped below the surface, to let the men get some rest. But the net was a new and even more serious obstacle to the passage.

There was, however, a gap at the bottom of the net, and Nasmith and

Boyle got through after some nasty moments; E7, on the other hand, was caught, and after a desperate 12-hour battle, was forced to surface and surrender. The others continued to batter away at the net, and by the end of the year it had been effectively destroyed. The British and the French had a total of 13 submarines engaged at one time or another in the Marmara, of which 8 were destroyed; the passage of the Dardanelles was made 27 times. The Germans had over 40 U-boats in the Mediterranean, but they were concentrated to the west, and never seriously threatened the Allied transports.* It is not surprising that von Sanders waxed sarcastic about the contribution of the German Navy to the defence of the Dardanelles.

While the battle was raging on the Peninsula, Boyle in E14 and Nasmith in E11 had been spreading havoc in the Marmara.

They shelled Turkish reinforcements, sank a number of transports and the battleship *Barbarossa Harradin*, and Nasmith returned to Constantinople to torpedo a collier tied up at Haida Pasha Station quay; Nasmith's First Lieutenant, d'Oyley Hughes, swam ashore to blow up a railway viaduct, and when Boyle returned after battering through the net across the Narrows, his place was taken by E2 (Lt.-Commander Stocks). It was an astonishing story, and added to the already legendary exploits of the British submarines in the Marmara.

When Hamilton visited de Lisle's headquarters on the 18th he found a more optimistic and aggressive atmosphere. The Turks had made no serious attempt to attack, and three days of intensive activity had greatly improved the British positions. De Lisle had now veered from the depths of gloom to the heights of optimism. Reinforced by the 29th Division—'we saw them coming ashore', Sergeant Hargrave has written. 'They looked pretty grim and woebegone. In fact they looked like the rest of us'—and the 2nd Mounted Division (to be used as infantry) under General Peyton which had arrived from Egypt, he originally only proposed to attack the W Hills. But he was so encouraged by the improvement in the situation in the past few days that he conceived a more ambitious plan, embracing the capture of Kiretch Tepe and Tekke Tepe. It was now Hamilton's turn to preach caution, and he refused to sanction anything more than a limited attack.

The attack took place on August 21st, and in terms of numbers was the greatest battle fought in the campaign. The 29th Division advanced from a point near Chocolate Hill towards Scimitar Hill, the 11th Division attacked the W Hills, while a composite Anzac force of 3,000 men under Cox attacked Hill 60. The offensive was timed for early afternoon so that the

---

* Their only important success was the sinking of the transport *Prince Edward* on August 13th, in which 861 British officers and men were drowned. 15 Australians were drowned on September 2nd when the transport *Southland* was torpedoed. 1,048 Allied troops were killed at sea in the campaign either as a result of enemy action or other causes.

men would advance with the sun behind them, but a totally unexpected and unseasonable mist fell shortly after noon, and the battle was fought in a veil of swirling haze and stifling heat. By 4 p.m. the main attack had been completely held up, and de Lisle ordered Peyton's Yeomanry to 'push through' to the objectives.

They left the shelter of Lala Baba and marched across the Salt Lake in open formation, seven yards between each man. The light was beginning to fail, but the Salt Lake silhouetted every man. The shrapnel began to burst over them. When the remnants reached Chocolate Hill at about 6.30 p.m. they were ordered forward blindly into the fearful gloom. It was almost dark when they began to climb Scimitar Hill. Sir John Milbanke, V.C., a Harrovian friend of Churchill, told his officers; 'we are to take a redoubt. But I don't know where it is and don't think anyone else does either; but in any case we are to go ahead and attack any Turks we meet.' And then he led the Sherwood Rangers into the evil murk, and oblivion.

Hamilton, watching the battle high up on Kiretch Tepe, saw the whole advance. So did almost everyone else, especially the Turks. When the battle finally ended, the Turks had been forced to bring up their last reserves, but the British, at the loss of over 5,000 casualties, had advanced not at all. Churchill's brief and poignant sentences admirably summarise this terrible battle. 'The British losses, particularly of the Yeomanry and the 29th Division, were heavy and fruitless. On this dark battlefield of fog and flame Brigadier-General Lord Longford, Brigadier-General Kenna, V.C., Colonel Sir John Milbanke, V.C., and other paladins fell. This was the largest action fought upon the Peninsula, and it was destined to be the last.'

On the following day, Birdwood and de Lisle met Hamilton to discuss a proposal put forward by Guy Dawnay to evacuate the Suvla position; even Aspinall was shocked by the suggestion, Hamilton described Dawnay as 'defeatist', de Lisle considered that British prestige could never survive such an admission of defeat, and Birdwood opposed the withdrawal as it would endanger his left flank. The fact that the proposal had even been seriously put forward was ominous. A week later, Cox's composite force of Australians, New Zealanders, British and Gurkhas at last abandoned the attempt to capture the insignificant mound known as Hill 60 after they had seized what they thought to be the summit, only to find that the actual summit was still held in strength by the enemy. At one point, an Australian battalion was ordered to make an attack 'with bomb and bayonet only'; when the Colonel pointed out that they had no bombs, he was told 'that they must do the best that was possible without them'. For connoisseurs of military futility, valour, incompetence and determination, the attacks on Hill 60 are in a class of their own. In one of the assaults the present author's uncle—to whom this book is dedicated—was grievously wounded. He lay for hours in the scrub. Soon after dusk he was discovered by two Australians. One kicked him. 'Aw, leave the dead 'uns till later,' said the other. Made forcibly aware of their error, they carried the wounded subaltern with rough tenderness to the shore. Three weeks or so later he arrived in England, with nothing save the pyjamas he wore, to be informed by a cross officer that as officially he had been sent to Egypt, he had no right to turn up in England.

Lieutenant Lemon left behind him a nightmare scene on the torn slopes of Hill 60. 'The whole place is strewn with bodies—Gurkhas, Australians, Connaught Rangers,' Allanson wrote in his diary on the 23rd; 'the smell, another of the minor horrors of war, is appalling, the sights revolting and disgusting. Our work is so heavy that we cannot add to it by burying the bodies.'

'The local fighting goes on without cessation,' Major Prigge wrote; 'day and night the rifles bark, guns and howitzers boom here and there. The flash of guns and searchlights, the bright red light of exploding bombs of every type, give the dark nights a characteristic note, or on light nights show up clearly against the soft crescent of the moon.' Both sides were utterly exhausted. 'Courts martial became very frequent at Helles', Lord Rochdale reported. 'The crime was almost exclusively for sleeping on sentry duty.' 'Four calendar months since we landed on Gallipoli,' Major Davidson (now at Suvla) wrote on August 25th; 'and not much progress made yet.' 'I want no more of the glories of war,' Allanson wrote in his diary on the 22nd after burying three young officers on the slopes of Hill 60. '. . . I hope we may not be yet in for another advance.'

Hamilton's admission of defeat, and the chilling request for a further 95,000 men, arrived in London at a black hour for the Allied cause. 1915 had been a year of almost unmitigated disaster. On the eastern front the Russian armies were reeling backwards after losing half a million men and over 3,000 guns in a series of heavy defeats at the hands of the Austro-German army. In the Balkans, Bulgaria hovered on the brink of entering the war on Germany's side. On the Italian front a strong offensive had been bloodily repulsed. In France, Joffre had persuaded Kitchener to sanction another enormous autumn offensive.

Hamilton's own reputation had taken a series of very heavy blows; his breezy optimism in his letters to the King, Kitchener and Asquith now grated as much as it did on his exhausted and demoralised staff on Imbros. He subsequently wrote that 'as a result of the battles of August 1915, we had gained elbow-room and inflicted enormous losses on the enemy—how enormous we did not know at the time. But we had not succeeded in our main aim; to get command of the Narrows. The spirit of the Turks had, however, been broken, and they had been thrown entirely on the defensive.' Self-deception could hardly go further. Some of his staff officers now spoke openly at G.H.Q. of engineering his removal. He had lost over 40,000 men in under three weeks, and had gained little or nothing; ugly stories were circulating about the treatment of the wounded. In August, 43,553 men had been evacuated, of whom 12,968 were suffering from dysentery; the 1st Australian Division, which had landed 13,300 strong and received reinforcing drafts of 7,700 men, was now reduced to a *total* of 8,500; the evacuation rate for sick alone was 1·7 per cent at Suvla, 5·1 per cent at Helles and 7·5 per cent at Anzac. Stopford, as soon as he reached Imbros, prepared a lengthy series of charges against G.H.Q. which he submitted to the War Office on his arrival in London, and which required careful examination. But Ministers were not yet in a position to consider withdrawal; the prospects were grim, but even the most convinced opponents of the Dardanelles operations—Lloyd George, Bonar Law and Carson—shrank from so drastic a step. Hamilton was promised some reinforcements, and Byng brought new vigour into the exhausted Suvla troops.

From this moment, however, the Gallipoli story sinks into an ugly welter of accusations, personal spite, dashed hopes and despair.

The French provided the first brief flurry of excitement by suddenly proposing to land six divisions on the Asiatic shore of the Straits. 'From bankrupt to millionaire in 24 hours . . . *Deo volente* we are saved; Constantinople is doomed', Hamilton wrote joyously. The mirage quickly disappeared. The reasons which had prompted the French to offer four new divisions under General Sarrail were entirely political; Sarrail was the only sound anti-clerical Republican among the higher ranks of the French Army.* The offer was made on September 1st, and the British had scarcely recovered from their astonishment when it was discovered that Joffre had only agreed to their diversion to the Dardanelles on the condition that he should retain them until the results of his new offensive in Champagne were known; this was not due to begin until September 26th. One of the lighter features of the tedious series of conferences which now ensued in London and Paris was the demand of the French Naval Chief of Staff that no troops should land on the heavily defended Asiatic shore until the landing-places had been properly prepared for them; these essential preparations included the construction of piers and the landing of stores! This was not the voice of Guépratte, and the removal from the Dardanelles of that indomitable fire-eater at this time was significant.

By the last week in September the whole plan collapsed when Bulgaria mobilised. The clandestine dispatch of German arms to Turkey could be

---

* He had been appointed to command the French forces at Gallipoli when Gouraud had been wounded, but had refused to serve under Hamilton, and had insisted on an independent command.

greatly increased now that King Ferdinand had finally made up his mind who was going to win. Greece and Serbia asked for 150,000 men to guard the Greek eastern border, and France and Britain agreed. Mahon's 10th Division and a French division had to be withdrawn from Gallipoli and sent to Salonika. On the Western Front, Joffre's offensive slumped bloodily to a halt. The British Government now had four major theatres of war on its hands; France, Gallipoli, Salonika and Mesopotamia, and the moment for establishing priorities could not, it appeared, be long delayed.

It was inevitable that Ministers should look increasingly askance at Hamilton's conduct of operations. Stopford's report had been examined by four senior generals; Hamilton was given no chance of seeing and commenting upon Stopford's allegations, and although the committee of enquiry rightly refused to come to any definite decision on the matter in these circumstances, Kitchener informed Ministers that the review of the Suvla operations had resulted in 'considerable criticism of Sir Ian Hamilton's leadership'. General Mahon, an old friend of Sir Edward Carson, wrote severely to him about the conduct of operations at Suvla. From Egypt, Maxwell contributed his share of criticism of Hamilton's leadership, writing to Kitchener in August; 'I hear stories and criticisms of his staff which would make his hair stand up if he heard them !' Birdwood, while complaining to Fitzgerald on August 10th (the very day Chunuk Bair was lost) about Hamilton's first dispatch on the April landings, added tartly, 'G.H.Q. I understand arranged Stopford's landing, in which I hear improvement might have been made.'

On top of these surreptitious streams of criticism there came the extraordinary episode of the Murdoch Letter. Keith Murdoch was a well-known Australian journalist on his way to London to act as the representative of various Australian newspapers and had been asked by the Australian government to report upon the postal arrangements for Australian troops in Egypt, which had been the subject of frequent complaints. He wrote an obsequious letter to Hamilton from Cairo, asking for permission to visit the Peninsula, and Hamilton reluctantly agreed.

There was undoubtedly something badly wrong with the relationship between the soldiers—particularly at G.H.Q.—and the few war correspondents attached to the army. The soldiers had a strong dislike for journalists, and Birdwood had issued an order before the landings that 'officers and soldiers are forbidden to give any military information to press correspondents. . . . All civilians whose conduct gives rise to suspicion will be arrested, whether they have passes or not.' Ashmead-Bartlett, perhaps not surprisingly in view of this order, was arrested the moment he landed at Anzac Cove on April 25th, and, he relates, thought for a moment that he was going to be shot out of hand. The Standing Orders of the M.E.F. stated that 'officers and soldiers are forbidden, without special authority, to communicate to Press Correspondents any information relative to military events, plans or dispositions. Correspondents, unless they have received previous sanction from the Chief field censor, are prohibited from asking officers or men to impart any such information.' The correspondents themselves, with a few exceptions, of whom Henry Nevinson and Bean were perhaps the most notable, did not help their own cause, and the flood of official complaints to London from G.H.Q. about their private conduct and their professional capacities makes interesting reading. One correspondent, although paid considerable sums by his newspaper, was at Imbros for only a month, and never ventured near the front lines. His lack of personal familiarity with the Peninsula did not inhibit him from subsequently publishing lengthy commentaries on the campaign containing much criticism of Hamilton and his staff. Ashmead-Bartlett, although a highly capable journalist and personally no coward, had long since maddened the staff by his chronic pessimism. He had at least been depressing from the outset, and his unconcealed lack of optimism had particularly struck some Australians who had met him on April 24th, on the voyage from Mudros to Anzac. It was averred that his dispatches were read out to the Turks to encourage them. A report of a conversation with Compton Mackenzie had resulted in Ashmead-Bartlett being given a final warning as to his future conduct. He took the rebuke badly, and was more surly and hostile than ever. He despised the G.H.Q. staff and most senior officers, and thought, and said so repeatedly, that the landings should have been made at Bulair. 'He is not to be trusted', Hamilton wrote of Ashmead-Bartlett on October 12th. 'He has the habit of criticism and sees everything from a most pessimistic standpoint.' The fact remained that he had much to be pessimistic about.

Murdoch confined his attentions to Anzac. As Hamilton subsequently wrote in an admirably restrained and dignified answer to his accusations, 'he resisted the temptation to visit Helles, twelves miles distant, despite his original "intense anxiety" to visit the sacred shores of Gallipoli, and despite the fact that transport was always available and that he had my full permission to go anywhere and see everything.'

Murdoch had, however, seen quite enough. Even to hardened soldiers, Anzac came as something of a shock, and after the August battles, with men being evacuated in great quantities with dysenteric complaints, everyone sick to death of the monotonous food, the flies and the shelling, Anzac was no longer inspiriting. On his return to Imbros he met Ashmead-Bartlett, and at once found that they spoke the same language. Between them, they concocted a plan whereby Ashmead-Bartlett would write a letter and Murdoch would see that it got to the authorities in London. Henry Nevinson

overheard their discussion and alerted Hamilton; Murdoch was met at
Marseilles by a military escort and forced to hand over the letter before proceeding to London.*

On arrival in London, Murdoch acted with great speed and effect. It
would appear that he saw Lloyd George after he had prepared a lengthy
diatribe on the Gallipoli operations; but it is certain that Lloyd George
seized his opportunity. Murdoch first saw Carson, who took him quickly
to Lloyd George, who urged him to lay what information he had
before the Cabinet. Murdoch subsequently saw Grey, Bonar Law, Balfour,
Churchill, F. E. Smith and Hankey. Lloyd George wrote to Carson on
September 25th:

> I saw Murdoch the Australian yesterday. He struck me as being exceptionally in-
> telligent and sane. That makes the account he gave me of his visit to the Dardanelles
> much more disquieting . . . I agree that Murdoch's report does not differ in essentials
> from that furnished to us by Colonel Hankey. He simply dots the i's and crosses the t's
> of some things said by Hankey. . . . As you know, I always opposed this Gallipoli
> enterprise, and so have you. I opposed it at the start, and you have opposed it since you
> have joined the Ministry. . . .

Murdoch's letter was addressed to the Australian Prime Minister, Andrew
Fisher, and included a contemptuous dismissal of Hamilton—'I like General
Hamilton, and found him exceedingly kindly; I admire him as a journalist,
but as a strategist he has completely failed'; Braithwaite was 'more cordially
detested in our forces than Enver'; Birdwood 'had not the fighting qualities
or the big brain of a great general', and so on. He said he had seen one staff
officer 'wallowing' in ice while wounded men were dying of heat a few
hundred yards away (a reference to the *Aragon* and the Australian hospital
on the shore); 'sedition is talked around every tin of bully beef on the peninsula'; orders had been given at Suvla to shoot any loiterers; the New Army
troops were 'merely a lot of childlike youths without strength to endure or
brains to improve their conditions'. Only the Anzacs, to whom gushing
tributes abounded, came well out of Murdoch's impressions of three days
at Anzac and Ashmead-Bartlett's information.

Many commentators have expressed surprise that Asquith should have
had this amazing document printed on the duck-egg blue stationery of the
Committee of Imperial Defence and circulated to the Dardanelles Committee.
In the circumstances, it is difficult to see what else he could have done.
Lloyd George, Carson and Bonar Law were profoundly restive, and Asquith
himself was entertaining serious doubts about Hamilton, a fact which has
never been appreciated. 'I have read enough to satisfy me that the Generals
and Staff engaged in the Suvla part of the business ought to be court-

---

* According to the late Lord Burnham, it was destroyed at the War Office.

martialled and dismissed from the Army', he had written to Kitchener on August 20th on reading Hankey's moderate and fair report. Two other important features of the Murdoch Letter have been given insufficient emphasis. In the first place, Murdoch was not a minor figure in Australian journalism; he had actually been runner-up to Bean in the ballot among Australian journalists for the position of official historian to the Australian forces. In the second, the fact that his letter was addressed to Andrew Fisher made the possibility of suppression doubly delicate.*

But a far more important agent than Murdoch had been at work. On August 30th Hamilton told Kitchener that he was sending Guy Dawnay back to London. 'He has an old head on young shoulders, and is one of the most sound and reliable staff officers I have ever struck. He knows all our most intimate plans, ideas and dangers.' Dawnay's mission, never fully related before, is a far more remarkable and important episode than that of the Murdoch Letter, and must be recounted in some detail.

Dawnay, like Aspinall, Lloyd and Wyndham Deedes, had been on the Gallipoli staff since Hamilton had been appointed in March. Between them they had prepared the staff appreciations which had formed the basis of Hamilton's plans for the April and August landings. Perhaps they ascribed too much to themselves, but they had come to regard themselves, not without justice, as the only officers with an accurate realisation of the situation. The fiasco at Suvla had been a terrible shock, and, significantly, their anger was directed not at Stopford or Hammersley but against Hamilton and Braithwaite. Their deep personal affection for Hamilton remained, but their confidence in him as a commander had absolutely gone. It would be unprofitable and painful to set out in detail or at length the views which they expressed in correspondence and conversation at this time on the subject of the Commander-in-Chief and his Chief of Staff.

Between them, they concocted a plan. Someone, they felt, must go to London to 'tell the truth'; Hamilton's telegrams, which had all been seen by Orlo Williams, the chief cipher officer, filled them with despair. 'The point being that neither dispatches nor telegrams from here represent the case as it is', Deedes wrote. 'They are all written in the sanguine, optimistic vein—which is again due to nothing but, on the one hand, we firmly believe, ignorance and inability to grasp the truth, and, on the other, the desire to keep up the semblance of a rosy situation to enable certain people to keep their seats. . . . . G. L. [Lloyd] and Dawnay and I determined, for the sake of the hundred thousand men out here, that the *truth* should be known.'

* There is an amusing footnote to this curious episode. In the Second World War, Lord Burnham—who, as Harry Lawson, had seen much of Murdoch in the autumn of 1915—met him in Gibraltar. Lord Burnham was then Director of Public Relations in the War Office; Murdoch was Sir Keith Murdoch, and a rich man. 'Brought any letters with you this time?' Burnham enquired. Murdoch was singularly unamused.

It was not difficult to persuade Hamilton that it would be useful for one of his staff officers to go to London, although he was of course completely unaware of the purpose of the mission. Aspinall was the first suggestion, but Dawnay's personal friendship with the Royal Family and the Asquiths was the decisive factor.

In London, Dawnay saw everyone from the King—who was by now vehemently anti-Hamilton—downwards and wrote to Deedes that he was 'aghast at the fog of war, lack of grip, and want of direction'. Kitchener was furious when he heard that Dawnay had had secret discussions with Asquith and Lloyd George without informing him, but, apart from fixing him with his deepest scowl at an unhappy dinner-party at 10 Downing Street, there was little he could do to repair the damage. Dawnay had suffered agonies of conscience before setting out from Imbros, but had been steeled by the exhortations of his friends and by his conviction that a great disaster was imminent. 'A really strong man, he said, would perhaps go home and get them both stellenbosched (i.e. Sir Ian and C. G. S.)', Orlo Williams records of a conversation with Dawnay on September 2nd. 'I said to him plainly I thought at this time the nation's good was much more important than the reputation of Sir Ian. Asked him what kind of telegram went home last night, and he replied "Hopeless". He and Aspinall tried over and over again to get a proper version of things sent but it was useless. I asked "what view then does the blessed man himself take of things?" He replied, "Oh, Mr. Micawber's exactly".' Dawnay conducted his difficult task with great delicacy, as Callwell has testified; 'Dawnay . . . was loyalty itself to his chief, but the information that he had to give and his appreciation of the situation as it stood were the reverse of encouraging.' He said clearly and firmly that the situation was grave, and even desperate. Ministers were impressed by the weight of his evidence and his transparent integrity. Murdoch could possibly be laughed off, but not Dawnay. In all the history of the Gallipoli campaign, nothing is more surprising than the spectacle of this exceptionally competent young staff officer advising Ministers to over-rule the authority of his own commander-in-chief.

Hamilton was given a chance to save himself by sacrificing Braithwaite. 'There is a continuous flow of unofficial reports from Gallipoli and in much the same strain criticising adversely the staff and your headquarters and complaining that the members of your staff are much out of touch with the troops', Kitchener wrote warningly to Hamilton on October 2nd. 'The present arrangements do not appear quite satisfactory . . . and I would suggest to you the possibility of some important change in your headquarters staff; for instance, if you agreed, Kiggell might change places with Braithwaite. Should you however not do so and desire to remain as at present, may we assume that we are quite safe in regarding these unofficial statements as not representing the true feelings of the troops?' The onus of proving the falsity of the 'flow of unofficial reports' was therefore, most unfairly, put on Hamilton. He indignantly refused to sacrifice Braithwaite. 'My confidence in him is complete', he replied. 'I did not select him; you gave him to me, and I have always felt most grateful to you for your choice.'

This characteristically generous action settled his fate. On October 11th the Dardanelles Committee sought Hamilton's views on the possibility of evacuation. Hamilton reacted with an emotional outburst which cooled on the morrow, when he sent an estimate of the loss of half the men and all their guns and stores; as he subsequently told the Dardanelles Commission, 'because evacuation to me was unthinkable, I wanted to show in my opinion that any idea of the sort should not be entertained at all.' Ministers were jaded and anxious; the voluntary system of enlistment was clearly doomed, the war was going badly everywhere, the munition situation was bad, criticism of the Coalition was growing, Carson had resigned— although the news had not yet been published—Members of Parliament were clamouring for a committee of enquiry into the operations and, on top of all this, German airships were bombing London; the raid of the night of October 13th–14th was the most serious yet, and considerable hysteria was engendered. On the 14th the Dardanelles Committee met. Both Bonar Law and Lloyd George had circulated lengthy memoranda on the 12th, strongly opposing the retention of Gallipoli, and both were contemplating resignation if what Lloyd George categorised as 'strong Dardanellian influences' prevailed; the Committee insisted that Hamilton must go, and left Kitchener to break the news.* On the same day, to emphasise the severe pressure under which Ministers were working, Lord Milner openly advocated the evacuation of Gallipoli in the House of Lords.

Few professional soldiers ever reach the position of high command. For he who does, there is one period of supreme responsibility. If he succeeds, through fortune and competence, his entire life and personal sacrifices have been justified. Honours and tributes are showered on him. Sustained by the enthusiasm of his army, the gratitude of a nation, and the pride of his family, he can look forward to a distinguished and prosperous retirement. But for the commander who is given his chance, and has missed it, there is nothing. His career is ended, his achievements forgotten, his inadequacies magnified. He is too often driven to self-justification with unhappy consequences. Hamilton himself once wrote that 'the man who commits himself to paper is building a house for his reputation to inhabit—and too often, when he was

---

* Moorehead (*Gallipoli*, 312) describes Hamilton decoding Kitchener's message 'with the cipher book and the device like a bowstring for decoding cables.' This is clearly a misinterpretation of Hamilton's account in *Gallipoli Diary*, II, p. 271. Hamilton was referring symbolically to the old Turkish custom of executing criminals by strangulation with a bowstring.

finished, he finds he has been at work upon a tomb.' To many, *Gallipoli Diary* was such a book.

Controversy still rages about Hamilton's conduct of the Gallipoli campaign. 'I can't look upon him as a very big man,' Birdwood wrote on November 12th, 'as he is really *shallow* by nature —artistic if you like it too, but I don't know that he could ever concentrate himself very deeply in thinking things out. I may be wrong and I certainly like him very much.' 'It is interesting to hear that Sir Ian is thought to be badly used', Guy Dawnay wrote to his wife on November 10th. 'He probably was, in the sense that the authorities' reasons for recalling him may have been all wrong. But the salient fact is that he was *no use*.' Many years later, in a private note, Dawnay wrote: 'Sir Ian was of the old chivalrous school; his war was to be "run on gallantry" —the Englishman never knows when he is beaten, and all that. And so he blinded himself to the truth.'

Few commanders can have aroused such vividly differing estimates of their capacities among those who fought under them as Hamilton has done. Examining these varying judgements, the historian is struck by their vehemence. To his many admirers Hamilton was a shamefully ill-used commander, on whom no shadow of censure should fall; to his very numerous critics he was the embodiment of incompetence. His *Gallipoli Diary* enraged as many survivors of the campaign as it impressed others; his published dispatches aroused similarly conflicting reactions. Today, fifty years after the campaign which ended his career, it is becoming increasingly difficult to form a balanced judgement from the opinions of contemporaries. They are either all for Hamilton, or all against him.

Hamilton possessed almost every conceivable qualification for a great culmination to an exceptional career. He was a finished professional, at a time when amateurism was too prevalent in the British Army. His experience of war was perhaps longer and wider than that of any contemporary. He had devoted his life to the study of arms. He had seen active service under almost every possible condition. He had immense mental and physical courage and resilience. To depict him as a dilettante or intellectual is an absurd distortion of the man's capacities. He was experienced, daring, imaginative—every quality which should combine perfectly. What, then, had gone wrong?

The argument that he never had a fair chance cannot be seriously sustained. He had had his chances, and he had missed them. Captain Falls has conjectured that perhaps there was 'a touch of unsteadiness of purpose, of inconsequence, somewhere at the back of that interesting mind.'* Most commentators have fallen back on comparably baffled ponderings. It is necessary, however, to probe deeper.

* Cyril Falls: *The First World War*, 110.

The difficulties with which he had to contend were enormous. The operation bristled with hazards and problems utterly new to everyone. The Mediterranean Expeditionary Force and de Robeck's Fleet contained many commanders of outstanding capacities, but they also contained many who were hopelessly unqualified by training, attitude or inclination for the tasks they had to perform. With the exception of the 29th Division, Hamilton's army consisted of relatively raw and imperfectly trained units. Many a general has been saved by his subordinates; in the Gallipoli campaign, Hamilton was often badly let down by them. This was often demonstrated in extraordinary ways. One brigade commander, a Peer, suddenly claimed parliamentary privilege and left his brigade and the Peninsula by the first boat for England. He was threatened by Kitchener with close arrest and court-martial, but when he returned to the Peninsula his place had been filled. Mahon's petulant departure from Suvla when his division was engaged in a desperate battle was perhaps understandable, but hardly admirable. Hamilton's fetish that he should not interfere once battle was joined was by no means theoretically unwise, but became a serious deficiency in circumstances where the subordinates on whom he placed reliance were inadequate to their tasks. In this respect, he was undoubtedly a very unlucky commander.

But it cannot be denied that he added to his own difficulties. His optimism and enthusiasm were unquenchable, even in the darkest hours, and were a great asset to him as a commander-in-chief and to the whole expedition, but the border between optimism and wishful thinking is perilously narrow, and it was one which Hamilton too frequently crossed. It was this failing above all others which lost him the confidence of his staff at a very early stage indeed of the campaign, and which eventually disillusioned not only Ministers but Kitchener himself. On reading his telegrams and private letters to Kitchener, one is struck again and again by his inconsistency. On one day he is firm and clear, but on the next vague and almost arch; on one, he sees all sunshine, on the next, all gloom. His letters to Asquith demonstrate his flamboyant and somewhat precious literary style at its worst.

At no stage of the entire campaign did he act like a commander-in-chief. The plans for the first landings were prepared almost entirely by his staff; at the landings, his only decisive intervention was in response to Birdwood's appeal; the Helles operations were almost entirely handed over to Hunter-Weston; the Anzac plan was Birdwood's, and although Hamilton deserves great credit for seizing it eagerly, at no point did he really initiate operations. The April landings and the August campaign were conceived and planned by his subordinates. Birdwood always blamed Hamilton rather than Stopford for the Suvla failure; 'he should have taken much more personal charge,' he wrote to his wife, 'and *insisted* on things being done and really taken command which he has never yet done.'

His grasp of detail was imperfect, and in this he was not assisted by Braith-waite's attitude towards the administrative staff. Many of his most severe critics have attacked his lack of ruthlessness, and in particular have suggested that he should have been more brutal with incompetent subordinates. This argument ignores the climate of opinion and atmosphere of the old British Regular Army. The concept of dismissing an officer out of hand was alien to that atmosphere; to say that it was a foolish attitude is really irrelevant; the fact was that it existed, and Hamilton was particularly susceptible to it.

Sir Ian Hamilton shared the fate of many British generals whose mis-fortune it has been to rise to high command early in a great war, but few have had such tantalising opportunities for glittering triumph. His great personal charm, his courage and daring, his independent outlook, his unequalled experience, imagination and zest were such that the tragedy of his failure is felt more deeply than in the case of any other British commander of the time. Misfortune had dogged his steps from the day he left London; few commanders have been expected to do so much with so little; few, perhaps, would have tried. Aspinall's judgement is probably the most fair. 'The enthusiasm, self-confidence and personal courage demanded of the military commander-in-chief he possessed in full measure. But he lacked the iron will and dominating personality of a truly great commander. . . . Hamilton's optimism, too, inclined him to over-confidence in battle. He left too much to his subordinates and hesitated to override their plans, even when in his opinion they were missing opportunities.' Hamilton wrote his own epitaph many years later when, describing how he kept asking himself at Gallipoli what Roberts would have done in comparable circumstances, he wrote sadly, 'Lord Roberts had not succeeded in grafting on to me his gift for taking the bull by the horns.'

Hamilton left Imbros on the 16th, and after a farewell dinner on *Triad*, boarded the cruiser *Chatham*. 'He is, I must say, most wonderfully good about it', Birdwood wrote to his wife. 'No ranting and raving that it is some one else's fault, etc., but just saying that he has not been fortunate enough to succeed and that there is an end to it. He of course must feel it very much, but shows it much less than I thought he would.' Birdwood, Byng, Davies, de Robeck, Keyes, the French and Hamilton's own staff assembled to bid him good-bye. A cold drizzle had begun to fall, making the scene even more desolate. It was a severe test of character, which Hamilton did not fail to meet. His account concludes:

> The adieu was a melancholy affair. There was no make-believe, that's a sure thing. Whatever the British Officer may be his forte has never lain in his acting. . . . I wrung their hands. The Bo'sun's whistle sounded. The curtain was falling so I wrung their hands once again and said good-bye. . . . A bitter moment and hard to carry through.
> Boarded the *Chatham* and went below to put my cabin straight. The anchor came up,

the screws went round. I wondered whether I could stand the strain of seeing Imbros, Kephalos, the camp, fade into the region of dreams—I was hesitating when a message came from the Captain to say the Admiral begged me to run up to the quarter-deck. So I ran, and found the *Chatham* steering a corkscrew course—threading in and out among the warships at anchor. Each as we passed manned ship and sent us on our way with the cheers of brave men ringing in our ears.

Hamilton's successor was General Sir Charles Monro, commander of the Third Army in France. A more remarkable contrast could hardly have been found. 'He was born with another sort of mind from me', Hamilton himself wrote. Shrewd, practical and determined, Monro would not be rushed and he would not be pushed. He refused to leave for the Dardanelles before he had spent several days at the War Office examining the available data and conferring with Kitchener on four occasions. Monro did not believe in 'side-shows'; he had been fighting on the Western Front since the beginning of the war, and had seen the British effort grow from a relative handful of superlatively trained but inadequate divisions into a massive army. But if he was not the obtuse 'Westerner' that he has been depicted by many supporters of the Gallipoli operation, it would be equally foolish to pretend that he came to Gallipoli with an entirely open mind. As Callwell has written of Monro's attitude before his departure from London, 'in so far as he understood the situation before satisfying himself of the various factors on the spot, he leant towards complete and prompt evacuation.' His staff contained several ardent opponents of the whole Gallipoli enterprise; what is not generally realised is the fact that their views were fully shared by an influential section of Hamilton's staff at Imbros and by all the senior British generals on the Peninsula with the exception of Birdwood.

While Monro was carefully examining the papers at the War Office, Roger Keyes arrived in London. Keyes came as the ardent advocate of attack; if the Army could not advance, the Navy would do so. To securing authority for the renewal of the naval offensive he brought all his vigour, enthusiasm and formidable pertinacity. De Robeck had firmly telegraphed to the Admiralty on August 22nd: 'To attack Narrows now with battleships would be a grave error, as chances of getting even a small efficient squadron past Chanak [are] very remote.' But he generously permitted Keyes to go to London to lay his scheme before the Admiralty. Balfour and Jackson listened carefully and were sympathetic, but no definite decision could be reached before Monro's report was received.

Monro's instructions, unlike Hamilton's, were precise; he was to report fully and frankly on the military situation in Gallipoli; he was to consider the best means of removing the deadlock, and to report 'whether, in his opinion, *on purely military grounds** it is better to evacuate Gallipoli or to

* My italics.

make another attempt to carry it'; he was to estimate the probable loss that would be incurred in evacuation and, alternatively, the number of troops required for victory. The wording of his instructions and the order of priorities were highly significant.

When Monro arrived at Imbros he was handed a memorandum drawn up by the General Staff which had been prepared in the interregnum period since Hamilton's recall. It estimated that a total of 400,000 men and plentiful ammunition would be required to capture the Straits; this attack could not begin until the spring, and meanwhile major military operations would have to be undertaken to secure the vulnerable Suvla position. If evacuation were decided upon, it would be unwise to reckon on a smaller total loss than 50 per cent of the fighting personnel and 66 per cent of the guns. Monro was impressed by the thoroughness of this document, although Aspinall states that Monro told him that he was sorry that it had not helped him more by 'plumping' more definitely in favour of evacuation. It is difficult to see how much farther the memorandum could have gone in this direction; in its form and content it was a definite and unanswerable case for evacuation, and the officers who had prepared it knew it.

The relationship between a new commander and the staff of his dismissed predecessor can be embarrassing and difficult. Monro has consistently been given less than justice in accounts of the campaign, and nothing was more remarkable than the rapidity with which he earned the affection and admiration of the staff at Imbros. 'I don't know that we made a very good impression,' Williams subsequently wrote, 'being many of us run down with the usual internal troubles of the Dardanelles, with our rough camp and our rough kit. Matters were made a little more difficult by the fact that the poor Generals had been pushed off in such a hurry that they, being used to French châteaux, had got no camp equipment, and there were even no beds or basins for them at first.' In spite of these unpropitious circumstances, Hamilton's staff took to their new chief almost at once. 'I am getting a great admiration for him', Dawnay wrote of Monro to his wife. 'A perfectly delightful man, genial, great sense of humour, and wonderfully sound judgement of men and affairs, and one who sees down to the *root* of things— sweeping irrelevances aside !' Dawnay, Aspinall, Lloyd, Deedes and Williams are united in their praise for him; his personal kindness, his brisk professional- ism and meticulous hard work quickly removed any feelings of resentment which may have existed in Hamilton's staff. Birdwood and Byng were soon on the very best of terms with him, and with his chief of staff, General Lyndon-Bell.

In all the circumstances, Monro kept a remarkably open mind on the vital question of the future of Gallipoli. Churchill's account of Monro's mission in *The World Crisis* was cruel and unfair. 'General Monro was an officer of swift decision. He came, he saw, he capitulated. He reached the Dardanelles on October 28; and already on the 29th he and his staff were discussing nothing but evacuation.'* This version of events is harsh and untrue. On the 28th Monro cabled his first impressions of the situation to Kitchener; these contained no hints of evacuation. He said that he had seen the corps commanders and had been impressed by their not unfavourable accounts of the situation; he asked for experienced company commanders to be sent out at once, and for adequate materials required for preparing the trenches for winter; he had inspected an Australian brigade at Mudros, and had been greatly taken by them. It was, in all the circumstances, a fair and cool document, and which has been conveniently ignored by his critics.

It was Kitchener, not Monro, who forced the pace. Before Monro had been at his new post for 24 hours Kitchener impatiently telegraphed: 'Please send me as soon as possible your report on the main issue at the Dardanelles, namely, leaving or staying.' The peremptory tone in this telegram was unmistakable. Taken in conjunction with the tone of the instructions Monro had received in London, it contained an implication of what the decision was expected to be. Kitchener's fatal habit of dashing off peremptory telegrams, which had so misled Hamilton in March and May, again distorted events at the Dardanelles to a significant extent. The telegram arrived on the evening of the 29th, and on the 30th Monro set out on a visit to Helles, Anzac and Suvla.

Monro's many critics make much of the fact that he never went beyond the beaches and that Lyndon-Bell never visited the Peninsula at all. In fact Lyndon-Bell had sprained his knee, and Monro would never have made such a brief examination of the three zones if it had not been for Kitchener's peremptory cable. Such has been the effect of Churchill's account of Monro's activities that he is now regularly cast in the familiar role of the block-headed 'Westerner', intent only on getting out of Gallipoli and back to France, a portrait which entirely ignores the facts of the situation. Kitchener was applying the scourge from London; the army on the Peninsula had no chance of advancing without massive reinforcements; almost all of the most influential members of Hamilton's old staff were convinced that evacuation was now almost inevitable; the entry of Bulgaria into the war meant that greatly improved guns and ammunition would be pouring into Turkey from the Central Powers; the one fact on which everyone agreed was that if the Turks had had adequate artillery support they would have blasted the Allies off the Peninsula months ago.

* Sir Ian Hamilton's subsequent comments on Monro also lacked charity: 'A General of the most blameless, sealed-pattern type was ordered out from France to assure the sailors and soldiers on the spot that they were licked.' (*The Commander* [posthumously published essays, ed. by A. H. Farrar-Hockley]).

Monro's professionalism was considerably ruffled by the scenes at Helles, Anzac and Suvla. The troops had long since accustomed themselves to the open beaches, the rickety piers, the choking dust, the patter of shrapnel, the shells, the long lines of mules, the hazards of landing everything by hand, the scruffy dug-outs, the dumps of miscellaneous stores and the glaring sun. Almost every new arrival on the Peninsula was disconcerted by the primitiveness of everything, the need for constant improvisation, and the almost complete absence of materials no less than by the danger, the noise and the tension. The ability of the British soldier to acclimatise himself rapidly to his new environment, whether it be desert, jungle, or mud, is one of his outstanding qualities, and the appearance of chaos on the Gallipoli beaches was deceptive. To see old news-reels of the fighting in France in 1916 and 1917 is an unforgettable jolt to those used to warfare in the second half of the twentieth century. It is not merely another war, but another, and a primitive, world. Yet 1916 saw a vast advance in technology and experience on the Western Front over the battlefields with which Monro was familiar when he arrived at Gallipoli, but even he was astounded by what he saw there. This fact, perhaps more than any other, brings home to a modern student the ramshackle primitiveness of Gallipoli. At Anzac, Monro glanced ruefully at Aspinall; 'Like Alice in Wonderland,' he remarked, 'curious and curiouser.'

At each of the three bases Monro visited the headquarters and briefly looked over the country. His critics say that he should have spent longer, and travelled farther; but the fact that each of the three positions could be seen almost at a glance was sufficient commentary on the precariousness of the Allied position. To each divisional commander Monro put two questions. Were his troops fit for a sustained effort on the enemy's position, and, if no reinforcements arrived and the Turks were reinforced with German guns and ammunition, could they hold on throughout the winter? It has been argued over and over again by Monro's critics that these were 'loaded' questions, designed to furnish him with the replies he wanted to recommend evacuation. Aspinall, for example, who accompanied Monro, has written that if Monro had told the commanders that massive reinforcements were on their way and that the Government had resolved to see the business through, their answers would have been very different. No doubt. But this argument ignores the unpalatable facts that Monro had just come from London and that he knew only too well of the doubts and hesitations there concerning the future of the campaign, and that the resources of the Empire were being stretched to their uttermost limits. It also evades the critically important point that both Davies and Byng were uncompromising supporters of evacuation, and had been so from their arrival on the Peninsula.

As it was, the senior officers told him the blunt truth; the guns were now rationed to two shells per gun per day; there was no equipment to conduct a winter offensive; almost every unit was badly below strength; there was a grievous shortage of good officers, particularly at major and captain levels; the troops were worn out by the fighting, the sickness and the unending chores of keeping the army supplied, and were incapable of more than 24 hours' sustained effort; if the Turks received great quantities of improved ammunition they could only say they could do their best. One glance at the positions was enough to persuade Monro that that best would not be good enough. Perhaps Monro looked at the Gallipoli positions too much with the eyes of a soldier used to conditions in France; on the other hand, everyone at the Peninsula tended to regard them in Gallipoli terms, where an advance of 50 yards was a major victory. Monro saw that Achi Baba was as far away as ever it was; that the Suvla troops were trapped on the fringe of a plain overlooked by the enemy at every point; and that there was virtually no hope of another surprise thrust at Anzac.

Monro returned to Imbros with his mind made up firmly for evacuation, and telegraphed to Kitchener to that effect on the following day (October 31st). 'Well I remember the pages of foolscap, written in pencil in the General's most illegible hand, as it was enciphered by the light of a feeble lamp in one of the Staff officers' tents,' Williams has related. 'Very few people knew the contents of that telegram. To those who did it gave the first ray of hope for the future—a hope that wise and definite decisions would be made at once, that a waste of energy and lives on useless ends would cease, and that the force would not long remain the lame, uncared-for thing, looking out doggedly but dully on a grey future, that it now was.' 'There was no sane alternative, from a military point of view, to immediate evacuation', Aspinall has written: '. . . In all the circumstances of the case, therefore, so far as they were known to the army in Gallipoli, there was no fault to be found with Sir Charles Monro's bold recommendation . . . the fact that Monro had thus quickly made up his mind, and had forwarded a report which might compel the Government to act, was a matter for relief and thankfulness.' Monro himself was under no illusion about the reception his report would have in London, where 'powerful Dardanellian influences' remained in the Dardanelles Committee; he remarked in the secrecy of his staff officers that he expected to be recalled forthwith. For a highly ambitious officer, promoted to high command in a critical area, to submit a report which he expected would result in his immediate dismissal—with little or no expectation of getting another comparable command—was an act of courage which has received little praise from historians of the campaign and brought upon his head Churchill's grotesque invective.

Meanwhile, Roger Keyes had been active in London, and had managed to fan the rapidly dying flames of enthusiasm for the enterprise. Once again, the vision of the Navy crashing through the weakened Dardanelles defences to the Marmara danced hauntingly in front of Ministers. A victory somewhere was desperately needed, and such a spectacular conclusion to the whole campaign would be a glorious one.

This, of course, was quite unknown to the army on the Peninsula. Their feeling of abandonment was becoming acute. The Turks were not particularly active, but the strain of maintaining exposed positions was continuous. At Suvla, even more than Helles, one felt naked in that great exposed plain, eyed by the sentinel hills. 'The area is tightly packed with mules, horses and men', a British chaplain wrote; 'streets and lanes of boxes piled 15 to 20 feet high, barges and lighters unloading at roughly thrown-out jetties; pyramids of baggage, mountains of forage, above all the din and noise a faint moaning is heard, growing rapidly louder and deeper—thud, bang—and up goes a column of dust and debris. The air clears, heads bob up, and where there had been a pile of biscuit boxes there remains a shell crater, with a litter of scrap tin, matchwood etc., and the work goes on.' At Anzac, the new positions on Rhododendron and in the Sari Bair foothills were difficult to reach, and were extremely dangerous to occupy. At The Apex and The Pinnacle, only a few yards separated the Turkish and British positions. 'Perhaps the truest indication of one's present frame of mind is that waking up to a perfectly divine morning, when the sea is a jewel and the wind ambrosial, and the mountains tinted so delicately, all one thinks is—"another bloody day!"' Orlo Williams wrote in his diary.

New arrivals at Lemnos, en route for the Peninsula, had any illusions of war quickly dispelled; it was not only the depressing surroundings, the flies, or the climate which were responsible; the most dispiriting feature was the attitude of the troops 'resting' after returning from the Peninsula. 'They resembled in some respects the survivors of an earthquake,' a young New Zealander, Alexander Aitken, has written of the remnants of the New Zealand Infantry Brigade on Lemnos; ' . . . it was significant that the prime cause, Gallipoli, was under a taboo and barely mentioned.' 'So weak, couldn't stand', a British private at Suvla wrote on October 20th; ' . . . simply crawled about, so reported sick. Had injection of emetine and castor oil, but did not relieve me at all. Shall do something desperate soon, I can't stand it. Had terrible night—in port for the last week—when possible I've had to sleep by the latrines—waterproof sheet and one blanket. It's all for your King and country!' The first sight of the Peninsula was an unforgettable sensation, recaptured by Aitken in his account of landing at Anzac early in November:

. . . we made out the black mass and ridgy back of the Gallipoli Peninsula, pinpointed with tiny lights, as from a camp of gold-miners on a slope, visible to us but not to the Turks. The water, unseen below, must have been in a flat calm, for desultory

326

rifle-shots and the rat-a-tat of a machine-gun sounded across it with extraordinary distinctness. Fifteen miles to the south a warship was firing at periodic intervals; to the north, a line of green lights with a red cross in the middle undulated above its shimmering reflection, a hospital ship at anchor, south of Suvla. In low tones old hands identified the contours: 'Quinn's Post just about there', 'Chunuk Bair up there', 'Hill 971 away to the left'. New-comers took it all in, silent and subdued.

There followed, in Aitken's case, a long awful trudge up to Rhododendron and The Apex. Before dawn the magic of the approach to the shore had vanished; by first light they had suffered their first casualties; by dusk their entire existence was dominated by a hard, dispiriting, false security and the tingling, tense boredom of trench life.

Kitchener's reaction to Monro's recommendation to evacuate had been one of complete consternation, and he had at once telegraphed to Monro to ask for the views of the corps commanders. Both Byng and Davies whole-heartedly agreed with Monro's judgement, and both had been advocates of evacuation almost from the time of their arrival, but Birdwood, although agreeing that the chances of making any progress were remote, advised against evacuation; uppermost in his mind were the probable effects on British prestige in the East, and the great dangers of evacuating at a time of year when the weather was unreliable. On the previous evening the destroyer *Louis* had been blown ashore at Suvla and broken in half in a fierce gale from the south-west, an unpleasant foretaste of what might now be expected. Telegraphing these views to Kitchener on 2nd November, Monro added that his opinion remained unaltered, and that the estimated loss was estimated at between 30 and 40 per cent in personnel and material. He then left for Egypt to consult Maxwell, leaving Birdwood in temporary command, and having already drawn up provisional plans for a joint military and naval committee to handle the evacuation.

Kitchener now clutched at the last hope of salvaging something from the Gallipoli imbroglio by fervently espousing Keyes' plan for another 'grand slam' assault on the Narrows. Balfour made it clear that the Navy might be prepared to carry out the attack 'if the army meant business'. It was the old story. The Fleet would not budge unless the Army attacked; the removal of troops to Salonika meant that this was out of the question. Inter-service friction had been remarkably absent throughout the campaign, but it is easy to detect from the private diaries and letters and confidential dispatches that the old mutual confidence had been sadly eroded. As a confidential joint naval and military Report of the operations subsequently guardedly stated, 'one must not be led by the frequent mutual expressions of confidence, admiration and eulogy to be found in the despatches and reports to think that on no occasion was there any impatience or criticism of the methods or work of the other arm.' Keyes himself felt bitterly that the Navy had never played its full part since March 18th, and had abrogated its responsibilities to the soldiers, an emotion fully shared by many of the soldiers.

In the small hours of November 4th, Birdwood was awakened by his acting chief of staff with a cipher telegram from Kitchener marked 'Most secret, Decipher yourself'. Birdwood could not handle the cipher, and the message was decoded by his staff. It was a staggering communication. Kitchener was about to sail for Gallipoli. He absolutely refused to sign orders for evacuation, 'which I think would be the gravest disaster, and would condemn a large percentage of our men to death or imprisonment'. The Navy was to force the Dardanelles if the Army could deliver an equivalent attack. Birdwood was to examine the ground near Bulair for a new landing. To provide the troops the garrisons at Helles, Suvla and Anzac were to be reduced to the lowest possible size. Birdwood himself was to have complete command over the force; while Monro was to be sent to Salonika. Hard on the heels of this telegram came an official notification from the War Office stating that Birdwood had been appointed to command the Mediterranean Expeditionary Force.

It was another flash of the old Kitchener, imperious, sweeping and unconsidered. Birdwood, however, did not react as might have been expected. He was appalled by the summary dismissal of Monro merely for giving a military opinion, and he was equally horrified by the suggestion of a new landing at Bulair. His great personal admiration and affection for Monro also played an important part. He begged Kitchener to think again, and suppressed the announcement of his appointment. Later on the same day he received a very different message from the Secretary of State. 'I fear that the Navy may not play up . . . . The more I look at the problem the less I see my way through, so you had better very quietly and very secretly work out any scheme for getting the troops off.' Birdwood replied that he was for staying on, but that if evacuation was to be carried out it was even more important that Monro should remain in command.

From this point, the chances of staying at Gallipoli remorselessly faded. The combination of Lloyd George and Law in the Cabinet was immensely powerful. On November 2nd Asquith, in a speech in the House of Commons, bluntly admitted that the campaign had failed. Kitchener's reputation had fallen so low with his colleagues that Asquith eagerly espoused the proposal to send him out to Gallipoli to report on the situation there. 'We avoid by this method of procedure the supersession of K as War Minister, while achieving the same result', he wrote to Lloyd George. Law at first agreed to Kitchener's mission, but then, sensing the possibility of Kitchener reversing Monro's advice, changed his mind; but, by then, Kitchener had gone. For those like Keyes, Birdwood and Wemyss who wanted to stay, it was a period of alternating wild hope and black despair. At one moment all would seem to be well, and they persuaded themselves that something of the old enthusiasm was to be discerned in London and Paris; within a few hours, the evacuationists would be in control again.

In Mr. Robert Blake's felicitous phrase, 'a ferocious paper warfare convulsed the Cabinet. Memoranda flew to and fro. Resignations were frequently threatened. It seemed that the Government could never survive.' The best chance of the 'stayers' slipped by when Keyes was invited to join Kitchener at Marseilles to discuss the naval plan on their way to the eastern Mediterranean; at the Admiralty it was assumed (wrongly) that as Keyes could not hope to reach Marseilles in time there was no point in forwarding the message to him. Keyes, after discussing plans with the new French Minister of Marine in Paris, travelled out via Naples, and by the time he reached Mudros, Kitchener had at last reconciled himself finally to evacuation. 'When you didn't turn up at Marseilles,' he told Keyes later, 'I made up my mind that the naval plan was dead.' It is unlikely that this episode had much significance; as soon as Lloyd George and Bonar Law had Monro's telegram in their hands, nothing short of the disintegration of the Government could have stopped evacuation. On November 8th Asquith averted Law's resignation by promising to support him over evacuation, and the die was virtually cast.

Monro and his staff were in Egypt when he learnt of his supersession from Maxwell after a gay champagne dinner at Shepheard's Hotel. He kept his feelings to himself, but those members of his staff who heard about it were furious. 'As he was that morning in Cairo,' Orlo Williams has written of Monro, 'he had literally nothing but what he stood up in, no staff, no A.D.C., hardly any kit—nothing but the prospect of seeing Lord Kitchener. . . . To us who had accompanied General Monro, although we only heard the bare facts, the whole procedure would have seemed astounding if it had not been so dramatically typical.' 'Can such a thing be conceived?' Dawnay wrote indignantly on November 6th. 'You put in a Commander, ask his advice as to the course to be pursued, and because he answers your question (as he is *ordered* to do) you turn him out! . . . I am specially discouraged because I believe in Sir Charles; I absolutely believe in his judgement; I think him a big man . . . I had anticipated a gradual clearing up of the mess here, under his guidance . . . Who is it that commits these atrocious fatuities?'

The evacuationists now steadily increased in size and influence, and, at this point, secured a priceless tactical advantage. Maxwell shared Birdwood's apprehensions about the moral effect of evacuation, and, with Birdwood, was insisting that if the Peninsula were evacuated there must be another landing elsewhere as soon as possible. Monro's staff quickly discerned that it did not particularly matter where the landing was to be, and between them they concocted a wholly bogus plan to land at Ayas Bay, in the Gulf of

Iskanderun. Kitchener had himself started the idea when he had mentioned this possibility in a telegram to Maxwell, and Guy Dawnay assisted by T. E. Lawrence, then in Cairo, 'rattled out a scheme in 36 hours for a new landing in Ayas Bay. . . . This was all a pure bluff.' Monro had a pretty shrewd idea of the motives which lay behind Dawnay's detailed proposal, and hesitated to sponsor it as a serious proposition. 'I had the greatest trouble to get old Monro even to put it forward,' Dawnay relates, 'because he thought it dishonest to put forward a scheme which he knew to be impracticable, even with the admirable object of securing time for K. to make up his mind to evacuation.'*

As a *ruse de guerre* the Ayas Bay scheme was spectacularly successful. When Kitchener arrived at Mudros, Birdwood, de Robeck, Maxwell and Sir Henry MacMahon (the High Commissioner in Egypt) were already almost reconciled to evacuation. 'Feeling very low all day at the very thought of giving up Anzac', Birdwood wrote in his diary at this time; 'Monro's arguments are, however, sound.' 'The need for diplomacy was obvious,' writes Williams; 'whatever view was to carry the day, persuasion would be necessary. Those who knew, but had merely to watch and devil, watched with keen interest the thickening of the diplomatic atmosphere. Conferences took place; now this pair, now that, would pace the short quarter-deck in earnest conversation.' After Kitchener arrived, he made the battleship *Lord Nelson* his headquarters, and reigned in the Admiral's drawing-room. Orlo Williams worked in the dining room, and has recounted that, 'an observer, seated at the green baize table, could remark all the coming and going, the *empressement*, and the subtle changes of temperature and atmosphere, which are the same in all ante-rooms of the great. Glimpses were caught of the conferences, of Lord Kitchener massive and overwhelming, General Monro with his warrior's face set hard as a rock, the portly carriage of General Maxwell, the keen features and slight figure of Sir Henry MacMahon. There was amusement, too, to be derived from the entourage, which brought a whiff of Whitehall incense into this far-off theatre of war. . . . When I hear the words "I am no politician, only a plain soldier", I laugh. I have seen a combination of the two.'

The Ayas Bay scheme placated the fears of Maxwell and MacMahon completely, and Birdwood, although becoming reconciled to evacuation, became so obsessed by the futility of undertaking another landing that most of the heat that would have been generated in arguments over evacuation was in fact dissipated on the Ayas Bay plan; as Williams has commented,

* The best account of the origins and execution of the Ayas Bay scheme is to be found in a private letter from Dawnay to Colonel Wavell (then engaged on the official history of the Mesopotamia campaign), dated June 6th, 1926, made available to me through the kindness of Lt.-Col. C. P. Dawnay.

'it served as an admirable solvent for conflicting views which, but for its influence, might have come into fiercer opposition.' This, of course, was the object of the whole exercise. Monro was embarrassed and ill at ease by this gigantic tactical hoax, and Dawnay sometimes found it difficult to keep a straight face as the great men earnestly argued. The French said it was impossible; the General Staff in London emphatically rejected it. This, in itself, was something of a shock; 'it was then for the first time that a suspicion crossed certain minds that, incredible as it might seem, the war might end with a different Secretary of State for War from him with whom it so greatly began', Williams has whimsically written. 'As it was, there was some asperity. The ante-room atmosphere was heavy and ominous.' By the time that Kitchener had reluctantly abandoned the idea the vital principle of evacuation had become almost tacitly accepted. Not the least comic aspect of the arguments for and against the Ayas Bay scheme is the intense seriousness with which it has been discussed by successive historians of the campaign.

On November 15th Kitchener telegraphed home his impressions of the position on the Peninsula, which he had examined on November 12th, 13th and 14th. He was considerably depressed by the precarious hold of the Army on the Peninsula and by the almost impregnable nature of the Turk defences; on his return from Anzac he espied Guy Dawnay, whom he had last met at 10, Downing Street at the celebrated dinner-party. Going up to him, Kitchener gruffly remarked, 'Young man, you were right.' His telegram of November 15th, although it made no clear recommendation, showed that he was now thinking seriously of evacuation; he added that he considered that it could be accomplished with far less loss than had been previously thought, an opinion increasingly shared by the joint military and naval committee set up by Monro to draw up an outline scheme for withdrawal.

Four days elapsed while the Cabinet brooded over Kitchener's telegram. Williams noticed that Kitchener was 'very fidgety', and the restlessness was shared by everyone. On the 19th the reply came; the Ayas Bay scheme was dead, two more divisions were to go to Salonika, and Kitchener was to give his considered opinion on evacuation without any *quid pro quo*. With a heavy heart, Kitchener definitely advised the Cabinet on November 22nd that Suvla and Anzac should be evacuated, and Helles retained 'at all events for the present'. This was a compromise which Monro was prepared to accept temporarily, particularly in view of the fact that General Davies now believed that his troops had established a definite moral superiority over the enemy and that there were simply not enough ships to undertake more than one evacuation at a time. Kitchener had no illusions that it was merely a method of 'saving face'. Monro was to command all forces in the Eastern

Mediterranean except for Gallipoli, where Birdwood was to be in charge of evacuation; de Robeck was to be replaced by Wemyss. Asquith telegraphed that the War Committee was in favour of total evacuation, and Birdwood was ordered to prepare for this eventuality. Already, significant preliminary work had been done in removing all surplus stores and ammunition.

Carden, Hamilton, Stopford, Braithwaite and Hunter-Weston had now finally left the scene; of the original commanders, only Birdwood and Paris were left. On November 11th it was announced that the War Committee, as it was henceforth to be known, had been reconstituted; Curzon and Churchill, the two leading opponents of evacuation, were excluded. Churchill's career had reached its nadir; on November 15th he left the Government, to serve with the Army in France. It had been a shattering eclipse. Of the original participants in the drama, only Kitchener—his authority now gravely undermined—Birdwood, Wemyss and Keyes remained. The curtain, if somewhat jerkily and hesitantly, was beginning to fall.

13

The End of the Adventure

Now snowflakes thickly falling in the winter breeze
Have cloaked alike the hard, unbending ilex
And the grey, drooping branches of the olive trees,
   Transmuting into silver all their lead;
And, in between the winding lines, in No Man's Land,
   Have softly covered with a glittering shroud,
The unburied dead.

   Malcolm Ross: 'The Unburied' (The Anzac Book)

For several weeks, the weather had been superb. 'It is impossible to convey any adequate impression of the sweetness of the mornings, as the flush of dawn over the sea faded in the growing light, and the dew-clouds, hiding the islands all save the higher peaks, like vast banks of whitest wool, vanished at the touch of the sun', a Scottish chaplain wrote; 'the days were bright, and the skies unclouded. The heat was tempered by cool breezes, now from the south and again from the east. It looked like compensation for all we had endured in months past.' Drummond Fish, the artist, wrote of Suvla at this time that 'the colours were the most wonderful thing about Gallipoli. There were mornings when the hills were as rose as peaches—times when the sea looked like the tail of some gigantic peacock, and the sands looked like great carpets of glittering cloth of gold—the place was an inspiration in itself, and if beauty could have stopped a war, that scenery would have done it.' There had been one or two ominous storms, which had whipped up the sea and torn at the wooden jetties; in Suvla bay the wreck of the destroyer *Louis* testified to the force of the sea.

On October 7th a fiercer storm had severely damaged the piers on the beaches. Captain Pawson, the M.L.O. at W Beach, wrote in his diary that

333

'next morning we found poor old W Beach looking very battered and weather beaten. . . . The shore by No. 1 pier was all under water, and the tramlines hung in the air with all their foundations washed away; a hole was cut right through No. 2 pier and on the beach close by lay our precious motor boat with a hole in her side, whilst further away a small store ship swung on a rock with her back broken and a gash in her bottom. And yet the sea had never really been rough nor the wind very strong except for a couple of hours.' On November 17th the main piers at Anzac and W Beach were smashed by high seas. 'All along the beach above the roar of the waves could be heard the crash of the great barges as the sea hurled them again and again against the shore,' Pawson relates of the scene at W Beach; 'they seemed to be trying to escape, but always the waves dragged them back for another blow.' When the troops at Helles surveyed the wreckage of the camps, stores and piers, they saw that the prow of *Majestic* had also disappeared. But these had been brief affairs, although fierce while they lasted, and had been followed by days of ambrosial warmth. There was relatively little activity on any of the fronts. 'So far, it is one of the most peaceful wars that one could imagine,' a newly arrived subaltern wrote in his diary at Helles, 'and it hardly ever occurs to one that we are out here to kill each other.'

On November 27th a violent thunderstorm broke. 'The sea was roaring like a vast monster under the lash of the tempest', the Scottish chaplain wrote. 'Then a mighty sheet of flame would flash across the heavens, torn by gleaming, twisted and broken lines, and for a moment the wide welter and turmoil of foaming waters, with the white hospital ships riding at anchor, leaped into view.' There was a brief hailstorm, when lumps of ice lashed down, and then torrential rain, which swept away stone parapets, animals and men. At Suvla a torrent came boring down from the hills, carrying the bodies of drowned Turks, and sweeping everything before it. One officer, sheltering in his dug-out, noticed 'a curious slapping noise in the slit outside, and a great snake of water came round the curve, breast high, and washed me backwards'; another, clambering hurriedly on to a parapet, saw two dead mules, one live mule, two dead Turks and a quantity of débris sweeping down the trench he had just vacated. In some trenches the water was over three feet deep, and men were struggling in filthy water up to their chests. Turks and British jumped on to the parapets in full view of each other to escape the flood. All thoughts of fighting vanished in the general *sauve qui peut*. 'No Man's Land was a lake', writes one eye-witness. 'No attack would come over that for some time. North and south the front trench was full of sullen brown water, and behind it was no sign of life . . . [A few men nearby] were all blue with cold, shivering and wild-eyed.' A British private, sent with a message to brigade headquarters, found the brigade major sitting crosslegged on the top of a table with two feet of water below him; the trenches were feet deep in water, and the messenger walked along ground which was open to the fire of both sides without a shot being fired. 'Ha, my boy', the major remarked. 'Is this your first experience of the pomp and glory of modern warfare?' 'It was indeed a hopeless dawn,' a British soldier wrote of the dawn of November 28th; 'nothing could be seen but demolished and water-filled trenches; equipment and debris was scattered everywhere. No food was forthcoming, as apparently all the ration parties had been swept away'.

The men had not begun to recover from the storm when the wind veered round to the north and an intense blizzard raged for two days. The men had hardly any protective clothing; most were soaked through before the snow fell, and supply arrangements were in chaos. The snow and frost hit the army with the force of a blow. Many Anzacs and Indians had never even seen snow before; blankets were frozen solid, rifles jammed, sentries were found frozen to death. 'Men staggered down from the lines numbed and bemused with the intensity of the cold', Nevinson relates. 'They could neither hear nor speak, but stared about them like bewildered bullocks. . . . Many were frostbitten; many lost their limbs; some, their reason.' A young officer of the Worcesters found no less than 30 men on the firesteps of a trench, frozen to death.

Both sides lit fires, and the men gathered round them, all thought of fighting gone. When the severity of the cold eased, a British machine-gun opened up on some wandering Turks, the enemy replied, and the war was resumed. An attempt was made to get liquor to the front lines, with catastrophic results in some places. At Suvla, some troops broke into the rum stores, and went berserk. 'The effect on empty stomachs and in that cold was simply devastating', a captain of the Herefordshire Regiment recorded some days later in his diary: 'Filled with a spurious warmth, they lay on the ground, and in many cases took off their coats, boots and even tunics ! . . . I remember finding one man in particular in only his shirt and trousers, holding an empty mug in a perfectly stiff arm, quite dead. Coming on top of everything else, it was heart-rending.' The same officer also described in his diary the gathering together of his men. 'Men were pretty badly knocked about by now, as we hadn't much food all day, on top of the previous night, and they slept and fell all over the place. We even had some casualties from this. We arrived some time and were directed to a resting place, a bleak stretch of snow-covered sand dunes, with sundry clumps of a sort of gorse. When I had shepherded in the last straggler, I felt like lying down and dying.'

At Suvla there were over 12,000 cases of frostbite and exposure, nearly 3,000 at Anzac, and about 1,000 at Helles, where the conditions were nothing like as bad. 280 men died as a direct result of the storm and the blizzard. 'I shall never forget the look of most of our men after the first and second nights' frost,' a young Newfoundland officer, Lieutenant Owen Steele, wrote almost immediately afterwards; 'the men's faces were nearly all as black as niggers from sitting over the smoking fires all night, and what with their eyes and woe-begone looks, they presented a really terrible sight.' 'More terrible scenes could not be pictured than those existing from the first to the second line of trenches,' writes a British soldier, 'dead lying about in hundreds all swollen and black and in every conceivable place and attitude, trenches broken down and filled with water, and equipment of all sorts everywhere.' 'Draggled men are squatted on the firing platform, and draggled sentries are peering stoically into the periscope mirrors,' another eyewitness records; 'in the saps, fed-up grenadiers are slinging bombs over the barricades. Officers in burberries chew damp cigarettes, and wonder when their spell is coming for a holiday at Mudros. Everyone speculates on the chance of the cooks' fire bearing up against the weather. And so the weary day drags through.' An Australian private at Anzac, Thomas Dry, wrote at this time of life at Anzac: 'We could not get water or tea to drink for nearly a fortnight. So bad did our thirst become that we had to go down to the cooks and get a drop in the middle of the night at the risk of getting into serious trouble, as they had sentries stationed all round. Then the snow came and we ate it, but it takes a lot to quench your thirst. . . . No matter where we go now, it will never be as bad as Gallipoli.' In their dazed condition, it seemed to many of the men that there was nothing to stop the Turks driving them into the sea. 'I had visions of long columns of prisoners winding their way into captivity in bleak Anatolia or somewhere in Asia Minor', a Scottish subaltern wrote.

The storms inevitably put the question of evacuation in a new and ugly light. Monro at once telegraphed to London on December 1st: 'Experience of recent storms indicates that there is no time to lose. General Birdwood telegraphed yesterday that if evacuation is to be made possible it is essential to take advantage of every fine day from now. If decision cannot be reached very shortly, it may be equivalent to deciding against evacuation.' Keyes, supported by Wemyss, was still fighting to make one last supreme effort; Wemyss telegraphed to the Admiralty on November 28th: 'General Monro places the probable losses at 30 per cent: I do not think he exaggerates. I am, however, strongly of opinion that such a disaster should not be accepted without an effort being made to retrieve our position. I consider that a combined attack by Navy and Army would have every prospect of achieving decisive results.' Monro's patience, which had been sorely tried in the past month, very nearly broke under Keyes' provocations. The tension at Imbros between the military and naval staffs became acute.

'Unless I am mistaken,' Monro wrote icily to Wemyss on December 1st, 'it appears to me that you have been conferring with my Army and Corps Commanders on matters of military import the decision in respect to which rests with me. This is a proceeding which is not regular and which I obviously cannot accept . . . I am particularly anxious not to introduce any heat into this question. But you would not approve of my approaching your subordinates without your knowledge and consent'. Wemyss—described by Orlo Williams in his diary as 'a hearty, rather choleric individual with an eyeglass rather like George Grossmith'—took the rebuke badly, and the relationship between Wemyss and Keyes on the one hand and Monro and Lyndon-Bell on the other deteriorated even further. Birdwood skilfully stayed out of this unhappy personal row between the senior naval and military commanders, and found it all 'hateful'. 'I am having a horribly anxious time of it here, which I have no wish ever to go through again', he wrote miserably to his wife.

On December 1st Monro urgently cabled London for a definite decision. The subject was now almost common knowledge in political circles; Carson told the House of Commons that 'the Dardanelles operations hang like a millstone round our necks', and Lord Milner returned to the topic in another speech in the Lords. 'Really,' Birdwood wrote despairingly to Monro about this unwelcome publicity, 'it hardly gives us even a fair sporting chance!' But in spite of the hostility of Lloyd George and Law to the retention of Gallipoli, the Cabinet—confronted with a lurid portrait of catastrophe by Lord Curzon—was wobbling once again. 'Conceive the crowding into the boats of thousands of half-crazy men, the swamping of craft, the nocturnal panic, the agony of the wounded, the hecatombs of slain', Curzon wrote. He received powerful support from Hankey, whose memorandum was in a very different tone, drawing attention to the possible unfortunate consequences of withdrawal, including the signing of a separate peace by Russia. Could not the four divisions in Salonika be returned to Gallipoli?

To this question Monro bluntly replied that they would make no difference to the situation on the Peninsula. On December 4th Bonar Law made a decisive intervention by submitting a counter-memorandum to Curzon's, urging an immediate decision. Curzon had spoken of troops 'in despairing tumult' on the shore and of 'a welter of carnage and shame'. Law retorted curtly that he could not conceive of British troops behaving in this manner and that the perils of remaining were immeasurably greater; he went on to assault the whole concept of the 'stayers' with the withering phrase: 'It seems to be assumed, by a strange process of perverted reasoning, that by merely holding on at Gallipoli we should paralyse the whole offensive of the enemy in the East.'

Nevertheless, as the long days dragged on, Monro began to have serious doubts, and, on the same day that Law's memorandum was circulated, remarked to Keyes, 'Well, we are in for it—we are going to do it; you have got your way.' For a moment it seemed as if this might be the case, and that Hankey's proposal to bring back the Salonika troops to Gallipoli might win the day. But it was another mirage; the French and the Russians would not hear of it, and on December 7th Monro was at last ordered definitely to evacuate Anzac and Suvla. At this point it even appeared that the British might have two evacuations on their hands, as Mahon's gallant 10th Division had begun its painful retreat from Lake Doiran. Monro hastened to Salonika in a destroyer, to find the harbour and the future of the Salonika army enmeshed in a thick fog. Fortunately, the situation had already eased, and Monro could devote his full attentions to Gallipoli again.

Wemyss made a last attempt to reverse the decision. He complained, with some justification, that he had not seen any of Monro's appreciations on the situation. 'The Navy', he telegraphed on December 8th, 'is prepared to force the Straits and control them for an indefinite period. . . . The Navy here is prepared to undertake this operation with every assurance of success.' In a private telegram to Balfour he blamed Monro for having an obsession with France and killing Germans: 'He looks upon any action which does not have the above for its immediate objective as a waste of effort.' Balfour replied on the 10th that he personally agreed, but no one else did. De Robeck had been called into a meeting of the War Council on December 2nd, and his opposition to a renewal of the naval attack had made a strong impression. Wemyss' intervention, which might possibly have had an effect even a fortnight before, was too late. Purely military considerations were no longer uppermost in Ministers' minds; the decision to evacuate was essentially a political one, and by December 8th the politicians had at last resolved on it. Nearly six weeks had elapsed since Monro had made his first recommendation to evacuate; at last the 'stayers' knew they had lost.

Monro's foresight in ordering preliminary plans for evacuation now paid enormous dividends. The final plan was largely the work of Aspinall and Lt.-Col. White, a very capable Australian at Anzac. Monro's headquarters were established on the *Aragon* of ill-repute, which was crammed with staff officers in addition to the Lines of Communication staff. *Aragon* had lost all her luxury; 'she smelt like a bad drain, the food was nasty, the stewards (who subsequently struck) discontented, and the office accommodation for a Commander-in-Chief's Headquarters preposterous', Williams records. '. . . Many of us will always look on the succeeding month as a nightmare.'

In spite of these disadvantages, Monro had at least brought his General Staff and Administrative Staff together, and the results give some indication of what might have been achieved if Hamilton had done the same. Their task was to evacuate some 80,000 men, 5,000 animals, 2,000 vehicles, nearly 200 guns and enormous quantities of stores from Suvla and Anzac from under the eyes of the enemy. At Anzac, the problem was not quite as acute as at Suvla, and the fact that it had been possible to smuggle ashore 25,000 men in three nights in August showed that it should not be impossible to smuggle a similar number away if strict secrecy were preserved and all embarkations done at night.

The plan was for a gradual and secret withdrawal, until only a small garrison, to be taken off on one night, was left. The boats were assembled, stricter security precautions than ever before were taken—without repeating the folly of leaving everyone in the dark until the last possible moment—and elaborate time-tables drawn up. As it was impossible to conceal from the men what was happening, they were told that the garrisons were being reduced for the winter; work was pressed forward on improving the trenches and dug-outs, which not only kept the men occupied but made the story about 'thinning' the garrisons even more plausible. On about December 12th, the pretence was abandoned. 'It is now a certainty that we are evacuating,' Lt. Steele wrote in his diary on the 15th, 'for stores are being shipped off all the time, also small lots of troops. . . . We are all hoping and expecting to have no difficulty in getting off without an action at all.' The reactions of the men when they were told the truth were mixed; a few, like Birdwood, said that they would rather die than leave, and Birdwood relates that one Australian said to him, nodding towards one of the ragged cemeteries, 'I hope *they* won't hear us going down to the beaches.' A captain of the Herefordshire Regiment, which left Suvla on December 12th, wrote: 'It was impossible to help noticing the contrast—that brilliant August morning, the Battalion full of fight and high endeavour 750 strong!—this dark December night, slinking away, under 100 strong, weary, dirty, blasé, disillusioned. And yet, I was sorry to go.' Most, however, were glad that at least some firm decision had been taken, and the majority probably were intensely glad to get away.

By the end of the second week in December the evacuation was well advanced. The weather had improved wonderfully after the blizzard, and seemed settled. The accursed flies had gone, and conditions were almost as good as in early May. Every night the flotillas of small boats would creep into Suvla Bay and Anzac Cove; by morning, the seas were empty again. Tents were kept standing, the remaining guns kept up a regular rate of fire, and every possible step was taken to give the appearance that a large army still remained. The men entered into this part of the deception willingly, although their officers noticed a natural reluctance to take unnecessary risks now that the end was so near. By December 18th only 40,000 men remained, and the Turks apparently suspected nothing. Using their experience of the attack on Number Three Outpost in August, the commanders established a regular routine of what were known as 'silent stunts', when the front was silent for several nights. The Turks became suspicious, and launched occasional local attacks, which were firmly repulsed. The Turks quickly accepted the silent stunts as a new feature of the Anzac fighting, and were grateful for the respite. Kemal had now finally left the Peninsula; if he had still been there it is possible that his suspicions would have been aroused and a more aggressive attitude adopted. As it was, the Turks were almost completely quiescent. Major Zeki, the saviour of Lone Pine, subsequently told the Australians that 'towards the end a lot of movements were noticed, but we couldn't make out if you were landing troops or taking them away.... It was reported, first, that the number of tents was decreasing; second, that the guns were firing less and that fire was being undertaken by the ships instead; third, that there were some days of silence. . . . But some of us, even at the end, thought that you were preparing to attack.'

Throughout, White had insisted that the final withdrawal should be as quick and total as possible; the last 40,000 men were to be evacuated on two final nights, December 18th/19th and 19th/20th. Thus December 19th found 20,000 men left at Suvla and Anzac. The tension was now acute in the deserted labyrinths of trenches, saps and dug-outs. One could walk for what seemed hours without meeting anyone. 'Everything looking very deserted,' a British soldier at Suvla wrote, 'there being now only a few people left, and nothing but empty dug-outs and rubbish left behind.' The trench floors were dug up to soften the noise when the men finally left them, and long white lines of flour, salt and sugar were laid from the trenches to the beaches. Various forms of self-firing rifles had been designed and tested; the most common one was a contraption whereby a tin was filled with water with a hole in the bottom, through which the water dripped into a lower tin, attached to the trigger; when the bottom tin was full it over-balanced and fired the rifle. Engineers and miners made the last preparations to explode a large mine under the Turk trenches at The Nek, where the bones of the light horsemen still littered the scarred ground. Ammunition and bombs were buried (usually in the latrines), tarpaulins destroyed by pouring caustic soda over them, and even cooking utensils smashed. It was impossible not to have memories, and for many they were bitter ones. Most of the last to leave were buoyed up with excitement, but oppressed with physical exhaustion and nerves. 'No one closed his eyes even momentarily during those nine lingering hours', an Australian light horseman has written. 'Sleep seemed as impossible as the whole proceeding. It seemed incredible that everything should go off successfully; that the enemy should not guess that all that remained to oppose them was a handful of calmly desperate men.' Birdwood paid a last visit to Anzac, and stood for several minutes in Anzac Cove, now absolutely empty. Two large water

340

THE END OF THE ADVENTURE

condensers had been installed on the beach, but had been hit almost at once by a shell, and stood like gaunt sentinels over the flotsam of equipment which littered the beach.

At last, darkness fell, and men began to converge softly down the saps and gullies and well-trodden paths on to the beaches. Tiny red lights glowed at important intersections, and there was a regular system of 'traffic officers' to guide the parties to the beaches. There was a slight drizzle of rain, and the scene was as eerie as on that Sunday morning an eternity ago when the original invaders slipped, wraith-like, into the small cutters which were to take them to the beaches. When the men reached the beach they were quietly embarked on the little tugs and lighters which operated with remarkable silence and efficiency.

'The great *massif* of Sari Bair towered above us, and now and again could be seen through a gap in the fog which lay low and only close to the shore', an officer of the Lines of Communication Staff, in a boat off-shore, relates; '. . . we watched the routine guns flare out as they had done at intervals for many nights before, and we could also see the flare of the answering Turkish cannon. It was a ghostly scene. . . . How quiet the vessels were! Hardly a shout, and only now and then a megaphone boomed.' On the cruiser *Grafton*, another eye-witness wrote in his diary: '8.30 p.m. . . . The big whale-like shape of Sari Bair against the faint misty sky. A fire or two burning steadily. One of our field-guns at Suvla is firing. The rattle from Anzac is like a low-crackling fire; that at Suvla like a kettle of water boiling. A bomb has flashed on The Nek—then a dull report. The ship is at anchor on a perfectly silky sea. A destroyer is moving across the surface of it—very slowly, like a black cat—about 200 yards to port. I can hear the rustle of her bows moving thro' the silky water. A bomb at Hill 60.'

Extreme tiredness now overcame many of the men. 'All they desired was sleep,' wrote one officer, 'and to be left alone. All the Turks in the world did not interest them. Persuasion was useless, and time was slipping by. There was nothing left but to ply the boot to the fleshy part of the anatomy. We literally booted some of them along to, and on to, the last boat.' By 3 a.m. the night had become very cold, and as the last men to leave had neither greatcoats nor blankets, they were thoroughly chilled by the freezing night air before the welcome orders were quietly whispered that their turn had come. The trench-floors were covered with torn blankets and coats to deaden their footsteps and many men had socks or torn-up sand-bags over their boots; every now and then one of the self-firing rifles cracked out and a Turk responded; as the men went they drew barbed wire across the paths behind them. At 2.40 Lone Pine was abandoned, and Courtney's and Johnston's Jolly at 2.45 a.m.; at 3.25 the last men on Walker's Ridge withdrew; at 3.30 the order was given for the mines to be exploded at The Nek. The explosion rocked the beach, and a great column of flame and smoke rose over the head of Monash Valley, killing over 60 Turks. By 4 a.m. there was no one left at Anzac, and the Suvla evacuation was nearly completed. At 4.10 the last boats left Anzac Cove. A huge store of food and equipment was set on fire at Suvla, and the flames lit up the bay. Not one man had been left behind.

Monash, one of the last to leave, writes:

> The strain being over, the reaction came in wild and hilarious greetings, mutual felicitations and hearty hand-shakes all round. The steamer got under way for Lemnos, and the sights and sounds of Gallipoli dropped back into the past. Gradually the ship's company, worn out with want of sleep and the tremendous strain of the closing hours, fell asleep in all sorts of attitudes, on saloon tables, on decks, in alleyways, and on hatches. I got a bunk in the pantryman's cabin, but found myself quite unable to sleep, so decided to write down my impressions while they were still fresh. It is now 6.30 a.m. and we are just dropping anchor in the outer roadstead of Mudros Harbour, and a new day is breaking.

The news of the completely successful evacuation of Suvla and Anzac came as a thunderbolt. German and Turkish reactions were a mixture of relief and astonished mortification. German military commentators were not sure whether the evacuation was a victory or a defeat, and von Sanders and his staff were equally perplexed. The Turk troops, although delirious with excitement and relief, had so healthy a respect for their enemies that the possibility of another landing could not be entirely ruled out. 'As long as wars last,' a German military commentator wrote at the time with remarkable generosity, 'the evacuation of Suvla and Anzac will stand before the eyes of all strategists as a hitherto unattained masterpiece.'

As soon as it was absolutely certain that Anzac and Suvla had been safely evacuated, Monro telegraphed to Kitchener to urge the abandonment of Helles; two days later, the General Staff at the War Office advised in the same sense. At this point, Monro was ordered to return to command in France; Sir Archibald Murray was to exercise general supervision over the forces in the Dardanelles and Salonika, and, in his turn, was to be succeeded as C.I.G.S. by Sir William Robertson. The first realisation of what this meant occurred when G.H.Q. at Imbros was to submit all reports to Robertson personally, and not to the Secretary of State. On December 24th, however, Monro was told to stay until Murray arrived, and it was not until New Year's Day that he and his staff left Mudros.

Von Sanders, chagrined by the bloodless escape of the British and Anzacs, ordered a close watch to be kept on the Allies at Helles, while he tried to collect every available man for the southern front. 'It was thought possible that the enemy might hang on there for some time', he has written. 'That could not be permitted.' He had reckoned without two extremely important factors—the high morale and determination of the British at Helles, now thoroughly rested and well prepared, and the low morale and will to win of the Turks. For some time the British at Helles had been convinced that the Turks were a beaten army, and it was significant that whenever a Turk attack was ordered it was conducted with nothing like the old élan. The Turk infantryman was now convinced that the British were going, and did not relish the prospect of impeding their departure. A significant episode was the reaction of the Turks to the explosion at The Nek. They were not particularly angry, but were very surprised and, in a curious way, offended at such gratuitous and unnecessary killing at the last moment. An Australian historical mission in 1919 found the Turkish officers they interviewed still puzzled and hurt at such a stupid and ungentlemanly act. Something of the same fatalistic lethargy which had so maddened von Sanders and Kannengiesser in March and April was again easily apparent in the Turkish troops.

These facts made the situation confronting the British slightly more promising than might otherwise appear. The Navy and G.H.Q. had the invaluable experience of Suvla and Anzac behind them if evacuation were ordered, and if it were decided to hold on to Helles there were enough men and materials to make it (in theory) 'a second Gibraltar'. On the reverse of the medal, the Turks now had 21 divisions available on the Peninsula, and two batteries of Austrian artillery. Ominously, the weather had broken 16 hours after the evacuation of Suvla and Anzac, and a series of fierce storms ripped up the flimsy piers and battered the stone jetties; at times the road from W Beach to Gully Beach was impassable, and Gully Ravine degenerated into an evil-smelling bog; conditions near the front lines were not dissimilar to those experienced in Flanders, with carts bogged down to their axles, trench floors awash with slimy, glutinous mud, and horses struggling through the mire. The Turkish shell-fire now became more consistent, accurate and effective than at any time since the beginning of the campaign. 'Christmas Eve', Pawson writes, 'was the worst day which anyone can remember on the Beach since the Landing.' On the 28th he wrote: 'Weather has been perfect since the 23rd and still holds. Everything else is getting steadily worse.'

The French had insisted on the withdrawal of their troops from Helles, and Birdwood had to call upon the 29th Division, only recently evacuated from Suvla, to fill the gap. The 'Incomparable 29th' was now a shadow of its former self; since August 20th it had suffered over 12,000 casualties, of whom nearly 2,500 were killed or missing; the division had also lost a great deal of its equipment in the Suvla storms, but doggedly returned to take over the familiar Helles line once again.* Birdwood was convinced that the

* In the Gallipoli campaign the 29th Division suffered 34,011 casualties, of whom 9,042 were killed or missing; 10,993 were wounded in action, and 13,977 incapacitated through sickness or disease.

only chance of success at Helles lay in a policy of aggressiveness, and it was a remarkable tribute to the resources of determination in VIII Corps that the response to this order was so spirited. The Turkish command was also urging an aggressive policy of patrolling and local attacks, but the reaction of the Turk infantry was very different. Within a week of the Suvla and Anzac evacuation the British at Helles had obtained a tactical superiority over the enemy which remains one of the least-publicised but crucial triumphs of the entire campaign. Apart from their artillery bombardment, at no time in the whole of 1915 were the Turks so unaggressive.

Preliminary plans for evacuation were already well advanced when the Cabinet at last agreed on December 27th. This time there were no opponents of evacuation in the staff or in the army. 'What is to happen now?' Aspinall had written to Guy Dawnay on December 23rd, 'For God's sake, get me away from the Dardanelles! It has far too many shattered hopes and unhappy memories.' The British position at Helles was already serious, and by the time that von Sanders managed to gather his full strength together, it would be critical. Monro urged upon Birdwood the vital importance of speed, and Birdwood decided that the final garrison of 22,000 men should be embarked in two successive nights, 15,000 to be taken off on the last night. Weather permitting, it was planned that the final stages should be undertaken on the nights of January 7th–8th and 8th–9th, assuming that the weather did not wreck all calculations.

In spite of elaborately prepared and well-distributed orders of the day to the troops about the high honour of defending Helles for the Empire, as soon as the embarkations began in earnest early in January it was clear to everyone what was afoot. 'In a close community, such as we were, we scented something in the wind', a Scottish subaltern has written. 'At Helles, rumours generally assumed tremendous priority in our thoughts. Indeed, they were our life. The bigger and better the rumour, the more the troops liked it, until like a bubble they generally burst—but not this one.' All the subterfuges and devices employed at Suvla and Anzac were used again; men marched round in full view of the Turks on the open roads, no tents were struck, the guns fired their regular quantity of shells, the patient mules toiled daily to the lines. On January 1st Pawson wrote in his diary: 'Breakfast at 8.30, shells falling all over the place, huge piles of baggage and stores on the beach with weary Tommies sleeping on them; wind in the north and getting stronger; temperature low.' Every night the ships slipped out of Mudros, took on their loads at W Beach, V Beach and Gully Beach, and slipped away again before dawn. The official accounts of the campaign describe the evacuation as if it had been a well-ordered and perfect operation. The accounts of participants are less flattering. 'Never have I seen such a conglomeration of stores thrown about', Captain Laman of the South Wales Borderers indignantly wrote of the scene on W Beach on January 4th: 'No order; no method. No one seems to be running the show.' The shelling was now really heavy, and tempers were frayed. When the Navy failed to turn up on time at one beach, Laman —who, it will be remembered, had been in the S Beach landing on April 25th and had served at Suvla—wrote angrily that inter-service co-operation was 'extremely rotten', and added, 'I only remember the Navy being up to time once.' But in spite of the confused appearance of the evacuation, the important thing was that the men were getting away, and getting away undetected. By January 7th the garrison was down to 19,000 men and 63 guns.

On that day von Sanders launched what was intended to be the first blow in the final massive assault on the Helles front. It was delivered at the British salient on Gully Spur, and was not, as has been implied in some accounts,* a general attack all along the line. At midday a tremendous bombardment fell on the units of the 13th Division holding Gully Spur, and appeals for artillery support brought warships hurrying to the western shore of the Peninsula. At Imbros a brigade was hurriedly alerted, and held in immediate readiness to be rushed to the Peninsula.

At four o'clock, the Turks exploded two big mines on Gully Spur, the bombardment increased to a new intensity, and the attack seemed imminent. Nothing like it had been seen throughout the campaign, and some observers with subsequent experience of the Western Front have said that they never saw a more concentrated bombardment. The British guns, although few in number, had unlimited ammunition; the warships fired off literally every shell and cartridge in their magazines, being replenished by consort ships. The troops remained calm in the midst of this tumult, and as soon as bayonets were seen above the enemy parapet the British rifle and machine-gun fire exploded with a deafening crash. Only at two points did the Turks even leave their trenches to be mown down as soon as they emerged; officers could be seen trying to drive them forward unavailingly; when the bombardment subsided by six o'clock the crisis was over. The Turk commanders were badly shaken by the ferocity of the British response and the refusal of their men to attack, while the morale effect of the naval bombardment was almost comparable to that at the beginning of the campaign. British casualties were only 164 killed and wounded, and the Turks admit to cruel losses. That night another 2,300 men were evacuated, and the final stage had been reached.

De Robeck had returned to the Dardanelles, Wemyss having been posted to the East Indies. Once again, as in April, he had to make the final decision. January 8th was bright and calm—'beautiful morning,' Captain Laman wrote, 'and one could hardly believe that there was such a thing as war'—and

* See, for example, Moorehead, *Gallipoli*, 351-2.

although the glass was falling, it was expected that the next 24 hours would be fine. De Robeck gave the order for the operation to begin.

At Helles the day passed quietly, but with agonising slowness. The systematic slaughter of horses and mules greatly upset the men, to the extent that Keyes even suggested to Birdwood that if the army remained on the Peninsula for a few more days the animals could all be evacuated; but at this stage this was quite impossible. As soon as darkness fell, the long lines of men began to converge on the beaches, while the dark sea again filled with every type and variety of vessel. Cruisers and monitors took up their allocated positions, their guns trained on the areas through which the Turks would have to pass if they pursued the evacuating troops. At nine o'clock the wind was blowing at 35 miles an hour, and the sea was rising. By magnificent seamanship and devoted work by parties of engineers, the embarkation proceeded with few mishaps. By 2 a.m. the weather was becoming very bad, and there was a heart-stopping moment when *Prince George* reported that she had been struck by a torpedo which had not exploded; there was a flurry of anxiety, but *Prince George* had merely bumped some flotsam.

By 3.30 only the last units remained; the seas were crashing against the piers, and the scene was wild and desolate. The Turks suspected nothing: 'Hour-long quiet and silence', a German account of the night relates. 'From the narrow no-man's land there came no message from the patrols stationed there. The night service of the telephone had nothing to do.'

At 3.45 a.m. the last barge waited at W Beach for General Maude, who had insisted on returning to Gully Beach to collect his valise, which he had left on a stranded lighter when the beach had become impracticable for embarkations. Lt. Steele, the young Newfoundland officer, was sent to look for Maude. It was pitch-dark, and he knew the main magazines would explode in half an hour. The British trenches were now empty, and Steele felt wretchedly isolated, wandering about in the dark, shouting Maude's name. Maude's party had been held up by having to cut its way through the barbed wire placed across the tracks, but eventually Steele found it. Trundling his bag on a wheeled stretcher, the general arrived at W Beach just after the commander of the boat had said that he could wait no longer.

Just before the boat pushed off the first magazine blew up with an immense roar, scattering débris over the men in the last lighter but fortunately wounding only one man. The sea was now so rough that it was proving difficult for the lighter to get away, and it was barely a hundred yards offshore when the main magazine blew up, 'like St. Paul's Cathedral being fired out of a howitzer', as one witness laconically described it. 'By now,' Steele relates, 'there were fires everywhere, and it was really a wonderful sight. . . . We were now all ordered to get below, for it was very windy indeed, and the sea was beginning to crash over the lighter.' Rockets rose from the Turkish lines, and a violent bombardment fell on the empty beaches and piers. A total of 35,268 officers and men, 3,689 horses and mules, 127 guns, 328 vehicles and 1,600 tons of stores had been evacuated in just over a week without the enemy command being aware of the fact that anything unusual was going on.* On the morrow the Turks could count their booty; for the moment, they could only try to urge their men forward into empty trenches, which, until a few hours earlier, had been death-traps.

'And thus', as one of the beach officers who had been at the Anzac withdrawal, wrote to his fiancée, 'ended another evacuation.' 'How strange it was to feel safe,' wrote a Scottish chaplain on Lemnos; 'to walk out without the expectation that a bullet or fragment of a shell might find you at any moment.'

---

* 508 animals were slaughtered or left behind, 15 guns and 1,590 vehicles were wrecked and abandoned, and an unspecified quantity of baggage and stores left on the Peninsula. Von Sanders states that these were of enormous quantity, and took two years to gather up. Turkish accounts state that they fed and clothed four divisions for four months with the food and equipment abandoned at Helles, Suvla and Anzac; one account adds that 'one soldier died through eating too much English marmalade'.

Epilogue

The winds are high, and Helle's tide
Rolls darkly heaving to the main;
And Night's descending shadows hide
That field with blood bedew'd in vain.
Byron, 'Don Juan'

The Gallipoli campaign had lasted for eight and a half months. It is extremely difficult to estimate the casualties of either side with any precision. Turkish records were very loosely kept, and it is certain that their official figures of 86,692 deaths and 164,617 wounded and sick are a considerable underestimate of their actual losses. One Turkish source even places their casualties as high as 470,000, but a more probable estimate is about 300,000. Estimates of British and Dominion casualties also vary considerably from 198,340 to 215,000; including the French casualties, and deaths from drowning and accidents, the total Allied casualties were probably 265,000, of whom some 46,000 were killed in action or died of wounds or disease. This toll may appear small beside the holocausts on the Western Front; by any other previous standards of modern warfare, it was horrific.

Godley, with a characteristic tactlessness, had ordered the New Zealanders to parade immediately after they had been withdrawn from the Peninsula, in order to impress upon what one of them has described as 'the handful of decrepit, homesick, thoroughly verminous and blasphemously fed-up scarecrows' the fact that 'the war had only just begun'. But, for most of the Gallipoli troops, it was only too true. Contrary to one statement,* a great number of them served in France, including the 29th Division, the Anzacs and the Royal Naval Division. Many who survived Gallipoli fell on the Western Front; Brigadier Street, Patrick

* Moorehead, *Gallipoli*, 361.

348

Shaw-Stewart, Private Dry, Lt. Steele of the Newfoundlanders, and the New Zealander, Sergeant Pilling, were among their number. Eighty-four regiments of the British Army include Gallipoli on their battle honours.

Thus, for many of the men who served in the Gallipoli campaign, it was only the beginning. Four future Field Marshals (Birdwood, Slim, Harding and the Australian, Blamey) had fought on the Peninsula, as had a future British Prime Minister, Attlee. Birdwood, Monash, Walker, de Lisle, Hunter-Weston, Wemyss and Keyes went on to senior commands in the First World War. The careers of Nasmith, Boyle and Freyberg prospered greatly. Slim joined the Indian Army, fired by the example of the 1/6th Gurkhas on Sari Bair, and created for himself perhaps the most enduring reputation of all the British commanders in the Second World War. Freyberg commanded the New Zealanders in the Middle East and in Italy in the Second World War, and subsequently became Governor-General of New Zealand, an almost legendary figure, with a V.C. and three bars to the D.S.O. he won at Bulair on April 25th. His death in 1963 marked the end of the small band who buried Rupert Brooke on Skyros. He has been succeeded as Lieutenant-Governor of Windsor Castle by Slim, who previously had been Governor-General of Australia, as also had Hore-Ruthven.

But for many other survivors, Gallipoli was the end. Some professionals, like Allanson, Unwin and Dawnay, resigned from the services at the end of the war. Others, like Orlo Williams—who resumed his interrupted Clerkship at the House of Commons—Compton Mackenzie, Arthur Behrend and A. P. Herbert, returned to civilian life at the end of the war. Hamilton, Stopford, Hammersley, Sitwell and Maxwell were not asked to serve in the field again. Maxwell was perhaps the most unfortunate. Relieved of his Egyptian command early in 1916, he was sent to Ireland to handle the Easter Rising in Dublin. It is not to exaggerate to say that his severity in executing the leaders of the uprising destroyed any last hopes that remained of conciliating Ireland. Gallipoli had destroyed Kitchener's position, and had temporarily crushed Churchill; in the long run it had also ended Asquith's leadership. The campaign had indeed been, as Moorehead has written, 'a mighty destroyer of reputations'.

Sir Ian Hamilton lived to be 94, and died on October 12th, 1947. He had survived all the Gallipoli commanders except Birdwood, who died at the age of 86 in 1951. His appeals for another chance went unheeded. 'I would most loyally assist you', he once wrote to Kitchener; 'I talk both French and German, and you know I can use my pen'. He became Lieutenant of the Tower of London, was elected Rector of Edinburgh University, and published several more books. He bore the deaths of his devoted wife and of their adopted son, killed in action in the Second World War, with characteristic fortitude. Almost to the end he was an elegant, gay, lively and charming companion. Few men can have been surrounded with such devotion and respect. Nothing that he wrote, nor anything written about him, has adequately explained the mystery of his personal failure at Gallipoli. It is a measure of the man that it is still a subject about which people care.

The British returned to Gallipoli at the end of 1918 as ultimate victors. The Turkish armies in Palestine and Mesopotamia had been crushingly defeated; the Ottoman Empire had ceased to exist; Talaat and Enver had fled the country, and were destined for violent deaths. But the British had not heard the last of the Dardanelles. The terms proposed by the British Admiral on *Agamemnon* in Mudros Harbour were generous; those inflicted by the politicians were harsh. Kemal raised the standard of revolt in Anatolia, and bore it all over Turkey. The Greeks were routed in battle and ignominiously bundled out of the territory granted to them around Smyrna by the Allies. At Chanak, Turkish and British troops once again confronted each other. Lloyd George and Churchill were again in power. The Dominions were again asked for support. Britain awoke with astonishment to find herself almost at war. Fortunately the heads of the soldiers were cooler than those of some Ministers in London. The 'Chanak Incident' marked the last convulsive twist of the Lloyd George Coalition, and heralded Lloyd George's abrupt and final descent into the political limbo. Down with him fell Churchill, who even lost his seat in the House of Commons. He had to begin a long and weary climb back into the political uplands which would probably never have succeeded had not the Second World War occurred. Thus, the Dardanelles Question had twice within ten years delivered near-mortal blows to Churchill's career. Gallipoli reverted to the Turkish people.

As one eminent military historian has remarked,* 'no episode of the war is more poignant than the effort to force the Dardanelles'. None, certainly, has aroused fiercer controversy. Sir Edward Grey once wrote that 'nothing so distorted perspective, disturbed impartial judgement, and impaired the sense of strategic values as the operations on Gallipoli.' The same could well be said of the innumerable commentators on the campaign. There is something about it which still affects historians and authors. Dispassionate and sober judgements seem to waft away whenever the subject is raised.

Within a few months of the evacuation the inquests began, and have continued to this day. In 1916, the Government agreed to the appointment of a Royal Commission to pick over the bones. It interviewed almost every individual concerned in the initiation of the campaign and in the conduct of the naval and military operations, with the conspicuous exception of Lord Kitchener, who had been drowned in the cruiser *Hampshire* in the North Sea. The Commission presented two heavily censored Reports, in 1917 and 1918; the evidence that it received has never been published. Its conclusions were that the operation had been ill-conceived and ineptly executed, with

* Cyril Falls: *The First World War*, 107.

the vain expenditure of thousands of valuable lives; only the heroism of the men and the wisdom of Monro received commendation.

A confidential joint Services study of the naval attack was also set in train; its findings were never published, and for many years it was a strictly classified document. 'The principal lesson to be learnt from a study of the naval attack on the Dardanelles defences would appear to be that it is essential that operations of this nature should be based on a previously well considered estimate of the sea, land and air forces necessary to obtain the results desired', it concluded, rather lamely. It even advised against a single commander-in-chief for amphibian operations of this type and scale.

There were many who refused to accept the verdict that the campaign had been disastrously conceived. Three more years of attrition on the Western Front, the collapse of Russia, and the long and difficult campaign in Mesopotamia, all combined to throw a new light on Gallipoli. The admission of the Turks that they had been very close to complete defeat on at least three occasions materially assisted this process. By the mid-twenties a formidable and fierce controversy was being waged. Hamilton published his *Gallipoli Diary*, Churchill presented his case with matchless eloquence in *The World Crisis*, Aspinall carried the rehabilitation of Gallipoli further in his admirable official history.

Perhaps this process was carried too far. John Masefield flung a romantic pall over the whole enterprise with a best-selling book first published in 1916 and frequently reprinted; Ernest Raymond's minor classic, *Tell England*, also depicted the campaign in a heroic light. Among many who had taken part there was an understandably desperate attempt to prove that it had all been worthwhile. Even Aspinall succumbed: 'The drama of the Dardanelles campaign,' he wrote in 1932, 'by reason of the beauty of its setting, the grandeur of its theme and the unhappiness of its ending, will always rank amongst the world's classic tragedies.' He took as the theme of his official history the words of Aeschylus; 'What need to repine at fortune's frowns? The gain hath the advantage, and the loss does not bear down the scale.' As John North has justly remarked, 'no battleground so easily lends itself to retrospective sentimentality'.

But other pens were at work. A. P. Herbert's novel *The Secret Battle* was astringent and bitter. Bean's official Australian history was almost chilling in its curt factuality; the only reference to Troy concerned an Australian sergeant of that name. Ashmead-Bartlett's highly censorial and controversial *The Uncensored Dardanelles* appeared in 1928. Sir William Robertson's memoirs presented the 'western' point of view with disconcerting moderation and skill, and as late as 1932 Edmund Delage was indignantly enquiring, 'Superb Anzacs, nimble Gurkhas, laughing Senegalese, sailors who fought under Guépratte and de Robeck, soldiers of France and of all the counties of England, you! all of you, what heroes! But—to what end did you die?'

By 1939, an enormous library on the campaign had accumulated. Churchill, Fisher, Lloyd George, Hamilton, Keyes, Guépratte, Wemyss, von Sanders, Prigge, Mühlmann, Kannengiesser, Ashmead-Bartlett, Mackenzie, Nevinson, Callwell and Samson, among others, had published their personal accounts; a host of further memoirs and commentaries arose, of very varying quality. In 1956 Alan Moorehead dramatically revived public interest with an account of the campaign which, although based almost exclusively on published accounts and containing some judgements which were, to say the least, controversial, set out the varying fortunes of the battle with a vigour and lucidity which attracted the attention of a very wide audience. Other books—notably Hankey's discreet but revealing memoirs—have subsequently appeared.

Thus, judgements on the campaign have varied greatly. Immediately after the 1914–18 war the general opinion was that it had been an unmitigated catastrophe, for which Churchill was personally responsible. Bean wrote that 'through a Churchill's excess of imagination, a layman's ignorance of artillery, and the fatal power of a young enthusiasm to convince older and slower brains, the tragedy of Gallipoli was born'. Churchill retaliated angrily by describing this judgement as 'crude, inaccurate, incomplete and prejudiced'. Bean, however, stuck firmly by his judgement. But in 1934 Roger Keyes was writing, 'In the light of our knowledge today, can anyone doubt that the forcing of the Dardanelles would have shortened the war by two years and spared literally millions of lives?' almost without serious challenge.

But very recently, opinion has been hardening against the whole operation and against Churchill's part in its initiation. As new information slowly emerges it is being more widely realised that The World Crisis is an incomplete account, which has hitherto received inadequate critical analysis. It is doubtful if any serious student of the campaign would echo the brutal portrait of Churchill's part in the campaign presented by an American historian in 1926: 'Brilliant in conception, blithely willing to accept responsibility in matters of which he was ignorant, impatient of detailed analysis or plan, living not only for the present generation but continually posing, almost strutting, for his portrait for posterity, he jockeyed the ageing Fisher from one position to another, and finally overcame all opposition to the Dardanelles Expedition except that offered by the Turks.' But the more sober and fair words of J. F. C. Fuller, written in 1956, represent the significant shift in informed opinion which has taken place since the 1930's: 'Mr. Churchill forced his Dardanelles card on the Government, and the Government was incapable of playing the hand. The result was that the British Empire not so much drifted but was pushed into a campaign which in the end proved as disastrous as that of Saratoga.' Even more recently, A. J. P. Taylor has described the Dardanelles and other projects of the time as 'cigar-butt strategy', 'designed to evade the basic problem—that the German army could be beaten only by an antagonist of its own size'. Although it would be grossly unfair to heap the blame for the Gallipoli disaster on Churchill, it is equally foolish to contend, as some of his more apoplectic admirers have done and still do, that his part was uniformly wise and justified by events.

Churchill himself has written of Gallipoli that 'the terrible "ifs" accumulate'. What Lloyd George could no doubt dismiss as 'strong Dardanellian influences' have argued incessantly that the Allies came agonisingly close to a great triumph. While this is undeniably true, the reverse of the coin is equally important. Orlo Williams has written of the first landings that 'a sudden change in the weather, a quicker reinforcement from Bulair, or a proper supply of ammunition for the Turkish field-guns on that day, and the next might well have driven us into the sea'. If von Sanders' dispositions south of Achi Baba had been only fractionally different on April 25th, or if the mass attack on Anzac on May 19th had been properly directed, the consequences might well have been one of the most grievous defeats ever inflicted on the British Army. It is best to state the fact that it was a desperately close fought campaign, waged with superlative perseverance and courage by both sides, which ended in a tactical draw; regarded strategically, it was a major defeat for the Allies.

It is of course of endless fascination to dwell on the might-have-beens of Gallipoli, of which the most intriguing is the question of what would have happened if Turkey had been snuffed out of the war and the Russians had taken control of Constantinople and the Straits. The indications are that their occupancy would not have been unmolested. Supporters of the campaign have said blithely that the Allies could have 'poured' munitions into Russia, ignoring the simple question of where they were to come from. The more the question is considered dispassionately, the more does it appear that little could have been effectively done by the Allies to bolster up the tottering Tsarist regime or to have averted the German victories on the Eastern Front.

Nevertheless, it is not difficult to see why Gallipoli exerts such a powerful grip on the interest and imagination of the British people. The setting, the challenge and the response to that challenge are alike enthralling. As Orlo Williams has written: 'A wonder; yes. That is the word for those days. The scenes, the men, the actions, the great ships, the smell of thyme mixed with the reek of cordite, the knowledge that immortal history has been made before one's eyes. I do not praise War, but there I saw deeds rise fully to the heights of a great issue, in a noble setting, giving a quality to those days, with all their suffering, that aeons of grey evolution can hardly attain.'

These things are difficult to comprehend, and even more difficult to communicate. As Private Gilder wrote at the end of his Gallipoli diary; 'no diary or thrilling narrative, accompanied by photographs, can convey to those at home the slightest appreciation of what the conditions were like. . . . It is only the Tommies themselves who underwent the many and varied trying ordeals that beset them who know of these conditions.' The truth of Gallipoli is locked in the memories of those who fought there, and their number sadly declines with every year. The memory often plays false tricks, and every man recalls different aspects of Gallipoli. For some, it was a nightmare interlude in life, to be pushed back into the recesses of memory; for others, the memories are of comradeship, courage, humour and a brief sense of heightened living, to be treasured; others are still cast down by the recollection of lost friends, and this, in a way, is the nearest a man may get to immortality.

Certainly, there is little romantic or heroic about Gallipoli itself. In early summer, when most visitors come, it is deceitfully beautiful. But by August it is a place of grilling heat, sinister silences and aloof hostility. The grass has vanished in the sad little cemeteries, the hills glare in the harsh light, the fine sand covers everything, the Salt Lake at Suvla cruelly assails the eye. Sedd-el-Bahr is still a pile of stones, although the old castle moulders slowly. Apart from the garrisons quartered on it, the Peninsula is almost deserted.

One does not have to search far for traces of the fighting. At Anzac the preservation of the débris of the campaign is the most spectacular, but on the Achi Baba slopes one has only to leave the road and plunge into the scrub to find evidence of the campaign everywhere. Near Sedd-el-Bahr a light railway, complete with trucks built in Birmingham, is piled into a hollow; at W Beach a steam tractor decomposes with reluctance; at Helles the demolished Turk guns lie around in clumsy attitudes; off Anzac Cove a man and a boy make a living by scooping up shells, grenades, rifles and bayonets off the clear sand. Apart from a new lighthouse above W Beach and the cemeteries and war memorials, the Peninsula can barely have changed in 50 years.

Of the 34,000 British and Empire troops who lie on the Peninsula, only some 7,000 have known graves; of the French dead, which totalled nearly 10,000, over 6,000 were never found. Every year the winter rains reveal more bodies; if they are on the Allied side of the old front lines they are buried by the officers of the Commonwealth War Graves Commission; if not, they are left. The Turks never buried their dead, and their remains lie thickly in the scrub.

Perhaps this is what gives the Peninsula its grim atmosphere. It is not a place which invites visitors, and, as John North has feelingly written, 'even those who return to the Peninsula to keep an appointment with the dead intrude upon its loneliness, its shattering silence'. If ghosts walk, they walk in Monash Valley and Gully Ravine, and guard eternally the rocky escarpment of the Gallipoli Peninsula.

Memorials were unnecessary, but, inevitably, arrived. The British and the Australians were first on the scene, closely followed by the New Zealanders and the French. The clearing of the battlefields was an awful business, particularly on the Sari Bair heights, where the cooler atmosphere had hideously delayed the decomposition of the bodies. Small cemeteries were hacked out of the rough ground and planted with grass and shrubs, with pine-trees surrounding them. Few contain many actual bodies. The task of keeping them tidy and preserving the headstones and memorials from the acute contrasts of the climate is borne by the devoted officers of the Commonwealth War Graves Commission, who wage an unending contest against an acute water shortage, labour problems and obscurantism on the part of some local officials. The Commission's representative at Çanakkale has to be a horticulturist, water-diviner, engineer and diplomat. By high summer the cemeteries, although neat, are drab; the headstones glitter in the arid soil; a few tufts of the spring grass feebly survive near the shadow of the few bushes. From time to time graves are found to have been dug up and rifled, in a ghastly quest for identity discs and gold fillings, but official protests have long since been abandoned as useless.

For the Turks find all this devotion to the dead very strange. Recently, an enormous Turkish memorial has been erected at the tip of Morto Bay, above S Beach, on the exact spot where the South Wales Borderers surprised and dislodged a Turkish platoon 50 years ago on April 25th, 1915. There are other small memorials dotted about the battlefields, commemorating individual achievements at The Nek, Lone Pine and elsewhere. Kemal, when once asked why there was then no Turkish memorial, curtly remarked that 'the greatest memorial is Mehmedchik [the Turkish equivalent of "Tommy Atkins"] himself.'

This is perhaps the best note on which to leave Gallipoli. The historian can only supply his narrative of events, and draw upon the fragments of material which have survived the storm, the wreckage and the years, arriving on his desk like the jetsam of a long-sunken ship. He cannot assemble a solemn list of results achieved by the Gallipoli campaign, in the manner so beloved by those with trim departmental minds, in which everything can be processed and analysed with satisfying completeness. There is no profit and loss account for Gallipoli. In the words of Caxton's Original Preface to Malory's *Le Morte d'Arthur*:

EPILOGUE

I, according to my copy, have done set it in imprint, to the intent that noble men may see and learn the noble acts of chivalry, the gentle and virtuous deeds that some knights used in those days. . . . Wherein they shall find many joyous and pleasant histories, and noble and renowned acts of humanity, gentleness, and chivalries. For herein may be seen noble chivalry, courtesy, humanity, friendliness, hardiness, love, friendship, cowardice, murder, hate, virtue, and sin. Do after the good and leave the evil, and it shall bring you to good fame and renown.

NOTES ON SOURCES

Notes on Sources

These notes do not include material in official archives.

UNPUBLISHED COLLECTIONS

MAJOR COLLECTIONS

Kitchener Papers. Public Record Office.

Birdwood Papers. Now deposited at the Australian War Memorial, Canberra.

Papers of General Sir Ian Hamilton. In the possession of Sir Ian's literary executor, Mrs. George Shield.

Papers of Colonel W. G. Malone. In the possession of his son, Mr. D. G. W. Malone.

Gallipoli Papers of Colonel Sir Henry Darlington. In the possession of his widow, Lady Darlington.

Gallipoli Diaries of Dr. Orlo Williams, D.C.L. Deposited at the Imperial War Museum; only available for inspection with the permission of Dr. Williams, who is the last survivor of Sir Ian Hamilton's original Staff.

Gallipoli Papers of Major-General Guy Dawnay. In the possession of his widow, Mrs. Guy Dawnay.

Gallipoli diaries and letters of Major C. Allanson. Also includes documents sent to, and correspondence with, Major John North.

MINOR COLLECTIONS

Mafeking and Gallipoli Letters of Sir Alexander and Lady Godley. War Office.

Diaries and letters of Lt.-Col. H. V. Gell. In possession of his widow.

Diaries and journals of Corporal Alec Riley. Imperial War Museum.

Letters of Lt. Desmond O'Hara, D.S.O. In possession of Mrs. A. Bruce.

Journals of Capt. A. C. Pawson. In possession of Mr. Pawson.

Journals of Lt.-Col. C. F. Jerram. Royal Marines Museum.

Gallipoli letters of Major-General Sir Andrew Skeen. In possession of his widow.

Gallipoli and other memoirs (typescript) of Commander Dix, R.N. In possession of his widow.

Journal of Commander H. R. Tate, R.N. In possession of Commander Tate.

Diaries of Capt. E. K. Laman. In possession of his daughter, Mrs. Kirkland-Laman.

Diaries of Capt. C. Hawkes, M.B.E., M.C. Deposited at the Imperial War Museum by his widow, Mrs. G. M. Hawkes.

Diaries of C. P. O. F. W. Johnston, D.S.M. In possession of Mr. Johnston.

Diaries of Lt. O. W. Steele. In possession of his sister, Miss E. Steele.

Diaries of Pte. C. W. Gilder. In possession of Mr. Gilder.

Diaries of R. M. Gale. In possession of Mr. Gale.

Gallipoli memoirs (typescript) of Lt.-Col. J. S. Millar. In possession of Lt.-Col. Millar.

Diaries of Captain Hon. Claud Lambton. In possession of Hon. Claud Lambton.

Diaries of E. Ewart Fieldhouse. In possession of Mr. Fieldhouse.

Diaries of E. G. Law. In possession of Mr. Law.

Diaries of Lt. D. T. Houghton, R.N. In possession of his daughter, Mrs. Restell.

Diary of Lt.-Col. A. R. Chater, R.M. Royal Marines Museum.

Diary of Lt. (Acting Capt.) N. V. Holden. In possession of his sister, Mrs. D. E. Carr.

In addition to the documents referred to, I have received and read a large number of Gallipoli diaries and letters of great interest which have contributed greatly to the book indirectly, and which have affected the treatment of certain episodes without being directly quoted in the narrative. In addition, I have seen a very large number of original photographs and scrap-books, which have been of value in my researches.

SELECT BIBLIOGRAPHY

For reasons of space, I have not included the very numerous unit histories which deal with the campaign.

I am most grateful to the authors, executors, or publishers possessing the copyright of those works marked with an asterisk for their permission to make quotations.

* Adam, Colin Forbes: *Life of Lord Lloyd* (Macmillans, 1948).
* Aitken, Alexander: *Gallipoli to the Somme* (Oxford, 1963).
* Arthur, Sir George: *Sir John Maxwell* (Murray, 1932).
* Ashmead-Bartlett, E.: *The Uncensored Dardanelles* (Hutchinsons, 1928).
— *Despatches from the Dardanelles*(Newnes, 1915).
* Aspinall-Oglander, C. F.: *Military Operations; Gallipoli* (2 Vols., with 2 Vols. of appendices, Heinemann, 1929, 1932).
— *Roger Keyes* (Hogarth, 1951).
* Asquith, H. H. (Earl of Oxford and Asquith): *Memories and Reflections*, Vol. 2 (Cassells, 1928).
Barrow, Sir G.: *The Life of Sir Charles Monro* (Hutchinsons, 1931).
* Bean, C. E. W.: *Official History of Australia in the War: The Story of Anzac* (2 Vols., 12th Edition, Angus and Robertson, 1941).
* — *Gallipoli Mission* (Australian War Memorial, 1948).
* Beaverbrook, Lord: *Politicians and the War* (Revised edn. Oldbourne, 1960).
* Behrend, A.: *Make Me a Soldier* (Eyre and Spottiswoode, 1961).
* Berrie, G. L.: *Under Furred Hats* (Penfold, Sydney, 1919).
* Brereton, C. B.: *Tales of Three Campaigns* (Selwyn and Blount, 1927).
* Brodie, C. G.: *Forlorn Hope, 1915* (W. J. Bryce, 1956).
* Brownrigg, Sir, D.: *Unexpected* (Hutchinsons, 1942).
* Burton, O. E.: *The Silent Division; New Zealanders at the Front, 1914–1918* (Angus and Robertson, 1935).
* Bush, Eric: *Bless Our Ship* (Allen and Unwin, 1958).
* Butler, A. G.: *Australian Army Medical Services in the War of 1914–18* Vol. 1 (Australian War Memorial, Revised edn., 1938).
Byrne, J. R.: *New Zealand Artillery in the Field* (Whitcomb and Tombs, 1922).
* Callwell, C. E.: *The Dardanelles* (Constable, 1919).
* — *Experiences of a Dug-Out* (Constable, 1920).
Cayley, Sir W.: *Memories of an Eastern Division* (1920).
* Chatterton, E. K.: *Dardanelles Dilemma* (Rich and Cowan, 1935).
* Churchill, W. S.: *The World Crisis*, Vol. 2 (Butterworth, 1923).
Cooper, Sir B.: *The Tenth (Irish) Division in Gallipoli* (Jenkins, 1918).
Corbett, Sir Julian: *Naval Operations*, Vol. 2 (Longmans, 1921).
* Creighton, Rev. O.: *With the 29th Division in Gallipoli* (Longmans, 1916).
* Cutlack, F. M. (Ed.): *War Letters of General Monash* (Angus and Robertson, 1935).
* *Dardanelles Commission:* First Report and Supplement, 1917, and Final Report and Appendices, 1919 (H.M.S.O., Cd. 8490, Cmd, 371).

* Darlington, Sir H.: *Letters from Helles* (Longmans Green, 1936).
* Davidson, G.: *The Incomparable 29th and the 'River Clyde'* (Bisset, 1920).
Dawson, R. M.: *Winston Churchill at the Admiralty* (Oxford, 1940).
* Delage, Edmund: *La Tragédie des Dardanelles* (Translation, Bodley Head 1932).
Deygas, F. J.: *L'armée d'Orient dans la guerre mondiale* (Payot, 1932).
* Djemal: *Memories of a Turkish Statesman* (Hutchinsons, 1922).
* Einstein, Lewis: *Inside Constantinople* (Murray, 1917).
Ermin, A.: *Turkey in the World War* (Oxford, 1930).
* Ewing, W.: *From Gallipoli to Baghdad* (Hodder and Stoughton, 1917).
* Fallon, D.: *The Big Fight* (Cassells, 1918).
Falls, Cyril, and MacMunn, Sir G.: *Military Operations: Egypt and Palestine* (H.M.S.O., 1928).
* Feuille, H.: *Face aux Turcs* (Payot, Paris, 1934).
* Fisher, Lord: *Memories* (Hodder and Stoughton, 1919).
* Fuller, F. J. C.: *Decisive Battles of the Western World*, Vol. 3 (Eyre and Spottiswoode, 1956).
* Guépratte, Admiral: *L'expédition des Dardanelles* (Payot, 1935).
* Hamilton, Sir Ian: *Gallipoli Diary* (2 Vols., Arnold, 1920).
* — *Listening for the Drums* (Faber, 1944).
* — *The Commander* (Ed. by A. Farrar-Hockley) (Hollis and Carter, 1957).
* — *Gallipoli Dispatches* (H.M.S.O., 1915–16).
* Hankey, Lord: *The Supreme Command*, Vol. 1 (Allen and Unwin, 1961).
* Hanna, H.: *The Pals at Suvla Bay* (Ponsonby, 1917).
Hargrave, John: *At Suvla Bay* (Constable, 1916).
* — *The Suvla Bay Landing* (Macdonald, 1964).
* Herbert, A. P.: *Half-Hours at Helles* (Basil Blackwell, 1916).
* — *The Secret Battle* (Methuen, 1919).
* Herbert, Aubrey: *Mons, Anzac and Kut* (Arnold, 1919).
Higgins, Trumbull: *Winston Churchill and the Dardanelles* (Heinemann, 1964).
* Housman, Laurence (Ed.): *War Letters of Fallen Englishmen* (Gollancz, 1930).
* Idriess, Ion: *The Desert Column* (Angus and Robertson, 1932).
Jeans, T. T.: *Reminiscences of a Naval Surgeon* (Sampson Low, 1927).
* Jerrold, Douglas: *The Royal Naval Division* (Hutchinsons, 1923).
* Jones, Rev. D.: *Diary of a Padre at Suvla Bay* (Faith, 1917).
Jones, H. A.: *The War in the Air* (Oxford, 1928).
* 'Juvenis'; *Suvla Bay and After* (Hodder and Stoughton, 1916).
* Kannengiesser, Hans: *The Campaign in Gallipoli* (Translated by Major C. J. P. Ball, Hutchinsons, 1927).
Kearsey, A.: *Notes and Comments on the Dardanelles Campaign* (Gale and Polden, 1934).

* Keyes, Admiral Roger: *Naval Memoirs*, Vol. 1 (Butterworth, 1934).

* Knox, R.: *Patrick Shaw-Stewart* (Collins, 1920).

Larcher, M.: *La Guerre Turque dans la Guerre Mondiale* (Chiron (Paris), 1926).

Les Armées Françaises dans la grande guerre, Tome 8 (Paris, 1923–7).

* Lloyd George, David: *War Memoirs*, Vol. 1 (Nicholson and Watson, 1933).

* Mackenzie, Compton: *Gallipoli Memories* (Cassells, 1929).

MacMunn, Sir G.: *Behind the scenes in many wars* (Murray, 1930).

Macpherson, Sir W., and Mitchell, T.: *General History of Medical Services in the Great War* (H.M.S.O., 1924).

* Magnus, Philip: *Kitchener* (Murray, 1958).

* Marder, A. J. (Ed.): *Fear God and Dread Nought*, Vol. 3 (Cape, 1959).

* — *Portrait of an Admiral* (Cape, 1952).

* Masefield, John: *Gallipoli* (Heinemann, 1916).

* Montgomery, Ina: *John Allen of the Gallant Company* (Arnold, 1919).

* Moorehead, Alan: *Gallipoli* (Hamish Hamilton, 1956).

* Morgenthau, Henry: *Secrets of the Bosphorus* (Hutchinsons, 1918).

* Mühlmann, C.: *Der Kampf um die Dardanellen* (Oldenburg, 1927).

* Mure, A. H.: *With the Incomparable 29th* (Chambers, 1919).

Murphy, C. C. R.: *Soldiers of the Prophet* (Hogg, 1921).

* Nevinson, H. W.: *The Dardanelles Campaign* (Nisbet, 1918).

— *Last Changes, Last Chances* (Nisbet, 1928).

* North, J.: *Gallipoli, The Fading Vision* (Faber, 1936).

Patterson, J. H.: *With the Zionists* (Zion Mule Corps) *in Gallipoli* (Hutchinsons, 1916).

Peaudeleu, Dr.: *Aux Dardanelles* (Payot, 1924).

Pemberton, T. J.: *Gallipoli Today* (Benn, 1926).

* Perk, Major Kadri: *The History of the Dardanelles Campaign*, Parts II and III (Military Review, Istanbul, 1940).

* Pilling, E. G.: *An Anzac Memory* (Stanton, Dunedin, 1933).

* 'Presland, John' (Mrs. Gladys Skelton): *Deedes Bey* (Macmillans, 1942).

* Prigge, E. R.: *Der Kampf um die Dardanellen* (Kiepenhaver, 1916).

* Puleston, W. D.: *The Dardanelles Expedition* (U.S. Naval Institute, 1927).

* Ribblesdale, Lord: *Charles Lister, A Memoir* (Fisher Unwin, 1917).

* Robertson, Sir W.: *Soldiers and Statesmen* (Cassells, 1926).

* Samson, C. F.: *Fights and Flights* (Benn, 1920).

* Sanders, Liman von: *Five Years in Turkey* (U.S. Naval Institute, 1927).

* Serman, E.: *Mit dem Türken an der Front* (Scherl, 1915).

* Spender, J. A.: *Life, Journalism and Politics*, Vol. 2 (Cassells, 1927).

Statistics of the Military Effort of the British Empire in the Great War (H.M.S.O., 1922).

Stewart, A. T., and Peshall, C. J. E.: *The Immortal Gamble* (Black, 1917).

Stoker, H. G.: *Straws in the Wind* (Herbert Jenkins, 1925).

* Subin, J.: *Uncensored Letters from the Dardanelles* (Heinemann, 1916).

Thomazi,: *La guerre navale aux Dardanelles*, Vol. III (Payot, 1926).

* Vassal, J.: *Impressions et souvenirs de guerre, 1915–16* (Plou-Nousset, 1916).

Vedel, V.: *Nos Marins à la guerre* (Payot, 1916).

Waite, F.: *The New Zealanders at Gallipoli* (Whitcombe and Tombs, 1921).

* Wedgwood, Hon. J. C.: *Essays and Adventures* (Allen and Unwin, 1924).

* Wemyss, Lady W.: *Life and Letters of Lord Wester Wemyss* (Eyre and Spottiswoode, 1935).

* Wemyss, Lord Wester: *The Navy in the Dardanelles Campaign* (Hodder and Stoughton, 1924).

MISCELLANEOUS

* *Diaries and Gallipoli memoirs of Mustafa Kemal* (Translation; typescript, Imperial War Museum).

* Rayfield, Lt.-Col. F. A.: *The Dardanelles Campaign* (typescript and manuscript with numerous appendices). A most detailed and lengthy study of the campaign, based on prolonged research, most kindly made available to me by the author.

* Allanson, Major C.: *Personal Diary, July–December 1915* (Privately printed). This important document, of which only 50 copies were printed, is dedicated to, among others, my late Uncle.

* *Chronicle of the War Services of the 1st Battalion the Herefordshire Regiment* (Typescript, edited by A. G. Parfitt, 1962). Only 250 copies were made.

* *Brigadier-General C. Aspinall-Oglander; miscellaneous letters and notes concerning the Official History of the Gallipoli Campaign*. These letters and notes have been culled from many sources, particularly from the papers of General Guy Dawnay, Major Allanson and Col. Malone.

* Miles, Major Sherman: *Notes on the Dardanelles Campaign* (U.S. Coast Artillery Journal, Vols. LXI–II, 1924–5). Apart from the interest of Major Miles' comments and researches, these notes also contain some interesting comments by Sir Ian Hamilton.

* Egerton, Major-General G.: *Annotated Copy of Official History of the Gallipoli Campaign* (Imperial War Museum).

* Wylly, H. C.: *Neill's 'Blue Caps'*, Vol. 3 (Privately published, Gale and Polden, 1923). Records the war services of the 1st Battalion, the Royal Dublin Fusiliers; includes several excellent personal accounts of the V Beach landing.

* Williams, Dr. O. C.: *The Evacuation of the Dardanelles* (National Review, 1920). Dr. Williams, as chief cypher officer at G.H.Q., was closely involved in the campaign from the very outset; this long article is perhaps the best personal day-to-day account of the discussions on the possibility of evacuation from October to the end of December.
* Williams, Dr. O. C.: *The Gallipoli Tragedy, Part One* (Nineteenth Century, July 1929). Contains some interesting criticisms of, and comments on, the first volume of the Official History.
* Williams, Dr. O. C.: Article in *Radio Times*, April 24th, 1931.
* *Account of commanding officer of 3rd Battalion, the 26th Regiment, of the Turkish defence of Sedd-el-Bahr, April 25th–26th, 1915* (Translation; typescript; Imperial War Museum).
* Willis, Major R. R., V.C.: *The Gallipoli Landing* (Talk on BBC, April 24th, 1934). Major Willis was one of the six officers and men of the Lancashire Fusiliers awarded the Victoria Cross for the landing at W Beach.
* Turkish General Staff, Historical Section: *A Short History of Turkish Operations in the Great War*, Vol. 1 (Constantinople, 1922).
  Mehat Bey: *The Battles of Sedd-el-Bahr* (Turkish War College, 1920).
  Izzedin Bey: *The Battles of Ari Burnu* (Ibid, 1920).
  Selaheddin Bey: *The Naval Battles at the Dardanelles* (Ibid, 1920).
* Slaymaker, H. E.: *The Dardanelles Campaign* (Typescript, Imperial War Museum).
* *The Anzac Book* (Cassells, 1916).
* *The Gallipoli Gazette* (Journal of 1st Battalion, the Lancashire Fusiliers).
* Striedinger, O.: *Cape Helles—A Retrospect* (R.A.S.C. Quarterly, Vol. XII, 1924).
* Allen, Capt. C. R. G.: *A Ghost from Gallipoli* (Journal of Royal United Service Institute, May 1963). In this important article, Capt. Allen fully disclosed for the first time the details of the negotiations with the Turks in February–March 1915 for a separate peace treaty.
  Russell, W.: *The Gallipoli Campaign, A Personal Reminiscence* (National Review, October 1926).
  Wilson, H. W.: *Mr. Churchill and Lord Fisher at the Admiralty* (National Review, June 1923).
* MacMunn, Sir G.: *The Lines of Communication in the Dardanelles* (Army Quarterly, April 1930).
* Anonymous: *Work of a Trawler in the Aegean Sea* (Naval Review, Vol. VI, 1918).
* Smith, Capt. B. H., R.N.: *Dardanelles Details* (Naval Review, Vol. XXIV, 1936).

NOTES ON SOURCES

* Murray, H. W.: *The First Three Weeks* ('Reveille', Australia, April, 1955).
* Savige, S. G.: *Farewell to Lone Pine* (Ibid).
* Howe, H. V.: *Belated Query* ('Stand-To', Australia, September, 1962).
  Farmar, Major, H. M.: *The Gallipoli Campaign* (Lecture; summarised in Journal of R.U.S.I., November, 1923).
* 'Zachabona': *Six Months in the Dardanelles* (Blackwood's, February, 1916).
* Black, C. S.: *Cape Helles, December 1915* (The Nautical Magazine, December, 1919).
  Commonwealth War Graves Commission: *War Graves of the British Empire; Gallipoli.*

INDEX

Index

INDEX

assumes that he is to be C.-in-C., 44
convinces Kitchener that military operations are necessary, 47
prepares plans for Helles landing, 51
reverts to command of Anzac Corps, 52
his character, 60, 63, 81, 87, 91
his landing plans, 102, 103
orders Navy to cease landing artillery at
Anzac, 128
opposes evacuation, 131
determined to advance, 167
last major attack (May 2nd/3rd), 179 ff.
his part in defence of Anzac, 181
proposes that Australian 1st Div. shall
lead August attack, 242
opposes idea of withdrawal, 309
his opinion of Hamilton, 318, 319
to supersede Monro, 328, 330
pays final visit to Anzac, 340, 349
Birrell, Surgeon-General W. A. (Director of
Medical Services), 93, 136, 222,
248
his estimate of casualties, 137
Biyuk Anafarta, 244, 295
Blamey, Major, 183, 242, 349
Blizzard, 335
Bloody Angle, 275
Boer War, 240
Boghali, 75, 76, 103, 111
Bolton's Ridge, 109, 168, 174
Bomba Sirt (Bomb Ridge), 189
Bombs, see Grenades
Bombardment, Air, 158
Bouchet Redoubt, 155
Bouvet (French) sunk, 61
'Boxing Day Memorandum', 26
Boyle, Lt.-Cdr. E. G., V.C., 203, 308, 349
Braithwaite, Major-General Walter, 52, 53
his character, 59, 82, 87, 123, 129, 200
his complacency, 282, 283, 294
confirms Stopford's objections to attack,
304
Dawnay suggests recall of, 316
Braund, Lt.-Col. G. F. (Anzac), 115
his defence of Russell's Top, 167, 169, 172
Brereton, C. B. (qu.), 95, 116, 152, 169, 174,
179, 219
Breslau (German), 9, 10, 21; 2
Bridges, Maj.-Gen. W. T., 128, 129
killed, 180
British aircraft, 46, 47, 77, 84, 158
British fleet, see Allied Fleet
British Forces, see Allied Forces
Brodie, Admiral C. G., 46, 47, 59, 65, 66
Brodie, Lt.-Cdr. T. S., 85
Brooke, Rupert, 94, 95, 213, 349

Browne, Denis, 94, 213
Brown's Dip, 109, 168, 264
Bulair, 11, 15, 74-7, 81, 86, 101, 127, 277, 283
Bulgaria, 6, 11, 27, 42, 310
enters the War, 323
Buller, General Sir Redvers, 240
Bully-beef, 281
Bush, Midshipman Eric, 104, 278
Byng, Lt.-Gen. Hon. Sir J., 240, 306

Callwell, Maj.-Gen. C. E., 10, 52, 316
memoirs, 352
Canning, Sir Stratford, 4, 5
Canopus, H.M.S., 61, 204
Canterbury Battalion (R.N. Div.), 219
Carden, Vice-Adm. S. H., 28 ff., 34, 40
opens naval attack on Outer Defences, 41,
44, 46
collapses and leaves command, 58
Carson, Sir Edward, 215, 247, 317, 337
Casualties
War Office estimate of probable, 94, 110
British, at W Beach, 119
French, 135, 155; 45
Allied, before Krithia, 141, 147, 150
Australian, before Krithia, 154
29th Division, 153, 343
Anzac, 170
Royal Naval Division, 203
VII Corps, 262
88th Brigade, 262
Australian at Lone Pine, 267
at The Nek, 276
British and New Zealand at Chanak Bair,
268
Suvla and Anzac Battle, 301
Final Allied and Turkish, 348; 40
Caucasus, 17
Chailak Dere, 220, 267, 270
Chanak, 1, 13, 35, 53, 74, 143, 254, 350
Charlemagne (French battleship), 61
Chatham, H.M.S., 320
Chatham Battalion (Royal Marines), 170
Chelmer, H.M.S., 204
Chessboard, The, 173, 179; 37
Chocolate Hill, 239, 242, 243, 244, 246, 255
captured, 281, 309; 56
Christian, Rear-Admiral A. H., 282
Chunuk Bair, 2, 102, 111, 112, 219, 220, 235,
237, 242, 243, 267; 37, 53
Turks under Kannengiesser on, 274
captured by N.Z. Wellington Battalion,
284, 291
all Allied defenders killed in Turkish dawn
attack (August 10th), 299

373

Churchill, Major John, 55
Churchill, Lord Randolph, 19, 21
Churchill (Sir) Winston, 3, 10, 18
  The World Crisis, 11, 28, 30, 351, 352
  examines plans for seizing Gallipoli, 11
  relations with Fisher, 23 ff., 35
  introduces plan for joint operations against
    Dardanelles, 25, 37, 40
  his personal difficulties with the War
    Council, 41
  on Ian Hamilton (qu.), 55
  dismayed by failure of de Robeck's plan, 68
  his confidence in ultimate success, 94
  his precarious position, 192 ff.
  resignation requested, 197
  member of new Dardanelles Committee,
    215
  his Memorandum urging a new effort in
    Dardanelles, 216
  prevented by Cabinet from visiting
    Dardanelles, 249
  still opposed to evacuation, 332, 349, 350
Clayton, Captain, 118
Collingwood Battalion (R.N. Division), 212
Committee of Imperial Defence, 10
Commonwealth War Graves Commission,
  182, 355
Conservative Party, 192, 193
Constantine, King of Greece, 10, 11, 50
Constantinople, 4, 5, 8, 27, 33, 35
  panic in, 42, 48, 53
  submarine exploit at, 308
Cornwallis, H.M.S., 61, 115, 117, 123; 61
Coronel, Battle of, 21
Courtney's Post, 109, 115, 168, 173, 182,
  184
  abandoned, 341
Courts martial, 310
Cowans, General (Q.M.G.), 225
Cox, Maj.-Gen. H. V., 148, 200, 243, 248,
  277, 284, 289
Cradock, Admiral, 21
Cressy, H.M.S., sunk, 21
Crete, 6
Crewe, Marquess of, 18, 24, 215
Crimean War, 4
Cunliffe-Owen, Lt.-Col. C., 53, 55, 80, 129
Cup, The, 264, 266
Curzon, Lord, 20, 215
  against evacuation, 332, 337

Daily Telegraph, 191
Dallas, Captain J. S., killed, 269
d'Amade, General, 47, 79
  urges Hamilton to let him re-embark, 134

orders evacuation, 135
warns Hamilton that French troops are at
  breaking-point, 147
Damakjelik Bair, 268, 291
Dardanelles, 1, 10, 11
  fortifications, 14
  ammunition shortage at, 49
  minefields, 15
  mobile batteries, 15, 45, 66
  Churchill's first proposals for attack on, 25
  plan for naval operations against, 32
  Carden opens attack Outer Defences, 41, 44,
    47
  de Robeck opens attack, 60
  Turkish defence preparations and disposi-
    tions, 71 ff.
Dardanelles Commission appointed, 24, 38,
  54, 65, 94, 225, 282, 350
Dardanelles Committee, 215
  seeks Hamilton's views on the possibility of
    evacuation, 317
Dardanos, Fort, 47
Darlington, Col. (Manchester Regiment),
  161, 199, 200
Davidson, Major (RAMC), 226, 310
Davies, Gen., replaces Hunter-Weston as
  G.O.C. VIII Corps, 234
Dawnay, Major Guy, 61, 89, 161, 180
  on sinking of *Majestic*, 206
  his report on Suvla situation ignored by
    GHQ, 283, 294
  proposes evacuation of Suvla positions,
    309
  sent to England to report on the grave
    situation, 316
  his verdict on Hamilton, 318
  his opinion of Gen. Monro, 322, 330, 331,
    349
Dead Man's Ridge, 109, 168, 173, 179; 38
Deal Battalion (Royal Marines), 170, 219
De Bartolome, Commodore, 29, 34, 68
Dedeagach, 48, 51
Deedes, Captain Wyndham, 41, 82, 89, 244
Delage, Edmund, 351
De Lisle, Maj.-Gen. H. de B., 201, 218
  convinced of futility of daylight frontal
    attacks, 231
  replaces Stopford as G.O.C. IX Corps,
    306
  Birdwood's estimate of his abilities, 307,
    349
De Lotbinière, Col. Joly, 91, 281
Dentists, lack of, 223, 252
Denton, Corp (N.Z.), 219
  succeeds Carden as C.-in-C. of naval force,
    59 ff.

INDEX

June the Fourth, Battle of, 211 ff.; **41–43**

Kanli Dere (Achi Baba Nullah), 151
Kannengiesser, Colonel, on Turkish 5th
    Army (qu.), 72, 144
  orders cessation of attacks, 147
  despairs of success, 213
  commands divisions south of Gaba Tepe,
    253
  ordered to Sari Bair, 273
  his memoirs, 352
Kelly, Clegg, 94
Kemal, Mustapha, Lt.-Col., 75, 76, 111, 112
  calls up 19th Division, 114
  attacks, 143, 166, 167, 171
  suicidal night attacks at The Nek, 189
  convinced that British will advance up Sazli
    Dere, 254
  commands all Anafarta formations, 292
  remains confident, 298
  leaves Peninsula, 340, 349
Kenna, Brig.-Gen., V.C., 309
Kephez Minefield, 49, 50, 85
Kephez Point, 35
Kereves Dere, 140, 141, 149, 152, 229; **44**
  Spur, 151
Keyes, Adrian, 134
Keyes, Commodore Roger, 50, 59, 63–67, 75,
    123
  shocked by inactivity of Navy, 191
  advocates new naval attack on the Narrows,
    321
  arouses enthusiasm in London for new
    naval offensive, 325, 329, 349
  memoirs, 352
Kilia Liman, 204
Kilid Bahr, 1, 2, 11, 14, 35, 47, 51, 53, 63, 85,
    143, 192, 202, 290
Kiretch Tepe, 238, 243, 246, 255, 278, 280–2,
    298; **52**
Kirkpatrick, Pte. (Anzac), 176
Kitchener, Lord, 10, 18, 19, 24, 32, 33, 36,
    40–43
  picks Hamilton for command, 52–4, 93
  orders 42nd Division to Gallipoli, 143
  his fury at withdrawal of *Queen Elizabeth*,
    194, 195
  pessimistic message to Hamilton, 201
  orders dispatch of 53rd and 54th Divisions,
    217
  worries Monro for a report on the pros-
    pects at Gallipoli, 323, and re-
    places him by Birdwood, 328
  goes to Gallipoli to inspect the situation,
    328; **60**

returns to London with a depressing view,
    331
  advises that Suvla and Anzac be evacuated
    and Helles held, 331
  his death, 350
Knox, Col., 17
Koe, Lt.-Col. A. S. (K.O.S.B.), 125, 133
Koja Chemen Tepe, 2, 112, 237, 242–4, 256
  attack on, 270 (map), 273, 287, 295; **52**
Kress, Lt.-Col. von, 9, 16, 17
Krithia, 89, 125, 134, 136, 139, 184
  First Battle of, 140 ff.
  Second Battle of 150 ff., 209
Krithia Nullah, 151, 261
Krithia Spur, 151
Kum Kale, 1, 11–15, 45, 74, 89, 101, 102
  French land at, 126
  confusion as to situation at, 134

Lala Baba, 239, 243, 255, 278, 283, 295,
    309
Lalor, Capt. J. P., 111, 114
Laman, Capt. E. K. (qu.), 345
Lancashire Fusiliers, 95, 96, 117, 149, 278,
    279; **14**
'Lancashire Landing' (W Beach), 149; **14**
Landing craft, Fisher's armoured, 33, 79, 239
Landing forces, general deployment of, 96
Lansdowne, Lord, 215
Law, Andrew Bonar, 19
  his opinion of Churchill, 193
  hears of Fisher's resignation, 196, 197
  joins new Dardanelles Committee, 215,
    216
  opposes retention of Gallipoli, 317, 328,
    329
  for evacuation, 337
Lawrence, T. E., 330
Leane's Trench, 256
Legge Valley, 107, 108, 114, 168, 266, 270
Le Marchand, Lieut., 289
Lemnos, 34, 39, 40, 43, 50, 58, 119, 227,
    250
  Australian hospital, 137
  low morale at rest camps on, 228, 326
  medical services on, 137, 306
Lemon, Lieut. R. L., 310
Lice, 223
Limpus, Vice-Adm. A. H., 10, 13, 15, 63,
    66
Lindley, Maj.-Gen. Hon. J. E. (53rd Division),
    leaves at own request, 307
Lines of Communication, 203
  inefficiency and unpopularity of the Staff,
    225–7

INDEX

reorganization of, 227
H.Q. set up on *Aragon*, 338, 341
Lister, Charles, 94, 206
Little, Sgt., 40
Lloyd-George D., *see* George, David Lloyd
Lloyd, Lord (qu.), 5
  on incompetence of GHQ, 229
London, H.M.S., 64, 103–6
Lone Pine, 109, 168, 174, 184, 243, 263
  the fight for, 164, 265, 266, 270
  abandoned, 341
Longford, Brig.-Gen. Lord, killed, 309
Lord Nelson, 61, 63
Louis, 333
Louis of Battenberg, Prince (First Sea Lord), 22
Loyal North Lancs. Regiment, 297
Lusitania, sinking of the, 216
Lutzow (transport), 138
Lyndon-Bell, Maj.-Gen. A. L., 322, 323, 337

McCay's Hill, 109
McKenna, Mr. Reginald, 18, 215
Mackenzie (Sir) Compton (qu.), 164, 212, 214, 349
  memoirs, 352
McMahon, Sir Henry (High Commissioner for Egypt), 330
Mahon, Lt.-Gen. Sir Bryan, 240, 245, 247, 262, 280, 304
  refuses to serve under de Lisle and replaced by Hill, 307
  retreats with 10 Division from Lake Doiran, 338
Maidos Plain, 11
  Village, 3, 15, 75, 76, 102
  27th Turkish Regiment stationed at, 107, 184, 254
Majestic, H.M.S., 45, 62, 85, 205, 334
Mallet, Sir Louis, 8, 10
Malone, Col. W. G. 167, 169, 175, 183, 188, 190, 284
  killed, 286
Mal Tepe, 85, 102
Manchester Regiment, 161, 199, 213, 263, 278, 280; **42, 43**
  casualties, 119
Manica, H.M.S., 85
Manitou (transport), 91
Margetts, Lieut., 113, 114
Marmara, Sea of, 1, 30, 46
Masefield, John (qu.), 91, 351
Matthews, Lt.-Col. G. E. (R.M.), 45, 125, 133, 134

Maude, Maj.-Gen. F. S., 346
Mauretania, 216
Maxwell, Sir John (C.-in-C. Forces in Egypt), 16, 42, 43, 44, 47, 51, 79, 82
  his misgivings, 83, 84
  objects to movement of 42nd Division from Egypt to Gallipoli, 143
  strained relations with Hamilton, 251
  meets Monro for conference, 327; **60**
  relieved of Egyptian command and posted to Ireland, 349
Medical services
  incompetence in dealing with dysentery, 221, 222
  preparations for Suvla operation, 248
  inadequacy of, 306
  see also: Wounded
Mendere River, 126
Messudieh, blown up, 13
Milbanke, Col. Sir John, V.C., 309
Miles, Capt. Sherman, 74
Military Landing Officers, 175
Millington, Sgt., 40
Milner, Lord, advocates evacuation of Gallipoli in House of Lords, 317, 337
Minefields, 15, 49, 50, 62, 63, 65, 85
Minesweepers, 49, 50, 63, 84, 85
Mining, 188, 340
Minneapolis, 279
Mohammed, V, Sultan, 7
Moltke (qu.), 3
Monash, Brig.-Gen., 177, 190, 222, 227, 242, 271, 272, 285, 287, 342, 349
Monash Valley, 109, 111, 114, 115, 168, 170, 175, 179, 274, 342; **18, 38, 39**
Monro, General Sir Charles
  succeeds Hamilton, 321; **51**
  makes favourable impression on Staff, 322
  shocked by situation on Peninsula, 324
  makes up his mind for evacuation, 325
  his estimate of probable casualties, 327
  superseded by Birdwood, 329
  returns to Gallipoli, 329
  rebukes Wemyss, 337
  ordered definitely to evacuate Suvla and Anzac, 338
  urges withdrawal from Helles, 342
  ordered to return to French Front, 342
Moorehead, Alan, *Gallipoli*, 52, 92, 104, 134, 235–6, 237–8, 267, 271, 273, 284, 290, 297, 317, 348, 352
Morale, 177, 178, 228, 326
Morgenthau, Henry, American Ambassador to Turkey, 7, 12, 48, 70

379

INDEX